THE PINEWOOD STORY

GARETH OWEN WITH BRIAN BURFORD

Foreword by HRH The Princess Royal
Introduction by Sir Norman Wisdom OBE
Preface by Sir Roger Moore KBE
Afterword by Lord Attenborough CBE

Reynolds & Hearn Ltd
London

**In memory of J Arthur Rank and
Desmond Llewelyn – greatly missed.**

First published in 2000 by
Reynolds & Hearn Ltd
61a Priory Road
Kew Gardens
Richmond
Surrey TW9 3DH

The James Bond films are made by Eon
Productions Ltd, and the views expressed by the
authors and contributors herein are not necessarily
shared by the producers.
The 007 logo and films are © Danjaq LLC and
United Artists Corporation.

A CIP catalogue record for this book is available
from the British Library.
ISBN 1-905287-27-5.

Designed by Paul Chamberlain and Chris Bentley.

Printed and bound in Great Britain by Biddles Ltd.

Front cover:
main picture –
Sean Connery and Honor Blackman in *Goldfinger*
(Eon Productions/MGM/UA) © Konig/Rex Features
side bar –
Kenneth Williams in *Carry On Again Doctor* (Rank Film
Distributors), Angelina Jolie in *Alexander* (Warner Bros/
Intermedia Films), Tom Hanks in *The Da Vinci Code*
(Columbia/Imagine Entertainment), Judi Dench in
Casino Royale (Eon Productions/MGM/UA), Natalie Portman
in *V for Vendetta* (Warner Bros/Silver Pictures), Clive Owen
in *King Arthur* (Touchstone Pictures/Jerry Bruckheimer Films),
Johnny Depp in *Charlie and the Chocolate Factory*
(Warner Bros), Natascha McElhone in *Ladies in Lavender*
(Take Partnerships/Scala Productions), Daniel Radcliffe in
Harry Potter and the Goblet of Fire (Warner Bros/Heyday Films)

Back cover:
left (top to bottom) –
Sidney James, Peter Gilmore and Barbara Windsor in
Carry On Henry (Rank Film Distributors), Roger Moore and
Barbara Bach in *The Spy Who Loved Me* (Eon Productions/
MGM/UA) © Chris Capstick/Rex Features, Tom Hanks and
Audrey Tautou in *The Da Vinci Code* (Columbia/
Imagine Entertainment)
side bar –
Pierce Brosnan in *Tomorrow Never Dies* (Eon Productions/
MGM/UA), Sophia Myles in *Thunderbirds* (Universal/
Studio Canal/Working Title Films), Kevin Spacey in
Beyond the Sea (Archer Street/Quality International/
Trigger Street Productions), Jude Law in *Alfie* (Paramount),
Sharon Stone in *Basic Instinct 2* (MGM/C-2 Pictures/
Intermedia Films), Halle Berry in *Die Another Day*
(Eon Productions/MGM/UA), Colin Farrell in *Alexander*
(Warner Bros/Intermedia Films), Jason Statham in *Revolver*
(EuropaCorp), Nicole Kidman in *The Hours*
(Miramax/Paramount/Scott Rudin Productions)

FOREWORD: HRH THE PRINCESS ROYAL — 5
INTRODUCTION: SIR NORMAN WISDOM OBE — 6
PREFACE: SIR ROGER MOORE KBE — 7

ONE: THE EARLY DAYS — 9
TWO: OPEN FOR BUSINESS (1936–1938) — 21
THREE: THE WAR YEARS (1939–1945) — 27
FOUR: BACK IN BUSINESS (1946–1949) — 35
FIVE: THE DAVIS ERA PART ONE (1950–1956) — 47
SIX: A LITTLE WISDOM — 65
SEVEN: IS THERE A DOCTOR IN THE HOUSE? — 73
EIGHT: THE DAVIS ERA PART TWO (1957–1962) — 79
NINE: A RIGHT CARRY ON — 97
TEN: 'BOND … JAMES BOND.' — 109
ELEVEN: BOOM (1963–1969) — 125
TWELVE: BUST (THE 1970S) — 135
THIRTEEN: SUPERMAN, SAVIOUR OF THE WORLD (AND PINEWOOD) — 149
FOURTEEN: PINEWOOD GOES COMMERCIAL (THE 1980S) — 155
FIFTEEN: SET FOR THE FUTURE (THE 1990S) — 165
SIXTEEN: A NEW ERA — 181

AFTERWORD: LORD ATTENBOROUGH — 204
BIBLIOGRAPHY AND ACKNOWLEDGEMENTS — 205
FILMOGRAPHY — 206
INDEX — 231

CONTENTS

I very much doubt that, back in 1936, either J Arthur Rank or Charles Boot envisaged their new film studio enjoying more than 60 years of film-making excellence. Pinewood Studios rates as one of Europe's leading production facilities, and is still expanding, despite the many ups and downs the British film industry has endured over these years.

Pinewood is a name synonymous not only with British films and filmmakers, but also with some of the biggest and most successful American films ever made. Many of Hollywood's highly acclaimed filmmakers return time and time again to the studio, with multi-million dollar productions, and that speaks volumes in itself. Additionally, of course, we should not overlook the fact that their return to Pinewood also ensures further substantial investment in the film industry as a whole, and in the thousands of production personnel employed within it.

There is little doubt that this magical film-factory, tucked away in leafy Buckinghamshire, has a fascinating story to tell – and this is it. I hope all who have worked at Pinewood in the past and those that will do so in the future will enjoy its history. ■

HRH The Princess Royal

FOREWORD

It's amazing to think that my association with Pinewood goes back almost 50 years – I was a child star you know! – and I'm ever so pleased that my chums Gareth and Brian have done such a smashing job in putting together this history of my favourite studio. They have brought back so many of my fondest memories in the process.

I suppose it would be difficult to single out any one event at the studio, but I'll never forget dear Marilyn Monroe and how she kissed me in the corridor, nor my golfing pal Sean Connery when he learnt that *A Stitch In Time* had knocked his second Bond film off the top spot. Mind you, he's done quite well since.

I feel tremendously proud to think that my Pinewood films are still as popular now as they were when they first came out at the cinema (they're all available on video you know, from all good retailers) and it still brings a little lump to my throat when I see those six famous words tagged on the end … 'Made at Pinewood Studios, London, England'.

Let's hope they'll be seen on many, many more films for a great many years to come – I'm sure they will! ■

Norman Wisdom.

Sir Norman Wisdom OBE

INTRODUCTION

The first time I set foot in Pinewood was in 1947. I was a young lieutenant serving in Germany and was given a week's leave to come to England and test for *The Blue Lagoon*. I tested with Claire Bloom, who was not actually going to get the part as Jean Simmons had already signed, but they wanted some footage of her.

Testing on the same day was, among others, a young actor known as Larry Skikne. He went on to become very successful under the name of Laurence Harvey. Neither of us got the part; it went to Donald Houston.

After leaving the Army, I was given three spits and a cough as a stage door johnny in *Trottie True* and we shot locations in the grounds of Pinewood at the back of the admin block. That was in 1948.

Many years elapsed before I was back at Pinewood again. In 1970 my partner, Bob Baker, suggested that we shoot *The Persuaders!* television series at Pinewood, and I was to spend over a year on L & M Stages. A very pleasant period in my life.

In 1972, I returned yet again to start shooting my first Bond, and every other year after that we shot interiors for six more Bonds. I lie! We missed out on *Moonraker* which was based in Paris.

In between Bonds, I shot some of *Gold*, *That Lucky Touch*, *North Sea Hijack* and *The Curse of the Pink Panther* at Pinewood.

I have kept an office at the studio for the past 35 years as I consider that Pinewood is my second home, and hope it will be so for many more years to come. So many friends, so many happy memories…

Thank you Pinewood, for being such a major part of my life. ■

Sir Roger Moore KBE

Left: *J Arthur Rank, First Baron Rank of Sutton Scotney and the guiding force behind Pinewood Studios.*

Below: *Heatherden Hall circa 1934.*

1

Hidden from the road by a screen of trees – 20 miles west of London, 15 minutes from Heathrow and closer still to Britain's major motorway network – lies a former country estate now known as Pinewood Film Studios.

The studios were expressly designed to constitute not only a leading filmmaking facility but also to create a tremendous working atmosphere which, to this day, hasn't been emulated in any other studio. The magical quality of this once stately home in leafy Buckinghamshire has been enjoyed by many famous stars, such as Lord Attenborough, Sir Dirk Bogarde, Pierce Brosnan, Michael Caine, Charlie Chaplin, Sir Sean Connery, Tom Cruise, Jamie Lee Curtis, Peter Cushing, Kirk Douglas, Dame Edith Evans, Jack Hawkins, Christopher Lee, Lord Olivier, Sir John Mills, Marilyn Monroe, Roger Moore, Julia Roberts, Moira Shearer, John Wayne, Sigourney Weaver and Sir Norman Wisdom – to name only a few.

A huge number of films have been brought to life within the hundred-acre site, and many long-running series such as the James Bond and *Carry*

On pictures have made Pinewood their home time and time again. Although many films are recognisably made at Pinewood – by virtue of perhaps using the famous double-lodge entrance, or the main house itself – the majority are not, as is only fitting for a truly flexible film 'factory'. But the conclusive proof comes with those six famous words ... 'Made at Pinewood Studios, London, England.'

As well as being steeped in history, Pinewood is also very firmly geared for the future with two new state-of-the-art stages and healthy bookings in the diary. But how did it all start? How did Europe's – indeed, one of the world's – leading film studios come into existence and survive so strongly to this day? To answer that question, we have to go back 65 years to the pioneering days of Charles Boot, Lady Yule and Joseph Arthur Rank.

In the 1930s, London and its suburbs boasted something like 20 film studios: Beaconsfield, Bushey, Denham, Ealing, Hammersmith, Pinner, Shepperton, Shepherds Bush, Southall, Twickenham, Teddington, Walton-On-Thames, Welwyn, Wembley and so on. Over at Elstree and Borehamwood, meanwhile, there were a further five studios. Some were bigger than others and several rapidly disappeared – they were old, badly designed, poorly situated and could no longer offer the facilities then required by filmmakers. The troubles facing British films were many, with the dominance of American pictures making British ones look like a poor investment. The story had been the same for decades and remains so to this day.

One of the greatest names in British filmmaking history was one of the most unlikely: Joseph Arthur Rank, millionaire flour miller and devout Methodist. He was a regular speaker at his local Sunday School but not a particularly stimulating one, as he admitted himself. One Sunday he decided to screen a religious film and it proved a

THE EARLY DAYS

great success. Further films followed and, when the supply was exhausted, Rank decided that he would make one of his own.

In 1933 Rank formed the Religious Film Society and his first film, *Mastership*, was completed in one week at Merton Park Studios, ran for 20 minutes and cost £2,700. As Rank's intention was to 'spread the word', the next step was to take his film around churches to interest them in screening it. Though never shown commercially, *Mastership* was an immediate success. Rank made arrangements for further films to be made and after a couple of years moved production to the Rock Studios (later British National) at Elstree, which were deemed far superior to those at Merton Park.

Lady Yule, millionairess widow of jute baron Sir David Yule, became active in the film industry in the early 1930s. She had inherited an estimated £9m upon her husband's death in 1928. Horses were her main interest in life and she expended every luxury on them at her Hertfordshire stud farm. Her interest in film was merely, she said, 'to combat boredom'. She had very little interest in whether a film made a profit or not; in fact, she had very little interest in any financial matters relating to production. Like Rank, however, she was religious.

In 1934, Rank formed British National Films with Lady Yule and the young producer John Corfield. The following year they produced *Turn of the Tide* in response to a challenge from the *Evening News* to the *Methodist Times*. Attacking the low moral standard of modern films was all very well, maintained the *Evening News*, but why didn't the Methodists produce 'family' films of their own? Rank took up the challenge and Corfield produced what turned out to be Rank's first feature.

The story was based on Leo Walmsley's 1932 novel *Three Fevers*, which was inspired by the author's life in Robin Hood's Bay on the North Yorkshire coast. It was reported that Rank knew Robin Hood's Bay from childhood visits and, having read *Three Fevers*, saw the opportunity to provide a true reflection of everyday life in Britain as opposed to the Hollywood-style stories coming from Alexander Korda at Denham, which Rank believed bore little relation to British life and val-

ues. The story is a simple one based on the rivalry between two fishing families, the Lunns and Fosdycks, after the Lunns acquire an engine for their boat. This prompts the Fosdyck family to start sabotaging lobster pots and to keep their daughter away from John Lunn, with whom she is romantically involved.

The film was superbly photographed by Franz Planer and boasted a fine cast which included Wilfrid Lawson, Moore Marriott and Geraldine Fitzgerald. However, *Turn of the Tide* struggled to get a theatrical release and was ultimately issued as the second half of a double-bill. Rank deemed this highly unsatisfactory, particularly because his costs had not been recouped. Another valuable lesson had been learnt: producing films was all well and good, but one had to have control of distribution and exhibition in order to make a profit.

Around this time, Corfield introduced Rank to C M Woolf, who had just left Gaumont-British and was considered a leading name in distribution. Woolf took the flour magnate under his wing and

Right: *The*
Ornamental
Gardens circa
1934 - hardly
changed to
this day.

Right: *The Ornamental Gardens circa 1934 - hardly changed to this day.*

together they formed, with William Portal of the General Cinema Finance Corporation, General Film Distributors. GFD's logo was the now legendary 'man with the gong'; Bombardier Billy Wells was the first to assume a role which was to grace all of Rank's future films.

Initially GFD concentrated on modest spy and comedy pictures, all of which made money, but Rank would move on to bigger things when Woolf died in 1942. And, despite building an empire that subsequent British filmmakers have been unable to match, he maintained his interest in religious films right up until his death in 1972. In a business dominated by rogues, charlatans and spivs, he was unique.

In the early 1930s the wealthy Sheffield building tycoon Charles Boot (of Boots the Chemist fame) was drawn into the world of film with a view to establishing and building a British studio to rival those of Hollywood. Writing in the 1 October 1936 edition of trade paper *Kinematograph Weekly*, he said: 'It came about this way. Sir Auckland Geddes had been touring the United States and had closely studied Hollywood, its studios and its film production activities, and he came back enthusiastic regarding the growing possibilities of a similar Film Industry in Great Britain. He and another far-seeing man [Sir John Henry] discussed in a definite and detailed manner the organisation which would be necessary to ensure success.'

Initially, plans were made to build a complex at Elstree, but the project fell through thanks to Boot's then considerable business interests in, and frequent travels to and from, Greece. His interest in a film studio, however, did not diminish. In 1934, Heatherden Hall, a lavish mansion in Iver Heath, Buckinghamshire, came up for auction on the death of its Canadian owner, Lt Col Grant Morden. Formerly the MP for Chiswick and Brentford, and a multi-millionaire in his own right, Morden had been declared bankrupt and left only £10 in his will.

The first recorded owner of Heatherden Hall was Dr Drury Levin, towards the end of the nineteenth century. He was noted for hosting very popular garden parties and for his one-upmanship. To make one of his parties better than one lately hosted by a friend, for example, he brought in the Hillingdon and Uxbridge Brass Band. A very wealthy man, he owned a magnificent 'coach and four' and a private yacht.

It is unclear what happened between Levin's tenure of the Hall and that of its second tenant, the famous cricketer K S Ranjitsinhji. After the Ranjitsinhji era, the house remained empty for some time before Morden's acquisition of it, when he spent thousands of pounds on adding a magnificent 76 ft ballroom, 30 ft high with a sprung polished floor and a ceiling heavily moulded in the Grindling Gibbons style; a swimming pool 44 ft long and 24 ft wide with dressing rooms, shower

Right: *The studios' club bar, scene of the ratification of the Irish Free State treaty in 1921.*

Below: *The original auction brochure from the 1934 sale.*

baths and a spectators' gallery (thought to be the first in a privately owned house in Britain); a Turkish bath; billiard room; glass-covered squash courts; tennis courts and ornamental garden.

Morden was very keen on gardening. He had 10,000 roses planted and funded expeditions to the Himalayas to bring back rare rhododendrons. He also brought trees, shrubs and plants from Japan, Canada, India, Australia and other exotic climes, many of which are still in the gardens at the studio: a Judas Tree, Wellingtonias, Tulip Tree and a magnificent Lebanon Cedar. Morden also owned borzoi dogs and deerhounds, and regularly held grouse and pheasant shoots in the grounds for his guests. Unsurprisingly, the Hall became a popular retreat for politicians and diplomats and was valued at £300,000.

The house made history on 3 November 1921 when the Irish Free-State treaty was signed there (in the room which is now the studio's main bar)

by the Rt Hon Earl of Birkenhead; the Rt Hon Viscount Long of Wraxhall; the Rt Hon Viscount Younger of Leckie, Chairman of the Conservative and Unionist Party; Sir Malcolm Fraser, Principal Agent, the Conservatives and Unionist Party, and Lt Col Grant Morden himself. A plaque commemorating this historic event was placed over the room's huge fireplace but fear of IRA attacks in the 1970s resulted in it being removed.

However, that wasn't the first great political event in the Hall's history because in 1917 the Colonel had hosted another momentous meeting

when Mr Walter Long finally agreed to join Lloyd George's first government. Many of his colleagues joined soon afterwards and it was stated that the decision made in that room that day paved the way for coalition.

After Morden's death, the auction of Heatherden Hall was held on 25 September 1934 by Goddard & Smith of London. The auction brochure described the property thus: 'Luxuriously appointed imposing Georgian Mansion (upon which vast sums have been spent from time to time) with its very valuable furniture and contents ... It contains: Porte Cochère entrance, Outer, Inner, Lounge and Staircase Halls, 4 Reception Rooms, Billiard Room, Magnificent Dance Room (76 ft by 30 ft), 39 Principal, Secondary and Staff Bedrooms, 2 Marble Bath Rooms, 9 other Bath Rooms, Exceptionally Fine Swimming Bath, Turkish Bath Room and adequate Offices.'

The brochure went on to describe the decorations as 'tasteful and costly throughout' and that there was 'main electric light, company's water,

central heating and telephone.' In addition there were 'three drive approaches each with Lodge entrance, spacious garage and stable premises with two flats over. A range of dog kennels, Bailiff's house, 4 cottages and Bungalow.' The grounds were 'richly timbered with ornamental water and boathouse, hard tennis courts, grass tennis courts, covered racquet court with electric light, walled kitchen garden, glasshouses, orchards, woodlands and park and grassland; the whole embracing about 158 acres with long valuable frontages to Parish, private and estate roads, affording profitable building development without spoiling the amenities of the mansion.'

Boot bought the house and grounds for what must have seemed a bargain – about £35,000. The estate agent in his brochure had considered it 'suitable for hotel, institution or clinic.' Ironically, the main house did later function in all three capacities ... for the purposes of filming, at any rate. A land tax (ground rent) of 'about £10.4s.3d' per annum was also payable on the property. A guided tour of the Hall in 1934 would have encompassed:

> a magnificent *porte cochère* entrance, supported by eight stone columns with three stone steps leading to the porch.
> an inner hall, which was approximately 18 ft by 11 ft with a polished oak floor above which was...
> the gallery landing with its ellipse-shaped top light.
> the lounge and staircase hall measuring approximately 33 ft by 23 ft.
> a stone-paved veranda of 50 ft by 14 ft overlooking the garden terrace and supported by 10 columns.
> the drawing room (34 ft by 17 ft) with three French windows leading to the veranda and terrace, a carved white marble mantelpiece and marble hearth, oak flooring, panelled walls.
> the magnificent dining room, which faced south and boasted five French windows, a carved wooden mantelpiece and overmantel.
> the library, or Irish room, boasted a stone mantelpiece with column jambs supports and an overmantle with carved coat of arms "te pie reponi".

> the ballroom, which again boasted a handsome stone mantelpiece and overmantel with the same coat of arms embossed.

> the swimming pool room, which measured 70 ft by 28 ft. The pool was made of white glazed brick and was 44 ft long and 24 ft wide with brass and marbolite steps, diving board and gangway at the side of the pool. Panelled doors lead to dressing rooms with shower baths and WCs, and an iron staircase lead to a spectators' gallery. The Turkish bath room was also entered from this room.

> the billiard room – with oak panelled walls throughout, massive oak beam ceiling supports and polished oak floor – was located on the ground floor.

> the first floor had six main bed and dressing rooms, and two bathrooms.

> the mezzanine floor housed four bedrooms and one bathroom in the east wing, and in the west wing a further four bedrooms and two bathrooms.

> the second floor contained seven guest bedrooms and a marble bath room.

> the 'domestic offices' on the ground floor were completely concealed from the entrance hall and comprised: a butler's pantry; housekeeper's room; kitchen, with four ovens and two fire grates; a tiled floor scullery; servant's sitting room; store room; larder; refrigerating room and dairy.

> the stables and garages were to the north of the house with five boxes, a harness room and a two bedroom flat.

> the grounds featured an ornamental lake spanned by an ivy clad bridge, with rose gardens and enclosed kitchen garden. There were also three lodges along with two smaller cottages.

> the Bailiff's House (also known as the Heath Farm) had four bedrooms and a garden that fronted the Fulmer Road.

After Boot purchased Heatherden Hall, the ballroom was transformed into a luxury restaurant with its French windows opening onto ornamental gardens, the bedrooms were turned into first class suites and a country club was established. Another brochure from the time states that 'It contains 80 bedrooms, including large private suites, has handsome lounges, drawing room, billiard room, library, restaurant, swimming pool and squash courts, and is surrounded by sixteen acres of superb ornamental gardens.'

'I am one of the very few', says Sir Anthony Havelock-Allan, 'and perhaps the only surviving person, to remember staying at Heatherden Hall when it was a country club, some 20 years or more before anyone thought of buying it for a film studio. It was a delightful venue with marvellous facilities, particularly the restaurant, and it was a wonderful place to stay. I recall vividly news of the signing of the Anglo-Irish agreement in what was then the smoking room of the Hall.'

W G King, a gardener at the Hall, remembered with fondness the early days on the estate. 'Heatherden Hall was functioning as a country club under the management of a Major Rawlings. The garden staff was increased to 18 (from six) under the supervision of Ian Morrison, the son of the head gardener of Mr Boot's estate in Derbyshire. The gardens were transformed from the wilderness they had become to their former glory. Where Car

Right:
Pinewood's
boardroom was
once the Hall's
library. The oak
panelling comes
from the
SS Mauretania.

Below: *The
150ft long
picture gallery
- said to be
haunted by
the Pinewood
ghost.*

Park One is now situated, a vast area of glass houses stood along with a vineyard, peach house and so on. This was surrounded by a two-acre walled kitchen garden where the walls were covered with fruit trees of every variety. The Heath Farm was once a fully operational farm; also in that area was the generating plant attended by the estate electrician, engineer Fred Clifford. The water came from the tank on the lot and supplied the ornamental lake in the garden, with the little waterfall which tumbles over the rock, behind the bridge which crosses the lake. The Deer Park was the grassed area outside the front door of the old Hall which, in those days, came within 12 yards of the porch with its stately pillars. Eventually, the progress of

the British film industry changed the landscape of Heatherden Hall, and we were privileged to see the start of Pinewood Studios. Soon, everything north of the Hall had gone.'

Indeed, Boot's plans for a film studio were advancing. He had at his disposal 'the experience of every leading studio manager, designer and engineer.' Having studied the latest and most efficient developments in studio planning, Boot placed his ideas before his colleagues at Henry Boot Ltd and H S Scroxton, an architect of 'outstanding ability', was engaged to work with A F B Anderson on finalising the scheme.

Boot's idea was simple: build a studio to rival the best that California had to offer. So with his general manager James Sloan he set to work designing his new studio complex. Sloan was a perfect choice for the developing Pinewood. He graduated from variety in 1919 and became assistant studio manager at the former Lasky studios in Islington for three years. Having assisted many directors in his years there, he then became a production manager for Pathé, Blattner (who invented the sound system Blattnerphone), Basil Dean and British National. Jimmy, as he was known, was an unassuming man with tremendous knowledge of studios in Britain, France and Germany as well as all aspects of production.

J Arthur Rank had made no secret of his annoyance at the inefficiency of small studios. Some only had one or two stages and a great deal of

Left: *The famed Tudor double-lodge, now the main entrance to the studios.*

Below, right: *A film studio under construction - Phase 1.*

time was wasted when sets needed to be moved and replaced by new ones. After all, Rank reasoned, be it a flour mill or studio, one 'factory' is much the same as another and similar principles should apply in running it. Rank desired better facilities with a view to producing his subjects efficiently and effectively, and Charles Boot was able to offer them.

Unsurprisingly, Rank and Lady Yule soon joined forces with Boot and became major shareholders in Pinewood Studios Ltd. The name Pinewood was chosen, according to Boot, because 'of the number of these trees which grow there, and because it seemed to suggest something of the American film centre in its second syllable.'

The first of the sound stages were designed to have offices and dressing rooms adjacent, in a covered area containing workshops, props, wardrobe etc – a fully self-contained department. The main house saw many bedrooms and bathrooms converted into executive offices and the new administration block was constructed behind it in a design in keeping with Heatherden Hall.

The entrance to the Hall, underneath the large studio clock, is in fact a large sixteenth-century fireplace which was bought from Allam Hall in Derbyshire, where it is said three generations of one family spent 30 years carving the solid oak. The library, now boardroom, and restaurant were decorated with oak panelling from the luxury liner, SS *Mauretania* – sister ship of the *Lusitania* – when the ship was decommissioned and broken up. It cost £185.18s.3d to transport to the studio. The ship's sun deck was also used to provide the

wooden floor (now carpeted) of the picture gallery – all 150 feet of it – which joins the old house with the administration buildings. Film stills hang now where paintings once did. This corridor is also said to be haunted by the 'Pinewood ghost'. A relation of one of the Hall's former owners committed suicide in the house, and it is said that she paces the corridor late at night.

Externally, two new entrances into the grounds from the Fulmer Road, which was later re-named Pinewood Road, were constructed in addition to the original drive (which, although still in existence, is only used occasionally and mainly in productions). The famous 'Tudor style' double-lodge now forms the main studio entrance although, with only an eight-foot clearance, a second entrance for larger vehicles was built a hundred yards further along the road.

Right: *Phase 2.*

Below: *Phase 3.*

The first bricks of the new studio were laid in December 1935, and a new stage was completed every three weeks. By September 1936, the first film was shooting. The cost of building the studio ran to over £1 million.

Five stages were initially constructed (A, B, C, D & E): three large (A, D & E with dimensions 165 ft by 110 ft by 35 ft) and two small (B & C with dimensions 110 ft by 81 ft by 34 ft). Several ingenious ideas were incorporated such as the routing of electrical cables overhead, rather than underground, and the provision of enclosed water tanks (in larger stages), capable of holding up to 65,000 gallons which could be heated to any reasonable temperature. The tanks were covered by sectional flooring, and any section, large or small, could be removed as desired. Compressed air was also laid on for paint spraying and effects purposes in all five stages and there were two large exterior sunken tanks on the lot.

Another innovative feature incorporated into each stage was the portable remote control switchboard, which operated the camera motors, recording cameras, rising and falling doors, ventilation controls, warning lights and telephones. Covered walkways connected stages to production offices and the main house, meaning it was possible to walk anywhere around the studio while fully protected from the elements. Underground power lines were routed through the gardens – from the powerhouse which could generate up to 10,000 amps – and another interesting feature was a 100-yard wide ramp with a gradient of 1 inch in 8 inches: particularly useful for sky-line shots. Along with its own powerhouse, the complex also boasted its own water supply courtesy of two artesian wells – 550 ft and 450 ft deep – which pumped up to 12,000 gallons per hour of clean and pure water.

The administration block boasted 65 offices, including self-contained suites for producers, each comprising a large private office, bathroom, assistant's and secretary's office. Opposite the stages were the 'spiders' – a row of seven individual houses connected to the main corridor. Four of them, two storeys high, were devoted to dressing rooms – two star players and featured players' suites and two capable of accommodating some 1,500 extras. The star suites contained a reception room, dressing room, maid's room and bathroom.

Pinewood was on course for becoming a state-of-the-art filmmaking complex.

Production at Pinewood began after a mishap

SOME CONSTRUCTION AND EQUIPMENT FACTS AND FIGURES

Men employed during construction:	1,500
Steelwork erected:	2,300 tons
Concrete:	20,000 cubic yards
Patent glazing:	25,000 sq ft
Asphalting:	15,000 yards
Thatchboard:	24,000 yards
Sound-proofing:	300,000 sq ft
Floor area of buildings:	7.5 acres
Bricks used:	6,000,000
Ventilating trunking:	3,300 ft
Capacity of air inlet fans:	8,100,000 cubic ft / min
Feet run of heating pipework:	50,000
Number of radiators:	700
Heating surface of radiators:	25,000 sq ft
Electrical wire:	60 miles
Bare aluminium conductors:	2.5 miles

(source: *Kinematograph Weekly*, 1936)

Bottom: *The 'spiders' to the left face the main administration block.*

Wilcox now had more money than ever, thanks to his insurance claim. The studio's first equipment was purchased from B&D and transferred from Elstree. It cost £75,545 which included the sum of £61,999 for sound equipment supplied by the Western Electric Company Ltd.

The news was announced in the *Kinematograph Weekly* on 28 May 1936: 'Shareholders of the British and Dominions Film Corporation at an extra-ordinary general meeting held on Tuesday approved unanimously the scheme under which B&D will become part-owners of the Pinewood Studios by virtue of an investment of 50 per cent in the capital of the studio owning company ... The present share capital is £150,000 which is to be increased to £300,000, of which B&D is to take £150, 000 ... It is proposed that the directors of B&D join the board of the Pinewood company and that Captain R Norton be appointed managing director. Captain Norton has agreed to apply part of the remuneration payable to him by Pinewood towards reducing the remuneration payable to him by B&D. Certain of the equipment and stores at Elstree which were not affected by the fire will be taken over by the

at another studio. A fire at Elstree early in 1936 persuaded the director Herbert Wilcox to transfer his British & Dominion (B&D) productions to Pinewood, after brief stints at 'Sound City' (Shepperton) and Warner Bros Studios in Teddington. It was said that with the whole of his studio gutted – bar the vaults and cutting rooms –

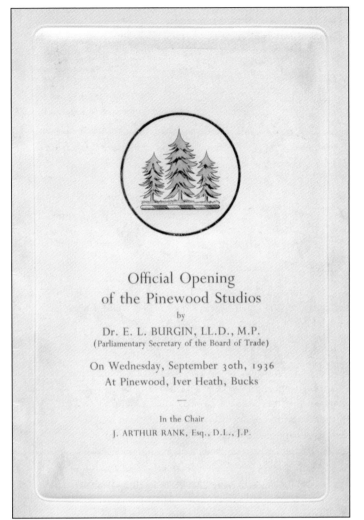

Official Opening
of the Pinewood Studios
by
Dr. E. L. BURGIN, LL.D., M.P.
(Parliamentary Secretary of the Board of Trade)

On Wednesday, September 30th, 1936
At Pinewood, Iver Heath, Bucks

—

In the Chair
J. ARTHUR RANK, Esq., D.L., J.P.

Pinewood Studios, and B&D will also manage Pinewood Studios for a term of 10 years.'

With a background in banking, Captain Richard Norton (later Lord Grantley) had been in charge of production at United Artists in the early 1930s prior to joining B&D. In 1936 he was appointed the first managing director of Pinewood. The monocle-wearing aristocrat and his assistant, Anthony Havelock-Allan (himself later knighted), were charged with keeping the studio busy – which wouldn't prove as easy as they first thought.

Havelock-Allan had begun his career in the entertainment business as a cabaret manager and subsequently as a casting director, giving him an extensive knowledge of actors, both established and up-and-coming. Richard Norton persuaded him to join B&D and now, through a twist of fate, Havelock-Allan found himself back at Heatherden Hall, although this time it was to be his home for two years.

'We moved to Pinewood in the early part of 1936,' he remembers, 'when there was only one stage and the dressing rooms completed. Captain Richard Norton and I took suites on the top floor of the old house and Pinewood became our home until the end of 1938. It was absolutely ideal for me, as I could get out of bed and be at work almost immediately. I can honestly say that as well as being a lovely studio, I was tremendously happy there and, indeed, met my first wife Valerie Hobson there. It was the happiest period I have ever had in the film business. The ease and comfort of being there was wonderful.'

Having transferred with Wilcox's B&D outfit, assistant editor Richard Best (who went on to cut such notable films as *Ice Cold in Alex*, *The Dambusters* and *Woman in a Dressing Gown*) recalled the first day in 1936. 'Pinewood had an air of relaxed efficiency – the same as it has today, only less bustling. The first impression on entering was of its elegance and good planning, emanating not only from the original house and grounds but in the choice of pale-whitish brick work and off-white stages. The car park was finished in light gravel to match and was surrounded by a low chain rail.'

On 30 September 1936 a special opening ceremony was performed by the Parliamentary Secretary of Trade, Dr Leslie Burgin. According to a report in the *Daily Film Renter*, 'Guests are being taken down to Iver from Paddington by special train, and motored thence to the studios. A strong muster of trade and production celebrities is expected.' Over 1,200 guests assembled for the event and a special lunch was served on D Stage. A guided tour of the stages, dressing rooms, power house, workshops, administration buildings, and the club house and gardens followed. Herbert Wilcox was shooting *London Melody*, which was already partly completed before transferring to Pinewood, and the guests were allowed a peek at the first film ever shot at the new studio. (Released by GFD in 1937, *London Melody* was dubbed by *Variety* an 'excellent compilation of bromidial mush, beautifully produced and directed.') The day's events ended at 4.00pm when 'vehicles [were] available to convey guests to Iver Station.' ■

OPEN FO

Left: *Carol Reed, who directed*
Talk of the Devil.

Right: *Herbert Wilcox, whose 1937 film*
The Frog *was produced at Pinewood.*

2

The second film to arrive, Carol Reed's *Talk of the Devil*, was the first to be filmed completely at the studio. The studio's first operational year, or rather half-year, was deemed both successful and busy, with the facility playing host to eight pictures, several of which were 'quota quickies' designed to fulfil B&D's Paramount contract.

The 1927 Cinematograph Films Act – which purported to enhance and increase British film production by requiring a certain number of British films to be shown at cinemas – meant a great deal of hastily produced quota-fillers, or 'quota quickies', appeared. The act was introduced after US producers were shown to be earning £50m a year from British cinema-goers and the quota films, it was hoped, would go some way to reducing that sum. They were of no more than 75 minutes in duration and generally cost around £6,250 each. Often shot in two weeks, they were then edited and dubbed in another two weeks.

'They paid one pound per foot of film, and wouldn't pay any more if you went over one hour fifteen, as that was 6,250 feet!' recalled Sir Anthony Havelock-Allan, who was responsible for all of B&D's quota films. 'Quotas were not really regarded with much affection, apart, of course, from those who got their start in them. Vivien Leigh made two, although she always denied it; Rex Harrison first appeared in one, as did Wendy Hiller and Margaret Rutherford. George Sanders got his first starring role in one too. Young writers also got a break: Terry Rattigan and Robert Morley wrote scripts for me before they became famous.'

Simplicity was the key to these productions. There was no heavy camera coverage, post-synchronisation or sound effects recordings. Library tracks were used for both music and effects. They were usually well cast, with reasonable scripts, and proved a springboard for many famous names of

the future. Actors in the Pinewood films included Patrick Barr, Greta Gynt, Jimmy Hanley, Wendy Hiller and Edward Rigby.

Conversely, just as they were a starting ground for many aspiring filmmakers, they also marked the end of the line for some of the great silent movie directors, George Pearson being one. Film director and Oscar-winning lighting cameraman Freddie Francis worked on many of the 'quota' films, two of them with George Pearson, at the beginning of his Pinewood career. 'He was a strange chap,' says Francis, 'as he always used to wear his overcoat and trilby hat on set. He never really came to terms with sound either, as he would quite often talk in the middle of a scene or shout out directions.'

But what of the other filmmakers? 'There were many people around the studio at that time,' continues Francis, 'who really knew very little about making films and I have to admit I learnt a lot from their mistakes! They just found themselves in the situation of having to make these films and muddled their way through as best they could. Of course, the in-joke with the quota films was that nobody other than the cleaners at the Plaza would

USINESS (1936 – 1938)

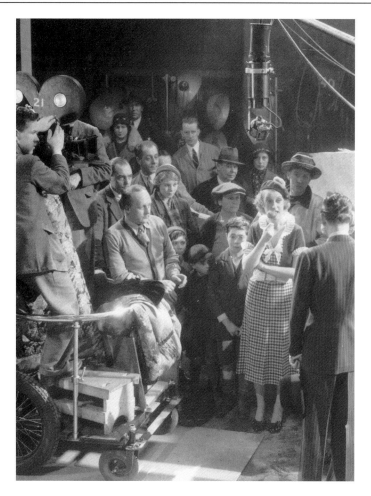

ever see them, as the films were often run in the mornings to fulfil the requirements of the quota act – but they were a good training ground.'

The ten-year life span of the 'quota quickies' came to an end in 1937, the same year in which J Arthur Rank bought out Lady Yule's share in Pinewood, when she became unhappy with Woolf's plans to bring together British National with GFD. Rank in turn sold Lady Yule his shares in British National, which she then ran with John Corfield. Rank now found himself with ever-greater interests in production and distribution.

Pinewood was fast making its mark as a remarkably modern production centre. Yet the refined elegance of the once stately home was not lost as the art gallery, drawing rooms, guest rooms and gardens were beautifully maintained. It was, however, a difficult time for filmmakers and, as they suffered, so too did the rental spaces that so desperately relied upon their activity. Denham struggled under Korda, who found himself £1m in the red owing to poor box-office on the likes of *The Four Feathers* and *Elephant Boy*. Twickenham Studios found it impossible to stay in business too. It was a bad time to be in film ... unless your name was Mr Rank.

Gaumont-British, which owned more than 300 cinemas, was floundering in the American market. Woolf had left the company to form GFD and Michael Balcon went over to MGM. The three Ostrer brothers – Isidore, Maurice and Mark – were responsible for the day-to-day operations of Gaumont-British and as such they owned 51 per cent of the stock. The other 49 per cent had been sold to Fox in the early 1930s. In a bid to control the spiralling losses, a deal was struck with Rank and Woolf to absorb Gainsborough Productions, with GFD releasing future Gaumont-British product. Rank and Woolf now became the country's biggest and, some would say, most powerful distributors with GFD.

However, dwindling production activity was the immediate problem to overcome, though Pinewood itself kept reasonably busy. Of some 24 productions in 1937, *The Frog* was produced by Herbert Wilcox and, despite being described by critic Graham Greene as the sort of production one might see 'produced in country towns by stranded actors', it spawned a sequel in 1938 called *The Return of the Frog*. *Lancashire Luck*, a Paramount quota quickie, launched Wendy Hiller's career while Alfred Hitchcock shot his first Pinewood film, *Young and Innocent*. In it he achieved what was considered to be one of the best and longest tracking shots ever – right the way around a dance floor and ending up on the twitching eye of the band's drummer. Hitchcock wouldn't return to the studio until 1971.

Also in 1937, Sinclair Hill directed *Midnight Menace* for his own company, Grosvenor Sound Films, from a treatment called *War On Wednesday*. This had been submitted in an unusual form by its authors, Alexander Mackendrick and his cousin Roger MacDougall. With no idea of how to write a film script, cartoonist Mackendrick and saxophonist MacDougall storyboarded the film in cartoon format, speech balloons and all. The film exploited the highly topical threat of aerial invasion by Fascist aggressors, with Germany thinly disguised as Grovinia, and featured alarm-

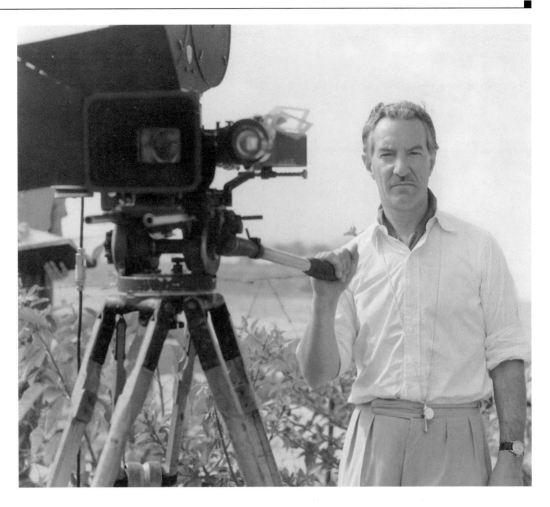

ing scenes of Piccadilly Circus under bombardment, just as Korda's *Things To Come* had the year before. The famous German actor Fritz Kortner, who had been Louise Brooks' co-star in Pabst's *Pandora's Box*, was brought over to take the lead, while the young hero – a cartoonist, appropriately enough – was played by Charles Farrell. Mackendrick later became a distinguished director; one of his most memorable films, *The Man in the White Suit*, was written by MacDougall.

In 1938 a new Films Act was introduced to rid the screen of quota quickies. A 'treble quota' system was brought in, the idea being that producers would opt for more expensive or better films, but certainly fewer than under the previous Act. It provoked a massive crisis: investors were wary and fewer and fewer films were made. Richard Norton developed an idea to keep the studio busy and technicians employed. Pinebrook Films was formed to make low-budget films when there were gaps in studio bookings. Anthony Havelock-Allan began his 'big picture' career with these films.

Along came such pictures as *Lightning Conductor* with Gordon Harker and *Spot of Bother*,

starring Roberston Hare and Alfred Drayton. One of the most successful productions was *The Lambeth Walk* with Lupino Lane and Sally Gray, directed by Albert de Courville. Thought to be one of the many 'lost' films of the period, the discovery and remastering of a French-subtitled copy was greeted with jubilation in the mid 1990s. The stage revival of *Me and My Girl*, source of 'The Lambeth Walk', still plays to packed houses on both sides of the Atlantic, while Sir Anthony Havelock-Allan still receives enquiries about the film, including one about the rights to the property from Hollywood star Paul Newman.

Better was to follow with *This Man is News*. Shot for £14,000, it made almost £150,000 at the box-office. But the Pinebrook venture proved to be a double-edged sword. Studio staff wages still had to be paid and Norton found it a struggle. He then persuaded his cast and crew to take a lower salary and invest the remainder in the film. If the film made a profit, then salary deferment would earn a sizeable amount. *This Man is News* was the first film ever to offer profit participation, rather than just a straight fee. It is interesting to note

that Pinebrook never lost money.

One of the non-Pinebrook productions of the year, *The Mikado*, was a glorious Technicolor version of the Gilbert and Sullivan operetta with Martyn Green. The new colour technology was bulky and awkward. The camera was the size of three ordinary film cameras and worked by exposing three separate strips of film.

Meanwhile, playwright George Bernard Shaw was being cajoled into allowing one of his plays to be made into a film. He had turned down many previous requests but a 40-year-old Hungarian called Gabriel Pascal persuaded him otherwise. He was a very canny producer. From studying farming at the Hungarian National Economy college and serving as a lieutenant in the Hungarian Hussar Regiment during the Great War, he progressed to producing silent films in Italy and decamped to Britain in the mid-1930s. He won Shaw over against all the odds, and when C M Woolf rejected the opportunity to distribute the film and hence guarantee the finance, Pascal manoeuvred himself in the direction of Richard Norton (who was no great friend of Woolf) and arranged a meeting with J

Arthur Rank himself. Ignorant of Woolf's decision, Rank agreed to back the film.

The splendid result, *Pygmalion*, starred Wendy Hiller and Leslie Howard, who co-directed with Anthony Asquith. The film was nominated for four Academy Awards – Best Picture, Script, Actor and Actress. It also caused some controversy when Wendy Hiller delivered what was then considered an outrageous line: 'Not bloody likely!' It was the first of Pascal's collaborations with Rank and was box-office dynamite. Rank had evidently made a wise decision.

Dame Wendy Hiller fondly remembered the early days at Pinewood in a 1986 TV interview. 'I didn't realise how lucky I was to be virtually living in a country house. The "big house" still had that feeling – the atmosphere, furnishings, lovely pictures – the feel of a lived-in country house. The staff were very efficient and attentive and it was lovely to be able to walk through the gardens, beautifully planted and maintained, to make-up and get into my chair to have my hair set and have a white-coated waiter bring me my breakfast. That was filmmaking ... or rather, that was filmmaking

at Pinewood! We made *Pygmalion* in seven or eight weeks. I had to work Sundays; Mr Howard didn't, and I called him Mr Howard all the way through filming, as he was the established star! I did move from Mr Asquith to "Puffin" [his nickname] but that was very daring!'

Film producer Euan Lloyd was heavily influenced by Pinewood's early output, including *Talk of the Devil* and *The Gang Show*. He remembers *Pygmalion* in particular, because 'It provided diction lessons for me as well as Eliza Doolittle. From this I learned how to enunciate, improve my table manners and, yes, to respect the law. I believed I learned more in the cinema of the thirties than in the classroom. It also gave me a determination to enter the wonderful world of cinema – in any capacity.'

Pascal, meanwhile, went on to produce Shaw's *Major Barbara* at Denham before he struck a further deal with Rank in the 1940s. His first under the new deal, *Caesar and Cleopatra*, was another Shaw subject and had the dubious honour at the time of being the most expensive British film ever. It was also very controversial and spelt the end of Pascal's career with Rank

and, indeed, in Britain.

Over at Korda's Denham Studios, problems worsened. His big-budget pictures couldn't deliver the box-office he so desperately needed. Ever-increasing debts stretched the patience of Korda's 'patron', the Prudential Building Society. Rank saw his opportunity to move in. Working with Prudential, Rank bought out Korda's interests in Denham and combined the studio with Pinewood. It was a further six years before Rank bought out all of Prudential's interests in the studio.

The amalgamation of Denham and Pinewood was brought to fruition with the formation of D and P Studios Ltd. It had been registered as a private concern with a nominal capital of £750,000 in £1 shares. The objectives of the company were listed as being to 'acquire London Film Productions and Pinewood Studios, and it will adopt agreements with (1) London Films and Prudential Assurance Company, and (2) Pinewood Studios and Equity and Law Life Assurance Society.' The eight appointed directors were E Ronald Crammond, E H George, Sir Connop Guthrie, E H Lever, Captain R Norton, J Arthur Rank, Spencer M Reis and P C Stapleton.

On Christmas Eve 1938, however, Pinewood Studios closed its doors. Lack of productions and mounting operating costs had rendered it non-viable. Rank moved all production over to the busier Denham Studios. His interests in other areas of film, meanwhile, were growing further. When Oscar Deutsch, of the Odeon chain of cinemas, needed further investment to fund his 'invasion' of North America, the vital missing link in Rank's empire was finally put in place.

The son of a Hungarian scrap merchant, Deutsch started building his cinema establishments in 1933. Odeon, it is believed by some, stood for Oscar Deutsch Entertains Our Nation. From his first cinema in Perry Barr, Birmingham to the chain's Leicester Square flagship, Deutsch's empire grew rapidly and he had almost 200 of them by the time Rank took his seat on the board early in 1939.

By that time, however, war was looming in Europe. ∎

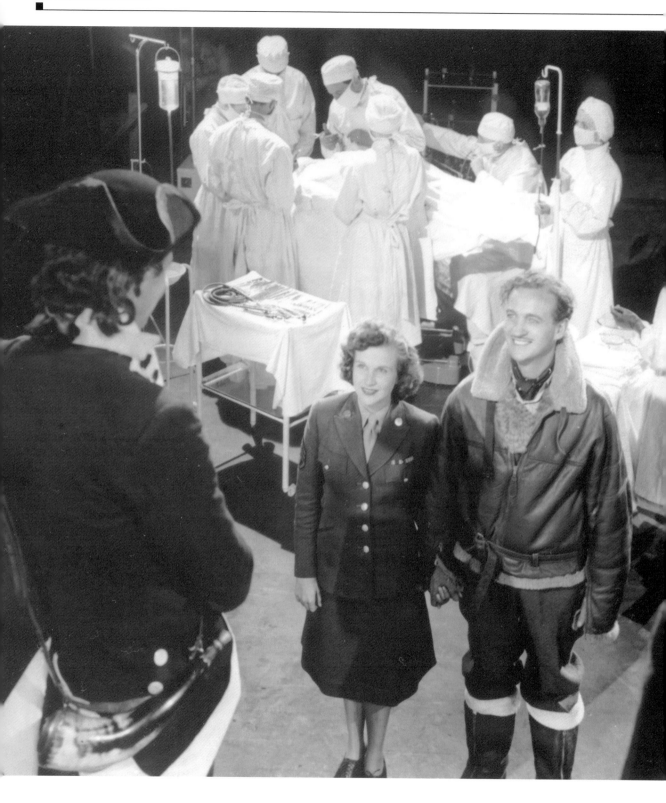

3

TH

Left: *The Archers' production of* A Matter of Life and Death *starring David Niven and Kim Hunter.*

Right: *One of the 'extravagant' coaches laid on to transport Lloyd's staff to and from work.*

When war finally arrived in September, Pinewood Studios were requisitioned by the Army. Denham was still open thanks to Pascal and *Major Barbara*, which by then was over-running its schedule.

As well as the Army using Pinewood for storage purposes, the Royal Mint moved onto one of the stages and Lloyd's of London were installed in the main house and admin building. Lloyd's, in fact, moved into the studio the weekend before war was declared. Some 500 staff, mostly women, were involved in the move and every one of them was offered a local billet. Five thousand such billets were secured through house-to-house canvassing in anticipation of the whole city market evacuating; wherever Lloyd's went, it was assumed, the Marine Insurance companies and brokers in other sections of the market would surely follow. On 4 September 1939, Lloyd's opened for 'business as usual' at its new base.

Staff who were not billeted locally took advantage of the daily long-distance coaches, which carried them to and from their homes. However, when it became impossible to continue such an 'extravagant' service, buses ran only to the local London Underground station in Uxbridge. Meanwhile, eight vans were used on a daily basis to transport documents to and from the City.

The decor of the studio was now transformed dramatically. Gone were the off-white colours and in their place was camouflage paint. Several members of the Lloyd's staff had received ARP training in London before war was declared, and these men and women formed the nucleus of a Lloyd's Pinewood Fire Guard which developed into an enviable team covering fire, first-aid and wardens' duties. There were no air-raid shelters at the studio at the time, so the staff were given rather vague instructions to 'disperse into the surrounding woods on warning being sounded.'

The first year of the war, the 'phoney war' as it was dubbed, gave valuable breathing space during which the question of shelters, blackouts, warning signals and fire-watching rotas could be tackled. And with the formation of the Local Defence Volunteers – the Home Guard – came Pinewood's own formidable unit: the 10th Bucks Battalion, No 5 (Pinewood) Platoon.

In 1941, the Crown Film Unit, Army Film and Photography Unit (AFPU), Royal Air Force (RAF) Film Unit and the Polish Air Force Film Unit made their base at Pinewood, and had use of the studio and general production area. A wire fence was erected diagonally across the car park and the road alongside the administration building in order to separate the house and gardens from the main studio area. The wire fence didn't prevent a certain amount of fraternisation with Lloyds' female staff, especially when American servicemen arrived in 1942.

The orderly room and officers' and sergeants' mess were all situated on the corridor later occupied by the art department. Regular roll call parades took place in the car park in the mornings, many of them conducted by future producer Anthony Nelson Keys. Army boots and gaiters were then changed to civilian shoes for production work. The Lloyd's staff often watched in amusement as they arrived for work on the other side of the wire fence. There were also cross-country runs across the Pinewood estate, again much to the amusement of the civvies on site.

'All the technical personnel were automatically given the rank of sergeant,' says John Aldred, who

WAR YEARS (1939 – 1945)

Right: *Eight of these all-important document vans ran between the studio and city every day.*

served as a sound engineer with the AFPU, 'and an officer was put in charge of each section such as camera, sound and editing. Civilian staff were employed for set building, lighting and props etc and since a large proportion of both Army and RAF personnel had been drawn directly from the film industry, we found that most of us had known each other in civilian life only a few months before. We had been on Christian name terms then, but it was considered bad form to address an officer by his first name – except in private.

'Our billets were the dressing rooms in Blocks A, B, C and D, and included ATS and WAAF personnel. The majority of sergeants and officers didn't live far away, and so were able to return home at the end of each day; but those who had to live in had batwomen to look after them, even to the extent of being served early morning tea in bed! We never went short of anything, except for the canteen not opening for the traditional mid-morning tea break. However, the problem was solved in rather a novel way as over in Gerrards Cross [a few miles from the studio] there was a branch of the British Federation of Women Zionists who ran a mobile canteen, and it was arranged that they should come over to Pinewood each day. Queues formed and trade was brisk – they became known as "The Women of Israel"!'

From his first day at Pinewood as assistant Crown Film librarian – and later film editor – John Legard remembers the routine. 'One would enter the studio via the second [timekeeper's] gate and collect a meal ticket from an RAF chap, as it was the RAF who had the administration of the studio, for a two-course lunch. It cost one shilling. The RAF canteen was located in an upstairs room over what are now the studio general stores.

'My job was looking after, filing and cataloguing all the MOI library material. Crown was the Ministry's own film unit and made films connected with all aspects of the war effort, from high-powered propaganda to straightforward information films. My work could be boring at times, but gave one a wonderful opportunity of handling film and therefore was excellent training. On the first morning, in 1943, Frank Capra came into the library for some footage, as he was producing a series called *Why We Fight*. It was, for me, a good start.

'The lady in charge of the library, which was on the ground floor of the main cutting rooms, was a trim little creature called Adelaide Pentecost. She was originally a film negative cutter at Elstree, where David Lean was one of her boys! Bernard Gribble was one of the others in the library with me. He later became a distinguished editor at Ealing on films like *The Man in the White Suit*, and later Hollywood where he is now based. We were paid £2 10s 6d a week.'

Dubbing Theatre 1 was occupied by the RAF sound technicians under Flight Lieutenant Bill Sweeney, whilst Theatre 2 was used by the AFPU under Captain D P Field. Both theatres were still equipped with the Western Electric recorders from 1936. The Crown Film Unit also used Theatre 2, but because they employed another system (RCA), they also had to have their own re-recording equipment and projector.

Although war was very much on everyone's minds, the atmosphere at Pinewood was very relaxed and the conflict sometimes seemed rather remote. On one occasion Princess Marina, the Duchess of Kent, paid an official visit to Pinewood. Several editors and production personnel were presented to her, including the young Richard Best, who had been fortunate to transfer to the AFPU in 1941 after starting at Pinewood on day one back in 1936.

With the constant air attacks on London, however, it was inevitable that at least one bomb would fall near Pinewood. It was a V2 missile which exploded in a field about half a mile down Pinewood Road. Lilli Palmer and Rex Harrison were living in the road at that time and, according to Palmer, the

'bomb landed in front of the house and the huge rhododendron bush took the full blast and prevented the house from being severely damaged.'

John Trumper, an assistant in the editing rooms, recalls the V1 and V2 missiles vividly. 'I remember while coming from Uxbridge up the short steep hill, at the front of the top deck of a double-decker bus, watching a V1 passing over at a low level only a short distance ahead. Then during the film *A Diary for Timothy*, a V2 fell in a field just to the south of Pinewood and the blast blew in the window where I was working, filling my hair with scraps of broken glass.'

Preliminary damage to Pinewood was minimal, but the knock-on effects were still being felt days later. 'I remember someone of fairly high rank in the studio,' says John Legard, 'working in his office about a week after the V2 dropped when the ceiling suddenly collapsed and he was knocked unconscious!'

Thankfully, that was the first and only time the Third Reich came near Pinewood. Extra 'fire watching' duties were introduced on the roof of A [now D] Stage – which had an unobstructed view in the direction of London, where any future fire bomb attacks were expected to come from. Pinewood's Chief Fire Officer, Mr Semple, had been at the studio ever since it opened and his eyes never missed a thing. He was somewhat advanced in years, however, and often reminisced about his war experiences – not the current war, nor the Great War of 1914-18, but the Zulu War in South Africa at the end of the nineteenth century, when he fought in the infantry.

The studios formed the base for many service cameramen, who were posted to all corners of the World War. Rushes were regularly returned to the studio: reels of footage covering all aspects of life behind the lines and at the front. The turnaround was speedy. For instance, the first rushes of the D-Day landings arrived at Pinewood within three days. Of course, by comparison to today's instant news and pictures, it was pretty slow, but for the time it was almost miraculous.

The atmosphere at Pinewood during these years was imperative to the success of the films and personnel involved, as Hugh Stewart testifies. 'I found myself in charge at the studio, in company with the RAF and Crown Film Units, training a bunch of sergeant cameramen to go overseas. There was one major snag: I didn't have the slightest idea how to photograph a battle, let alone tell anyone else how to. Thanks to the atmosphere at Pinewood we somehow managed to invent a training scheme. Army Film Units, with a very high level of morale and efficiency, went out to cover campaigns in the Western Desert, North Africa, the Far East, France and Germany. Pinewood was always fun to come back to.'

Many future greats of British filmmaking were based at the studio at this time, among them Roy and John Boulting (Army and RAF) and Jack Lee, Pat Jackson, Jack Holmes and Humphrey Jennings (Crown). David MacDonald and Hugh Stewart led the Army cameramen; Stewart later returned to produce 19 features for the Rank Organisation, including three Morecambe and Wise films and a dozen with Norman Wisdom. Also present were John Aldred, Richard Best, Frank Clarke, Johnny Guthridge, John Howell, Gil Taylor, Bob Verrall and Harry Waxman.

A great many documentaries were produced by the units reflecting wartime Britain – both civilian and military – at home and abroad, among them:
Desert Victory – Montgomery's successful attack at El Alamein and the follow-through along the North African Coast.
Burma Victory – the Burma campaign, including General Wingate's activities.
Left of the Line – the Canadians' role in the D-Day landings.
Malta GC – the story of Malta's stand under horrific bombardment.

A Harbour Goes to France – how Churchill's concrete 'Mulberry Harbour' was planned, built and towed to Arromanches in Normandy to act as a supply base.

Tunisian Victory – the American and British continuation of the desert war.

The True Glory – the story of the build-up and eventual invasion of Normandy by British, Canadian and American troops.

All the above were made by the AFPU. *Journey Together* – the story of flying crew training – was produced by the RAF.

Roy Boulting's unit won an Academy Award for *Desert Victory*. In fact, it was pure luck that led Boulting to become involved with the production. Rommel had driven the British Eighth Army over the Egyptian border and was now at El Alamein. Egypt and its oil wells were the prizes for Rommel should he smash the British. If the Germans had seized control of these, Britain would have been weakened and Rommel would have been able to drive up to the Crimea and join Paulus's army. This battle would affect the whole course of the war, one way or another.

At the War Office Boulting met Major Woolley, whose job it was to keep records on the Middle East campaign. The subject was then discussed and Boulting returned to his Pinewood unit, knowing what was required. Within ten days, on 5 November 1942, Rommel was in retreat, the Italians surrendered and David MacDonald shot almost one million feet of film, recording Britain's first major victory of the war. Boulting's team edited the material under his supervision. Because the initial night advance of the battle was so dramatic, Boulting himself recreated it on one of Pinewood's stages; night shooting in the desert was impossible owing to the limitations of contemporary film stock. These scenes were intercut with the footage from the front.

The sound effects also proved a challenge for the AFPU team, as John Aldred – later Oscar-nominated

for his sound on *Mary Queen of Scots* – recalls. 'We tried letting off a thunderflash firework in a dustbin at the carpenters' shop to simulate gunfire, but it was not entirely successful. So we ended up travelling to Lark Hill on Salisbury Plain to record real gunfire, and also to Chobham Common to record tanks on their testing ground. We also visited several munitions factories in Wolverhampton to obtain sound effects for sequences showing the manufacture of tanks and armaments. We had our own portable recording equipment, a Western Electric 'Q' channel, mounted in what was originally an Army bread van on an AEC chassis!'

The film opened at the Odeon Leicester Square to cheering applause. It remains a tremendous feat of filmmaking. Macdonald was promoted from Major to Lieutenant Colonel overnight, and the film's editor, Richard Best, was awarded the British Empire Medal – although it didn't drop through his letterbox until 1949.

Garson Kanin and Carol Reed's *The True Glory* was the biggest war documentary made at Pinewood; it was a combined effort by the AFPU and the American Photographic Corps, and Colonel Frank Capra came over to supervise the post-production and assume overall control in the dubbing theatre. The film covered all aspects of the war in Europe from events leading up to D-Day, the invasion itself, the capitulation of the German forces on 4 May 1945 and the official end of the war in Europe on 8 May. Peter Ustinov provided the film's commentary. To accommodate the fantastic amount of extra film editing required when the American units arrived, additional cutting rooms were constructed along the corridor adjacent to D Stage.

Among the many American servicemen who came to Pinewood to work on *Tunisian Victory* and *The True Glory* was Frank P Keller. He later became a famous Hollywood editor and won an Academy Award for *Bullitt*. As well as Capra, Garson Kanin and Irwin Shaw also spent a lot of time at the studio.

Previous page: *An AFPU roll call.*

Left: *At work in the cutting rooms (left to right) - Merrill White, Richard Best and Frank Clarke.*

The Army Film Unit also employed some distinguished writers and composers. The novelist J L Hodson wrote the narration for *Desert Victory*, which was spoken by Leo Genn. Frank O'Connor and Laurie Lee also wrote commentaries. William Alwyn composed the *Desert Victory* score, Alan Rawsthorne scored *Burma Victory* and Sir Arnold Bax *Malta GC*. Several noted actors were at large, too – Richard Attenborough, John Justin, Edward G Robinson, David Tomlinson and Jack Watling appeared in *Journey Together*, which was directed by John Boulting.

John Trumper worked with the celebrated documentarist Humphrey Jennings on several of the Crown Film Unit productions. 'I had a short nervous breakdown, caused by Jennings's habit of finding the shot he wanted by unspooling 1,000 feet of unslated rushes onto the floor until he found and tore out the relevant section, leaving me to clear up the mess!' Trumper also cut his first film during this time, of Myra Hess playing the first movement of Beethoven's Appassionata Sonata. The 10-minute film is now available on video.

The Crown Film Unit was very large compared with other documentary companies, and producers in charge included Ian Dalrymple and later Jack Holmes and Basil Wright. Some of the other notable Crown films made during these years were:
Fires Were Started – the story of the wartime Fire Brigade.
Listen to Britain – a superb evocation of wartime Britain.
A Diary for Timothy (with narration by Michael Redgrave) – an account of the period, with hopes for the future generation.
The Silent Village – the tragedy of the annihilation by the Germans of the Czech village of Lidice, re-enacted in and by a Welsh community (all the above were directed by Humphrey Jennings).
Coastal Command – the story of the Sunderland and Catalina flying boats guarding the sea convoys.
Close Quarters – a chronicle of the submarine service.

Perhaps Crown's most outstanding film was Pat Jackson's *Western Approaches* – the story, filmed in Technicolor, of the North Atlantic convoys. John Aldred was 'loaned' to the unit from the AFPU to record certain sounds. 'They required some sound effects of a submarine for the film, so we took our Army sound truck up to Scotland and off-loaded our equipment into a submarine at the entrance to Loch Long. We then sat at the bottom of the loch whilst a destroyer approached from a distance of three miles dropping depth charges all the time! We clearly heard the screws as they passed overhead, and then they dropped a few more charges. It shook us up a bit, but the only damage suffered was from pieces of cork lining flying about in all directions. After we had surfaced there were quite a number of fish floating on the surface that had been stunned by the explosions. We had fresh fish for lunch that day!'

Other highlights of these years were a little more relaxed. There were regular evening film shows in Theatre One laid on by the RAF projectionists, usually showing the current feature films. Although the projectionists received no extra pay for the evening duty, at the end of each show they screened the following title:
Just a thought for your reflection,
A show like this needs good projection.
So don't forget before you go,
The backroom boys who run the show.

Right: *Fire-watching on A Stage, now D Stage.*

Everybody willingly parted with their shillings and pence. Other memorable moments included the lunch-time musical recitals in Theatre One, organised by Ken Cameron (chief of sound for the Crown Film Unit). Muir Mathieson was musical director and also conducted the music for many of the wartime films, continuing with Crown until it moved out of Pinewood in late 1946 to Beaconsfield Studios.

Ken Cameron recalls how the lunchtime recitals came about. 'I used to go to many of Myra Hess's concerts at the National Gallery, as she was a great friend of mine. One day we were chatting and she said that she would love to come over to Pinewood for a little concert. So I arranged it and it was an astonishing success! From there, others followed like Denis Mathews and Solomon, and sometimes the RAF Symphony. If I wasn't able to arrange a "classical" piece, we quite often would have something light or even a gramophone record.'

During the last year of the war, Crown produced a short film with the London Symphony Orchestra called *Instruments of the Orchestra*, also known as *The Young Person's Guide to the Orchestra*. 'The music for it was actually recorded at Wembley Town Hall,' says Cameron. 'We had to play the instruments over the completed film and it was all with very primitive technology. On one side of me I had Muir Mathieson and on the other Benjamin Britten ... That was quite a day!'

All of the wartime documentaries and films made at Pinewood are held at the Imperial War Museum, and many are available on video. They make amazing viewing, especially when one thinks that this was the first time in history that such a comprehensive visual and aural record was made possible.

Sadly, many film technicians lost their lives in action. A plaque stands to their memory in the main corridor leading to Pinewood's stages.

J Arthur Rank did not sit idle during the war years. The man who maintained that he was 'guided by God' saw his empire go from strength to strength. Rank's Denham studios were kept busy when war broke out, with the appetite for home-grown product becoming greater than ever. Dependence on Hollywood films decreased and, despite losing many technicians to the war effort, the British industry boomed. It was estimated that the majority of the population were visiting the cinema at least once a week.

In a stroke of genius, Rank had bought the newly completed Amalgamated Studios at Elstree in 1939 by writing a six-figure cheque from his own personal bank account. By eliminating delays in this way, he pipped John Maxwell, head of ABC, at the post. As if that wasn't enough, he then did a deal with the government to lease the studio for records storage at a very good return on his money.

In 1941, the troubled Gaumont-British fell into his hands too, when the Ostrer brothers sold out to Rank for three quarters of a million. The same year, his grip on the British film business was further tightened when Oscar Deutsch succumbed to cancer at an early age and his Odeon chain was acquired, much to the chagrin of Deutsch's family and associates, many of whom didn't particularly care for Rank. And when Lime Grove Studios re-opened for business Rank struck a deal with Michael Balcon to distribute all of Balcon's Ealing output, whilst guaranteeing the studio autonomy.

After the death of C M Woolf in 1942, Rank's other chief partners, Lord Portal and Lord Luke, gradually began to withdraw from the business. Within nine years, the millionaire miller had advanced from renting simple projectors at church Sunday schools to becoming Britain's most powerful and influential film mogul. Indeed, the government became worried about his and ABC's growing monopoly of studios and cinemas and commissioned the Palache Report in 1944. It found that, although Rank had growing interests, he by no means had a monopoly – less than half the operational British studios were controlled by Rank and he owned only 15 per cent of cinema screens. It was agreed that ABC and Rank should have to ask permission from the Board of Trade before opening further cinemas.

At Denham, Rank had funded a group of independent filmmakers in a film production pro-

gramme. Independent Producers Ltd comprised Ian Dalrymple and Marcel Hellman, Anthony Havelock-Allan and Ronald Neame, Leslie Howard, Frank Launder and Sidney Gilliatt, Michael Powell and Emeric Pressburger, David Lean and Alfred Watkins. The idea was to bring together distinguished filmmakers of the day, promote co-operation between them and enable them to make the best use of facilities and manpower. Rank also offered them a cut of the profits. They were very much independent, Rank funding their operations with the minimum of interference. Finance, creative freedom, stories, casting and 'final cut' were all part of the deal. All the more amazing: no party in the company was under any form of contract.

'Independent Producers was the brainchild of an agent called Christopher Mann – quite an extraordinary chap,' remembers Cineguild's production manager, Norman Spencer. 'He suggested that the leading filmmaking talent of the day should form a conglomerate where each would take a place on the board and, although they would make their own films, they would assist each other. Tom White was the general production manager and his assistant was Peggy Hennessey. I remember that each of the production managers from the various companies such as Archers, Cineguild, Wessex etc would meet every Monday in the Pinewood boardroom to discuss matters and how projects were running and so forth. It was a marvellous company with a tremendous unified spirit.'

Independent Producers Ltd operated from 1944 to 1947. James B Sloan had come over from Pinewood to act as chief production manager and the group's managing director was George Archibald. Their functions were administrative rather than creative and they took seats on the board with J Arthur Rank as chairman. Of the filmmakers, Leslie Howard died soon after the company's formation when a plane he was travelling in was shot down by the Luftwaffe over the Bay of Biscay. Marcel Hellman then left after making two indifferent pictures with the group, *They Met in the Dark* and *Secret Mission*. Alfred Watkins, meanwhile, did little but offer his production services and expertise. Even so, many notable productions came from the Independent Producers stable, not least *Black Narcissus*, *A Canterbury Tale*, *A Matter of Life and Death* (which was inspired by a government request to improve Anglo-American relations and became the first Royal Film Performance), *Great Expectations* and *Oliver Twist*.

Through all this, J Arthur Rank maintained that his film activities still stemmed from duty and obligation. He wanted to give the Americans a run for their money and was passionate about ensuring his films received good distribution throughout the world. Indeed, in the summer of 1945 he had visited Hollywood and was given an almost royal reception by the assembled moguls. The mild-mannered Sunday school teacher was an enigma to the American press: he controlled everything and yet appeared so unassuming, quite unlike his American counterparts. One of these – David O Selznick, the producer of *Gone With the Wind* – was so keen to work with Rank he formed a new company in England just to make one (unrealised) film. Rank was shown around Universal Studios, of which he was a shareholder, and was so impressed with American production efficiency that he later sent over his own technicians, producers and directors to study Hollywood methods. Pinewood was to benefit greatly from the expertise they brought back with them.

During this time John Davis, an accountant from Oscar Deutsch's reign at Odeon, was fast becoming a powerful figure within the Rank Organisation. He was a hard worker, with an unstinting loyalty to J Arthur Rank, and was considered to be the voice of prudence. Every penny should turn a profit, as far as Davis was concerned, and gone were the luxuries of uncapped Rank investments to support extravagant producers. ∎

4

BAC

Left: *David Lean's* Great Expectations.

Right: *The Archers - Emeric Pressburger and Michael Powell during the filming of* Black Narcissus.

In 1946, Pinewood re-opened for business. An immediate investment programme was embarked upon in the sound department, as the pre-war installations were by then considered antiquated. The two dubbing theatres were given a face-lift with new mixing consoles and recording equipment, and a new recording theatre was built for sound effects and dialogue post-sync.

The Crown Film Unit's old quarters became the studio's camera department, headed by Bert Easy, who had previously run the department at Denham. Pinewood owned all the camera apparatus in those days, but no studio could keep pace with subsequent developments and, when Panaflex cameras and lenses appeared on the scene, they were only available for hire. When Bert Easy retired, the department was closed in favour of on-site camera hire companies such as Samuelsons, who were able to offer a more cost-effective deal for the latest equipment.

The first film onto the stages was the Launder-Gilliatt production *Green for Danger*, starring Alastair Sim, Trevor Howard, Rosamund John and Sally Gray. The *Daily Telegraph* described this comedy-thriller set in a wartime emergency hospital as 'slick, witty and consistently entertaining.' A couple of the Independent Producers' films also made use of Pinewood, most notably David Lean's *Great Expectations* and Powell and Pressburger's *Black Narcissus*, the second film to shoot in Technicolor at the studio and winner of Academy Awards in 1948 for art direction and cinematography. The production recreated the Himalayas in the back lot and gardens, as Norman Spencer recalls. 'My office was on the first floor of the old house overlooking the gardens and one could really have been forgiven for thinking we were in the Himalayas, especially with the light at certain times of day. Hundreds of rhododendrons were brought in, as they are found in that area of the world in abundance, and the gardens looked fantastic; albeit with nuns everywhere!'

Great Expectations had started production at Denham. 'But we couldn't facilitate the paddle boat sequences at Denham,' Spencer points out, 'so decided to move over to Pinewood where we used the large tank. It was a tremendous sequence and took around ten days or so to film. After *Great Expectations* Cineguild moved to Pinewood full-time and completed all its future films there until David [Lean] and I left to join Korda at Shepperton.'

Anthony Havelock-Allan returned to produce Ronald Neame's *Take My Life*, a thriller in the Hitchcock mould with excellent performances from Hugh Williams, Greta Gynt and Marius Goring. 'The post-war atmosphere was much more professional,' he claims. 'There had been a "gifted amateur" feel to the place with the grand house and gardens before, which, although never inhibiting the making of films, was perhaps a little too pleasant on the whole. You got away from the fact that what

N BUSINESS (1946 – 1949)

you were doing was making an industrial product and probably the most risky one there is. You're putting a great deal of money into a piece of celluloid and nobody knows what might happen. But that industrial feel was present on our return, perhaps through the influence on Rank of John Davis.'

The first post-war year for Pinewood was a good one. But better was to come in 1947, for one of the greatest stories ever told was created on C Stage: *The Red Shoes*.

Powell and Pressburger, who had initially met at Denham, chose the story having completed *The End of the River*, which had been a strange departure for the filmmakers and a critical and commercial disaster. *The Red Shoes* was a very simple tale of a great ballet dancer and how she is torn between love (with Marius Goring) and her career

(with Anton Walbrook) and then driven to suicide when she has to choose between them. Nothing like it had been seen before; the subtle use of colours, the special effects and the wonderful characters and performances all combined to form a beautifully textured film. *The Red Shoes* received three Academy Award nominations for Best Picture, Best Story and Music; Brian Easdale won in the latter category. Powell and Pressburger were back on form. And of the many new techniques and effects employed in the film, the 'gunshot' travelling matte must rate as the best: Moira Shearer danced with a newspaper.

Editor Noreen Ackland collaborated on all of the Powell and Pressburger films at Pinewood and remembers *The Red Shoes* with particular affection. 'Micky and Emeric were wonderful. Exciting.

Everything was new and they made you a part of the whole company making it. I was only second assistant in those days but was made to feel just as important as the stars. Pinewood was a fantastic place to work – a truly magical film made at a truly magical studio. It will always be my favourite film and holds so many precious memories for me, and whenever anyone mentions Pinewood to me, *The Red Shoes* always springs to mind.'

Following the highly successful and critically acclaimed *Great Expectations*, Cineguild decided to film another Dickens classic, *Oliver Twist*. David Lean again took the director's chair but worried greatly about who should play Fagin, the film's most memorable and menacing character. Alec Guinness, who had played a cameo role in *Great Expectations* as Herbert Pocket, asked to meet with Lean at the Savoy. He asked outright to play the part. Lean frankly told Guinness that he was out of his mind. Unfazed, Guinness asked Lean at least to allow him to test for the role. Stuart Freeborn's ingenious make-up was based on the George Cruikshank's original illustrations and took three hours to apply; when Guinness walked on the set in full make-up and costume, Lean was overwhelmed.

The search for Oliver himself was a highly publicised one. Of 1,500 applicants, 80 were auditioned. John Howard Davies, son of the *Express* film critic Jack, was only eight-years-old and that created problems not only with the unions but also the educational authorities. But so determined were Cineguild that this boy was their Oliver that they forged ahead anyway. John later became a BBC executive, while his father went on to write the scripts for such films as *Paper Tiger* and *North Sea Hijack*.

'*Oliver Twist* was shot in its entirety at Pinewood,' remembers Norman Spencer. 'The fantastic, silent opening scene was all done on a stage and it was planned with military precision as each shot had to convey the mood of that scene – the girl's pain with the thorns, the cold night with the clouds and so on. John Bryan designed the set. David [Lean] said that he wished he could start every film with a silent sequence as he felt it was a real tension-builder. He used the analogy of a

Facing page: *Robert Newton as Sikes awaits 'Action!'.*

man sitting in the cinema just about to light a cigarette, but he can't because he's so grabbed with what's happening on the screen. The baby we used in the workhouse scene was in fact the daughter of a local doctor. I had to find a new-born baby, and the only thing I could think of was to phone a local doctor and enquire if any patients were soon to "produce". A lady doctor in Gerrards Cross, Dr Shipman, said that my luck was in as in two weeks she was due to give birth! The day after the child was born, we took the unit to her house and filmed the scene you see in the film. Incidentally, the baby was named Olivia, after the film's title.'

Kay Walsh, David Lean's second wife, played Nancy. Walsh had a significant involvement in creating the opening sequence and vividly remembers the cold early morning starts. 'Sometimes one just didn't feel like working at all, particularly when it was dark and raining, and I found myself almost having to force myself to get up and take the car to the studio. But the cheery welcome at the gate and then the wonderful greeting by the Sergeant at reception made one feel it was all worthwhile after all.'

Oliver Twist also marked Euan Lloyd's baptism at Pinewood. 'During the five years from 1946 to 1951 I worked as publicity director for GFD. Visiting the set of *Oliver Twist* added fuel to my fire to be involved in production. However, during my tenure I often found myself at Pinewood and at meetings held in the projection theatres I shared the responsibility for shaping advertising campaigns for new product. This brought me into contact with many stars of the day, some becoming life-long friends, and one lady in particular, a Rank starlet named Jane Hylton became Mrs Euan Lloyd.'

Three other films were shot at the studios in 1947, one of which, *Esther Waters*, was notable for its casting of a young Dirk Bogarde.

Independent Frame (IF) was a technical project that Rank invested in heavily. Plans were hatched for the project as far back as 1944. David Rawnsley was the leading force behind IF, which was expected to revolutionise filmmaking by shortening film schedules and saving money on set con-

struction and location shooting. The idea appealed to Rank, especially in light of the ever-increasing excesses of some producers, because it offered an inexpensive production process and, moreover, a welcome means of supplying his distribution and cinema companies.

Rawnsley's idea stemmed from working on *49th Parallel* where he had shot a multitude of background plates (the location shots that would be projected onto screens in the studio, in front of or behind artistes, to give the impression of the artistes actually 'being there'). He thought that by taking the process a little further, it would be possible to combine projection, matte effects and split screens into one great project: Independent Frame.

Painted backdrops would be wheeled in and out of the stages on Vickers rostra, and with the use of specially modified cameras all would combine to quicken the filmmaking process. Gone would be the lengthy construction times and changing of sets and stages and in would come a factory 'conveyor belt' system, as Charles Staffell, one of Pinewood's top special effects men, described it. The sets were wheeled in, the artistes followed, rehearsed and then shot the scene. Then they'd move to another stage while the sets on the first were being wheeled out and replaced, to shoot further scenes and so the process continued. There would, of course, be a massive 'library' of backgrounds for use in multiple productions.

Bernard Hanson, who was assistant stage controller on the IF films, explains the technicalities of shooting. 'The whole stage was divided up into squares and each had a number. I then had to mark up the squares, once I received details from the art director on where the cameras had to be placed – otherwise the shot wouldn't fill the screen properly. I was just a youngster in those days, and had to tell very distinguished cameramen where they would have to place their cameras!'

Alan Hume, who later went on to photograph many of the *Carry On* and James Bond films, was then a camera operator. 'Yes, the floor was marked up in yard-squares which were all numbered. We used to go on the floor and say "We're shooting scene 28." The reply would come back "That's

square 34 shooting towards square 19 and you'll be on the screen in such and such a position.'"

The first IF film made at Pinewood was the comedy-drama *Warning to Wantons*. Movement was severely restricted on the sets and the projection techniques were never totally satisfactory. It was a frustrating process synching the projector shutter frequency with that of the camera filming the action, and actors often had a give-away 'glow' around them in these scenes. The process was later modified and perfected by Charles Staffell, who won an Academy Award for his work in the projection process; the first and only Oscar awarded for technical work of this kind.

'Independent Frame was an ill-thought out project,' believes Norman Spencer, 'but Rawnsley was egged on by the likes of John Davis who wanted to save money on productions. Davis was never interested in films, but paid them lip service and always tried to cut expenditure. The only useful thing to come out of it were the rostra!' Director Guy Hamilton agrees. 'The only useful remains of that ridiculous experiment were those excellent Vickers rostra – they're still in use today!'

Bernard Hanson added: 'I do remember that a hexagonal rostrum was made too – it had a revolving centre. The idea being that the hex would sit in the middle of the stage and other rostra could square onto the edges. I don't recall that one ever being used though.'

'The rostra are marvellous, but you must also remember that some bloody good projection equipment was developed as well,' says Alan Hume, 'which became invaluable in many of my later pictures. Independent Frame wasn't the success they thought it would be, but a few good things did come out of it.'

Warning to Wantons cost £100,000 and took 35 days to make – almost double what was anticipated on both counts. Naturally, these excesses were put down to teething troubles. But Rank had spent over £600,000 developing the technology – principally at Pinewood – and the resulting films were often poor quality box-office disasters. The great white hope in film production was soon dead in the water.

Kay Walsh appeared in *The Red Peppers*, an early IF film that co-starred Ted Ray. Like many other IF artistes, Walsh has few fond memories: 'Movement was very limited. There were so many sets coming in and out all the time and I remember we were all nearly electrocuted when someone dropped a cigarette end down the side of the rostrum and it caught fire. David Rawnsley, whom I knew, was a very talented man but the technique needed much perfection.'

Around this time, the first creations from the Gaumont-British animation division came to life. In 1944, Rank head-hunted David Hand, a highly regarded American animator who had recently served as supervising director on Walt Disney's *Snow White and the Seven Dwarfs* and *Bambi* among others. His brief was to mould the division, based at Moor Hall in Cookham, into one that could rival the Americans and produce cartoons for British audiences, incorporating British humour.

This was to be a particularly difficult task. At one point thoughts of turning newspaper cartoon strips into animated films were considered but quickly dismissed. Competition was fierce: *Popeye*, *Tom & Jerry* and the like were massively popular. The result of Hand's efforts was a stilted and unoriginal hodgepodge with very little of the madcap fun the American cartoons could offer. The animated films cost around £10,000 each and lasted no more than 10 minutes. The division was closed down with losses of around half a million pounds.

Another ill-fated project was *This Modern Age*, on which some of Hand's animators were kept busy. This was Rank's attempt to better the American newsreel magazine *The March of Time*. Production started in 1946 with *Homes For All*, a documentary about homelessness and poor housing. The series tackled some 41 topical subjects in its four-year lifespan and Rank gave the editorial team complete freedom, as he had done with his Independent Producers, even though some topics and viewpoints were not to his taste. Initially popular, the series visited many countries and prided itself on its location shooting. One 21-minute film was produced per month and each featured music by Muir Mathieson. Every episode ended with the legend, 'The challenge must be met in This Modern Age.'

Bob Verrell, who edited many entries in the series, says, 'They were excellent little films with relevant subjects and, in my opinion, every bit as good as – if not better than – *The March of Time*. Their eventual downfall came because they were not supported by the distribution and exhibition circuits, as they ought to have been and as Rank hoped they would be. I know for a fact that J Arthur Rank was particularly saddened at the demise of the series, more so than anything else he had worked on setting up, because he was tremendously proud of the films and felt they said a lot about Britain.'

This Modern Age was eventually relegated to supporting programme time-filler status and, along with the cartoon initiative, was reluctantly discontinued.

Another idea of Rank's was the formation of the 'Company of Youth', which became known as the Rank Charm School. Rank had a strong contract artist division, and the Charm School was basically a finishing school for many of them: they would learn poise, screen techniques and all-round airs and graces. An academy was founded in a large house in Highbury, North London. Enrolment wasn't necessarily dependent upon acting ability, but rather looks, figure and potential. The most successful Charm School graduates included Joan Collins, Diana Dors, Jill Ireland, Christopher Lee, Roger Moore and Anthony Steel.

'When I left the Army I had no interest in acting at all,' observes Anthony Steel, 'although I did enjoy going to the theatre and films. But it was when I met up with two friends of mine, Guy Middleton and Taffy [Hugh] Williams, in Berlin that the seeds were sown. We were having a drink and they mentioned that Olive Dodds and the Rank Organisation were wanting to create some stars for the future. Unbeknown to me, they had already spoken with Olive Dodds and said that I was someone she should meet.

'I eventually met with Olive and she asked if I'd ever thought about being an actor, and – in all honesty – I said "No"! She said that she'd let me know and that was that. However, a month or so later I received a letter saying that they'd like to offer me a two year contract. The money they offered was considerably better than what my old Army chums were making, and although they all said I was mad, it seemed like a good opportunity.

'I then went into the Charm School. It was quite an eclectic crowd – all ages from 17 onwards – and I went to Highbury Studios. Molly Terraine, who was in charge with Olive, had been a very successful actress and took me under her wing. After six weeks I said that it didn't really interest me. What I wanted was some practical experience. After a couple of little bit parts which gave me that experience, I landed *The Wooden Horse* – as they were looking for an unknown to co-star – and it was a great success. I then re-negotiated a new contract with Rank and stayed with them for quite some time.'

Charm School artistes were paid £20 a week whether they worked or not. The contracts were renewable annually (on the company's side) and when the artistes were hired out, or 'sub-let', to other producers Rank had it written into the contract that his organisation was entitled to 50 per cent of any profits. With most of Rank's top stars being in high demand for public appearances, charity functions and the like, quite often one of the Charm School artistes would be sent in their place. It didn't seem to matter that they were not of equal status to, say, Dirk Bogarde or Jean Simmons: they were stars simply because of their association with J Arthur Rank and were besieged accordingly.

Euan Lloyd explains how he also used Rank's stars to help achieve better relations with other sectors of the industry. 'My job was to bring a closer understanding between Wardour Street and Pinewood's producers as Mr Rank could sense a gulf which was becoming harmful. Salesmen and moviemakers rarely see eye to eye. John Davis approved my plan to invite salesmen and certain key exhibitors to the studio to see how the supply lines worked. An extension of that plan culminated in my escorting Mr Rank to GFD's countrywide branches. Actors became involved too, led mainly by Trevor Howard, Jack Hawkins, Stewart Granger, as well as new faces like Donald Houston. Personal appearances by the stars became a regular event, often lifting the box-office results. Glamour prevailed.'

Although the Charm School was kept busy, its

graduates were not; there was no obligation for any of Rank's producers to engage them, which rather defeated the object of setting up the academy. Those who were engaged were often only used in small parts or walk-ons and many left the business as a result.

After the abolition of 'quota quickies' the 'B' picture industry had suffered in Britain. In 1947 Rank decided to revive the curtain raisers as he believed, in tune with the Palache report of 1944, that Britain needed a flow of inexpensive films to act as a training ground for up-and-coming filmmakers. He purchased the two-stage Highbury Studios for this very purpose and every five weeks, at a cost of £20,000, a movie was made by talented newcomers, with seasoned heads of department overseeing production and providing the experience and know-how. Former Ealing Studios filmmaker John Croydon was brought in to run Highbury, where he was extremely innovative and turned its many constraints to his advantage. Preparation was everything with Croydon. He emphasised that time spent on planning and preparing sequences was invaluable once you moved on to the stage.

Highbury produced some admirable films, many transcending the material on which they were based, and provided a valuable training ground for actors, directors and technicians alike. However, like the cartoon and documentary divisions, the B pictures did not make money. The mechanics of distribution and exhibition only permitted a second feature to earn a small fraction of the sum earned by the main film.

Rank also established a children's film company to supply new pictures, made specifically for children, to the cinema circuits' Saturday morning clubs. The film programme was only part of the morning activities; also on offer for 'the betterment of youngsters' were singing lessons and general instructional classes in safety, hygiene, good citizenship etc. Every member received a birthday card and free admittance voucher for the following week. Although moral messages were contained in the clubs' activities and films, Rank was careful not to preach: first and foremost he wanted to entertain. Although the division lost money,

Facing page: *A lavish ballroom scene from David Lean's* Madeleine.

Rank believed the social benefits outweighed financial gain. Under Mary Field, the division produced some good quality and entertaining children's films but, like many of Rank's initiatives of the 1940s, it ultimately failed to survive. The films stayed in circulation but took some 15 years to show any profits. Ironically, within a year of its closure, the government set up the Children's Film Foundation and appointed Rank as chairman, with Mary Field as executive officer.

In 1947, Britain was plunged into financial crisis as a consequence of an international 'dollar drain' and the government announced drastic measures to reduce imports and increase exports. Hollywood films were a major 'import' and substantial profits were flowing from British cinemas right back to the American producers. The ad valorem tax was rushed through Parliament, imposing a duty of 75 per cent on earnings of American films in Britain. Needless to say, the film industries on both sides of the Atlantic were furious. Rubbing salt into the wound, the Chancellor of the Exchequer stated that the tax would not be on actual earnings but predicted earnings, meaning that it would have to be paid in advance.

Hollywood reacted swiftly. The very next day an embargo was introduced preventing any new American films entering Britain. Rank was in America at the time, courting potential distribution partners, and American producers looked to him, the voice of reason, as the man who could turn around this ridiculous taxation scheme. He was unable to, and almost overnight his work in setting up distribution deals in America was brought into question. Added to that, his cinema circuits were starved of highly profitable and much-needed American product.

The government assumed that without American dominance of the British circuits, British filmmakers would be in a much stronger position; they would have to satisfy the demand by increasing production and would have nothing to fear from Hollywood. But did the post-war British film industry have the capacity to achieve this?

Pinewood was put into overdrive: six-day weeks and night-shifts were the norm as the pro-duction boom got into gear. It would be fair to say that although the 'quota quickie' legislation had been abolished almost ten years earlier, Rank was entering into that arena again with his new programme. Like the 'quota' films, it was destined primarily to feed the circuits and fill the gaps left by the American films.

In November, Rank announced plans for 47 feature films to be produced at Pinewood with investment of almost £10 million. But Rank's coffers were not as rich as he would have liked, and the investment programme could only be met by capitalising upon his other companies within the Organisation. J Arthur Rank announced plans that were effectively to involve Odeon shareholders in his production programme, which went totally against what Oscar Deutsch had stated when floating the company in 1937: 'This company will not engage in film production, either by itself or [through] any subsidiary company.'

Rank suffered at the hands of the financial press. They were particularly critical of his plans to absorb his General Cinema Finance Corporation into Odeon Cinemas, while merging that chain with Gaumont. And because Rank's programme could not be fully operational for several months – the projects needed to be developed before moving into production and post-production to exhibition could take a further six months – the ill-thought-out scheme proved an unmitigated disaster.

By March 1948, Harold Wilson – in his capacity as President of the Board of Trade – reached a new agreement with the Motion Picture Association of America. When the Hollywood embargo was lifted – just as the first of Rank's films was released – there was a massive influx of previously unreleased American pictures. Filmgoers opted for the lavish Hollywood productions in preference to Rank's offerings and the Rank Organisation plummeted towards financial disaster. The company's overdraft at the end of the 1947/48 financial year was over £16 million. Rank's hopes and plans for a thriving British film industry, on which he had worked so tirelessly, were in tatters. He was slipping more and more into the red with ever-mounting debts. It would seem that his Midas touch was

wearing off. Had it not been for the good will of the National Provincial, film production would have been abandoned altogether.

Eleven films were produced at Pinewood in 1948, including two Independent Frame films: the aforementioned *Warning to Wantons* and *Floodtide*, directed by Frederick Wilson and starring Gordon Jackson, Rona Anderson, John Laurie and Elizabeth Sellars in a drama about a young Clydeside ship designer. Other productions included *The Passionate Friends* and *The Blue Lagoon* from Cineguild and Individual respectively.

The Passionate Friends led to the demise of Cineguild. Ronald Neame was to have originally directed Eric Ambler's adaptation of the H G Wells novel. David Lean didn't feel that Neame had what it took to be a good director, despite his having directed *Take My Life*, and ordered the script rewritten. Start dates were set, however, and Neame commenced filming with half the new script in place, only to be supplanted by Lean a few days later. The whole débâcle spelt an unfortunate end

to one of Britain's most successful and talented production companies. Other members of the Independent Producers team were also showing signs of frustration and division. Powell and Pressburger were lured away to join Korda's revitalised enterprise, this time at Shepperton Studios; Launder and Gilliatt felt that they were losing their independence as the free reins they had so enjoyed were being drawn in; and Ian Dalrymple's Wessex Films made their last film at Pinewood with *Dear Mr Prohack*. David Lean made one more film at Pinewood in 1949 – the disastrous *Madeleine* – before he too left to join Korda. Anthony Havelock-Allan set up his own company, Constellation Films – it, too, ultimately controlled by Korda.

It was ironic that as Rank rose to great heights while Korda floundered during the war, the scales had now tipped the other way. Rank was struggling to keep his company afloat and his most prized and successful filmmakers were leaving to join Korda, who had sought and secured government funding. ∎

THE DAVIS

Left: *Kenneth More as Douglas Bader in Lewis Gilbert's* Reach For The Sky.

Right: *John Davis - the infamous 'JD'.*

In 1949, there were only seven British studios open and even they employed 2,000 fewer people than in the previous year. Rank lost more than £3m in production. Just as the early 1940s had seen Rank's empire rise to astronomical heights, the end of the decade witnessed it plunging to new depths. Highbury Studios and the Charm School were closed, the children's film division was wound-up and the Organisation was on the verge of collapse.

However, there was a man – or hatchet man – of the hour. John Davis, the young accountant who had joined Odeon in the 1930s, had worked his way up to the position of managing director of the Rank Organisation and, more importantly, had the total trust of J Arthur Rank. Charged with turning the Organisation around, Davis stepped in with ruthless efficiency. The closure of Gainsbrough's Islington and Lime Grove Studios (the latter sold to the BBC before being demolished in the early 1990s for a housing development) soon followed; Independent Producers was formally disbanded and George Archibald left; Denham Studios was wound down and all of the Organisation's production interests were transferred to Pinewood under the control of Earl St John. 200 jobs were sacrificed.

Earl St John was born in Louisiana, USA, in 1892. His first taste of the film industry came when he peddled films across Mexico for his uncle. After the Great War, he came to Britain working as an independent exhibitor in Manchester before Paramount appointed him 'head of exploitation' in London. St John began to expand their cinema circuit and when Odeon bought out Paramount cinemas, the company took over St John's contract. Just prior to World War II, he became personal assistant to John Davis. 'JD', as Davis was known, subsequently installed him as executive producer at Pinewood where he would eventually oversee some 131 films.

'My lingering memory of Earl St John,' says director Ken Annakin, 'was that he was a slow reader, and often if you needed a verdict on some scene or synopsis, you'd find he'd retire into the toilet to concentrate on the matter – a joke amongst us, but it seemed to work!' J Lee Thompson's verdict was that 'Earl was always full of fun and confidence and he always gave you the feeling that whatever you were making would be a huge success. He was truly delightful and became a very dear friend.'

Davis's 'cut and cut' mentality towards films made him a figure of hatred among production personnel, even, to some degree, Earl St John himself. 'JD was rude, arrogant and harsh,' confirms director Lewis Gilbert. 'That's a fact. His poor secretaries were often in tears as he treated them terribly at times. Most senior figures lived in fear of the man, even Earl St John. I remember going into a meeting with JD and Earl one morning and JD barked at Earl to get me a chair. I was relatively young at the time and Earl must have been in his sixties, so it was very embarrassing to see him dive off into a corner and rush a chair to me.

'But I always found that JD was the complete gentleman to non-contract filmmakers, such as me

RA PART ONE (1950 – 1956)

– I was never under contract – and when he agreed a deal it was a deal. It wouldn't change and there needn't be anything in writing: a deal was a deal. I started *Carve Her Name With Pride* without anything in writing, because I knew I had JD's handshake. He didn't know much about films and never pretended otherwise, but he knew what could work in terms of a deal and a story for his circuit. Never did he criticise a director or producer if the finished film didn't perform well at the box-office. He took responsibility for the good as well as the not so good, and that I admired in him.'

Ken Annakin agrees that Davis did have some redeeming features. 'I had many meetings with JD at Pinewood. He was the first of the hard-faced businessmen who have since come to run this industry and, basically, he wasn't a bad guy. He did try to understand the quality of film stories and encouraged those who made a good – and profitable – movie. If you managed to get into his good books, you were invited up to his suite for lunch-

es to impress journalists and top trade people. If you got into his bad books, then you just tried to cling on – usually through Earl St John. He may have made mistakes, but there have been many people in charge of studios, past and present, who have no interest in stories or the content of movies. I don't think he did well with the acting talent, though, as British stars seemed to get out of their contracts as quickly as possible! He was lucky to have Dinah Sheridan as his wife for many years; she certainly tried to fill the creative gaps in his make-up. He did many silly things, but gave us all good breaks and the chance to make a really good movie now and then.'

'I always got on famously well with John Davis,' recalls Rank contract director Ralph Thomas. 'He could organise a picture within ten minutes if he liked the idea, it was a good script and had a sensible budget – and it would be done on a handshake. If he didn't like the idea or package, then you'd never sway him! At least he was

Facing page: *Rank's executive producer Earl St John (left), talking to director Roy Baker.*

honest and up-front with you in that respect and wouldn't mess you around. He always came into the studio for one day a week and would see anyone with a problem or who wanted something done – he'd always happily meet with you.'

In the space of a year, the company overdraft was reduced by almost £4 million, thanks to Davis's measures coupled with the extreme patience of Rank's bankers. Davis slashed all budgets and imposed a maximum ceiling of £150,000 per film. He amalgamated Pinewood Films, Two Cities Films and Gainsborough under the banner of J Arthur Rank Productions Ltd at Pinewood, and was keen only to produce commercial films, avoiding the experimental initiatives that had cost Rank so dearly in the past. All Rank employees who survived the axe faced a 10 per cent pay cut, but even then were not guaranteed job security. 'You'd know whether or not you were long for the company at the annual Christmas dinner,' says Sir Donald Sinden. 'Long tables radiated from where JD sat, and one's seating at the tables suggested one's position in the "Rankery" for the following year. If within touching distance of JD, then your star shone brightly, but if you were at the far end, you didn't have long to go!'

Dinah Sheridan, who was married to Davis for 15 years, has few fond memories. 'I'll give you the fact that he did honour the deals he shook on, but that's all I'll give you. I divorced him for cruelty [in the end] and it took 15 minutes.'

Through all this upheaval, Pinewood remained busy. Captain Richard Norton, now Lord Grantley, returned to the studio as Chairman of Javelin Films – Anthony Asquith's company – to make *The Woman in Question*, following it with a celebrated adaptation of Terence Rattigan's play *The Browning Version*. Elspeth March visited the studios with her husband Stewart Granger around this time and remembers seeing some graffiti in one of the corridors. 'Someone had written "Richard Norton is a ..." – well, it was rather a rude word! He'd obviously seen it as he'd scrubbed across "Richard Norton" and written "Lord Grantley", leaving the expletive intact. It really was terribly funny!'

Ken Annakin and Harold French brought three of Somerset Maugham's stories to the screen in a compendium film called *Trio*. 'I loved the big stages at Pinewood,' he enthuses, 'and especially the one where they built the set of "my ship" which ran the whole length of the stage. I was at last in big pictures! It was wonderful to work in the country house surroundings and I felt very much at home because Arthur Alcott was in charge of all production. He had been my first feature production manager at Shepherds Bush – he was a great planner and I still use his methods to break down scripts. After *Quartet*, which I'd made with Betty Box at Islington – a very successful episodic film – there were very few British actors who wouldn't have given their right arm to play in the wonderful stories Maugham had written.' Indeed, the success of *Trio* resulted in a third Maugham compendium the following year. *Encore* was directed by Pat Jackson, Anthony Pelissier and Harold French.

The Clouded Yellow came from the Sydney and Betty Box stable: a Hitchcock-style thriller, it incorporated a chase across the Lake District. Ralph Thomas directed, and thus started a collaboration with Betty Box that would span a further 20 years. 'Betty mortgaged her house to keep *The Clouded Yellow* afloat,' he explains. 'You see, we had a contract with a company who were supposed to be financing films on behalf of the government and they withdrew after we'd started shooting. I was on a very complicated location in the Lake District when they pulled out and I needed money to keep going. It was three or four thousand pounds, which nowadays is nothing, but back then it was a lot of money and it was very brave of Betty and Peter [Rogers] to put their home on the line. She didn't tell me until the picture had finished, but then she made it all back plus some more. I'm rather proud of that film – Jean Simmons was lovely in it, and so was Trevor Howard. Sonia Dresdel was very good value for money too. They don't make them like her anymore. It's my favourite picture.'

In what was generally considered a positive move, the government introduced the British Film Production Fund in 1950, which became known as

the 'Eady Levy' after its architect, Sir Wilfred Eady. The fund, derived from a percentage of ticket sales, would make available £3 million a year for the film industry, half of which would go directly to producers making films in Britain. Ironically, it was to be the more successful producers who stood to benefit most from the scheme.

Although the Eady Fund was welcomed with open arms, a new crisis was on the way. In December 1949 the first provincial TV station began transmission in the Midlands and viewers were set to increase in millions over the next few years as TV spread across the whole of the country. There was, of course, an instant distrust of the new medium from filmmakers who feared not only shrinking cinema attendances, but also that – if their films were sold to TV – they would lose much of their quality when broadcast. This was a view shared by John Davis, who felt that a massive depreciation of the Rank Organisation's films would ensue should TV start broadcasting them.

The BBC had been short of programming in the late 1940s and was struggling to maximise its capacity. Rank was aware of the impending competition, and moved to see if a mutually beneficial compromise might be reached. His plans were for 'Cinema-Television', whereby live broadcasts were made to his cinemas offering more up-to-the-minute programming and news than film could provide. He saw this as the perfect compliment to cinema and as a public service. In exchange certain films from the library would be made available to the BBC.

Cyril Hayden was employed to bring together all of the Rank film negatives at Pinewood. 'They had the idea that all the films would be wanted for television, and there was a man called Alf Wilson who was employed just to examine all the negs, catalogue them, wrap them up in tissue paper and re-label them. A fantastic amount of work went into gathering negatives from all around the country – I remember some had even been stored in a barn somewhere.'

Both the government and the BBC were wary of the idea. They worried that if the scheme went ahead, Rank would eventually become more

Facing page: The Verger *was one of the vignettes from* Trio, *directed by Ken Annakin. Michael Hordern (as the vicar) is surrounded by co-stars Glyn Houston, James Hayter and Kathleen Harrison.*

interested in broadcasting his own programmes instead of buying in from the Corporation. So Rank was continually refused a broadcast licence. Ironically, however, Rank controlled Bush Radio which began producing and selling TV sets in addition to radios and proved to be one of his most successful interests.

Eventually, Rank was granted a short-period licence on the condition that he sold some of his films to the BBC. For several years broadcasts were relayed from Pinewood to the Crystal Palace transmitter and in turn to five of Rank's West End cinemas. Sadly, there were never large enough audiences to test the broadcasts on and Rank's attempts to compete with domestic television proved, in the long run, fruitless. It did, however, make Rank and Davis realise that TV was now a force to be reckoned with, rather than one they could work with. As a result, none of Rank's contract artistes were allowed to work on television, though Rank himself later invested in Southern Television, one of the first independent companies in the ITV network.

Rank's output in the 1950s was, rather unfairly, considered lacklustre and boring. While it is true that a great many films of the period were characterised by blandness, John Davis reported that Rank's pictures were performing better at the foreign box-office than ever. Dwindling domestic attendances made cinema closures unavoidable, however, but in those cinemas that survived – and many underwent modernisation programmes – a new market was booming: ancillary sales such as ice cream and sweets were, in some cases, making more profit than the films. In fact, it was reported that the Rank Organisation made a profit of £1m on sales of ice cream in 1951.

Ten films were produced at Pinewood that year. The most notable of these was Anthony Asquith's delightful production of Oscar Wilde's *The Importance of Being Earnest,* with the definitive portrayal of Lady Bracknell by Dame Edith Evans. Among the other films were Terence Young's *Valley of Eagles* and the David Niven vehicle *Appointment With Venus*, produced by Betty Box and directed by Ralph Thomas.

1952 proved to be a significant year, with the studio's first major 'renter' (a non-Rank associated company) arriving in the shape of Walt Disney. Under the guidance of associate producer Hugh Attwooll, Disney decided to capitalise upon the success of a couple of British films he'd produced by setting up a production programme at Pinewood. There was something special about Disney and his films that was summed up very succinctly by the late and much-missed Attwooll at the time of the studio's 50th birthday in 1986. 'Nothing went out of the studio that didn't have Walt's own personal stamp. I don't think he ever forgot what was contained in the script – he knew it mentally and visually. When he died, the films became the product of many people. They lost their magic touch.'

Ken Annakin concurs. 'Walt not only had his stamp on every picture, he was always an active creator. He had to okay all your storyboards and if you deviated he wanted to know why! A Walt Disney movie was always Walt's concept and you did your best to flesh it out and interpret it. That doesn't mean to say you were a slave director unless you chose to be, but you were making his movie and glad to have all the facilities he provided. Walt was a genius and I loved working for him.'

Disney's first Pinewood production was *The Sword and the Rose*, with Annakin directing Richard Todd, Glynis Johns, James Robertson Justice and Michael Gough in the story of young Mary Tudor. 'Disney had made *Robin Hood* in and around Denham Studios,' Annakin points out, 'but they closed after that production. *The Sword and the Rose* therefore came to Pinewood where facilities were pretty much comparable – one or two stages in Denham were bigger, but we had the same art director in Carmen Dillon, so the look of the pictures was the same except, perhaps, a little more lavish and with wonderful matte paintings by Peter Ellenshaw.

'Unfortunately, at the time of the shoot, we were in the middle of a National Electricians' Union strike. A go-slow strike. The shop stewards had decided to pull the breakers on us twice a day, and as I would walk across a set, one of the stewards would invariably bump into me and sneer "You

don't know when we're gonna shut you down, do you mate?" We survived, but it was very annoying and worrying since they could turn everything to black, and the cast might have been in very danger-ous positions – very unnerving. We were worried that it might have scared Disney away from the UK.

'There was one other nasty incident I remember on the film. I had just lined up a shot and was about to sit in my chair when something knocked me out. It was an electrician's spanner which came hurtling from the catwalk above and struck me a glancing blow on the right side of my head. My assistant, Clive Reed, grabbed me and told me that I was out cold for a couple of minutes. I came round, bewildered, and wanted to carry on, but was bundled into a car and driven to Uxbridge Hospital. After various checks, and some doping, they let me return to Pinewood. I had minor con-cussion for three weeks, but we carried on and got a fine movie. Whether the spanner fell accidental-

ly out of the electrician's pocket nobody knows; it could have been accidental as he asserted. We did have some problems with the unions, but you just had to battle on.'

Also in 1952, Pinewood played host to one of its most enduring and best-loved productions: *Genevieve*. The 39-year-old director Henry Cornelius began his career as an assistant to the famous French director René Clair and later enjoyed a couple of successes at Ealing Studios, particularly with *Passport to Pimlico*. He then took the unusual step of leaving to go independent. He worked on a story idea with Ealing's William Rose about a veteran car race in the hope of setting up the project with Michael Balcon. However, Ealing's schedule was such that Balcon could not bring Cornelius back into the fold. Instead, Balcon suggested that Cornelius go to Pinewood and meet Earl St John.

Cyril Howard, who became managing director of

the studio in 1976, recalls the conversation. 'Earl St John asked Cornelius what the film was about and when Cornelius told him it was about a vintage car race with this car called Genevieve, Earl said "Do you want to get me shot? You honestly expect me to put money into a film about an old car race – go on, get out!" That was that ... or so it seemed.'

But Cornelius's tenacity paid off and he secured financial support from the National Film Finance Corporation and then succeeded in persuading St John to 'green light' the project. The sterling cast included Kenneth More, John Gregson, Kay Kendall and Dinah Sheridan. 'It really was a wonderful film to work on and we had so much fun,' recalls Sheridan, 'but not with the director I might add – he was awful. I do think he was a very good comedy director, but the way he worked wasn't a pleasant one for us artists. We all loved the story and I think it was really for Bill Rose (the screenwriter) that we strived to make it as good as we possibly could. It was quite funny with Cornelius because Kay and I each had a whistle and when we saw him approach us, or head towards the dressing rooms at the studio, we'd blow our whistles and each head off in different directions so that he couldn't get hold of us!'

Shooting got underway in September 1952. The race was supposedly taking place over a summer weekend, but the weather was anything but summery, says Dinah Sheridan. 'It was freezing cold and one day towards the end of the shoot we were each given a tot of brandy to warm us up. When we asked who we should thank, Cornelius came over and said "I don't care if you're cold, but when you turn blue it affects my film!" So considerate! As we progressed through the film I got fatter and fatter with all of the extra clothes I was putting on. I was extra cold with fright too, as John Gregson couldn't drive and I had the job of telling him what to do out of the corner of my mouth. It was most unnerving.

'Because it was so noisy with the cars, we shot about 80 per cent of the film without sound and came back into the studio after Christmas to dub. That was quite difficult because we'd often be shivering with cold on film, and had to try and recreate that in the dubbing theatre.'

The race took place on the London to Brighton road, but the cast and crew rarely strayed more than an hour's drive from Pinewood and never even saw the Brighton Road. 'People always associate *Genevieve* with Pinewood,' says Sheridan, 'but the truth is we only shot around five per cent of the film at the studio, the rest was location – lots around Pinewood and Denham, and if you look closely you see the gates of Moor Park golf club come into view. The final sequences were to be shot near Westminster Bridge, and so we drove up the Embankment (which is in totally the wrong direction from where the Brighton Road is), where Kenny More was supposed to get his wheels stuck in the tram lines. But would you believe the tram lines had been removed! So we had to go elsewhere to get that shot.'

Everyone involved thought it was going to be a disaster. Cornelius insisted on numerous takes and often made last-minute changes to the script. The awful weather and budget over-runs understandably led to anxiety, but on the contrary *Genevieve* was a massive success, primarily through word of mouth, and was voted Best British Film of 1953. Larry Adler's wonderful harmonica score contributes greatly to the overall charm of the film, which was probably the closest Pinewood came to emulating the popularity of the Ealing comedies – but with two of Ealing's geniuses (Cornelius and Rose) on board, perhaps that was only to be expected.

'Adler's score really was very good,' Dinah Sheridan continues. 'I was so sorry that he wasn't nominated for the Oscar, but he was blacklisted and Muir Mathieson (the arranger) won the nomination in his place.' But there were compensations for Adler. "Us artists were paid a few thousand pounds flat fee – no profit share. When Adler was approached he named a fee, but the producer said "I'm afraid we don't have any money left." Anyway, Adler haggled and reduced his price but was still told that there wasn't any money. He really wanted to provide the music so suggested he take 2.5 per cent of the profits instead of a fee. He made a fortune and doesn't fail to remind me whenever I see him.'

Facing page: *Val Guest's* The Penny Princess *with Reginald Beckwith, Peter Butterworth, Yolande Donlan and Dirk Bogarde.*

Below: The Planter's Wife. *Left to right - Hugh Attwooll, Peter Hennesey, Gil Woxholt, David Harcourt, Jack Atchelor and Ken Annakin.*

Pinewood's other productions of 1952 included two Anthony Steel vehicles, Pat Jackson's *Something Money Can't Buy*, co-starring Patricia Roc and A E Matthews in a post-war comedy involving a young couple who set up a secretarial and catering company, and Ken Annakin's *The Planter's Wife*, a Malaysian-set drama in which a husband and wife defend their home against a terrorist siege, co-starring Jack Hawkins, Claudette Colbert and Ram Gopal. 'I had Peter Hennessey shoot a few establishing shots in Malaysia,' says Annakin, 'but the whole situation out there was far too dangerous, so we chose Ceylon for all the location shots – and found sites which matched what we had in Malaysia perfectly. We had a great location shoot (all the snake/mongoose stuff was staged there), then we came back to Pinewood and matched all the house and dug-out sequences. Claudette, who had always made pictures in American studios, was completely at home at Pinewood.'

Former Gainsborough Pictures screenwriter Val Guest directed Dirk Bogarde and Yolande Donlan in his first Pinewood film, *Penny Princess*, in which a New York shop girl inherits a tiny European state and boosts its economy by selling cheese and schnapps. 'When I originally brought the story to Earl St John, Yolande and I went to Hollywood to see if we could secure Cary Grant's interest,' Guest reveals, 'and we were also thinking about Michael Wilding. But one day Earl said to me "What's wrong with Dirk Bogarde?" "Well, first of all," I said, "Dirk has always played dramatic parts and this isn't that kind of part." "Make him funny then!" Earl barked. I must say, Dirk was lovely to work with and we got along very well, but I remember that in one of his books he wrote about the film and said "Poor Val – he wanted Cary Grant and got me!"

'For some reason they decided to launch the film at a big bash in Llandudno [North Wales] and, along with the cast, many of the top Rank executives attended, including John Davis. Someone else who came along, as a friend, was Dinah Sheridan and that was the night that she met JD and danced with him. Soon afterwards they married. I always say to Dinah that she shouldn't blame me!'

Next up was an all-star melodrama set in the fashion world, Compton Bennett's *It Started in Paradise*, and the young Muriel Pavlow went straight from that into Anthony Asquith's *The Net*, with James Donald, Phyllis Calvert and Robert Beatty.

John Paddy Carstairs, meanwhile, directed *Top of the Form*, starring Ronald Shiner, Harry Fowler, Alfie Bass and, in a minor role, Anthony Newley.

J Arthur Rank became more involved with the family flour business in 1952 after the death of his brother Jimmy Rank, and withdrew from the day-to-day running of the Organisation. John Davis then assumed responsibility for the whole of the Rank Organisation and expanded into other areas which, ultimately, proved far more profitable than film, namely Bush Radio and Rank Precision Industries, which manufactured products such as sound and projection equipment, cameras and lenses.

1953 witnessed the birth of two of Rank's most successful comedies. The diminutive British funny man Norman Wisdom made his début in *Trouble in Store*, the full story of which is recounted in Chapter Six, while *Doctor in the House* was the first of the successful Betty Box-Ralph Thomas Doctor comedies; the full story on those is told in Chapter Seven.

Lured to Britain by the Eady Levy, Albert R Broccoli and his producing partner Irving Allen had a major success with *The Red Beret*, directed by Terence Young at Shepperton. For their next picture, *Hell Below Zero*, they moved to Pinewood.

Based on *The White South* by Hammond Innes, the film was directed by Mark Robson. The action was set on whaling ships in Antarctica and that's where the cast and crew – but not the film's star, Alan Ladd – had to go for the location shoot.

Not long after completing *Hell Below Zero*, Broccoli and Allen returned to make *The Black Knight*, another vehicle for Alan Ladd. Ladd wasn't too keen though, according to Euan Lloyd. 'An American friend, whom I'd met during my tenure as joint press officer of the Variety Club of Great Britain, was back in London and asked if I would care to join him for lunch at Pinewood with Alan Ladd. He was shooting *Hell Below Zero* at the time. Alan Ladd and I hit it off from the start and our long conversations about the American West sealed a friendship that lasted until his death. He also became my mentor.

'Alan wanted nothing more than to get home to his ranch in California and resisted every effort to keep him here for the third film Broccoli and Allen wanted him to make. At the pool-side in Eden Roc in the South of France (where I had been invited to join the Ladd family), Allen and Broccoli, along with director Tay Garnett, made one final pitch to

get Alan's agreement to make *The Black Knight*. It was not a promising script, despite substantial doctoring by Bryan Forbes, but finally Alan relented. There was one condition: that they would get me a production job. Unbelievably, Allen said yes. I think he would have given his wife away to please [Columbia's] Harry Cohn. A deal was made and I found myself personal assistant to the now legendary duo, who proved to be the finest teachers any student of cinema could hope for. And I was back at Pinewood, working alongside Alan, Peter Cushing, the gorgeous Patricia Medina and some of the best technicians alive. From there I moved on to become an independent producer.'

Bryan Forbes recalled how he was drafted in to work on the script in his autobiography *A Divided Life*. 'Early in my screenwriting career I was a contract script doctor, called in to perform emergency surgery on terminal cases ... The most famous of these was *The Black Knight*, the brainchild of half a dozen parents. One Saturday afternoon the producers rang me to say that they had reached an impasse. "We've run out of pages," they said.

"Could I come up with something by Monday morning?" I was young and hungry, so with the misguided confidence which often goes with these two factors, I agreed and was shown footage of what had already been shot.'

At Broccoli's memorial service in 1996, Forbes told the assembled 2,000 people at the Odeon Leicester Square of one particularly awkward plot complication he had to contend with. 'Sue Ladd, Alan's wife, had script approval – that was in the contract. Every word uttered by Ladd had to first be approved by her. I came up with a few pages in which Ladd dodged a few arrows, vaulted from the castle battlements into a cart of hay, sliced a few of the villains in two with his sword, seized a horse and galloped across the rising drawbridge just in time. What was Mrs Ladd's verdict? "Alan Ladd does not steal horses." She went on to explain that if he did they would lose the Boy Scouts Association, the Daughters of the American Revolution and probably half his fan club. Everyone was dumbfounded. However, Irving Allen said, "Sue, he's not stealing a horse, he's bor-

Facing page: *'Anyone here lend me a horse?' Harry Andrews,
Alan Ladd and Peter Cushing in* The Black Knight.

Below: You Know What Sailors Are. *Costume designer
Julie Harris with producer Peter Rogers.*

rowing one." She was not convinced. So I came up with a line, when Ladd has done his vaulting and slicing, that he would deliver to a sentry – "Is this the horse I ordered?" He jumps onto it and gallops off. Sue agreed it! And that's what they shot.'

Also in 1953, Gregory Peck came over for *The Million Pound Note*. Adapted by Jill Craigie from a story by Mark Twain and directed by Ronald Neame, the film has Peck inheriting the titular note (of which half a dozen were 'minted' at Pinewood) and encountering great difficulty either in spending it or in changing it for smaller denominations. Although the main joke wears a little thin, the result rates as a very enjoyable comedy and co-starred Jane Griffith, Ronald Squire, Joyce Grenfell, A E Matthews and Wilfrid Hyde White.

Following this, the Rank Organisation next produced a charming film called *The Kidnappers* with Duncan Macrae, Adrienne Corri, John Whiteley and a young Vincent Winter, who won a special Oscar for his role. The story is set in a small Nova Scotia village at the turn of the century and follows a group of children who 'borrow' a baby after

being refused a pet and hide in a cave. After a few more pictures – most notably for Disney – the young Winter decided to turn his attention to the other side of the camera and, thanks to Disney's Hugh Attwooll, embarked upon an extremely successful career as an assistant director. In 1998, Winter took part in the American Academy's 70th anniversary line-up of previous Oscar winners. Tragically, he died soon afterwards, having contracted an illness while conducting a 'recce' for a film project overseas.

Next, Ken Annakin directed two films. *You Know What Sailors Are* was producer Peter Rogers' first movie – he later produced all the *Carry On* films – and boasted painted backdrops of the desert so vast that the studio could not rake up enough Brutes (large lights) to light them adequately. *The Seekers* was a New Zealand-set emigration epic with Jack Hawkins and Glynis Johns and also introduced Kenneth Williams to Pinewood.

Pinewood made the headlines on Monday 20 July when Rank threatened to close down the studios. All studio employees were given 14 days notice that

production would cease unless a dispute with the Film Artistes Association (FAA) was settled. Thankfully, the dispute was resolved before the two weeks elapsed and production continued.

After Queen Elizabeth II's coronation, the number of people who rented or owned television sets multiplied tenfold. The effects on cinema were painfully obvious – audiences were declining rapidly. One idea to lure people back was to produce three dimensional (3D) films. Another was to develop a new lens system – anamorphic – which produced a picture 2.5 times as wide as it was high. The process was dubbed CinemaScope and, unlike 3D, proved popular with both audiences and film-makers. The first film shot in CinemaScope was *The Robe*, a Biblical epic which provoked a massive row between Rank and 20th Century-Fox when the Organisation refused to install stereo sound in all cinemas at which the film played. Things were soon patched up, however, and, as a matter of course, all Odeon cinemas were fitted out with stereophonic sound equipment.

On Friday 20 November, Pinewood made the headlines again, this time over a daring £10,000 robbery. Thieves climbed a ladder across the canteen roof and entered a window on the first floor of the administration block. They broke into the cashiers' room and blew the safe open by putting a charge of gelignite into the key-hole and used cushions to muffle the explosion. Newspapers reported that 'The robbery was discovered shortly after 2.00 am by security officers when they were making an inspection. On each pay-packet was stamped J Arthur Rank Productions Limited.' The studio was in full production at the time but all 1,500 employees were paid as usual.

Director J Lee Thompson's first film at Pinewood came with *As Long As They're Happy*, the film version of a frantic stage farce starring Jack Buchanan and Diana Dors. 'I had known Jack Buchanan very well, as he was a close friend of the family,' Thompson recalls. 'In fact, I looked upon him as an uncle. So when I was asked to direct him in a film, you can imagine how excited

Facing page: *'I've heard about being left holding the baby ... but an alligator!'* Donald Sinden in An Alligator Named Daisy.

Left: *You always knew when Peter Finch was around - the Griffin's heads would disappear!*

I was. I often marvelled at his musical numbers as a child and thought I'd take full advantage of his skills in the film. So I decided that we would have a scene with him dancing along a balcony and down some stairs, through a ballroom and up another set of stairs. I'd had visions of this many weeks before the film started, and so the set was built; it was quite magnificent. Once the film had started, I told Jack about the scene and he was quite horrified. He said that all his life he'd fooled people into thinking he could dance, when all he could actually do was a little one-two-three step: he was no Fred Astaire and couldn't do what Astaire could. Bang went my plans! He did in fact do his little one-two-three step, but he made it look a hundred times grander.'

In 1955, Thompson returned to direct *An Alligator Named Daisy* with Donald Sinden, Stanley Holloway, Margaret Rutherford, Frankie Howerd, James Robertson Justice and Diana Dors again. 'That was a wonderful experience too, with a splendid cast. The only problems came with Daisy the alligator. Initially, we used a live one, which was quite tame. However, one day its trainer was bitten severely by the thing, and we all became very wary after that, so a battery-powered model alligator was later used and proved much safer to work with; and it didn't "escape" either, as the live one was prone to do.'

Donald Sinden vividly remembers his close encounters with the real alligator. 'I said "Nothing can scare me – I've worked with John Ford!" One

sequence involved a ballroom in full swing. The doors were supposed to open and reveal me, carrying Daisy. The band was then to stop, the ladies scream and everyone back away. It was all rehearsed and we were ready for the first Take. The door opened and I came through, but instead of screams I was greeted by howls of laughter. "Cut!" The director came over and suggested I look at Daisy. I looked down and saw that in the region of her belly a huge pair of bombdoors had opened and from them was hanging a long thing like a banana, but pink. Daisy was a boy! Nothing would make him retract it and we had a 150 extras hanging around waiting. "Couldn't you put your hand over it?" asked Lee. I didn't fancy that. He might have been outraged and turned nasty! Everyone who saw the film said "What a good model you used – it looked like a real alligator." Well, it was – very real!'

It was a busy time for Diana Dors; she next starred alongside John Gregson in Ken Annakin's *Value For Money*. Busier still, Peter Finch starred in *Simon and Laura* (for Muriel Box), *A Town Like Alice* (for Jack Lee), and the excellent *The Battle of the River Plate* from the Powell and Pressburger team. The latter was an account of the 1939 trapping and subsequent scuppering of the German pocket battleship *Graf Spee* in Montevideo Harbour. Finch played the sympathetic Commander Langsdorff and the cast also boasted John Gregson, Anthony Quayle, Bernard Lee, Ian Hunter and Christopher Lee.

'Peter Finch was a wonderful character,' says Devina 'Dizzie' Watson, former studio manager's assistant. 'His antics around the studio were legendary. He had a particular fascination with the two large stone griffins which sit either side of the fireplace entrance and, although he wasn't a muscular chap, he'd often pick them up and move them around the studio. He even put one in the boot of his car one day and took it home. On another occasion he was in the bar admiring a painting which used to hang there, and which Peter Rogers had just paid to be cleaned. It was of a Duke I think, and Finch took a cigarette, burnt a hole in the canvas around the Duke's lips, and put it in there. So there

hung this lovely, just-cleaned painting of a very distinguished chap, with Peter Finch's fag-end smoking away in his mouth! You always knew when he was around the studio, that's for sure.'

Up until 1955, Muriel Box was the only female director to make a film at Pinewood. However, that was set to change with *All for Mary* from director Wendy Toye: 'My contract was originally with Alex Korda and when he died it was transferred to J Arthur Rank and I made the move from Denham to Pinewood – it was quite a shock in some ways because whereas I considered Korda and Denham to be a very creative and interactive partnership, Pinewood seemed much more like a factory. Everyone there was lovely and very helpful, but it was a very business-like atmosphere, perhaps due to John Davis's influence.

'Many people ask if I found it difficult being a female director in those days. "No" is my answer. I never really had any problems, although I know Muriel Box often said she had trouble and didn't get the support she hoped for. I think it may have

been because she was Sydney's wife and the fact that she had moved from writing to directing and never really dealt with actors. I myself came into directing films through the theatre, and had been directing there since 1949. I'd also choreographed many dances in films, so I knew a lot of British crews through my work on those. I think I was more readily accepted because of that work.

'*All for Mary* was adapted from a stage play and one of the stars – David Tomlinson – had appeared in the stage version. When I heard that he'd been cast in the film with Nigel Green, I insisted he didn't play the same role as he had on stage. I knew David and realised that he'd bring very little freshness to the part. So Nigel took that role and David took the other leading role. It worked very well, apart from the fact that David insisted on giving Nigel directions! It was Leo McKern's first film and they weren't really keen on him being cast, but I was. Leo had a glass eye, and at every opportunity Nigel tried to stand on that side of him, to make the camera pick up on

Facing page: Tiger In The Smoke *director Roy Baker is adamant that Tony Wright, centre, was miscast.*

Left: *John Gregson and Cecil Parker were True As A Turtle.*

it. He was very naughty like that!

'The producer was Paul Soskin and had a very strange sense of humour, so much so we tried to keep him off the set by putting the red light up early. We had one shot where I was shooting through a window, four floors up, at David coming down on a sheet. The cardboard boxes were built up to the second floor though, so if he had fallen it wouldn't have been far. David put on a great show of being terrified about this and the sheet was creaking and he was saying "Oooh God, Oooh God!" but we did the scene and it was perfect. The red light went off and in came Paul, insisting we re-take it. I told him it was perfect but he was adamant. So up we went again. I called "Action" and there was a terrible tearing sound, an awful scream and the body of David Tomlinson went shooting past the window, bounced on the boxes and hit the floor. The minute it hit the floor, I realised it was a model because of the noise it made. I was in tears by then though, and it turned out to be the crew's idea of a joke! They'd dressed the dummy up in David's clothes and moustache and thought it was hilarious.'

Lewis Gilbert next brought the Douglas Bader story to the screen with *Reach for the Sky*, which he both wrote and directed. 'When I made *Reach for the Sky* there were only seven or eight stages at Pinewood,' says Gilbert, 'but it's grown a lot since then. We needed a couple of large stages for the film and there were only really two studios that could offer them – Pinewood and Shepperton. I much prefer Pinewood, so that's where we went. It

was a very enjoyable experience coming to make a film at Pinewood, and Kenny More loved working at the studio, so we were off to a good start. However, the problems came soon afterwards – not with Pinewood, but with two scenes I'd written. The first scene was when a soldier said 'bloody'. Now, this was 1954 and I couldn't get the censor to agree to pass it. I said "How can you have a soldier who doesn't say bloody? They used to say a lot worse." All he said was, "Well, can't he say ruddy instead?" I said no – we really fought for that one.

'Then after that I had a run-in with John Davis over a scene. It was when Kenny More, who played Bader, was trying to get back into the air force without his legs. He went in for his medical and in the outer office a warrant officer told him "You're wasting your time, they'll never let you back in." Having gone in and got his recommendation, Bader came back into the outer office, just looked at the warrant officer and put two fingers up at him. JD was horrified by this. He said he didn't like it and I should cut it. I said, "No, JD, this actually happened – it's the story." No more was said. However, the next day, JD sent his assistant Archibald over to see me. He said "You've got to take it out." I said, "Please – don't even ask. It's in the story, it's a bit of fun and it will get a laugh." At this point Archibald started to cry. He sobbed, "JD will murder me." I never really saw him around after that! But the scene stayed and it always got a laugh!"

In 1956 Roy Baker was at Pinewood with *Jacqueline* and *Tiger in the Smoke*; Ralph Thomas directed Anthony Steel, Stanley Baker and Odile Versois in *Checkpoint*, an industrial espionage thriller set in Italy, and Muriel Box directed *Eyewitness* with Donald Sinden and Muriel Pavlow – both of whom also starred in *Tiger in the Smoke* and *Doctor at Large* the same year.

'We became known as the Rank Rep Group,' says Muriel Pavlow of her threefold teaming with Donald Sinden, 'but I did so much like working with him. My only regret on *Tiger in the Smoke* was that Donald wasn't in the Tony Wright part – it would have worked so much better if they had switched roles.'

Regarding this contentious piece of casting, Roy Baker remembers *Tiger in the Smoke* as the

Facing page: *The cast and crew of*
The Prince and the Showgirl, with Marilyn
Monroe and Laurence Olivier centre front.

film in which he first felt the 'interfering' influence of John Davis. 'JD found himself being drawn more and more into production matters partly because of all the criticism the Organisation was getting regarding its film output. I dare say he did have some positive influence to offer, but his involvement in this film was disastrous. It was a wonderful story and a half-good film, but JD insisted that Tony Wright should play the lead. I wanted Jack Hawkins or Stanley Baker: the character was a ruthless and dominating bastard, and Tony didn't have that sort of personality. JD believed that Tony was set to become a massive star and became obsessed about our casting him. We relented, and cast him. It didn't do Tony any favours at all – he knew it wasn't working and I don't think his career ever recovered.'

Wendy Toye shot *True as a Turtle*, a smuggling comedy involving yachts crossing the Channel with John Gregson, Keith Michell, June Thorburn and Cecil Parker. 'We assembled a lovely cast for that picture, including Clement Freud in his one and only film. Two days into the shoot, I got a call to go and see John Davis. "We've got to get rid of Miss X," he barked. "She's no good." I told JD that I wasn't used to this sort of behaviour, and that if she went so did I. He grumbled a bit and then left it. In the event, she was excellent. I didn't have much to do with him after that, and when my contract expired, I concentrated on theatre work again.'

Two American stars, Bob Hope and Katharine Hepburn, visited the studio and played opposite each other in *The Iron Petticoat*. Miss Hepburn was deemed to be the consummate professional, but 'professional' to some meant 'temperamental' to others. On one occasion, she was on set blowing off steam about something or other and Bob Hope said 'If you don't behave yourself, I'll tell everyone that you are Audrey Hepburn's father!' She calmed down considerably after that.

The big film of 1956, however – and one that set the whole of Pinewood buzzing – was *The Prince and the Showgirl* starring Laurence Olivier and, in her only British film, Marilyn Monroe. Media attention was considerable to say the least, and often proved problematic – as did Marilyn

Monroe herself, often causing disruption to the filming, as production manager Teddy Joseph explains. 'It was hopeless. Olivier used to cry every day because we would have to stand around waiting for Marilyn, who he said was so unprofessional. He hated the business of her arriving at 9.00 am and meandering over to the set by 11.00 am, when everyone else had been ready hours before. I know she had some problems in her own life, but it was affecting the film greatly. We loved her, but hated the way she was.

'Olivier was totally the opposite. I was asked to meet him at least nine months before shooting was due to start, so I went to 146 Piccadilly – which is no longer there – and I remember that I had to be there at 3.30 pm, and naturally had my best suit on. Olivier said "You must take tea with me" and a butler arrived wearing white gloves and a silver tray along with a marvellous tea service. I was used to roughing it with a mug of tea from the canteen, so this was quite something! For an hour we chatted about the film and he wanted to be absolutely sure that I was the right person. When you consider that I was just the production manager, you realise the tremendous effort and detail Olivier went to in making sure everything was just so.

'Six months later I started setting up the film, which I think I must have then been on for a year. Marilyn arrived with Arthur Miller, her new husband, and the 'black widow' [drama tutor Paula Strasberg] – part of her entourage throughout the shoot. Olivier would be behind the camera and as soon as he'd finished directing the scene, Marilyn would turn to Strasberg and Miller and ask how it went. She never asked the director! They all had their input, every bloody day, and it became ridiculous. It was quite often the case that many of the scenes that could be shot 'around' Marilyn were – including Olivier's close-ups – and when she arrived it was just a case of shooting her cutaways and close-ups to insert with what had been shot around her.'

Norman Wisdom recalls meeting Marilyn when he was filming *Up in the World*. 'I remember that we were shooting on adjacent stages, and one day Marilyn Monroe asked if she could come onto mine and watch some filming. She wore a cream satin

dress, strolled onto the set with Laurence Olivier and then sat quietly to watch. It was electric! They then had a little chat with me before returning to their set, and Marilyn winked at me as she left. A few days later, I was walking back to my dressing room on the last day of shooting and met her in the corridor. I said it was my last day, and she then lifted me up and kissed me smack on the gob. I'll never forget that as long as I live and always remember her when I walk down that corridor.'

According to Donald Sinden, 'About a month before Marilyn was due to arrive, the number one dressing room was gutted and completely re-decorated in blue. A new carpet, curtains, couch, armchairs, dressing table were installed – all in blue. Then two weeks before she appeared a man arrived from Hollywood to vet the place and ensure that everything would be to her satisfaction. He pronounced "Miss Monroe does not like blue." Back came the painters, upholsterers and carpet fitters and in six days everything was made white. My dressing room was in the same block, four doors from hers, so I saw the comings and goings of the entourage. She was still suffering from the effects of the Method and one day I pinned up a notice on my door:

Registered Office of the
NAZAK ACADEMY*
Prof. Donald Sinden
'You too can be inaudible.'

Particularisation:
NEW EGOS SUPERIMPOSED
MOTIVATIONS IMMOBILISED
IMAGINARY STONE KICKING ERADICATED
UMS & ERS RENDERED OBSOLETE
FEES: Exorbitant but we can work on your minimum
Extra pockets provided by the school tailor
MOTTO: 'THOUGH 'TIS METHOD YET THERE'S MADNESS IN IT' (Bacon)

'I waited inside and eventually heard the footsteps of the entourage. They paused outside my door and from the entire group I only heard one laugh, immediately recognisable as Marilyn's. The door burst open and in she came. We introduced ourselves and from that moment she regularly popped in for a natter and a giggle.'

The film, based on Terence Rattigan's light comedy *The Sleeping Prince*, boasted excellent production values, with sets designed by Roger Furse and first-class photography by Jack Cardiff, resulting in a wonderful visual backdrop for the meeting of the two very different, yet arresting, star personalities in 1911 London. It is interesting to note, given tales of her unprofessionalism, that Marilyn Monroe's own company co-financed the picture. She reportedly received a massive 75 per cent of the profits. ■

*Kazan, as in Elia Kazan, spelt backwards.

6

At 15, Norman Joseph Wisdom secured the position of drummer boy with the King's Own Royal Regiment at Lichfield. He states categorically that he owes all his success in later life to the Army. After a hand-to-mouth childhood, they provided him with an education and a trade, as well as feeding him and paying him.

In the barracks one night, Norman started shadow boxing – as he often did in the gym – and had all his companions in stitches when he allowed the 'shadow' to hit him back, knocking him to the floor. He took the hint and made his first professional appearance at Collins Music Hall, after which he was invited to perform at the Victoria Palace on the same bill as Laurel and Hardy. His comic genius was immediately recognised and he was besieged by agents. Many stage and TV appearances followed and Norman fast developed a reputation as 'the new Chaplin'.

It was during the successful run of *Paris to Piccadilly* at the Prince of Wales Theatre in 1952 that Norman's agent burst into his dressing room one night and announced that the Rank Organisation had offered him a seven year film contract. Norman knew that Associated British Pictures Corporation (ABPC) were considering signing him up, but for Rank to offer such a contract without even an audition was something else. Agent Billy Marsh had, in fact, used ABPC's interest in Norman as a lever to clinch the deal with Earl St John.

The deal was that Norman would make at least three films in the first two years of the contract, the first of which would pay £5,000 – a princely sum in the early 1950s. Driving to Pinewood in his new Continental Bentley, he arrived at one of the smaller stages for test shots. Waiting for him were Petula Clark and director Ronald Neame, Wisdom recalls. 'I had to look into Petula's eyes and say to her "Your eyes are as light as gossamer." I couldn't believe it! What sort of test was this for a comedian, I thought.'

Norman didn't hit it off with Neame, the film was never made and Norman was paid off. The studio then became wary of their new signing and didn't really know what to do with him. Earl St John was persuaded to commission a script more suited to the actor's abilities, and Jill Craigie delivered a screenplay which became known as *Trouble in Store*. But when she heard it was Norman who was playing the lead, she demanded her name be removed!

John Paddy Carstairs was drafted in to direct and, along with Norman and screenwriter Ted Willis, did further work on the script. Maurice Cowan produced the film, set in a large department store where Norman is a stockroom assistant who not only aspires to be a window dresser but

A LITTLE WISDOM

also to win the heart of a young girl in the record department (Lana Morris). To bolster the film's anticipated popularity, and Norman's lack of experience, Margaret Rutherford was brought in to play a major role.

The opening scene of *Trouble in Store* very firmly established what was to follow. Shot without a word of dialogue at a set of traffic lights, the snooty new store boss (Jerry Desmonde) is sitting in his convertible Rolls-Royce waiting for the lights to change to green, with scruffy little Norman apparently seated beside him. When the lights change and the Rolls pulls away, we see that Norman is in fact perched on a bicycle. Many hilarious, and sometimes tear-jerking, scenarios ensue, some of which Norman had to fight for.

'There's a scene when I'm dressing a window with crockery and I started doing it all wrong – things upside down, cups hanging from teapot spouts etc. Paddy [Carstairs] came over and said "No, no, no – you're doing it all wrong." He wanted me to do it all straight and proper. I said that my way was funnier and with that he threw his cap on the floor and stormed off. I then said that I'd shoot it his way if he'd allow me to do it my way too and then the next day in rushes we'd see which worked best. He agreed. The next day, the rushes theatre was full to capacity – everyone had obviously heard about our disagreement. Paddy's version came on, raised a few titters and that was that. My version came on and the whole house was in stitches. Paddy looked at me and said, "Norman, from now on we talk!"'

The Rank Organisation were still wary of Norman and the film, and therefore arranged a preview on 25 November 1953 at the Camden Gaumont in North London. All the top executives turned out, among them Earl St John and John Davis, and Norman was greeted very formally, almost curtly. When the film started Norman concentrated on the audience – their facial reactions and body language. Mercifully, they were in hysterics and the film was a phenomenal success. Upon leaving the auditorium, Norman was greeted far more effusively by the assembled execs. 'That's called the bullshit of show business,' says Norman.

The press were equally congratulatory and *Trouble in Store* was a very big box-office earner, as well as earning Norman himself a BAFTA award. Naturally, another film was speedily put into production and Norman returned to Pinewood, and the same producer-director team, for *One Good Turn*, with a script by Ted Willis, Paddy Carstairs and Maurice Cowan.

Though criticised for its over-emphasis on pathos, *One Good Turn* is another solid entry in the Wisdom franchise. It's set in the orphanage where the odd-job man (Norman) was himself brought up. The would-be romantic interest is Shirley Abicair but Norman is more concerned about a young orphan named Jimmy, whose one wish is to own a large toy car.

Known for his great sense of humour on set, Norman demonstrated it in the sequence where he drives a car through a tunnel. Performing his own stunts again, Norman tore into the tunnel (actually a large drain) but, rather than exiting smoothly at the other end, miscalculated its curvature effect. 'I turned slightly left and over I went, upside down, with the car on top of me sliding down the tunnel. When I stopped sliding, I lay there, moaning in pain. I heard Paddy shout for someone to call an ambulance and then felt him patting my cheeks, undoing my shirt collar, trying to rouse me. This went on for a few minutes and I finally burst out laughing. Paddy drew back and hit me across the face and warned me not to pull a gag like that again. As he left, I heard him laughing! My cheek didn't half hurt though.'

Jack Gardner was a young second assistant editor on *One Good Turn* and recalled Norman's film technique. 'When it came to the musical number, the track would have been laid down a few weeks in advance and all Norman would have to do during the take was mime. When Paddy did his long shots of the scene, Norman would mime any old rubbish, out of sync. But as soon as Paddy went closer in, Norman was bang on sync. That way, of course, he ensured we used more close-up shots of him!'

Norman was on stage in the West End when *One Good Turn* opened and had been asked to make an appearance at the Odeon Leicester Square. 'I had

about half an hour between the two evening shows at the Palladium, so decided that was when I'd get into a fast car and head to the Odeon, say a few words, and return to the Palladium. What I didn't bank on was that the car wouldn't get through all the crowds. I got out and managed to make my way to the foyer of the cinema, between signing autographs and posing for photos. A quick few words followed, and then a mad dash back to the Palladium where I'd left a note on my dressing room door saying "Gone to the pictures, back in ten minutes." I just about made it in time for the second house. Talk about cutting it fine.'

In 1955 Norman returned with *Man of the Moment*. Lana Morris co-starred again but the producer was now Hugh Stewart. Norman's relationship with Maurice Cowan had never been particularly cordial whereas Stewart's association with Norman would span ten highly successful years. 'One of my first tasks was to convince Norman that the script was okay,' Stewart explains. 'That his

ideas would work and so on. He had always been a loner, you see, and never really believed that people were on his side. However, once he trusted you, you had a friend for life and that's why he worked so well with Paddy and later Bob Asher. He liked and trusted them.'

Paddy Carstairs directed three more Norman films – *Up In the World*, *Just My Luck* (which reteamed Norman with Margaret Rutherford) and *The Square Peg* – before expressing a desire to go back to making suspense thrillers. *The Square Peg* is one of Norman's favourites, and in it he had two roles to play.

'In the film, I get drafted into the Army and posted to the front with my boss Mr Grimsdale – the lovely Edward Chapman. There, one of the German generals turns out to be my double. Jack Davies [the scriptwriter] suggested I should play the dual roles, as I'm pretty good on accents. I thought it was a good idea but Paddy did not. He said it wasn't a comedy part but a straight acting

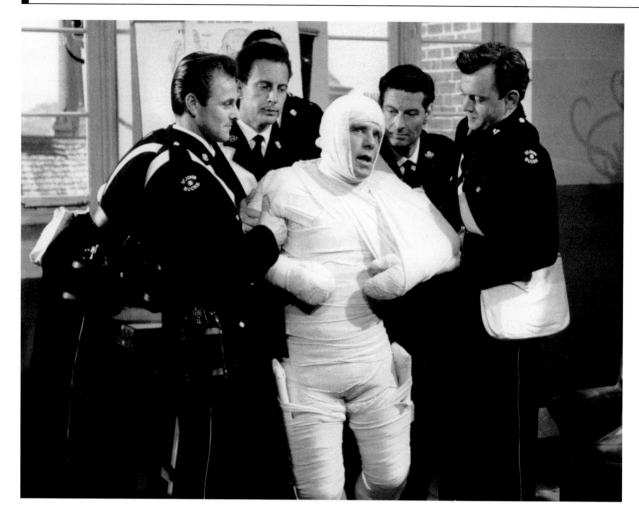

one. However, Hugh Stewart liked the sound of it and said we should go ahead. Paddy was reluctant but had to agree. On the day of shooting, he called "Action" and walked away to the back of the stage. I played the scene and noticed Paddy coming towards me. He shouted "Cut" and put his arms around me! What an apology.'

'The Square Peg was a massive success around the world,' Hugh Stewart observes, 'and particularly in the old Soviet Union states, where Norman is still idolised to this day.'

By this time, however, Norman was becoming a workaholic, driven by success and craving every opportunity to star on stage and in film. He would typically be filming at Pinewood during the day then go into the West End for his evening stage shows – and there were always two 'houses'. He would get home after midnight and rise again by 5.30 am to meet his studio car. It was a relentless routine which eventually saw Norman break out in a rash, complete with boils. Every time he fell over in his act, it was agony. 'Whenever I fell down, I'd hear a pffft! noise – it'd be a boil bursting. Then I'd

start slipping on the stage! It was horrible.'

Shortly after The Square Peg was completed, Norman went into hospital to have the boils lanced. He lay recuperating for a few days and was told by the matron that he was suffering from malnutrition. It was then he realised that he hadn't been giving himself time to eat properly – he was just too busy to think about stopping for food.

Follow a Star was Norman's next film, in 1959. Jerry Desmonde played opposite him again, this time as a faded singer named Victor Carew, who 'borrows' Norman's singing voice and revitalises his career. His miming to Norman's recordings (made mainly when Norman was singing in his bath) works well until Norman realises that he's being taken advantage of. Carew is finally exposed when miming to a record played at twice its normal speed. Robert Asher directed and June Laverick played the love interest.

Norman left the Stewart-Asher fold the next year to make There was a Crooked Man for producer John Bryan (financed by United Artists) and director Stuart Burge. However, he soon returned

Facing page: *All dressed up and nowhere to go. A Stitch In Time.*

Left: *Moonlighting as gardeners in Pinewood's grounds. Norman with Jerry Desmonde in The Early Bird.*

for *The Bulldog Breed*, a nautical comedy co-starring Edward Chapman. 'There's a scene in the film where you see me get into a ruckus with two sailors. Look carefully and you'll see that they're Michael Caine and Oliver Reed!'

Norman's second feature for John Bryan was *The Girl on the Boat*, based on a P G Wodehouse story and set on a liner in the 1920s. Sadly, the ingredients didn't come together as well as they had in Norman's Rank films but, back with Robert Asher, *On the Beat* re-established Norman's box-office popularity in 1962. He played dual roles again: Norman Pitkin, Scotland Yard car park attendant and car washer, and Giulio Napolitani, a criminal mastermind who maintains a camp hairdresser façade as cover. A wonderful supporting cast consisted of Raymond Huntley, David Lodge, Eric Barker, Terence Alexander and Dilys Laye.

But better still, in 1963, Norman became box-office dynamite in *A Stitch in Time*, knocking the latest James Bond adventure, *From Russia With Love*, off the top spot when the film opened in London. Set in a hospital, the comedy was again directed by Robert Asher, and had a script by Jack Davies, Eddie Leslie and Norman himself.

Norman Pitkin – in this incarnation – is an assistant in a butcher's shop. When a hold-up takes place, Norman swallows Mr Grimsdale's prized gold watch and chain to prevent it from being stolen and is promptly admitted to hospital. There, Pitkin, swathed from head to toe in plaster, falls off a table, into a wheelchair, down some stairs, through a wall and on to the top of a moving ambulance. Hanging onto the roof, he is eventually thrown off and ends up 'flying' into a hospital ward. The pay-off line comes when a doctor

(Patrick Cargill) enters the ward, looks at Norman and demands to know from the nurse what the patient is doing out of bed.

Robert Asher explained to Norman that the stunt sequence was far too dangerous and that a stuntman was being brought in. Norman wasn't happy but the director had the last word. So Norman, still in 'costume', just sat back and watched. The sequence started well but when the stuntman landed on the ambulance, he went flying straight off and broke his leg. Robert Asher was distraught. 'He knew I'd seen it all happen and said that he wouldn't be able to get another stuntman at such short notice. I just looked at him and smiled. He then said I could try it if I thought I could do it!'

Norman did everything the stuntman had done but took the precaution of hooking some springs to the ambulance roof to act as a brake when he landed on it. 'It worked like a dream and that's me throughout the entire sequence. I've always known how to fall so I've never really hurt myself apart from the odd bruise or two, and I didn't there either!'

The Early Bird (1964) was Norman's last film with Hugh Stewart and his first in colour. The first 15 minutes are silent and consist of an amusing collection of early morning 'get-up-and-out' routines between Norman, Edward Chapman and Paddie O'Neil. In the story that unfolds, Grimsdale's dairy is under threat from the massive Consolidated Dairies, whose head honcho is brilliantly played by Jerry Desmonde. Not only does Consolidated have most of the town's milk business, they also have electric floats – whereas Grimsdale's have a horse and cart.

Bryan Pringle plays one of Consolidated's milkmen, who systematically forces Grimsdale's out of business. Initially he smashes milk bottles, but progresses to poisoning Nellie the horse. Various showdowns ensue including Norman wreaking havoc in Jerry Desmonde's garden (actually the Pinewood gardens), on a golf course and finally in Consolidated's dairy. The Consolidated headquarters was actually the exterior of D Stage and Car Park One at Pinewood. Cliff Culley, an accomplished matte artist, 'painted on' the extras floors of the

THE NORMAN WISDOM FILMS AT PINEWOOD (year of release):

1953	*TROUBLE IN STORE*
1954	*ONE GOOD TURN*
1955	*MAN OF THE MOMENT*
1956	*UP IN THE WORLD*
1957	*JUST MY LUCK*
1958	*THE SQUARE PEG*
1959	*FOLLOW A STAR*
1960	*THERE WAS A CROOKED MAN*
1960	*THE BULLDOG BREED* (PART)
1962	*ON THE BEAT*
1963	*A STITCH IN TIME*
1965	*THE EARLY BIRD*
1966	*PRESS FOR TIME*

HQ. The same area had substituted for the rear of Scotland Yard in *On the Beat* a few years earlier.

Norman next appeared in Michael Bentine's ensemble piece *The Sandwich Man*, directed by Robert Hartford-Davis, but then returned to Pinewood with *Press for Time* in 1966. Robert Asher returned to direct, while Robert Hartford-Davis and Peter Newbrook produced, Newbrook also photographing the film. Gone was Pitkin, with Norman playing the Prime Minister's grandson posted to a small town on the coast out of harm's way ... they hope! But the film wasn't particularly memorable and marked the end of the classic Norman Wisdom comedies.

Norman then achieved massive success on Broadway in *Walking Happy*, a musical version of *Hobson's Choice*: so much so that he received the New York Critics Award and a Tony nomination. Richard Rodgers then offered him *Androcles and The Lion* opposite Noel Coward. His success in that led to William Friedkin casting him in *The Night They Raided Minsky's* for United Artists. The top-notch cast included Jason Robards, Elliot Gould, Denholm Elliott, Harry Andrews, Joseph Wiseman and Britt Ekland. Norman was on a roll

and won himself an Oscar nomination.

While in America, however, Norman's second wife Freda left him. Despite the promise of a Hollywood career, he decided to return home to his children. They became his first priority and his film career was put on hold. One more British film followed in 1969, however: *What's Good for the Goose*, a quite terrible attempt to put Norman into a modish sex comedy with Sally Geeson. Norman doesn't have many fond memories of the film, and none whatsoever of its director Menahem Golan. 'He was a shit,' Norman insists. 'He never let me try anything or make changes which I thought would improve the film. It was a horrible experience.'

It was 23 years before Norman made another film, during which time he kept busy on stage and TV. His film comeback was in a low-budget thriller called *Double X*, which received only a brief theatrical release before going to video. Co-starring Simon Ward and Bernard Hill, the film cast Norman as an ageing crook on the run from his old gang. The script and direction left much to be desired, but critical acclaim came Norman's way again with *Going Gently*, a BBC drama directed by Stephen Frears. In this moving play, Norman portrayed a terminally ill cancer patient – alongside Fulton Mackay as a fellow patient and Judi Dench as a nurse – and brought to the fore his impressive ability to play comedy and pathos almost hand in hand.

Norman remains a regular visitor to Pinewood – cries of 'Mr Grimsdale!' echo round the corridors whenever he's around – and still hopes to bring his next and much cherished film, *Adam and Evil*, to life at the studio. ∎

7

IS THER

Left: *Donald Sinden, Donald Houston, Kenneth More, and Dirk Bogarde were Doctors in the House.*

Right: *Ralph Thomas, one of Rank's busiest and most successful contract directors.*

Betty Box was the only female producer under contract with J Arthur Rank. In fact, until the early 1960s she was the only female producer of features in the business. She entered the film industry in 1942 working with her brother, Sydney, who was at that time making documentary films for the Ministry of Information and the British Council as well as training films for the Army.

Towards the end of the war, Sydney turned his hand to features and, after the tremendous success of *The Seventh Veil* (made at Riverside Studios in Hammersmith), he was asked by Rank to take over the reins at Gainsborough. But he was about to start another picture at Riverside called *The Upturned Glass* so Betty was thrown in at the deep end and effectively produced the film, though only taking an associate producer credit. Sydney took over Gainsborough's Shepherds Bush studios and Betty their Islington studios. After Betty had made around ten films, and Sydney about 40, the studios were closed and future production centred on Pinewood. Having arrived in 1949, Betty would stay until 1979.

Her first film at Pinewood was the stylish 1890s mystery *So Long at the Fair* (1949), with directors Terence Fisher and Antony Darnborough and stars Dirk Bogarde, Jean Simmons and David Tomlinson. But for her next film, *The Clouded Yellow*, she teamed up with director Ralph Thomas.

'They were such a wonderful team to work with,' says Muriel Pavlow, who appeared in two of the *Doctor* films. 'Betty seemed as though she was always having a ball; she was always tremendous fun to be with yet remained very shrewd! I loved and respected her and those wonderful qualities she possessed. Similarly Ralph. A wonderful director and one who knew exactly what he wanted, and how to convey it with ease to his actors. A genius. They both were.'

Ralph Thomas, brother of *Carry On* director Gerald and father of producer Jeremy, began his film career in the 1930s as an assistant editor and a test director. After the war he carved a very successful niche for himself as a maker of trailers. His early grounding in the cutting rooms provided invaluable experience, and Betty Box was so impressed with the trailers he compiled for *Miranda* (made at Islington) and *So Long at the Fair* that she asked him to direct her next picture.

Their fifth film together was *Doctor in the House*, based on the book of the same name by Richard Gordon. Box came across the novel at a book-stall in Cardiff railway station. By the time she reached Paddington, she was convinced it would make a good film. 'Betty always preferred to find her own subjects and stories,' explains her husband, film producer Peter Rogers, 'rather than just wandering down to the story department at the studio to see what was going. The material there had often been around for a long time and wasn't always particularly good!'

Nicholas Phipps came in to work on the script

DOCTOR IN THE HOUSE?

Below: *Jack Swinburne, Ralph Thomas, Gerald Thomas, Betty Box and Muriel Box in a production conflab.*

Facing page: *On location in Belgium for* Doctor at Large, *assistant director Peter Manley is left most with director Ralph Thomas centre, following the camera dolly.*

and Ralph Thomas went about casting good actors rather than professional funny men. 'We decided to cast the actors that we would have done if it was going to be a straight dramatic story about medicine,' he says. 'Dirk Bogarde, Kenneth More, Kay Kendall, Donald Sinden and Donald Houston all played it within a very strict, tight limit of believability. Of course, Kenny More was really far too old to be a student, but we thought he'd be very good in the film so Nick Phipps very cleverly wrote in the background story of how his character had to keep failing his exams year after year to maintain an allowance. Nick was a brilliant writer and made the very best of the Gordon books. Unfortunately, when he died we never recaptured the brilliance of his writing and the films never really rose above being just plain medical farces.'

For St Swithin's chief surgeon, Sir Lancelot Spratt, Box initially thought of Robert Morley but, unable to afford him, then struck on the idea of James Robertson Justice who, in the event, played the role with tremendous gusto. The budget was a modest £100,000 – originally it had been set at £119,000 – but, because there had never been a successful film about doctors and hospitals, the Rank Organisation were still very anxious. 'John Davis didn't like the title at all,' says Thomas, 'and suggested we change it to *Campus Capers* to hide the fact that it was about medics. But we stood by our title!'

Box did a deal with Guinness for a tie-in poster, in which all four leading actors were pictured standing at a bar drinking the black beer, above which was printed: 'GUINNESS IS GOOD FOR YOU, as good as *Doctor In The House*.' The poster appeared all over the UK, providing massive exposure yet not costing the production a penny. The film was a phenomenal success and recouped its costs in just six weeks at the Odeon Leicester Square.

'People used to hold medicine in great awe,' Ralph Thomas observes, 'but in our film people could identify with the funny situations they had seen, or that had happened to them as patients, doctors or nurses. It had an enormously wide common appeal – much wider than we understood when we were making it. The film was ridiculously successful and when I went down to Leicester Square the day after it premièred I was dumbstruck to see queues right round the square. It did very well in America for Republic Pictures and in Australia I remember it ran in one cinema for a whole year!'

'The film created a record,' recalls Sir Donald Sinden, 'by being seen by more people in its first year on release than any previous film: 17 million tickets were sold. Someone speculated that there were 34 million people of cinema-going age in the country, so why didn't the other 17 million go?'

The film's success guaranteed the Box/Thomas team greater creative control within the Rank Organisation and also meant that a sequel was almost certain, as Thomas explains. 'We promised to do another *Doctor* film and it was agreed that if we had other subjects – with reasonable budgets

and not too idiotic plots – they would let us do them too. It was a hugely cosy operation that served you well if you served *them* well. Betty and I had three long-term contracts with Rank and that allowed us to maintain the same key crew, which was ideal. We probably lost a little in fees because of the arrangement of having our team on the payroll for the whole year, but we had a great deal of comfort and a very nice atmosphere as a result.'

Dirk Bogarde reprised his role of Dr Simon Sparrow in the sequel, *Doctor at Sea*, much to the delight of his director. 'Dirk was a pleasure to work with because he always produced more than you asked of him. He was a great contributor.' Born Dirk Van Den Bogaerde of Dutch origin and raised in the Thames valley, Bogarde first found notoriety on the silver screen as the villain who murdered PC Dixon in *The Blue Lamp*. The Rank Organisation were eager to shake that image when they signed him up, moulding him instead into the distinguished aristocratic character he so epitomised in later films. Although he found success in *Campbell's Kingdom*, *A Tale of Two Cities* and *The Wind Cannot Read* as a hero and romantic lead, it was the *Doctor* films that catapulted

Right: *Maidenhead Town Hall doubled as St Swithin's, and later as hospitals in the* Carry On *films too.*

Below: *Bogarde returned to the series with* Doctor in Distress, *here attending a sick James Robertson Justice.*

him to new heights.

His co-star in *Doctor at Sea* was a very beautiful, but relatively unknown, French actress named Brigitte Bardot. 'We'd seen Brigitte in quite a few little French pictures,' Thomas explains. 'She was very beautiful and ever such a talented actress, and you could tell straight away that she was something special. We thought she could be good for the film and bring a lot of style to it with Dirk. Just after we'd cast her there was some scandal or other in France involving her husband-to-be, and she was quite a celebrity with all the publicity it generated, which helped us enormously when the film was released in Europe.'

The film was a big success and performed well across the world, particularly in Europe. Rank wanted more.

In 1956 *Doctor at Large* was put into production. With a script by Nicholas Phipps again, young

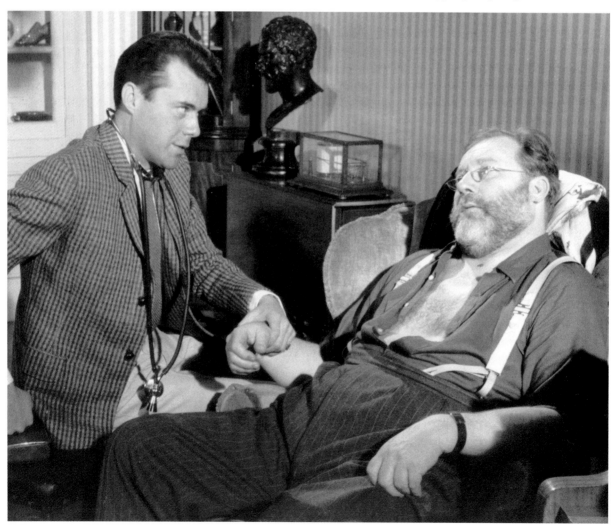

Simon Sparrow was this time launched into the 'real world' of medicine after Sir Lancelot refuses him the opportunity to practice surgery at St Swithin's. A starry cast included Muriel Pavlow, James Robertson Justice, Donald Sinden, Shirley Eaton, Michael Medwin, Edward Chapman and, in a three-day role, Lionel Jeffries. 'When the notices came out I shared top billing with Dirk Bogarde,' Jeffries remembers. 'He was furious!'

Muriel Pavlow had appeared in the first film and, though happy to return, felt this third instalment didn't quite have the same magic. 'I remember Dirk saying to me that we would have to work a bit harder on this one as we wouldn't have Kenny More's wonderful spirit. He was right. I wouldn't say the later films didn't work, because they did, but there was a certain something that the first one had that wasn't in the others. The ingredients and casting in *Doctor in the House* were sheer perfection and, like a good soufflé, it rose beautifully. That was certainly the benchmark film.'

Harbouring similar sentiments, Bogarde was keen to move away from his Simon Sparrow character and on to more challenging roles. The series continued, however, and in 1960 Michael Craig and Leslie Phillips (aka Doctors Burke and Hare) were *Doctor*[s] *in Love*. Although a weaker story – and lacking Bogarde – it still performed well at the box-office. 'It took a hell of a lot of money,' says Thomas, 'although admittedly it wasn't as good as the first three. When Dirk heard about it he was quite jealous. He said that if we had a script for another one, he wouldn't mind coming back to do it! He did come back for *Doctor in Distress*, although it wasn't as successful as his earlier ones. None of the later ones were, really, but they weren't unsuccessful either, as even the last one – which was a pretty bad picture – took

a lot of money.'

Doctor in Distress reunited Dr Sparrow with Sir Lancelot Spratt at St Swithin's (actually Maidenhead Town Hall), but did little to resurrect the charm of the first film; like the plot and jokes, it was wearing thin. 'Admittedly we were scrambling for new ideas by then,' says Thomas. 'We really didn't want to make farcical pictures. By this time the *Carry Ons* were coming in and that style didn't really tempt us, and Peter [Rogers] and Gerald [Thomas] were doing it so much better than we could have done anyway. The first films were about students and people learning to be good doctors – they were real people.'

Leslie Phillips reprised his role of Dr Burke for the two final films in the series, *Doctor in Clover* (1966) and *Doctor in Trouble* (1970), the former seeing his return to St Swithin's for a refresher course and the latter his return to sea when he inadvertently becomes a stowaway on an Atlantic cruise ship. The characters were becoming farcical and Leslie Phillips' increasingly lecherous Dr Burke was no real match for Bogarde's Simon Sparrow. The material dwindled into a collection of rehashed jokes and routines while saucy humour of the *Carry On* variety escalated. The time had come to draw a close to the series that had spanned 16 years, grossed millions of pounds and catapulted Dirk Bogarde to stardom.

Betty Box and Ralph Thomas remained the studio's busiest filmmakers during and after the Doctor films. In fact, they were the last two Rank contract filmmakers to leave the studio when the Organisation finally abandoned production in the late 1970s. Betty Box was honoured with an OBE in 1958 for her contribution to cinema. Sadly, she died early in 1999, still holding the distinction of being Britain's foremost and most successful female feature producer. On 9 June, Peter Rogers presented the Variety Club of Great Britain with a new Sunshine Coach in memory of his late wife.

The seven Doctor films are shown continually on TV around the world and even spawned two popular television series. They remain – like their creators – a distinctive feature of British cinema and Pinewood history. ■

8 THE DAVIS ERA

Left: *Just married! Dirk Bogarde and Yoko Tani in* **The Wind Cannot Read.**

Right: *The Rank premiere brochure for* **The One That Got Away.**

1957 – the studios' twenty-first anniversary – was a particularly busy year, with no fewer than 21 productions.

The first film into the studio was *Hell Drivers*, in which rivalry between haulage drivers leads to increasingly dangerous driving in a bid to reduce journey times. Cy Endfield pulled together an accomplished cast which included Stanley Baker, Patrick McGoohan, Herbert Lom, Sid James, Jill Ireland and – some way down the list – the young Sean Connery.

Stanley Baker then starred in Betty Box and Ralph Thomas's *Campbell's Kingdom*, a Canadian drama also starring Dirk Bogarde and Michael Craig. 'We were shooting in Cortina for winter because we couldn't use Canada,' remembers Ralph Thomas, 'and when we arrived there wasn't any snow. We must have bought all the cotton wool in Italy, and had men in from Milan to spray everything white. It all worked fine. But when we were finishing the picture we needed spring weather, and would you believe it started to snow! Well, we sprayed the snow green and all the women in the unit were making paper poppies to stick into the green-sprayed snow.

'We had a première in London and the Canadian High Commissioner attended with his wife. In the middle of the film they squeezed hands – he later said that it was because they recognised the location in Canada as Lake Luisa where they spent their honeymoon, and it was a very special place for them. We didn't have the heart to tell him it was shot in Italy!'

Box and Thomas made two further films later in the year, both with Dirk Bogarde. *A Tale of Two Cities* enjoyed a deluxe supporting cast including Dorothy Tutin, Cecil Parker, Donald Pleasence and an extremely hissable Christopher Lee, while *The Wind Cannot Read* (known around the studio as *The Illiterate Fart*) saw Bogarde marrying Yoko Tani prior to being tortured in a Burmese POW camp.

Ken Annakin, meanwhile, made *Across the Bridge*, based in part on a Graham Greene novel. 'This is still my favourite movie,' Annakin claims, 'because of the unique story and the great performances of Rod Steiger, Dolores the dog, Noel Willman, Bernard Lee – in fact, the whole cast. John Davis allowed me to make a most extensive recce in the El Paso area of Texas and across into Northern Mexico. We reproduced all the exteriors in the Granada/Seville area of Southern Spain and returned to Pinewood for the interiors – especially those on the train. Rod was an avid Method actor and used to insist on running round the stage before every shot in the railway carriage. I recall Bernard Lee watching and shaking his head. "Silly bugger," he'd say. "Why can't he just act?"'

On the other side of the lot, Roy Baker directed the groundbreaking *The One That Got Away*. 'The film was the first with a German hero,' says Baker, 'and you must remember that this was only a decade or so after the end of World War II. But

ART TWO (1957 – 1962)

Top right: *On location for* The One That Got
Away – *Hardy Kruger, director of photography
Eric Cross and the film's director Roy Baker.*

Bottom right: *Prepared for any eventuality!
Peter Manley on location in the Lake District.*

I was determined to make the film that way
because it was all true, and very dramatic. That's
why the casting was so important. Franz Von
Werra was played brilliantly by Hardy Kruger, but
there was tremendous opposition to playing a
German actor in the lead, particularly from John
Davis. He agreed to us doing the picture, but only
if we used a British actor in the lead. Fortunately,
we were able to buy some time while having the
script rewritten and eventually won him over.'

Peter Manley was Roy Baker's production manager and recollected the initial reconnaissance trip
in setting up the film. 'We started thinking about
The One That Got Away in December 1956, and
Roy and I went off to Canada to plot the course of
Von Werra. It was a factual story, and we were able
to follow all the ground he covered; it was fascinating. But it was minus 50 degrees in Canada and
impossible to work: cameras froze up and *we* froze
up! In the beginning of '57 we discovered that the
temperatures were more favourable in Sweden, so
we shot all the winter scenes there and came back
and shot the rest of the film in the Lake District
and at Pinewood.'

Hardy Kruger regards this film as the most
important in his career. 'The year before I met Roy,
my movie career in Germany was in danger as I had
rebelled against the low quality of German films. I
had seen some wonderful British, French and
American films and I dreamt of working in these
sorts of films, but I knew it was unlikely that anyone would come to me, a German actor, so soon
after the war. I tried my luck in Paris and London
but without much success. Having returned to
Germany I then thought about going to Hollywood,
but a call came through from the Rank Organisation
to set up a meeting with Roy Baker in Hamburg.
Roy then invited me over to London for the screen
test. I was walking on air when I got the job!

'It wasn't all plain sailing, however. When the
Rank Organisation finally announced that the film
would be made with me, they "paraded" me in front
of the press at the Odeon Leicester Square. The
press were, on the whole, very kind. There was
one journalist, however, Tom Wiseman, who
attacked me straight away and asked me if I had

Below: Pinewood receives the key of the door.

Bottom left: The Star, *30 September 1957.*
Lord Rank with Belinda Lee and June Laverick.

THE RANK ORGANISATION'S PINEWOOD STUDIOS CELEBRATE
21 YEARS OF FILMS FOR YOU

been a Nazi. I couldn't tell the press the complicated story of my life, but I had seen – to my disgust – that there were hardly any Germans who admitted to being a Nazi; they would say "I had nothing to do with them" or "I couldn't help it" and so on. I never took that attitude, and so I shocked Wiseman by immediately saying "Yes". It was a little more complicated than that, but I wasn't prepared to go into details and nor was I prepared to lie. The press then boycotted me and the film. The

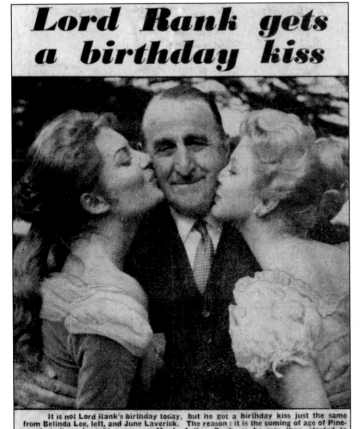

Lord Rank gets a birthday kiss

It is not Lord Rank's birthday today, but he got a birthday kiss just the same from Belinda Lee, left, and June Laverick. The reason : it is the coming of age of Pinewood studios where 21 years ago Mr J. Arthur Rank, as he was then, started to make his first film. Today he was honoured there at a mammoth party. (The Pinewood Story : See Page Eight).

Rank publicity department couldn't get my name or the name of the film into the press anywhere.

'As a result, people at Pinewood had a little problem with me. The stars and executives didn't shun me, but they were never seen with me either and I would always eat with Roy and Julian [Wintle, the producer] – we were always alone, nobody would join us. Then one day Finchie [Peter Finch] came in and said "Hi" to Roy and Julian, and he said to me "Are you that German fellow?" I said "Yes". "You're in deep shit, aren't you?" he said. I said "Yes I am!" "How about dinner tonight then?" he asked. That started a friendship that lasted until he died.'

The press boycott was deemed so serious that, halfway through location filming in the Lake District, Baker was summoned to Pinewood and told by John Davis and Earl St John that they were cancelling the picture. Baker stuck to his guns and, as Kruger puts it, 'The press and public loved the movie, I got fantastic reviews and my career was made, along with plenty of money for the Rank Organisation. I have to thank Roy twice – first for casting me and then for standing by me.'

Lewis Gilbert, hot on the successful heels of *Reach for the Sky*, next brought the biopic *Carve Her Name With Pride* to the studio. Violette Szabo, the British widow of a French officer who enlisted as a secret agent, was played brilliantly by Virginia McKenna in this highly dramatic film, directed with exquisite objectivity by Gilbert. In preparing for the picture, McKenna learned parachute jumping, judo and how to fire a Sten gun, as well as receiving invaluable guidance from Odette Churchill, as she explained in a 1986 interview for Thames TV. 'I was acting the part of someone who actually lived, and who died in a concentration camp, and no script or book could tell me what that was like. But Odette had lived through it. The courage of

Right: *Belinda Lee graces* Picturegoer *magazine's special Pinewood birthday edition.*

Facing page: *The engine room of doomed liner Titanic (actually Pinewood's power house) in* A Night to Remember, *with below, Kenneth More as Second Officer Lightoller.*

Week ending September 28 1957   EVERY THURSDAY   4½d

Picturegoer

THE NATIONAL **FILM** AND
ENTERTAINMENT WEEKLY

PINEWOOD SOUVENIR ISSUE
—celebrating the 21 years of Britain's No. 1 studio

ALL YOUR PINEWOOD FAVOURITES ARE INSIDE

BELINDA LEE

the women behind the enemy lines was remarkable and affected me deeply.'

On 30 September the grand 21st anniversary studio party was held at Pinewood. Lord and Lady Rank personally greeted all the guests, including 21 girls – all aged 21 – chosen from different parts of Britain, along with John Davis and his wife, Dinah Sheridan. The lawns were crowded with many of Rank's stars: Stanley Baker, Susan Beaumont, Dirk Bogarde, Phyllis Calvert, Jill Dixon, Anne Heywood, Jill Ireland, Belinda Lee, A E Matthews, David McCallum, John Mills, Kenneth More, Michael Redgrave, Flora Robson, Donald Sinden, Norman Wisdom and Tony Wright. 21-year-old Jill Ireland released hundreds of pigeons in the gardens before assisting Jill Dixon (also 21) and Norman Wisdom to launch 500 balloons – each one carrying an envelope which offered a prize to its finder.

More than 500 guests filled a huge marquee for lunch. The guest of honour was the Canadian High Commissioner, the Hon George Drew. In proposing a toast to Lord Rank, he said that he was 'one of the truly outstanding figures of the film world, whose ideals and integrity of mind and spirit have shown themselves in the quality of the films produced.' A set of curtains in front of a stage area drew back to reveal a huge birthday cake, complete with the appropriate number of candles. Kenneth More handed Lord Rank the knife to cut the cake – Anne Heywood assisted – while the assembled band played 'Happy Birthday'. Dirk Bogarde then took centre stage, pointing out that 'Lord Rank has a far bigger family than he thought and drawing Davis and Rank's attention to the two silver statuette cameramen adorning the cake. Deeply touched, Lord Rank said how much he appreciated 'this token of affection for us which we shall value all our lives.'

During the day's celebrations Lord Rank also paid tribute to his partner in the Pinewood venture. 'The person really responsible for the building of these studios is the late Mr Charles Boot. He, at the opening of this studio, said that if it had not been for me the project would have fallen down, but he made a mistake. He was responsible for it because I am sure that he would have found some other optimist to find the money.' The assembled guests then went on the studio tour. The Ravensbruck concentration camp, recreated on the backlot for *Carve Her Name With Pride*, was given a wide berth, however, so as not to offend or upset guests.

The celebrations were not just confined to Pinewood, as newspapers ran advertisements stating that anyone celebrating their 21st birthday on Monday 30 September should tell their local Odeon or Gaumont cinema. They then received a month's free pass to the cinema as 'part of Pinewood's coming of age celebrations.'

Production, meanwhile, continued apace and undoubtedly one of the greatest films to come out of Pinewood in 1957 – if not in its whole history – was *A Night to Remember*. Roy Baker's semi-documentary film of the *Titanic* and its fateful maiden voyage enjoyed much critical acclaim, brought great kudos to the Rank Organisation – which had been accused of only producing bland family films – and survives (James Cameron's 1997 blockbuster *Titanic* notwithstanding) as the definitive *Titanic* film.

The model sequences were shot in the Pinewood tank, over which the 007 Stage now stands, and many of the water sequences were shot at Ruislip Lido, a few miles from the studio. Half the deck was constructed on the backlot under the supervision of art director supreme, Alex Vetchinsky.

'The producer, Bill McQuitty, was very persuasive,' recalls Baker in accounting for Rank's decision to film a subject already handled twice before, in 1929 and 1953. 'He was also emotionally involved, being an Ulsterman, as the ship was built in the Ulster shipyards and his father took him to see the *Titanic* as it sailed down the river when he was a very young boy. He sold the idea to John Davis as a flag-waving project, with tremendous social issues and prestige at its heart. The society of the time had persuaded itself that a ship could be unsinkable and this film was to show the dramatic effect its sinking had on that society. We've received a lot of backhanded publicity for the film in the last couple of years after Cameron's *Titanic*. However, I'm *still* told by Bill that, somehow, our film has yet to go into profit!'

In another attempt to break into the US market, Rank Film Distributors of America was formed in 1957, and enjoyed a high-profile publicity launch. It remained the one elusive missing link in the Organisation's distribution network and would remain so, for the company was wound up after encountering 'considerable losses' (never disclosed) in the space of a year. Despite this setback, J Arthur Rank was ennobled the following year for his services to the British film industry. He became the First Baron Rank of Sutton Scotney.

The following year, Rank contract artiste Donald Sinden appeared in Jack Lee's *The Captain's Table*, co-starring with John Gregson, Peggy Cummins, Reginald Beckwith, Richard Wattis, Joan Sims and Maurice Denham. Based on a Richard Gordon novel, the screenplay was the work of playwright John Whiting and actors Bryan Forbes and Nicholas Phipps. Recalls Sinden, 'I was in the bar at Pinewood, which is where I got most of my jobs actually, having just finished *Rockets Galore*. I bumped into Joe Janni, the producer, and he started telling me about this script which involved three months' location work cruising

around the Greek islands. I said "Count me in" and didn't even wait to read it.

'A few weeks before shooting, he called to say that, unfortunately, the budget wouldn't stretch to the Greek islands. It was to be the Channel Islands instead. It still sounded good to me. However, a week or so before shooting I went for a costume fitting and the wardrobe man said "Shame about the Channel Islands, isn't it?" I didn't know what he meant. He then explained that the budget wouldn't stretch: the location was now Tilbury docks! We shot out to sea on one side, turned the ship around and shot the other way, and spent three months in those wretched docks!'

Sinden's reference to the importance of Pinewood's bar area is no exaggeration. 'Betty [Box] and I had our offices directly above the bar and restaurant area,' says Ralph Thomas, 'and you could look out of the window on a summer's evening and cast a whole picture with the people in the patio area! At the end of the day, everyone would gather down there and discuss the day's events, along with what was happening the following day. As we were all working for the same company, and being paid out of the same pot, there was a tremendous sense of co-operation and collaboration; anyone would do anything to help. I recall some producers literally borrowing sets from others when they were in trouble. That would never happen nowadays.'

Just as valuable a studio asset as the bar was the Commissionaire, Sergeant Arthur Munday. An avuncular figure, he knew who and who not to let in and was a veritable mine of information about what was going on around the complex, as Ralph Thomas explains. 'Arthur Munday was a great sorter-out of people and problems. He was in effect a "super prefect". If you needed to know anything, he was the one who knew or, if something needed sorting out, he'd do it – be it rustling up extras from the gardens after their extended lunch breaks or escorting someone around the studio ... or out of it!'

Also in 1958, J Lee Thompson popped over from Beaconsfield, where he was directing John and Hayley Mills in *Tiger Bay*, for some back projection and Independent Frame work; 'thoroughly

unpleasant' was his verdict on the IF process. The same year saw the arrival at Pinewood of another highly successful series, the *Carry On* films (which are dealt with in full in Chapter Nine). That year, too, the Rank Organisation was preparing to produce a film of *Lawrence of Arabia* – Anthony Asquith was to direct, Terence Rattigan script and Dirk Bogarde star – but, after recces in what were then very dangerous countries with volatile political conditions, the viability of the project was brought into question and it was cancelled. Rattigan got over his disappointment by turning his script into a successful stage play, *Ross*.

In 1959, a new addition was made to the studio's facilities for *Sink the Bismarck!* – the paddock tank, which to this day remains the largest in Europe, with the following dimensions: 221 ft (narrowing to 105 ft) wide, 198 ft long and 3 ft 6 in deep, and an inner tank measuring 51 ft by 40 ft by 9 ft. It has a total capacity of 764,000 gallons and a backdrop measuring 240 ft by 60 ft. Extensive model work was required in *Sink the Bismarck!* and all of it was carried out in the paddock tank. Lewis Gilbert's recreation of the sinking in 1941 of Germany's greatest battleship starred Kenneth More, Dana Wynter, Michael Hordern and Maurice Denham, while the set attracted many visitors, not least Her Majesty the Queen and the 12-year-old Prince Charles.

'It was a very low-key visit,' Gilbert maintains, 'and the Queen didn't travel with any entourage or bodyguards – just her and Charles. The young prince was at school in Cheam and had wanted to see a film studio. On arrival, the Royal party came to the paddock tank and watched some shooting. After a while, the Queen asked if there were any other films being made that she might visit. I said that I believed Betty Box and Ralph Thomas were on another stage [with *Conspiracy of Hearts*]. So we were walking down the corridor towards the stage and walking towards us was a chippie [carpenter] carrying a load of timber. "Alright guv?" he said as he approached. Then he did a double-take. He couldn't work out if it was the Queen or an actress made-up to look like her for a film. Suddenly it registered just who it really was and

Facing page: *Anna Massey and Carl Boehm in Michael Powell's disturbing thriller* Peeping Tom. *The film was savaged by critics on its initial release.*

the timber fell slowly out of his arms onto the floor in front of the Queen. She found it all very amusing. I finally took her on to the set and that was my greatest moment: the look on Betty's face was priceless. I introduced the Queen to the cast and she was absolutely delightful.'

'That's absolutely true,' says Ralph Thomas. 'It was just about tea-break time, in fact. I asked Her Majesty if she would care to join us and she said that she would be delighted to, on condition we made no fuss about trays etc – she wanted the same as everyone else. So, she sat on my chair with a cup and saucer in hand and it was a lovely afternoon.'

Thomas and Box were busier than ever. First up was a domestic comedy, *Upstairs Downstairs* with Michael Craig and Anne Heywood, and then came the excellent *Conspiracy of Hearts*, a World War II drama detailing how Italian nuns smuggled Jewish children out of concentration camps. The film avoids being over-sentimental and remained Betty Box's favourite. In the meantime, Lew Grade's TV arm ITC made its first Pinewood show –*Interpol Calling*.

One of the most controversial films ever made also came out of the studio in 1959 – Michael Powell's *Peeping Tom*. The film was berated on its release with one influential critic, Derek Hill, shrieking that it ought to be 'flushed down the nearest sewer.' However, those involved with the film saw it as a sad love story rather than a horrific thriller.

'I received a call from Mickey,' said editor Noreen Ackland, 'and he asked if I would like to cut his new film. I didn't need to think about it! When I read the script, I saw a very sad and tormented man in Carl Boehm's character and, while his methods were perhaps a little gruesome, it was by no means a "bad taste thriller". Mickey was devastated, as were we all, on its release when the reviews came in. They vilified the film. It really did have a severe effect on him and he never really recovered. Thankfully, the film is now rightly regarded as one of the best he ever made and has become something of a cult classic. I'm always being asked about it and it's always showing somewhere in the world; a remastered print enjoyed considerable success on its re-release in New York, mainly thanks to Martin Scorsese.'

The movie used Pinewood extensively, as part of the story was set in a studio punningly called Chipperfield. E Stage and its surrounding corridors, together with the double-lodge entrance, can be seen quite clearly in the film.

The story, written by Leo Marks, tells of how a photographer uses a spiked tripod to kill young girls while photographing the look of terror on their faces. The tormented Mark Lewis (Boehm) is revealed to have been 'scientifically' tortured and tormented as a child by his cruel father who filmed him day and night. (Powell himself plays Mark's sadistic father in these horrific flashbacks.) In retrospect, the horror content is tame compared with modern films, so one could be forgiven for not fully appreciating just how repugnant the critics of the day considered it.

The last film to shoot that year was *The League of Gentlemen*, which came from Allied Film-Makers, namely Richard Attenborough, Bryan Forbes, Guy Green, Michael Relph, Basil Dearden and Jack Hawkins. It is a classic example of the perfect British film encompassing ingenuity, originality, comedy, drama and action.

1960 went down in history primarily for the film that wasn't made at Pinewood: *Cleopatra*. Filming commenced on 28 September and, just over six weeks later, only 11 minutes of material was in the can when Elizabeth Taylor was taken seriously ill. It was by no means the film's first setback but proved the final straw for 20th Century-Fox, who decided to pull the plug on the Pinewood filming.

It was in the latter part of 1959 that Fox had agreed a deal with Pinewood, bringing in the biggest American production ever to be staged in Britain. Elizabeth Taylor had insisted on a European base for tax reasons and Fox were lured to Britain (after seriously considering Rome) because of potential Eady money. Peter Finch was cast as Caesar and Stephen Boyd as Mark Antony. The distinguished Russian-born director Rouben Mamoulian was hired and spent a year preparing for the task. However, it is said that he was apprehensive about the choice of Pinewood, and appalled to learn that the film's desert scenes were to be shot there too.

Right: *The fated, and magnificent, Alexandria set for* Cleopatra - *the Pinewood film that never was.*

Teddy Joseph recalled the early days of setting up the production, and how the shooting of the desert scenes at Pinewood came about. 'Rouben Mamoulian and Walter Wanger [the producer] sent me to Rome to see Dino De Laurentiis to try to reclaim some of the money they had spent on buying chariots and costumes when they were thinking about filming there. When I arrived, De Laurentiis met me and was very curt. He explained that Spyros Skouras at Fox had asked him to build two new stages at his studio six months earlier in order for the film to go to Rome. "There they are," he said. So here was I, not only telling him that the film wasn't going to Rome and we didn't need stages, but that we also wanted our money back!

'I reported back to London, and Wanger instructed me to go to Egypt on a recce with Mamoulian. Our party was met by Nasser's nephew, who was a stills man, and he was going to look after us during our stay. The next day we were escorted by an Egyptian air crew in a Russian-built aeroplane, which was in fact a cargo-cum-parachute plane without any doors, and in which we had to sit on the floor grasping onto a rope for support! We reached Luxor and Mamoulian started to collect pebbles – large ones, small ones – he just loved pebbles. So by the time we had finished the day's recce all of our pockets were full of these pebbles he'd collected and made us carry. They were everywhere; he was quite insane!

'I was left behind with Nasser's nephew to look for good desert (and there isn't much good desert in Egypt). We went about 40 miles out and arrived at a very large, empty Egyptian army camp. The only person there was a very old man, who I guess was in charge of security. Our guide went over to him and said "Do you know who I am, I'm Nasser's nephew." The old man was unfazed and refused us entry. So Nasser's nephew started beating him with a stick, quite violently. I couldn't stand for that. I reported his actions to the British Consulate and said that we couldn't possibly tolerate behaviour like this if we were going to bring a crew over. Within an hour I found myself ordered back to England and the Egyptian authorities took my passport away, saying that I'd only get it back

once I was on my way home. When I arrived back at Pinewood, I was summoned to meet Spyros Skouras in the boardroom. "I remember you," he said. "You were the one who didn't get my money back from Dino De Laurentiis!" He said that I'd messed everything up by upsetting Nassau's nephew, so we couldn't go back to Egypt to shoot. It caused quite a storm. The desert was then recreated on the lot!'

Cleopatra was certainly the most expensive and heavily publicised film ever to move into Pinewood. Sets of previously unheard-of dimensions were constructed on the backlot, but soon came the first of the many problems that dogged the production: a shortage of plasterers. The situation became so desperate that the studio finally resorted to advertising on prime-time TV to fill the vacancies.

The most impressive of all the sets was undoubtedly the harbour of Alexandria, which held one million gallons of water and was topped up further by the English rain. 'The Americans were enthusiastic about the big set on the lot once they had settled for the fact that it wasn't as big as they would have liked,' says Ernie Holding, Fox's man in London. 'They thought it was an excellent job of work and passed on their compliments to Pinewood.'

The size of the production was giving cause for concern. Before a foot of film had been exposed, the cost had easily exceeded £1m, and there was still a 16-week shoot to get underway. Elizabeth Taylor's arrival also brought problems for the studio, the main one being that she insisted on using her Hollywood hairdresser, Sydney Guilaroff. The British unions were up in arms and a dispute blew up that threatened to reach out to other studios. Eventually, a compromise was struck: Miss Taylor

English sortie was all but over. Miss Taylor's recuperation was a slow one, and what with the miserable British weather raining down on the sets day after day, the decision was made to transfer production, and Ancient Egypt, to Italy – where the climate was more conducive to Miss Taylor's health. The Pinewood sets were destroyed.

Joseph Mankiewicz was brought in to rewrite the script and direct the picture, and the result eventually made it to the screen in 1963. Rex Harrison and Richard Burton were re-cast as Caesar and Mark Antony respectively but even then, alas, the film didn't live up to the mass publicity and hype that had surrounded its production. Pinewood didn't receive a credit either.

In a very busy year for Peter Rogers Productions, *Carry On Regardless* was supplemented by Gerald Thomas' *Watch Your Stern* and *No Kidding*. Ralph Thomas and Betty Box moved on from *Doctor in Love* to the excellent political tale *No Love for Johnnie*, with Peter Finch and an all-star supporting cast.

Roy Baker's next assignment, meanwhile, was a rather unusual one featuring Dirk Bogarde and John Mills, plus veiled intimations of homosexuality, in New Mexico. 'After the success of *The One That Got Away* and *A Night to Remember*,' Baker remembers, 'I signed a three picture contract with Rank. Earl St John then handed me a book called *The Singer Not the Song*. I thought it was awful, and I told him so. I then came to the table with three other projects which were, one by one, rejected. Earl said that he really wanted me to do *The Singer Not the Song* with Dirk Bogarde. So I flew out to LA to see Dirk and we discussed the picture. For some reason he was very angry about Johnny Mills being cast to star opposite him – I never really found out why. It was a bit of a problem, as it caused tension on the set, but we soldiered through it and made it look as good as possible. However, as good as it looked, we finished up with a picture that was panned by everyone. They threw the book at it. The irony for me was that I was also given a producer credit, which meant I got a percentage of the profits ... if only!'

'When I was first offered that film,' says Sir

could have Guilaroff but only as supervisor to a British hairdresser.

The imminent arrival of 5,000 extras was the next headache. Pinewood's management laid on 28 extra tube trains from London to Uxbridge and 30 buses to shuttle to and from the station non-stop. Mobile lavatories were hired from Epsom racecourse and massive catering marquees were erected to house the mountain of food for meals. However, all the planning and organisation was wasted – along with 9,000 sausage rolls – when torrential rain forced shooting to be abandoned.

Then real disaster struck. Elizabeth Taylor became dangerously ill and had to undergo an emergency tracheotomy. Production was halted and Joan Collins placed on standby as a replacement. Fox were facing up to the fact that their

Top right: *Some of the cast and crew from*
The Singer Not the Song.

Bottom right: *Roy Baker's little-seen inter-
racial drama* Flame in the Streets.

John Mills, 'I was to co-star with Marlon Brando. I was very excited about it, but for some reason Brando pulled out and that's when Dirk came in. I know he wasn't happy about me being in it with him, but he was a damn fine actor!'

Baker then directed *Flame in the Streets*, again with John Mills, this time as a normally mild-mannered father confronted with the news that his daughter (Sylvia Syms) intends to marry a black man. 'A very controversial film,' says Baker, 'that Rank weren't particularly keen on pushing – they were frightened of it really as it was taken to be inflammatory. But in 1998 it was screened in Brixton to mark the 50th anniversary of the arrival of *Windrush*, the ship that brought a great many Caribbeans into Britain. The turnout for the screening was very good, and I think there were only a couple of white faces there. And the response was marvellous – they loved it. The film was a true reflection of what went on, you see.'

1961 was a slightly quieter year but with many interesting films, most notably *Victim* with Dirk Bogarde. A landmark film, in which Allied Film-Makers brought a homosexual hero to the screen for the first time in the character of a closeted barrister. Homosexuality was still illegal in 1961 and so the film met with a great deal of controversy – particularly in the United States, where it was refused the Seal of the Motion Picture Association of America, which is always required if a film is to receive a theatrical release. This intelligent and suspenseful film boasted an excellent cast, however, and had an immense impact, contributing to the homosexuality law being changed in 1967.

In his last interview (with BBC Radio 2), Sir Dirk Bogarde recalled that many potential co-stars turned down the script because of its homosexual angle and that 'We were not allowed to say homosexual, fag, faggot, poof, gay etc but when I asked the Rank spokesman what we *could* refer to him as, he suggested "invert"! Please! It was a very subdued set, but one day a carpenter was bending down to pick something up and someone shouted out "Watch your arse, Charlie!" That really lightened the whole atmosphere thereafter.'

Another well-remembered picture, *Whistle*

moment and said "Print them all!"'

The screenplay was based on the novel by Mary Hayley Bell (Mrs John Mills) and Forbes's delicate yet realistic handling created a believable, moving and quite enchanting movie in which three Yorkshire children stumble upon an escaped murderer (Alan Bates) in their barn and mistake him for Jesus Christ. Hayley Mills, John and Mary's daughter, headed the cast of otherwise unknown children.

'I'd just returned from America where I'd made *Pollyanna* and *The Parent Trap*,' she recalls, 'and going over to Pinewood was like coming home again – I'd spent a lot of time around the studio when I was young and often visited my father there, so it was a very familiar and happy environment. It was a particularly nice time to be at the studio because my father was on one stage making *Tunes of Glory* and my sister, Juliet, was on another stage with *No My Darling Daughter*, so I had a great sense of comfort knowing my family were just down the corridor. And the other chil-

Down the Wind, was due to be directed by Guy Green from a screenplay by Bryan Forbes. However, shortly before production commenced, illness prevented Green's further involvement and Forbes stepped in, making his directorial début. 'I wasn't very confident on the first day,' says Forbes. 'One of the first shots was with dear Norman Bird and I was so nervous that I totally lost my voice – I couldn't even say "Action". We did three takes and my continuity girl, Penny Daniels, asked which one we were going to print. I paused for a

dren in the film were absolutely wonderful – so talented. Little Alan Barnes stole every scene he was in. Bryan was so clever in his casting.'

'I journeyed to Clitheroe and sat in classrooms of local schools,' says Forbes, 'and observed.' There Forbes found a seven-year-old boy called Alan Barnes, and when he asked the youngster if he'd like to be in the film, Barnes said: 'I'm not bothered.' That dozy response clinched it. Diane Holgate was cast as his sister and together they stole many scenes. Forbes admits that he did have to make the occasional bribe, turning the whole film into a game for the children in order to surmount the boredom of the filmmaking process.

After his stint on the abandoned *Cleopatra*, Teddy Joseph turned his hand to producing *What a Whopper* with Adam Faith, Sid James, Spike Milligan and Carole Lesley. 'It's a marvellous family comedy that, after its initial run, was sold by the financiers to British Lion and then by them to TV,' says Joseph. 'I received accounts for a few years as I had a profit share but then heard nothing. When ownership reverted to me, I tried to track down the negative, but the labs and library had no trace.

To be quite honest, I was so busy with other work that I forgot all about it – until quite recently. My son phoned me to say that details had popped up on the Internet, courtesy of the British Film Institute. I got in touch with the BFI who told me that they had the negative in their archive, would you believe? So after more than 30 years I was reunited with my film.'

Comedy genius Peter Sellers headed the cast of *The Waltz of the Toreadors*, an adaptation of Jean Anouilh's savagely cynical stage comedy, while Disney brought one of their more ambitious projects to the studio, *In Search of the Castaways*. The poster proclaimed 'A thousand thrills ... and Hayley Mills' – and the film delivered on both counts. 'I think the joins show a little now,' says Hayley, 'but it was a fantastic experience with all the special effects going on and on the backlot were the remains of the *Cleopatra* set so it was like a giant playground for us all!'

This enjoyable South American-set adventure marked Maurice Chevalier's last screen appearance, playing an eccentric professor helping three children to track down their explorer father. Keith

Hamshere was one of the three children and later turned his hand to photography. He is now regarded as one of the film industry's finest stills photographers, with extensive experience of the James Bond and *Star Wars* movies.

The film took viewers through fire, ice and water and across several countries, or so it seemed. 'The furthest we travelled from Pinewood,' explained Peter Manley, the film's production manager, 'was three miles down the road to Fulmer, otherwise the entire film was shot in the studio – thanks to some clever special effects and excellent matte work. It's amazing what can be achieved when one tries!'

Disney remained busy the following year with *The Horse Without a Head* and the enchanting *The Three Lives of Thomasina*, both directed by Don Chaffey, while the heavyweight drama *Life for Ruth* came from Allied Film-Makers. Directed by Basil Dearden, this is an utterly absorbing story of how a young girl dies because of her parent's religious beliefs regarding blood transfusions. It gave Michael Craig one of his most challenging roles, rating alongside *The Angry Silence* as his best and proving a welcome change from the many bland leading roles he was offered under his Rank contract. Basil Dearden would return later in 1962 to direct Dirk Bogarde in *The Mindbenders*.

Also in 1962, Michael Winner made his Pinewood début with *Play It Cool*. "In the early sixties," he points out, "people said to me that you couldn't become a director until you were 40. It was a business in which everyone was very

British, wearing three-piece suits. However, the French new wave, with film directors in their twenties, changed all that. Suddenly, kids had a lot of buying power and they started to buy young people's music. Instead of buying Donald Peers, who was a man in his forties who sang in a dinner jacket, they created their own heroes. So, to direct these young 'heroes' the producers had to turn to young directors.

'I'd directed a nudist film called *Some Like It Cool*, which cost £9,000 and featured nudists playing volley ball – there was no sex in it at all – and the film made £120,000 in four weeks. Nat Cohen at Anglo-Amalgamated had seen some of my short films, and I'd written second features for him too, but I think what really amazed him was the fact that someone could make that much money in four weeks on a film that cost £9,000. He wanted in on that!

'So, through the producer David Deutsch, I was brought in to direct *Play It Cool* which Anglo financed. I'd never been in a studio in my life. I'd been making documentaries, short films and comedies, all on location, and the reason I made them on location was because I couldn't possibly afford to build sets. So you can imagine it was an incredible thing to be told that I was going to make a film at Pinewood. However, to be honest, I didn't really want to go to a studio because the film was about a young chap with a band of his own that played in coffee bars, and the story followed him around the new nightclubs in London, where he was hoping to find this heiress he was pursuing. As I knew these clubs, I said that's where we should be going to the real places, which would give us a really interesting documentary on life in London. They said no, no, films are made in studios and that's that.

'The film was really made because of Billy Fury, who was a very big star at the time. We were making what was meant to be Britain's first 'Twist' film, but the 'Twist' hadn't come to England in 1961 and so nobody 'twisted'! The few people who we found that could do it, were brought on as 'twist instructors' and they gave the kids – hundreds of them – lessons. I had a megaphone

Right: Play It Cool, *with Billy Fury (centre foreground) and Richard Wattis, Jeremy Bulloch, Keith Hamshere and Ray Brooks in support.*

through which I'd scream 'Everybody twist!' Then the sound man, Dudley Messenger, proceeded to play bloody Brahms or Beethoven through the loudspeakers. He was a real giggle. I was always using this loud-hailer, and one day I was shouting something through it and all of a sudden 26 loud-hailers came down from the ceiling on the end of some string. It was fun with Dudley!'

Fun it certainly was, and stories were rife about how enjoyable it was to be on this particular Pinewood set, so much so the *Daily Sketch* even ran an article: 'ALL PATHS LEAD TO MIKE THE MAGNET ... Actors leave their own films and join the crush ... What's going on? Why is Janet Munro, a few minutes ago sobbing glycerine tears in *Life for Ruth*, now laughing real salty tears? ... All you need is a few minutes on the set of *Play It Cool*.'

'I was rather exuberant you see,' Winner confesses, 'and it became the set everyone had to visit. I remember Roger Moore saying that he first met me on that set, as did Sean Connery. It was like a cabaret! It was a five-week shoot with a £72,000 budget. It wasn't particularly difficult to do, but then came the time to release it. There were two options open to you then: a run on the Odeon (Rank) chain or the ABC. If you couldn't get either of them, you were dead. Well, both chains refused to play the film, but Nat Cohen persuaded them to try it out on three screens, one of which was in Luton. It was actually one of the great moments of my life. We went to Luton and the cinema was besieged – you couldn't get in. The kids had been so starved of their own entertainment that they were fighting to see the film. It was an enormous success and then played the whole circuit. Unfortunately I didn't have a percentage share, just the £1,500 fee to direct.'

On the adjacent stage Terence Young was directing another film for Albert 'Cubby' Broccoli, who by this time was in partnership with fellow producer Harry Saltzman. This lavish spy thriller, featuring a relatively unknown leading man, was called *Dr. No* (see page 109). Also shooting, with an all-star cast that included Margaret Rutherford, Ron Moody, Terry-Thomas and Bernard Cribbins, was *The Mouse on the Moon*, in which the denizens of the duchy of Grand Fenwick accidentally discover a marvellous rocket fuel – their own home-made wine.

The film was admirably directed by Richard Lester, who later returned to Pinewood to direct the *Superman* movies. 'I got *The Mouse on the Moon* through Peter Sellers,' recalls Lester, 'as I'd worked with him on the Goon Show and he recommended me to the producer, Walter Shenson. The script was duly sent to me – I thought it rather good – and Walter then invited me to lunch at Pinewood. During lunch we agreed a deal and I signed to direct. Walter then asked if I'd like to see the sets. From the restaurant he led me out on to the backlot. There he proudly showed me Cornel Wilde's sets for *Lancelot and Guinevere*. "Here they are!" he said. Apparently, to save money, Walter had done a deal to buy the sets when Cornel's film wrapped – even though they were of a totally different period to our movie! That didn't seem to matter to Walter, and that was my first experience of Pinewood. Rather bizarre to say the least.'

Janet Munro starred as a Welsh girl who sets off in search of wealth and success in *Bitter Harvest*, while Oliver Reed took the lead in *The Party's Over*, which was later disowned by the Rank Organisation because of a necrophiliac sequence. Less controversially, 'Cubby' Broccoli and Harry Saltzman made their only non-Bond film for Eon Productions, *Call Me Bwana*, with Bob Hope, Anita Ekberg and Lionel Jeffries in a farcical tale set in the African jungle.

'We didn't get quite as far as Africa,' says Lionel Jeffries. 'More like Gerrards Cross golf course [a mile or so from the studio] and we shot it for Africa. They planted plastic palm trees and imported three giraffes, an elephant and a zebra. They used to let the animals out at night to roam around the course and just close the gate. Then we returned to the studio backlot in the freezing winter, knocked the snow off the potted palms and pretended it was Africa. It was crazy – I mean, it was so cold you could see our breath. But it was wonderful fun all the same.'

'The original intention,' recalls Clive Reed, first assistant director on the movie, 'was to shoot the entire film on location in Kenya, but the fun of the film was in the gags and facial reactions, which did not require the cast to be in an actual African location. A second unit shot various convoy shots travelling through the bush: actual jungle is not very plentiful in Kenya. The exterior camp sequences were shot on a large stage, the "jungle" sequences in Black Park with the addition of a few creepers and banana plants.' An in-joke followed in Eon's *From Russia With Love* (1963), where a hoarding concealing an escape route for one of the villains centres on Anita Ekberg's mouth in the poster for *Call Me Bwana*.

The period from 1952 to 1962 had seen a turnaround at Pinewood. No longer was the studio solely dependent upon Rank Organisation films to fill the stages; indeed, there were just as many 'renters' as Rank films coming in. The press, meanwhile, predicted an imminent upturn in cinema attendance and brought into question the

Organisation's closure of over half its cinema screens. Davis retorted that far from closing too many, he had not closed enough. But only 374 screens remained. Audiences were declining at an alarming rate and Rank films were not making the returns on investment that they once had. Had it not been for Xerox, the Organisation would have folded.

However, Davis's investment in Xerox was not the calculated business move he often claimed, but more a stroke of tremendous good fortune, according to Cyril Howard. 'Xerox was basically a dry printing process, and consisted of very basic technology at the time. Davis got on well with the man behind the idea [Joe Wilson] and decided to take a punt. He had no real idea of how successful it might become. I mean, would you – as a seasoned accountant and businessman – say that a dry printing process would provide more profit than a vast entertainment and leisure conglomerate? As luck would have it, it did.'

'Cyril is right about it being pure luck,' confirms Davis's ex-wife Dinah Sheridan, 'as I was in on the Xerox thing with JD and it was decided on the flip of a half crown coin – he couldn't decide whether to go in or not, and that decided it.

On 6 June 1962, Lord Rank announced his intended retirement as chairman and that he was to become the first Life President of the company. All Rank's employees signed a special commemorative book of thanks, totalling 28,066 signatures in all. Lord Rank was held in tremendously high regard by each and every member of his staff, especially John Davis, who succeeded him as chairman. Davis was consciously moving the Organisation, of which he now had almost total control, away from film production and was keen to concentrate instead on its more profitable divisions, including bingo and holidays. Lord Rank never interfered with Davis' running of the Organisation, but did keep in daily touch and always lent support and advice when required. The Organisation was now a very profitable proposition, worth almost £90 million. John Davis had certainly achieved what he was charged to do. ■

Left: Carry On Sergeant *with Norman Rossington and Kenneth Williams – they don't like it up 'em!*

Right: *Peter Rogers, the producer of the* Carry On *series.*

The Carry On series has filmed in every nook and cranny of Pinewood Studios, never venturing far from Britain's premier studio, as June Whitfield came to realise. 'I was delighted when offered a part in *Carry On Abroad* and wondered where in sunny Europe we would be filming. Alas, the location turned out to be a car park at Pinewood!'

Pinewood's exteriors have doubled for just about everything: the mansion as a hospital (*Nurse*), clinic (*Again Doctor*) and Indian high commission (*Khyber*); Car Park One as Sid James' taxi yard (*Cabby*); the timber yard as WC Boggs' toilet factory (*At Your Convenience*); the cherry orchard as camping fields (*Camping, Behind*) and an Army gun installation (*England*), to name only a few.

Peter Rogers was the creative genius behind the saucy series. His entry into the film business was initially as a writer, and he confesses that even at the age of 14 he used to write plays for his own amusement. Upon leaving school he joined a country newspaper in Kent, before turning to the theatre for a spell as Auriol Lee's assistant. During this time a couple of his plays were staged in London; one lasted a week while the other, a comedy, lasted ten days. And so the seed was sown – a career in comedy beckoned. After the war, and a bout of cerebro-spinal meningitis, Rogers concentrated on writing for radio. This lead to him being contacted by J Arthur Rank's Religious Films outfit, which he subsequently joined as a scriptwriter. After a spell in journalism, he was engaged as a writer by Sydney Box, having come up with ideas for Box's production *Holiday Camp*.

By the time the *Carry Ons* came around, Rogers had progressed through the ranks to become a prolific producer in his own right. He had also married Sydney's sister Betty, whom he had courted during his sojourn at the Box-run Islington Studios. Most importantly for the Pinewood story,

he became the first 'small' independent to move into the studio. It was also the studio to which Betty Box had moved when Rank amalgamated all his film interests under one roof. 'Betty and I had offices next to each other but we never met,' he recalls. 'We never discussed scripts at home or anywhere else. We were married rivals.'

Gerald Thomas was the younger brother of director Ralph and had gained experience of editing and second unit direction on his brother's picture *Above Us the Waves*. When Rogers was commissioned by the Children's Film Foundation to produce a picture called *Circus Friends*, he gave Gerald Thomas – who was under contract to him at the time – his first chance to direct. The film attracted good notices on its release in 1956 and so began a partnership that lasted almost 40 years.

Several features followed including the successful *Time Lock*, starring the young Sean Connery. The duo were casting envious glances at their relations' success with the *Doctor* films, however, and decided to take that form of comedy and expand upon it. A much-rejected treatment of R F Delderfield's *The Bull Boys* arrived on Rogers' desk. It dealt with the enforced enrolment into national service of a ballet company. He noted its

A RIGHT CARRY ON

potential and wanted his contract scriptwriter, Norman Hudis, to look over the treatment and replace the ballet dancers with a newly married couple who were desperately trying to consummate their union. The result? *Carry On Sergeant.*

They received backing of £75,000 from Anglo-Amalgamated, mainly owing to Stuart Levy's enthusiasm. 'I fixed up a television series, *Ivanhoe*, with Roger Moore at Beaconsfield,' says Peter Rogers, 'so there wasn't any room for my own picture. I had to come to Pinewood; I'd pushed myself out of my own studio!' Fellow filmmakers were critical of Rogers' relocation to Pinewood, feeling that the studio was far too expensive for a modest picture like his. 'When we first came here, people said to me that I was sticking my neck out,' reveals Rogers. 'I stuck my neck out in as much as I said that I only wanted a limited labour force. I didn't want them putting sparks and chippies on my set because they happened to have an empty set next door. And the works committee agreed on one condition. John Davis had banned end-of-picture parties at Pinewood. I came in as an independent and the union bosses said to me, "We agree to all this,

Peter, if you give us an end-of-picture party." And so they started up again.'

Production commenced on 24 March 1958 with the Queen's Barracks, Guildford, used for the Army locations. Bill Owen, who became best known in later life as Compo in the BBC's comedy series *The Last of the Summer Wine*, played Corporal Bill Copping. 'I remember that we weren't particularly welcome at Pinewood, with a limited time to make the film. If I remember correctly this was due to the type of film it was. A "corny comedy" was considered a little "below stairs" for Pinewood.'

Sergeant was a massive box-office success, however. Regular team members Charles Hawtrey, Kenneth Williams, Kenneth Connor and Hattie Jacques were part of the cast but it was TV's future *Doctor Who*, William Hartnell, who was top-billed as the abrasive Sergeant Grimshawe.

The second film, *Carry On Nurse*, was an even bigger success. It played for two-and-a-half years

Left: *Hattie Jaques in* Carry On Nurse - *that's a funny way to take a temperature.*

Bottom left: *Car Park One became Sid James' taxi yard in* Carry On Cabby.

in Los Angeles and launched *Carry On* fever. Shirley Eaton stole the headlines with her sexy performance and caused many a man's heart to flutter. *Nurse* ensured the future of the series and Rogers announced the titles for the next four films. 'I used to think up the titles in the bath,' he admits. 'Every one of them.'

Carry On Teacher followed in 1959 and then Sid James ushered in the dawn of a new *Carry On* era when he made his début in *Carry On Constable*. Many say that it was James who really became the epitome of *Carry On* humour. Indeed most of the best films feature Sid in such memorable roles as Gladstone Screwer, the Rumpo Kid, Sid Boggle and the Reverend Flasher, while his dirty laugh became the signature for the series. 'He was a kid at heart,' said Gerald Thomas in 1992. 'In *Carry On Cowboy* I would find him behind the scenery twirling a six-gun and trying to practice a

quick draw. And he liked a gamble. He would run a sweepstake every day on how many minutes of film we would shoot.

Constable was followed by *Carry On Regardless*, *Carry On Cruising* and *Carry On Cabby* (which was written as *Call Me a Cab* before it was decided to make it another entry in the *Carry On* series). *Cabby* marked the *Carry On* debuts of screenwriter Talbot Rothwell and series mainstay Jim Dale.

By this stage a regular team had been assembled on both sides of the camera. The acting regulars were later augmented by Bernard Bresslaw, Terry Scott, Barbara Windsor and Jack Douglas – the best of British comic talent. 'It was always a happy team,' says Rogers. 'It was like a repertory company. The restaurant staff used to look forward to a *Carry On* coming in because they would all lunch in there together. And it was hilarious. The laughter that went on was very noisy.'

The films were famed for coming in on time and within budget. Cinematographer Alan Hume recalls that 'We only used one camera, very seldom two. There were six weeks of shooting, five days a week and no overtime. We just had to work bloody quick. But Gerald Thomas was a very clever man. He was an editor first, so knew exactly what he needed'

For *Carry On Jack*, Peter Rogers originally cast Liz Fraser in the female lead but she was unable to take the part because of other commitments. In the event, the part went to John Mills's daughter Juliet in her only *Carry On* appearance. *Jack* is not such an innuendo-filled romp as the others in the series and is often overlooked as a result. However, Eric Rogers's music score captured the attention, with rousing versions of 'A Life On The Ocean Wave' and 'God Save The King'. Jack Gardner was assistant editor on many of the films and worked closely with Eric Rogers.

'He composed the music for all of the later films,' says Gardner. 'The music sessions were hilarious. We recorded at Anvil, down the road in Denham, and Eric would walk in every morning carrying a violin case. He'd go up to his podium and draw his musicians around him, then he'd open up the case to reveal two bottles of scotch and a dozen shot glasses. They were usually quite

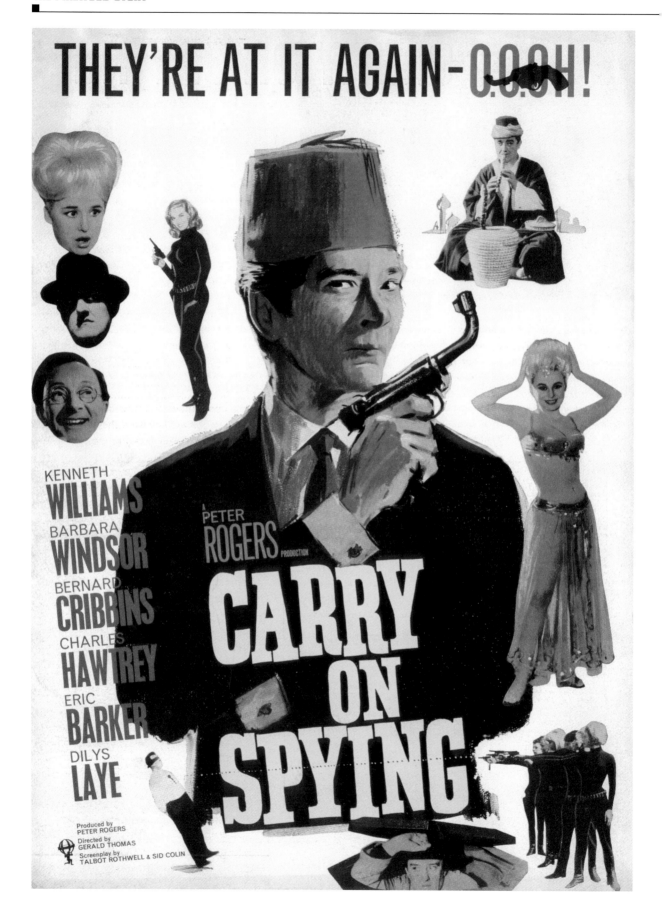

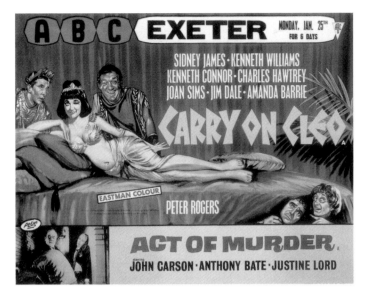

Below: *'Have you ever seen one like that before?' Cleopatra (Amanda Barrie) shows Mark Antony (Sid James) her asp in* Carry On Cleo.

merry by mid-day but played brilliantly!'

The popularity of the films reached a new high when they began sending up other popular films, the first example of which was *Carry On Spying* – which was also the first to feature Barbara Windsor. 'That's my favourite,' says Alan Hume, 'because it was a bit more challenging. It was a spoof on James Bond really. It was shot in black and white and was a bit more creative than the others.' But the Bond producers' feathers were ruffled. Harry Saltzman stepped in to prevent Charles Hawtrey's character from being called Charlie Bond 001 1/2 and it was changed to Charlie Bind 000. Moreover, he also complained about the poster artwork, which closely resembled that of *From Russia With Love*.

Carry On Cleo was next. The film is best remembered for the immortal line when Kenneth Williams' Caesar, realising that all his supporters are turning against him, declares 'Infamy! Infamy! They've all got it in for me!' Easily the most lavish in the series, this was Pinewood's sweet rejoinder to the fiasco that had attended Fox's Cleopatra epic when it occupied the studio in 1960. As with *Spying*, however, there were complaints about the poster artwork, creating a few

Right: *Happy birthday Kenny. On set* Screaming!
*with Harry H Corbett, Kenneth Williams, Tom
Clegg, Angela Douglas and Peter Butterworth.*

tense moments for Rogers when a court case was called to settle the dispute. The court found in favour of the *Carry On* team.

'We couldn't be at Pinewood without using the facilities here, the gardens and the vast lot of course, where they have now built the new stages,' says Rogers, 'but there was this thing known as the "Irish village" which we turned into all sorts of things. We had it as Cairo in *Cleo*. That's where this myth comes from about using other people's sets. You don't use other people's sets, you re-vamp them as stock.'

Following *Carry On Cowboy*, Harry H Corbett took time off from his role in the TV comedy *Steptoe and Son* to star in *Carry On Screaming!* – a spoof on the Hammer horror films. But more horrible things were happening behind the scenes. Following the death of Anglo's Stuart Levy, Rogers found himself at odds with Levy's partner, Nat Cohen. Levy had been a staunch supporter of the *Carry On* films, but Cohen had made no secret of the fact that he didn't like them and felt that they were bad for the company's image. During his long period with Anglo-Amalgamated, it was suggested to Rogers, many times, that he should leave Pinewood for a less expensive studio.

'I was pressured for a long time by ABC to go to Elstree because they exhibited the films and Anglo distributed them. I said "No, I'm not going to Elstree. If you want me to go there you won't have them." I told them that I knew Pinewood, I knew the working staff, I got on very well with the working committee and the people on the floor. I didn't want to go to a new studio and have to get used to new staff, new union bosses, new chippies. So I stayed here.'

The films' Pinewood base was cemented when Rogers struck a deal with Rank to finance the *Carry On* series after Levy's death. One of the first changes, albeit a temporary one, was to drop the 'Carry On' prefix – John Davis was nervous about being seen to use another distributors' title. The first under the Rank deal was originally called *Don't Lose Your Head* and was followed by *Follow That Camel*. Both were *Carry Ons* in all but name, and the prefix was restored for their third collabo-

ration, as well as being added to *Head* and *Camel* on their re-release.

Camel saw top American comedian Phil Silvers lead the cast. He took the part which was originally to have been played by Sid James, who was unavailable in the wake of a major heart attack. 'Rank's idea,' explains Rogers, 'was that in order to sell a picture in America you need an American artist, which I don't agree with. But when they're putting up the money you can't disagree with them. The film worked but Silvers didn't. He didn't become part of the team.'

Camel's script, a spoof on *Beau Geste*, was about the French Foreign Legion and the regulars, aware of the new financing deal with Rank, were hoping for glamorous Mediterranean sunshine. But they were disappointed to find that they would be going no further than Camber Sands in Sussex.

Alan Hume recalls problems they experienced there with the eponymous camel. 'It came from a zoo in Surrey and when it got down to Camber Sands and they took it out of the truck, they walked it towards the sands and it wouldn't go. It was so used to walking on tarmac that it refused to walk on sand! Eventually they cajoled it into doing so.' Adds Peter Rogers, 'We laid emergency airfield landing strips under the sand to be exact, and the camel was agreeable to walking on those!'

To many, *Carry On … Up the Khyber* represents the pinnacle of the series and both director and producer rated it as their personal favourite. 'It has fantastic production values when you consider the cost of it,' says Rogers. 'That dinner party

scene was shot on the smallest stage in the studio – not much bigger than my office.'

'That was a wonderful scene,' agrees special effects man Bert Luxford, 'and one I'll never forget for a very good reason. During all the chaos and gunfire, the room gradually falls apart and one sequence called for a bottle of wine that Sid James was pouring to be hit by a stray bullet and smash. So I made up a resin bottle with a little charge in the base and a trigger in the cork; I explained to Sid that all he had to do was press the trigger and it would go pop. He wasn't keen at all. He was afraid that it wouldn't look realistic and said "No, you've got to shoot it out of my hand." I couldn't believe it! He was insistent though. So there was I with a .22 rifle aiming at the bottle, shaking like mad, and I said to Gerald Thomas "Gerry, whatever you do, don't tap me on the shoulder!" (He usually did whenever he wanted me to do my bit.) Anyway, off we went. I hit the bottle; it exploded, the wine went all over Sid and Gerry came bouncing over saying how mar-

vellous it was. I was as white as a sheet.'

Beddgelert, at the foot of Mount Snowdon in North Wales, stood in for the Khyber Pass. Sixty local farmers were hired as extras and hostile tribesmen, prompting Thomas to comment that he felt like Cecil B DeMille. 'I had a letter from a man who had served in the forces and had been to the actual Khyber Pass,' swears Rogers, 'and he said he'd seen the film and recognised the area!'

Sid James went to the first screening of *Carry On … Up the Khyber* and reported: 'I never heard so much laughing from an audience in my life, they

killed themselves. In fact they were laughing so loud you could hardly hear the dialogue, a lot of it was completely lost, and it was one of those slightly blue jokes that got the biggest laugh of the night.'

Indeed, *Khyber* seemed to re-launch the series into a purple patch epitomised by the innuendo-laden banter written by Talbot Rothwell for Sid James and Barbara Windsor. And in *Carry On Camping* the bubbly blonde played her most notorious scene, in which Kenneth Williams presides over a rigorous exercise sequence and instructs the girls by yelling 'Now let's see those chests come out!'

'I'm always asked about Barbara's bra,' Bert Luxford laughs. 'I really can't understand the fascination. I mean, I've blown up houses and streets and nobody asks about them! Actually it was done with a snatch cord. It wasn't a fishing line as they say. You couldn't get a bra off with a fishing line – even if you had a very good sea rod. It had to be done with piano wire, a bit of wood and then the old-fashioned method of walking a few yards. I never saw a thing because I had my back to the scene. Once I got the tension, Gerry tapped me on the shoulder and then whoosh!'

Camping was set during the summer but was actually filmed in and around Pinewood during the autumn of 1968. The mud was sprayed green and the rapidly turning leaves were also painted to create the desired summer effect. The film was another huge success and is to 'contemporary' *Carry On* what *Khyber* was to the historical variety.

Sid James's final *Carry On* film was *Carry On Dick* in 1974. Although the series continued, a *Carry On* without Sid just wasn't the same. However, Thomas's ability to get the best out of his actors still left us with some wonderfully funny scenes from the later films. Audience figures were declining, however, and the films were feeling the heat from the even saucier *Confessions* pictures, starring Robin Askwith – who coincidentally had appeared in *Carry On Girls* in 1973.

Rogers' association with Rank ended with the compilation, *That's Carry On* (1977), which included scenes from the very best of the films and required highly skilled negotiations on the part of the producer in getting Anglo and Rank to agree to a 50/50 release deal. 'The idea came from the MGM compilation *That's Entertainment*,' says Rogers, 'and its success led us to thinking about further possibilities, but perhaps for TV.'

Meanwhile, mindful of the success of the *Confessions* films, Rogers announced plans for *Carry On Emmannuelle*, for which he received backing from Hemdale. It was a parody of the soft porn films starring Sylvia Kristel as (the slightly differently spelt) Emmanuelle. 'What we thought we'd do was try and make an X-rated *Carry On*,' Rogers remembers, 'but it wasn't X enough. That's

why the films were never very successful in France – because they do it and we talk about it.' The film performed poorly at the box office and left the series with an unsavoury and outdated image among prospective backers.

The eighties came and went without a single *Carry On* feature going into production. But the films continued to flourish on TV and video, despite the all-pervasive stranglehold of political correctness during that decade. Furthermore, the compilation shows *That's Carry On* and *What a Carry On* drew millions of peak-time viewers. 'Those compilations took nine months you know,' says Rogers. 'That was for a six-part series – and we did lots of series! So the *Carry On* films didn't disappear as such, because we were busy with the TV shows. There were millions of feet of film to go through for a start!'

Rumours continued to circulate of a new film in the pipeline. 'We had a let down with *Carry On Down Under*,' Rogers recalls. 'We'd been going to do *Carry On Dallas* but ran into legal difficulties. So I said, "Right – let's forget America, we'll go to Australia." We did the script, Gerald went over there and looked at some locations and the money was there. Then some bloody politician who got involved ran off with all the money! So we never made it.'

The fans finally got their wish, however, when *Carry On Columbus* was announced as the 31st film in the series. Says Rogers, 'John Goldstone brought it to us. He'd wanted to do a picture with Gerald for a long time. It was the anniversary of Columbus unearthing America.' It soon became apparent, however, that the old magic was gone. What was left of the old team – Jim Dale, Bernard Cribbins, June Whitfield, Leslie Phillips, Jon Pertwee and Jack Douglas – were back on board but the new comedy faces (Nigel Planer, Alexei Sayle, Maureen Lipman and the like) just didn't fit the bill.

'The scripts were nothing without the artists,' agrees Alan Hume, who was back as cinematographer, 'and of course by *Columbus* they'd all but gone. I'd worked so much with Peter and Gerald and owed them so much that I turned down a very big picture to do *Columbus*, and I'm very pleased I did really.'

'The script wasn't very funny,' admits Rogers. 'I

kept telling them that. The distributors and finance people insisted on all these new names – Rik Mayall, Julian Clary and all that lot – and I said they wouldn't fit in. I was right, apart from Sara Crowe. She's such a fantastic artist, she could fit in anywhere.'

However, there was still great fun to be had when making a *Carry On*, as Audrey Skinner, Peter Rogers' personal assistant, recalls. 'The film's production designer, Harry Pottle, stayed at a local guesthouse throughout his stint on the film. It's a lovely place, but run by nuns! They have quite a few Pinewood folk staying there, but told Harry that they'd never been to the studio – so he invited them over. Half the convent must have come. They walked down the main road outside the operating office, much to the bemusement of the studio manager, and down onto the stage where the boat sequences were being shot. Nobody knew that Harry had invited the nuns down, and so the cast and crew thought they were extras in the scene ... quite a few of them were seen to flick through their scripts trying to find where the nuns came into the sequence, and became quite concerned when they couldn't find mention!'

Columbus seems very much the end of the *Carry On* series, but Pinewood owes its longest-resident producer and his team a huge debt of gratitude. When the complex was short of product, there was always a *Carry On* just around the corner to fill the gap, prompting the legendary producer to admit that he benefited from the studio's

quiet times. And by exploding the myth that Pinewood was expensive, with all sorts of crew-members to put on a film's payroll, he ensured the studio's continued existence. Rogers still maintains his office at the studio, which he visits daily. 'I enjoyed making the *Carry On* films,' he reflects. 'They were very happy times. But, having made nearly a hundred films, I'll only be known for 31!'

In 1990, Rogers and Thomas received the Lifetime Achievement Award for Film Comedy at the very first British Comedy Awards ceremony, held at the London Palladium. Thomas died in 1993 and two years later the *Carry On* team received the London Film Critics' Circle Special Award for 'Carrying On' at their 16th annual awards ceremony.

And on 26 April 1995, the British Comedy Society held their first 'Pinewood Tribute' with a plaque unveiled in honour of Gerald Thomas. The brainchild of the British Comedy Society's Morris Bright, the event attracted 300 fans along with celebrity guests Bernard Cribbins, Suzanne Danielle, Jack Douglas, Fenella Fielding, Peter Gilmore, Valerie Leon, Norman Rossington and charity auctioneer Jim Davidson. Gerald's widow Barbara and their children also attended as did his long-time collaborator Peter Rogers with his wife Betty Box. The success of the event, during which the blue plaque in honour of Gerald Thomas was unveiled above the entrance to the administration block, prompted Pinewood to offer the corridor leading to the main stages to the BCS as a 'Hall of Fame'.

Facing page: Christopher Columbus (Jim Dale) leads the Carry On series into an uncertain future in Carry On Columbus.

Below: A right old Carry On. The series' 40th anniversary reunion at Pinewood.

Further annual tributes have been staged at the studios. In 1996, the *Doctor* films and the team behind them – Betty Box and Ralph Thomas – were honoured with cast members Shirley Eaton, Muriel Pavlow and (absent from Pinewood since 1963) Sir Dirk Bogarde in attendance. In 1997, the society paid tribute to Norman Wisdom on his 50th anniversary in show business; friends included the recently knighted Sir Donald Sinden, while Dame Thora Hird unveiled a plaque in the Hall of Fame and Norman's 89-year-old producer, Hugh Stewart, made a speech in the diminutive comedian's honour.

1998 was a particularly busy year for the BCS. In April, the official 40th Anniversary *Carry On* gala reunion attracted over 300 fans as well as Jack Douglas, Leslie Phillips, June Whitfield, Barbara Windsor and the writer of the first six films, Norman Hudis, who had flown in especially from his home in America. In October, at the end of interior filming, the world's longest running comedy series, *Last of the Summer Wine*, also achieved immortality in the Hall of Fame. The century was rounded off on 26 September 1999 with a special event in memory of Morecambe and Wise, who themselves made three features at Pinewood. The

new century began with the unveiling of a plaque in honour of Betty Box in January 2000. The BCS events at Pinewood have raised in excess of £100,000 for charity and welcomed over 100 celebrity guests and 1,000 fans and admirers. ∎

THE CARRY ONS (year of release):

1958 SERGEANT
1959 NURSE, TEACHER
1960 CONSTABLE
1961 REGARDLESS
1962 CRUISING
1963 CABBY, JACK
1964 SPYING, CLEO
1965 COWBOY
1966 SCREAMING!, DON'T LOSE YOUR HEAD
1967 FOLLOW THAT CAMEL, DOCTOR
1968 ... UP THE KHYBER
1969 CAMPING, AGAIN DOCTOR
1970 UP THE JUNGLE, LOVING
1971 HENRY, AT YOUR CONVENIENCE
1972 MATRON, ABROAD
1973 GIRLS
1974 DICK
1975 BEHIND
1976 ENGLAND
1977 THAT'S CARRY ON [COMPILATION]
1978 EMMANNUELLE
1992 COLUMBUS

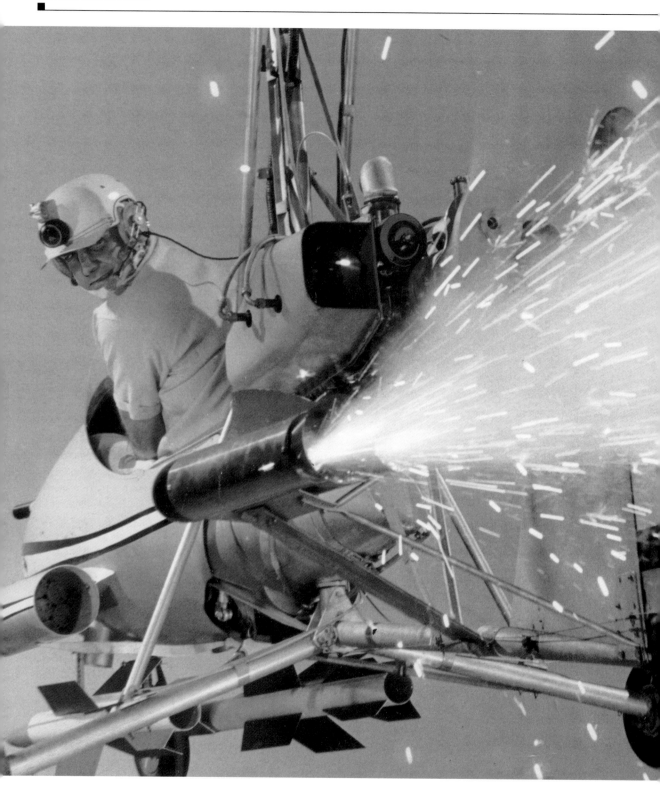

10

Left: *Aboard Little Nellie James Bond (Sean Connery) evades his SPECTRE pursuers in* You Only Live Twice.

Below left: *James Bond creator Ian Fleming (centre) with series producers Harry Saltzman and Albert 'Cubby' Broccoli.*

Below right: *'Bond ... James Bond.' 007 meets Sylvia Trench (Eunice Gayson) in* Dr. No.

Those famous words as uttered by Sean Connery in the first Bond film, *Dr. No*, have been called the greatest one-liner in cinema history. Twenty-one films spanning almost 40 years and box-office grosses running into billions confirm that 007 is the most successful film series ever shot at Pinewood Studios, or anywhere else for that matter.

Ian Fleming created secret agent James Bond in the 1953 novel *Casino Royale* and a further 13 books followed. His exciting mix of intrigue, action, adventure and sex, combined with travelogue-style narratives, seemed perfect for moviemakers. Despite this, the author experienced many years of disappointment in attempting to sell the film rights. Reactions to Commander Bond were decidedly cool to begin with, as Betty Box demonstrated by sending Fleming a rejection slip after reading *Casino Royale*, reportedly saying that the best place for the book was the waste-paper bin.

With the publication of *Moonraker* in 1955, however, things began to change. Actor John Payne offered $1,000 for a nine month option with a further $10,000 if the projected film went into production. Meanwhile, Ian Hunter of the Rank Organisation had begun negotiations of his own

regarding *Moonraker*. Payne grew tired of the endless wrangling that ensued and withdrew, leaving Rank in pole position. But Rank seemed unsure how to handle the Bond character and in 1959 Fleming's agent bought the rights back from them. The only *Moonraker* adaptation to surface was a production for South African radio the year before, with Bob Holness (latterly the avuncular quizmaster of *Blockbusters* and *Call My Bluff*) as 007.

Producer Albert 'Cubby' Broccoli had also made an attempt to obtain the rights during this period, but was let down by the unenthusiastic response of his then partner Irving Allen. But in 1961, the Bond opportunity came along again when Broccoli met the Canadian-born producer Harry Saltzman. Saltzman had experienced some success with the film versions of two John Osborne plays, *Look Back In Anger* and *The Entertainer*, but the option he held on the Bond stories was running out when he met Broccoli. They formed Eon Productions and set about securing finance for a series of films.

Broccoli's connections in Hollywood saw Eon emerge from a meeting with the top brass at United Artists with a $1m deal to bring the first James Bond adventure to the big screen. In his

'BOND ... JAMES BOND.'

autobiography, Broccoli admitted to feelings of apprehension. 'I couldn't ignore the fact that they [the books] had been around for a long time, and none of the leading British or American producers had made a serious pitch for them.'

Among the many actors said to be under consideration for the role of 007 were Patrick McGoohan, David Niven, Richard Johnson and Roger Moore. The producers plumped for a little-known Scottish actor called Sean Connery. 'Sean had the balls for the part,' Broccoli wrote. 'I was convinced he was the closest we'd get to Fleming's superhero.'

Terence Young, who had worked with Broccoli on *The Red Beret* and *Tank Force*, was an inspired choice for the director's chair and the film's distinctive look was the work of production designer Ken Adam. 'When *Dr. No* came up,' he remembers, 'I tried to persuade the producers to go to Shepperton. Pinewood was an enormous place and quite frightening to me because I'd just started in films. Up until that time I had worked in small studios like Riverside and Twickenham, so you can imagine how frighteningly large Pinewood seemed.'

Despite this initial wariness, Adam found that the studio was able to offer him more freedom of expression than he had ever experienced before. He had clear and original ideas for *Dr. No* which not only set the style for subsequent Bond adventures but also influenced numerous movies outside the 007 franchise. 'I wanted to come up with new ideas for Bond,' Adam continues, 'using new materials and new technology, and I thought it was about time someone made a film that expressed our technological era, while at the same time looking ahead with tongue-in-cheek.'

Given that the film's budget was $1m, there wasn't the relatively huge sum available for design that would become common in later years. Adam

was officially allocated £14,000. 'It was a ridiculous budget and I said I couldn't do it for that. The producers told me not to worry as they had £6,000 stashed away as contingency. I knew I couldn't rely on that being the case, as there were completion guarantees to meet and so on. But, in fact, I think it came to £21,000.'

Dr. No quickly recouped its costs and was a gigantic success. *From Russia With Love* was quickly lined up to follow. One of Fleming's finest Bond novels, it became one of the most realistic of the Bond films. The casting was conspicuously good and the film introduced the first pre-credit sequence, or 'teaser', which was to become a fixture of the series. Shot in the park-like gardens of Pinewood, with the administration building becoming the headquarters of the villainous SPECTRE, the sequence depicted a training mission where an enemy agent tracked and ultimately killed a Bond lookalike. Production designer Syd Cain made good use of Pinewood's exteriors, particularly its statues and ornamental bridge, in creating a very atmospheric, nocturnal setting. It was dubbed the 'renaissance garden', probably because director Terence Young's handling of the sequence was inspired by a similar setting in the 1961 art house classic *L'Année dernière* (*Last Year In Marienbad*).

The gardens played host to other scenes in the film. When SPECTRE agent Rosa Klebb (Lotte Lenya) arrives by helicopter to inspect assassin Red Grant (Robert Shaw), the house can clearly be seen in the background. The training camp was also constructed near the house, with the gypsy camp sequences set up on the exterior (paddock) lot.

Pedro Armendariz portrayed Bond's ally, Kerim Bey, and it emerged during filming that he was suffering from a terminal illness and was anxious to leave his family his fee from the picture. Instead of re-casting the part, the producers decided to shoot all his scenes in a two-week period, completing all his close-ups by June. 'We shot all his scenes out of continuity,' said Young, 'and then I played the part of Armendariz with Sean and all the other actors without him being there. We did the gypsy encampment last, and as we got the last shot I said "Cut it, print it. On your way, Pedro, go home and get some rest."' Armendariz committed suicide in his hospital bed before the film was released.

The first real Bond gadget was introduced in *From Russia With Love*, and it marked the first appearance of Desmond Llewelyn as 'Q'. (Peter Burton had played the part of 'the armourer', Major Boothroyd, in *Dr. No*, but was unavailable for the second film.) Q presents 007 with an attaché case which eventually comes into its own during Bond's fight with Red Grant on the Orient Express; it contains 50 gold sovereigns, a hidden throwing knife, a folding sniper's rifle and a tin of talcum powder concealing a tear gas cartridge. The task of creating the case fell to Bert Luxford in

Pinewood's special effects department, and so began his long association with the Bond films. There were two cases in reality, mainly composed of aluminium but with a chamois leather covering which, the unions decreed, had to be applied by upholsterers rather than Luxford himself. Luxford was also responsible for the mythical decoding device, the Lektor, on which the plot hinges.

The confrontation between Bond and Grant on the Orient Express remains probably the best fight sequence in the entire series. It was filmed at Pinewood and virtually all of it was choreographed by Young. Peter Hunt excelled himself with the fast-paced editing and also suggested the use of a third free camera which added an extra dimension to the footage.

From Russia With Love opened to even bigger box-office receipts than *Dr. No*. Despite starting pre-production work on the next film, Terence Young left to work on other projects and was replaced by Guy Hamilton, who had previously been offered *Dr. No*. Hamilton's *Goldfinger* was an international phenomenon. It is generally regarded

as the quintessential Bond film and is fondly remembered for 007's gadget-laden Aston Martin DB5 and the wonderful Fort Knox set. *Goldfinger* was more fantastic, more fun and more spectacular than anything that had gone before.

In the novel, Bond's Aston Martin DBIII has only a handful of 'extras' when compared to the cinematic version. 'The basic gadgetry was my idea,' says Ken Adam, who returned as production designer, 'but [special effects supervisor] Johnny Stears and his team made it all possible. Aston Martin were quite reluctant to let us have a car, because it wasn't one we needed but two. It was decided to get away from the Bentley [Bond's car in the previous film] and come up instead with the sports car of that period. Of course, after the picture came out their sales shot up by 50 per cent.'

Once again Bert Luxford found himself work-

ing on the gimmicks. 'It had so many gadgets to fit in,' he says, 'and yet if you lift the bonnet of a DB5 you'll see that there's only about four inches of space around the engine. They wanted guns coming out of the front, revolving number plates, a phone ... but there wasn't enough room for a radio, let alone anything else. So it all had to be hacked away. It was sacrilege to drill all those holes into a DB5. It was mostly hydraulics – the raising of the bullet proof shield was, as were the over-riders. The ejector seat, however, worked from pneumatics. The driver pressed the button and the lid of the car flew off and the seat shot out. In actual fact it was a tube going up the back of the seat and at the press of a button you had 100lb per square inch of pressure and – whoosh – up it went."

Many critics agree that once Bond pressed that

Facing page top: Route 2.

Facing page bottom left: The replica Fort Knox on Pinewood's back-lot.

Facing page bottom right: James Bond (Sean Connery) lays a trap For Goldfinger (Gert Frobe) during a round of golf.

button, the series changed irrevocably: the spectacular element of the stories would take precedence from then on. This pivotal moment took place near the carpenter's shop and was lit superbly by Ted Moore. 'Of course, it was a dummy that shot up,' Luxford points out, 'a proper mannequin dummy. If any human being had been in there, I doubt he'd have survived. The pressure was tremendous and I think it shot the dummy about 15 feet in the air.'

The famous DB5 chase took place around the studio complex, adjacent to E and A Stages; the same shots were taken from different angles to give the impression of a much bigger 'factory'. Black Park played host to the initial chase, resulting in the death of Tilly Masterson (Tania Mallet), and then it was into the studio and Goldfinger's factory.

Bert Luxford was present on the first night's shooting. 'Bob Simmons, the stuntman, had to drive the car down the main drag towards the powerhouse at Pinewood and crash into a false brick wall. What they didn't tell him was that behind the 'wall' was scaffolding. We'd just finished the car and he ruined it on the first night! Three months' work was destroyed in ten seconds when he drove into that scaffolding. John Stears and I went to the Aston factory in Newport Pagnell to see if they could help us out. They said "Don't worry, we'll have it fixed up in two days." They did too.'

The plot of the film concerned Auric Goldfinger's attempt to contaminate the world's largest gold depository at Fort Knox, and this presented Ken Adam with a major challenge. The filmmakers were not allowed to film inside the actual depository; not even the President of the USA is allowed in there. A young draftsman called Peter Lamont joined Adam's design team and, as he puts it, 'On the first day, Ken came in and placed a bunch of photographs of Fort Knox in front of me. And that was my first job – to design the exterior of the bank for construction on the backlot.'

A full-scale replica of the depository was built on the lot, including the main gate and metal facings and also part of the approach road. At the time it was the most expensive exterior set ever built at Pinewood and reportedly cost in the region of $100,000. The interior, by contrast, was a product of Adam's imagination. 'I quite liked that,' says Adam, 'because I thought it would have inhibited me if I'd seen the real thing. When the whole film deals with the biggest depository in the world, I felt I had to show gold to the audience.'

Broccoli described Adam's set as the work of a genius, with gold stacked 40 feet high, gleaming from behind prison-like bars. In reality, because of its weight, gold isn't stacked more than a few bars high, but, after the film was released, the producers received countless letters asking how they were allowed to film inside Fort Knox.

Among the other sets Adam designed for the film was Goldfinger's 'laser room', where Bond is strapped to a table at the mercy of a powerful beam. It was the first time that a laser had been shown in a film, replacing the rusty buzz saw of the novel. 'There was that famous interview at the time,' Adam continues, 'in the first *Observer* colour supplement. They interviewed me and Ronnie Udell [Pinewood's chief construction manager] and he said almost viciously, "Anything he can draw I can build." I took him up on that. It became our slogan. It was great because that's the sort of spirit that should exist in any film studio. Pinewood was lucky to have this incredible man, who really was unbelievable.'

It has long been thought that Adam would have won an Oscar if he hadn't insisted on being called 'Production Designer' rather than 'Art Director'. In those days only the latter category was recognised by the Academy. 'I wish – and I really mean this – that Ken Adam had won an Oscar for those early films,' says Peter Lamont, himself a winner, in 1998, for *Titanic*. 'He really deserved it as his sets brought so much to the films, and were so fantastic.'

Sean Connery developed his taste for golf on this film, as he had to learn the basics of the game for his match against Goldfinger. The scenes were filmed at Stoke Poges golf club, which is just a few miles north-west of the studio. Some 30-odd years

Left: *Bert Luxford's modified BSA was ridden by SPECTRE assassin Fiona Volpe (Luciana Paluzzi) in* Thunderball.

Below: *Ken Adam's vision of Blofeld's volcanic lair and (right) the stunning realisation.*

later, the Bond crew returned to the club for *Tomorrow Never Dies*, where the interior doubled for a Hamburg hotel.

The success of *Goldfinger* meant that Eon had a bigger budget than ever for the next adventure, *Thunderball*, on which Terence Young returned as director. Much of this film was shot in the Bahamas, with Pinewood used as a production base and for interiors. But the special effects team were once again kept busy creating the many gadgets for the movie, and in particular the BSA motorcycle, complete with front-firing rockets, used by beautiful SPECTRE assassin Fiona Volpe (Luciana Paluzzi). *Thunderball* was even more successful than its predecessor, and remains the biggest money-maker in the entire series.

For *You Only Live Twice*, Commander Bond travelled to Japan for one of his most ambitious adventures. However, it became apparent early on in pre-production that it would be impossible to find any of the locations Fleming had described. 'I spent three weeks with Cubby, Harry, Lewis Gilbert [the director] and Freddie Young [director of photography] in two helicopters, and we covered two thirds of Japan,' Adam remembers. 'We didn't find anything that Fleming had mentioned. Fortunately, almost towards the end of our scout, we found this volcano area in Kyushu, Southern Japan. And that triggered off

the whole thing about putting the villain into an extinct volcano.'

The volcano was then recreated at Pinewood at a cost which exceeded the entire budget of *Dr. No*. 'Cubby was amazing,' Adam continues. 'When he saw my design he asked how much it was going to cost. I had no idea, and just said "About $1 million." He didn't blink an eye! He said if I could do it for $1 million, I should go ahead.'

Once again, Adam was able to call upon the talents of the Pinewood workforce for an undertaking far more elaborate than anything he had previously designed. 'Thank God I had people like Ronnie Udell, because it wasn't a film set as such,' explains Adam. 'There were several hundred tons of steel and the tubular alone would stretch from London to Edinburgh. I had a great team with me – Chip Brown, the builders at Pinewood, the structural engineer and so on. Had it been the Empire State building, they would have known how to cope quite easily. But because this was an unusual structure – an artificial lake, 100 ft up, on a slope, 70 ft in diameter – it was a different kettle of fish.'

The safety aspects of such a set were of paramount importance, especially because a helicopter was required to fly in and out of it. 'That was a huge worry,' admits Adam. 'We nearly lost a Brantley helicopter in Japan as it disappeared for a few minutes after flying into the real volcano. We thought it had crashed. In fact, there were enormous down-drafts and the pilot had great difficulty in getting out. So I was really concerned as I didn't know what conditions we'd encounter in going from the outside into a closed set. I was

keenly aware that if anything went wrong, I would never work in films again. Ronnie had many sleepless nights!'

One of Bond's most memorable toys was an autogyro dubbed 'Little Nellie', which came about when Ken Adam heard a radio interview with Wing Commander Ken Wallis, its creator and pilot. Wallis doubled for Sean Connery in the aerial sequences, wearing only a short-sleeved shirt several hundred feet in the air. Wallis had earlier been invited to demonstrate 'Nellie' at Pinewood for the producers and used the backlot as a mini-runway. 'Nellie' was then equipped with a formidable arsenal to make it a kind of airborne DB5.

Bert Luxford was involved in making the rockets for the autogyro. 'We used the same rockets as I'd used on the *Thunderball* motorbike. We actually had a cluster of them on each side, and then there were two large ones. John Stears and I designed them, but had to take into account their weight. We contacted a firm called Schermuly, who made the flares for the bike, but the rocket-tubes they brought us weighed more than the actual rockets! Anyway, we took them out on the backlot at Pinewood and made a ramp to test these tubes. We had no idea how high the rockets would go, so pointed them at Black Park. John detonated one and off it went ... straight over the park, then it did a veer to port, then another and then another and, in fact, came straight back at us! We ran like mad and it landed about 20 feet away with its spike downwards."

Little Nellie's pilot admitted he wasn't too sure about the 'additions' to his autogyro. 'I did have reservations about some of the weapons,' he says. 'I wasn't happy carrying the flame-throwers on the tail and the large rockets were initially unstable, and we might have "met again" after firing.' In the event, the large rockets were removed for certain sequences and their absence can be spotted by eagle-eyed viewers.

However, there were considerable problems in Japan. The soaring temperatures and the fanatical press made life a misery for the crew, and the latter particularly perturbed Sean Connery, who announced that this would be his last Bond film.

But when the team returned to the familiar surroundings of Pinewood, it was a different story. 'It's quite amazing,' Adam notes, 'because when they were out in Japan they were having a lot of problems with riggers and plasterers who wanted extra money for all sorts of things, but when they came back and saw this set growing, they became more and more enthusiastic about it. The studio was so excited!'

In fact, it was reported that they had to close-off the set because so many people were coming along to look at the gigantic structure. 'It was huge!' exclaims Lewis Gilbert. 'It really was. Ken Adam was brilliant. I think the Bond films have lacked that kind of thing in recent years. Ken Adam made a big contribution to those early Bonds.'

The climactic battle sequence called for the use of a great many stuntmen, who were required to perform all kinds of abseiling into the set as Ninja commandos. Bob Simmons had the job of recruiting the men for the job, as he recounted in his autobiography *Nobody Does It Better*. 'Virtually every stuntman in England was brought into Pinewood for the battle sequence. Later, I had a crowd of 120 for the master shots. There were 40 specialists working on the ropes like Tarzans.'

Almost a decade would pass until the Bond producers made a further contribution to the Pinewood skyline. Meanwhile, Connery left and was replaced by Australian model George Lazenby for *On Her Majesty's Secret Service*, considered by many – despite misgivings about the leading man – to be the best film in the series. Connery was then lured back for the jokey *Diamonds Are Forever*, donating his $1m fee to charity and bringing a new camp sensibility to the series which would be perfected in later films. In 1972, Roger Moore, best known at the time as TV's *The Saint*, took on the role in *Live and Let Die*, recounting his adventures while filming in his published diary, *Roger Moore As James Bond*.

Below: *Pinewood's MD Cyril Howard (left) and guests with Sean Connery during the filming of his last Pinewood Bond film,* Diamonds Are Forever, *in summer 1971.*

Bottom left: *James Bond (Roger Moore) and Solitaire (Jane Seymour) are held captive by Kananga (Yaphet Kotto) in* Live and Let Die.

Bottom right: *The diamond-etched golden gun itself.*

The villain's underground headquarters were created on D Stage, with Moore bound to Jane Seymour's gorgeous Solitaire and suspended over a pool as potential morsels for a hungry shark. 'We filmed part of the cave scene in Jamaica in real underground caves,' wrote Moore, 'and there is only one thing missing from our carpenter's cavernous reconstruction at Pinewood: the bats, thank goodness. It is the biggest set I've ever worked on.'

Moore's second film, *The Man With the Golden Gun*, called for a very special prop, comprising a cigarette case, lighter, cufflink and pen – and

when it was accidentally broken, Bert Luxford was called in to save the day. 'We didn't make the original golden gun; it was made by the lighter people Colibri and it had to have special etching on the cigarette case. That was only done in one place – Ireland. On the very first day, it went on set and somebody dropped it. It just shattered! A gunsmith called Curly Kerrs and myself had to make a replica in double-quick time. It had to work, too, because the audience had to see Christopher Lee, as the $1m hitman Scaramanga, actually put it together. We did it in about a week,

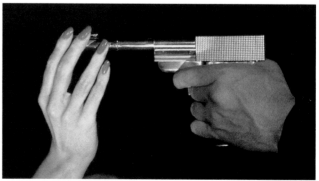

and then it went to Ireland for etching.'

The poster for the tenth film in the official franchise, Lewis Gilbert's *The Spy Who Loved Me*, claimed that it was the biggest Bond of all. We have already seen how the producers changed the studio's skyline, albeit temporarily, but this time they left a permanent reminder in the shape of the '007 Stage'.

The plot of the film – more or less a re-run of the spaceship hijacking routine in *You Only Live Twice* – involved the disappearance of nuclear submarines, swallowed up by a gigantic super-tanker belonging to the movie's chief villain, Stromberg (Curt Jurgens). During early pre-production, the search for a stage large enough to house three nuclear submarines was underway. 'We saw a lot of people and places,' Broccoli told *American Cinematographer* magazine. 'They couldn't promise anything. We told them we had to dig a big tank to take in the water and we'd have to have a guaranteed period. It became an

absolute farce. So it appeared to me that it was more sane, after talking to United Artists, to explore the possibility of putting up a new stage.'

United Artists took some persuading but Broccoli managed it. Production designer Ken Adam and young architect Michael Brown were brought together to design a stage. On the one hand, it had to be functional for the film, but on the other it needed to be operational as a stage in its own right, because Eon and Rank had agreed it would later be rented out to other filmmakers. This was the carrot that finally saw United Artists give it the go-ahead.

But where could it be built within the studio? Peter Lamont recalls that the idea was to position the new stage over the existing reservoir on the backlot. 'It only used to be 75 feet square, but we made it bigger for *Thunderball*. When *The Spy Who Loved Me* came along and we needed the large stage with a tank, we decided to extend the reservoir again and build the stage over it.'

PINEWOOD

007 STAGE

Facing page: *A brochure produced to celebrate the opening of the world's largest stage.*

Right: *Barbara Bach, Cubby Broccoli and Roger Moore on the* Liparus *set, contained within the huge 007 Stage; and (below) Happy birthday Curt! German actor Curt Jurgens (Stromberg) celebrates during the making of* The Spy Who Loved Me, *with Barbara Bach first up for a slice.*

Happily, planning consent was swiftly granted and the stage began to take shape throughout the scorching summer of 1976. Delta Doric, a building firm from nearby Uxbridge, took seven months to complete the world's largest stage, measuring 334 ft by 136 ft by 40 ft 6 in. Inside, the tank (measuring 297 ft by 73 ft by 8 ft 10 in) was the main feature of Stromberg's *Liparus* supertanker. 'It was surprisingly inexpensive to construct: $1,650,000,' observes Ken Adam, 'and I designed the stage to be part of the set with steel gantries and all that. I don't think UA ever regretted it as it's always been in use!'

The 007 Stage was officially opened on 5 December 1976. The ceremony was attended by former Prime Minister Harold Wilson and leading actors from the film. Several dignitaries from the Royal Navy were also in attendance, plus some top actors including Sir John Mills and Kenneth More. Cubby Broccoli's wife, Dana, broke the champagne bottle on the conning tower of the American submarine. A brochure was produced to promote Pinewood's new stage, with Pinewood's then MD, Cyril Howard, saying, 'The film industry has always cried out for a huge stage and now it has got one. I sincerely hope that producers will make use of the facility, which is unique.'

The Spy Who Loved Me was a huge success and Adam was nominated for an Oscar, losing out to *Star Wars* on the night. For Cubby Broccoli it was an extremely significant picture, as there had been much debate following his recent split with partner Harry Saltzman as to whether Bond would continue. Cubby had now left no doubt in anyone's mind. For Roger Moore it was the film that firmly established him as the new James Bond, and it remains the actor's personal favourite.

However, dark clouds were forming at Pinewood, as John Willis recounts. 'I was brought in for the publicity between the wrap of shooting and the première. It was tremendous fun. But the whole period was marred by the news that Cubby was having to give up his house in Green Street and move out of the UK because of the ridiculous tax laws that had been brought in. Pinewood was obviously very concerned because, at that time,

there wasn't a lot else going on and Bond was a lifeline. It looked like Cubby was going to take it all abroad, and there wouldn't be another one shot at Pinewood.'

Moonraker did in fact go to France, with Pinewood only being used for Derek Meddings' effects and post-production. It was Ken Adam's last Bond film, but only now is he receiving the recognition that his talents deserve, although Oscar success did come his way outside 007 with *Barry Lyndon* (1975) and, 20 years later, *The Madness of King George*. 'Today the early Bonds are such classics,' he says. 'We were all in the right frame of mind for it. We had such a great team and they overcame all of the logistical problems so well. We might have one unit in Rio, one in Paris, special effects in Florida and so on, but they all coped. That, I believe, was a major influence on American productions coming into Britain. They suddenly saw that we could deal with these big, big pictures. We became the kings of Pinewood, and the standards were very high on every level.'

Bond returned to Pinewood in the 1980s with *For Your Eyes Only* and *Octopussy*. However, during production on *A View To A Kill*, the next film in the official series, disaster struck. On Wednesday 24 June 1984, during the filming of Ridley Scott's *Legend*, the 007 Stage burnt down. In a matter of minutes, the world's largest stage

Right: *Tracy Bond's grave in* For Your Eyes Only *was situated in the cemetery of Stoke Poges Parish Church.*

Below: *Production designer Peter Lamont on one of his opulent* Octopussy *sets.*

was reduced to a heap of twisted, blackened metal. Ironically, all that was left of Ken Adam's superb design was the '007 Stage' sign. Fortunately, no one was injured as the production had already broken for lunch.

'I was lunching in the restaurant when someone rushed over and asked me if I'd seen the fire,' recalls Cyril Howard. 'I obviously didn't know what they were talking about, so when they told me it was the 007 Stage going up in flames, my initial thought was "How could it? It's a steel construction." But by the time I'd headed over to the stage to see for myself, it was almost gone. I'll never forget that sight: the structure was literally melted by the intensity of the heat. I'd never seen anything like it, before or since.'

John Glen, who had assumed directorial duties on the Bond pictures with *For Your Eyes Only*, was preparing for the new instalment when he heard the news. 'Cubby and I were having lunch in Curzon Street when halfway through the meal, the waiter came over and said that there was "a very important phone call from the studio for Mr Broccoli." Cubby wasn't pleased about having his lunch interrupted, but went to take the call. A few minutes later he returned, looking as cool and calm as ever, and continued with his lunch. Only after we'd finished dessert did he mention what the phone call was about. "They've only gone and burnt the 007 Stage down!" he said. Typical Cubby – never letting a problem disrupt a good meal!'

Peter Lamont, who had now worked his way through the ranks to production designer, soon realised the expertise was there to rebuild the stage. 'I was in my office in A Block when I heard the news, he recalls. 'I went up to the lot, and where the stage had stood was just ... well, nothing. I saw Michael Brown there – he was involved with the building of the original stage – and he said "I can rebuild it in 13 weeks from the time the site is flattened."

Twenty years after signing on as Ken Adam's draftsman on *Goldfinger*, Lamont now had the task of reconstructing his mentor's masterpiece. 'The original design was changed a little on the sides,' he says. 'There was a kind of drop at the edge of

the floor and we filled it in with concrete. We then put in a double-skinned roof to alleviate condensation problems. It was always a heavy load-bearing structure, not just a set cover, and a lot of work was put into making it a first-class one. We ran into delays with the health and safety people as they wouldn't allow us to build sets on the stage until they'd completed all sorts of checks first. We had to ship pieces of the mine set onto other stages, but it eventually came to a point where I couldn't do any more without the 007 Stage. We managed to get it pre-lit just before Christmas, to shoot in January. We re-inaugurated the stage the week after shooting had finished on it!'

At the dedication ceremony on a cold January morning, the facility was re-named 'The Albert R Broccoli 007 Stage'. Cyril Howard and MGM/UA's Frank E Rosenfelt joined leading members of the cast and crew on the day. 'We still do some renovation work on the stage,' reports current Bond producer Michael G Wilson, 'and still part-own it until 2004, when it reverts to Pinewood.'

In 1986, Timothy Dalton succeeded Roger Moore as Bond and his début feature, *The Living*

Below: *The grand re-opening of the Albert R Broccoli 007 Stage with (left to right) Fiona Fullerton, Cubby Broccoli, Roger Moore, Tanya Roberts, Christopher Walken and Alison Doody.*

Daylights, saw a return to the grittier and more realistic tone of the earlier films. The *Daylights* set played host to a royal visit when the Prince and Princess of Wales popped in on 11 December 1986. Diana 'crowned' Charles with a break-away prop bottle, much to the delight of the assembled press.

The film's release coincided with Bond's 25th cinematic anniversary but it proved to be the last 007 adventure to shoot at Pinewood for almost ten years. For Dalton's second movie, *Licence To Kill*, production was transferred to Mexico as the exchange rate was much more favourable and the film's storyline necessitated extensive location shooting in that part of the world. It was a big blow to Pinewood, which at that time was entering one of the bleakest periods in the history of the British film industry.

A lengthy court battle between Broccoli's company and MGM kept 007 away from the screen for the next six years, but in 1995 it was announced that a new film, *GoldenEye*, was in preparation and a new star taking on the part – Pierce Brosnan. Pinewood was unable to accommodate this seventeenth entry in the series, other than for post-production purposes, so Eon built their own studio at a disused Rolls-Royce factory in Leavesden, near Watford. Despite several 1990s adjustments being made to the Bond formula, one thing remained the same – it was a massive box-office success.

Ironically, when Brosnan's second outing came round in 1997, a new *Star Wars* film had booked Leavesden's facilities, leaving MI6's top agent

Below: *History repeating. More than 30 years on, 007 returns to Stoke Poges for a round (this time with new Bond, Pierce Brosnan).*

Right: *Peter Lamont's spectacular caviar factory set on Pinewood's paddock tank.*

homeless again. However, with *Tomorrow Never Dies* came another new studio: this time a disused warehouse near Frogmore was converted, but the team did return to Pinewood for the villain's stealth ship, using the 007 Stage for interiors and the paddock tank for exteriors.

Tomorrow Never Dies was the first Bond film to be made without the guidance of Cubby Broccoli, who had died on 27 June 1996 after a long illness. Taking the reins her father had handled so expertly for over 30 years, Barbara Broccoli continued the series alongside her stepbrother Michael G Wilson. The eighteenth official film was proudly prefaced with the legend 'Albert R Broccoli's Eon Productions Present' and went on to become another blockbuster success.

The World Is Not Enough was Pierce Brosnan's third Bond film, and with it the Pinewood connection was rekindled. 'I was asked to do *Tomorrow Never Dies*,' says Peter Lamont, 'but was on a sinking ship at the time, *Titanic*, and couldn't join the team. But after it was released, Barbara and Michael met up with me to congratulate me on my Oscar and asked if I'd like to do the next Bond. Naturally, I was delighted to accept. They asked me where we should do it – and I suggested Pinewood.'

Lamont and his team constructed an incredible set on the paddock tank for reformed villain Zukovsky's 'caviar' factory. The tank itself was

enlarged, with walkways and ramps constructed along its full length, to accommodate the huge plant, which was then completely surrounded by giant black backing for night shooting. 'We extended the paddock tank a lot,' says Michael G Wilson. 'I suppose it's never been bigger – it's in the tradition of Bond, the big sets like the volcano in *You Only Live Twice*. We have a lot of interesting action sequences taking place on this set too.'

'Although we had an outline script when pre-production started in the summer of 1998, there wasn't a "final" script until many months afterwards,' Lamont reveals. 'So although we had lots of preparation time, the period between my receiving a more advanced script and building the sets was quite tight.'

The choice of Michael Apted as director seemed an unusual one. He was best known for his absorbing *Seven Up* TV documentaries and movie dramas such as *Gorillas In the Mist* and *The Coalminer's Daughter*. 'I thought it was a joke when they first asked me,' exclaims Apted, 'because it's the province of an action director really. But then meeting with the producers made it all clearer to me, and I could see what they wanted. It was my first time as a director at Pinewood. I had cut a film – *The Squeeze* – here in the 1970s, but I've always avoided studio work as much as possible. Having said that, all my fears evaporated once we started shooting here. It was

Below left: Tomorrow Never Dies *director Roger Spottiswoode confers with producers Barbara Broccoli and Michael G Wilson.*

Below right: *Bond meets Bond - Pierce Brosnan and Samantha Bond (Miss Moneypenny) in* The World Is Not Enough.

THE EON JAMES BOND FILMS AT PINEWOOD [year of release]:

1962 *DR. NO*
1963 *FROM RUSSIA WITH LOVE*
1964 *GOLDFINGER*
1965 *THUNDERBALL*
1967 *YOU ONLY LIVE TWICE*
1969 *ON HER MAJESTY'S SECRET SERVICE*
1971 *DIAMONDS ARE FOREVER*
1973 *LIVE AND LET DIE*
1974 *THE MAN WITH THE GOLDEN GUN*
1977 *THE SPY WHO LOVED ME*
1979 *MOONRAKER* [PART]
1981 *FOR YOUR EYES ONLY*
1983 *OCTOPUSSY*
1985 *A VIEW TO A KILL*
1987 *THE LIVING DAYLIGHTS*
1989 *LICENCE TO KILL* [post-production only]
1995 *GOLDENEYE* [post-production only]
1997 *TOMORROW NEVER DIES* [PART]
1999 *THE WORLD IS NOT ENOUGH*

very intimidating during pre-production because there just seemed so much to do, and nothing was prioritised: it was *all* important, and it was a six-month shoot. Once we started shooting it kind of shaped out and we got it all done, and I had a great crew working with me.

'This one has a good story,' Apted enthuses, 'and lots of the great action you've come to associate with 007. I think one of the reasons the franchise survives is because they keep changing Bond. Although it's the same character, each actor brings something different to the part, and each film brings something different to the actor. But the audience knows that, along the way, they'll have the familiar elements too.'

Among the 'familiar elements' in the new film are 007's trusted colleagues Dame Judi Dench (M), Samantha Bond (Moneypenny) and Q (octogenarian Desmond Llewelyn). Another soon-to-be familiar face joins the team in the shape of John Cleese. 'I'm playing Q's assistant, whom Bond jokingly refers to as "R". I believe the idea is that I will eventually take over the gadget-man role when Desmond isn't able to carry on any longer.' Alas, this moment arrived all too soon when, in December 1999, Desmond Llewelyn tragically died in a car accident.

But, as 007 continues to grow in popularity and production values climb ever higher, will the series continue to make its base at Pinewood? 'In England, Pinewood is the major film studio,' says Michael G Wilson. 'I like working here because the British technicians have a certain style. We know them all so well. In England it's the best. Outside of England there's only really the US studios.'

Hollywood will always be a major player in the future of the series, not least because the films are financed by MGM. But it's clear that the producers view Pinewood not only as a facility but a home. A degree of emotional attachment to the place is clear from Peter Lamont's admission that he was once invited to take Bond to America but declined. 'I was asked over to the studios in America to conduct what they called a "feasibility" with regard to taking the Bonds out there. That was just before all the litigation in the early 1990s. But Pinewood will always be the home of James Bond.' ∎

11

Left: Hot Enough for June saw Dirk Bogarde working, unbeknown to him, for the intelligence services. Making good his escape, he nobbles a milk man.

Right: Kim Stanley leads the Seance on a Wet Afternoon.

The sixties were buoyant years for Pinewood, with more and more big American pictures basing themselves at the studio in the wake of Bond and Disney, and television production creating its first major impact, ultimately leading to new stages being constructed specifically for TV.

After *Doctor in Distress*, Dirk Bogarde teamed up with Betty Box and Ralph Thomas again in 1963 for *Hot Enough for June*. 'It was a mad comedy based on a very good book called *The Night of Wenceslas* by Lionel Davidson,' says Thomas, 'a sort of send-up of the early James Bond pictures and it worked very well. We originally wanted to call it *Agent 8 3/4* but Harry Saltzman wasn't too happy with that, so we changed it.'

It was also a busy time for Disney when both *Dr Syn Alias The Scarecrow*, with Patrick McGoohan and George Cole, and *The Moonspinners*, starring Hayley Mills, Eli Wallach and Peter McEnery, went before the cameras. Both were directed by James Nielson, but it was the latter which proved to be the publicity department's dream.

'Hayley's popularity at the time of *The Moonspinners* was phenomenal,' explains Disney's publicity man John Willis. 'You might say it was comparable with that of the Spice Girls today, so you can imagine what effect her first screen kiss had on the press! Everybody wanted to talk with Hayley and get the story, and even though she was still relatively young she handled everything and everyone with sheer professionalism.'

'I was actually quite terrified,' she confesses, 'because on the day of the "momentous" event, it seemed like half the world's press were on the stage floor. I was madly in love with Peter McEnery at the time, which further complicated matters – not that he knew. It made it even more terrifying for me as, not only did I have to kiss this man whom I thought was wonderful, but the cameras were clicking like mad at the same time.'

Bryan Forbes and Richard Attenborough next brought *Seance on a Wet Afternoon* to the studio. Kim Stanley played Myra Savage, a medium who manipulates her devoted husband Billy (Attenborough) into kidnapping a child so she can then appear to use her 'powers' to locate the girl. Stanley received an Academy Award nomination for her role as the unhinged psychic.

The production was designed by Ray Simm but one eerie set couldn't be recreated at Pinewood, as Bryan Forbes explained in 1994: 'I was sure I'd seen the perfect house for the seance scenes in Wimbledon, so I got in the car and drove over there. I immediately did a deal with the woman who owned the house, and she asked me who was going to be in the film. I said Richard Attenborough, and she then asked who was playing the female lead. I said that she probably wouldn't have heard of her as she'd only made one other film – Kim Stanley. She went as white as a sheet and said that Kim used to be her best friend and they hadn't seen each other for 17 years. She asked why I'd chosen her house, and I explained it was about a seance and the house had a turret room which I wanted to use. "Yes, I thought you would," she said. "The last owner committed suicide in that room."'

Bryan Forbes stepped in for Attenborough during the kidnapping scene, as Attenborough was suffering with a terrible cold at the time and the rain-soaked getaway was hardly conducive to shaking it. The substitution is only noticeable, however, if you look very closely.

1964 kicked off with two TV shows – *Topo Gigio*

BOOM (1963 – 1969)

and *Circus World* – with two more following later in the year, *Court Martial* and *One Day in London*. A new stage (H) was built for TV production and the *Court Martial* series was the first to move into the 89 x 37 x 28 foot space, as producer Bill Hill explains. 'The people at Pinewood built us our requirements as a self-contained unit. They gutted a whole block and reconstructed it, creating an admin block, completely self-contained and inter-communicating, plus dressing rooms, make-up, hairdressing and wardrobe departments. They modified three stages for our production. This went on during July and August. The unit of 150 people started to arrive ready to shoot on 7 September. When the

first four 48-minute episodes were sent over to New York, back came the order "Double the number, let's have 26." Each film was made in an average of 9 1/2 days, and that's not bad going.'

Richard Attenborough remained in front of the camera in *Guns at Batasi* and no sooner had Sean Connery completed work on Basil Dearden's *Woman of Straw* than he stepped back into 007 mode for *Goldfinger*, the benchmark Bond film. Meanwhile, Harry Saltzman, one half of Eon Productions, set about making another spy thriller, albeit with a less glamorous hero. *The Ipcress File* would launch Michael Caine to superstar status.

Those Magnificent Men in Their Flying Machines

boasted all-star cast, including Stuart Whitman, Sarah Miles, James Fox, Robert Morley, Gert Fröbe, Eric Sykes and Terry-Thomas, in a rip-roaring comedy set in 1910. Press mogul Lord Rawnsley (Robert Morley) puts up a £10,000 prize for a London to Paris air race. All manner of contraptions are entered, piloted by one of the most international (and funniest) casts ever to come together at Pinewood. The script (co-written by director Ken Annakin) was nominated for an Academy Award.

'The film was wonderfully serviced by Pinewood and every technical department attached to it,' recalls Annakin. 'We shot an amazing number of flying sequences against blue screen and the crews worked skilfully and patiently to get it right. Some people say it launched my "Hollywood career". Well, I never really had one, as most of my films were shot on locations all around the world. But I have been based in Hollywood since the 1970s, so I guess in that sense it did.'

Incidentally, Wing Commander Ken Wallis, who subsequently invented and piloted 'Little Nellie' in *You Only Live Twice*, supplied the aircraft sounds for the film by recording his deliberately spluttering autogyro engines and playing them back at different speeds.

Hugh Stewart and Robert Asher, in their first non-Wisdom collaboration, opted to bring television's most popular comedy double act to the big screen in *The Intelligence Men*. Eric Morecambe and Ernie Wise lost something in translation to the big screen. Although amusing in parts, this tale of two inept spies didn't succeed in recreating the dynamite so often displayed in the team's TV extravaganzas. 'When we came to Pinewood'" said Ernie Wise in a 1987 interview for Thames TV, 'we thought we were going to meet all the big film stars – we did see a few in the restaurant – but Eric thought that they'd all be popping by our dressing room and so he bought a big fridge and filled it full of booze. Nobody came! We were so disappointed. My biggest disappointment was on the first day on location, when I was sitting in my caravan, ready to do my first scene, and my lunch came in through the window on a paper plate. It was difficult for us not having an audience for the

first time, as the timing was in a sort of void, and that's why I felt our films were a bit diluted. If we could have had an audience and later cut them out, it would have worked much better.'

The last film to shoot in 1964 attracted some unwelcome attention from the press, thanks to the rivalry that existed between its two stars Kirk Douglas and Richard Harris. 'After working for Disney for many years,' recalls John Willis, 'I decided to become a freelance publicist and *The Heroes of Telemark* was my first. Talk about a baptism of fire!

'The film's director, Anthony Mann, had originally been signed to direct *Spartacus* but he and Douglas didn't get on and Mann was replaced by Stanley Kubrick. He'd also made a film with Richard Harris and didn't get along too well there, so bringing them all together wasn't perhaps the best idea. Douglas and Harris were very jealous of each other and were always bitching about who the 'star' was. Their demands became silly and seriously affected the running of the production. For instance, Harris rolled up at the studio one day with a tape measure, measured Douglas' trailer and then announced he was going home. Apparently, it was a little bigger than his own trailer. Another day, Douglas fired his chauffeur and Harris immediately turned round and hired him.

'It got worse. We were on location in Rome, and one evening we all attended a film première. Earlier in the day, the British papers ran a story about all the childish behaviour and petty rivalry between the two leads and Richard Harris was furious. He saw me in the foyer of the cinema, pushed everyone else out of the way and demanded to know who leaked the story. I said nothing! He threatened to hit me – and I wish he had done – but we were pulled apart. The most annoying thing for me was when, on the last day at Pinewood, both of them were in the corridor walking towards each other – it was a bit like *High Noon* – and I couldn't believe my eyes: as they met, they shook each other's hands like they were old friends!'

1965 kicked off with Terence Young returning to the Bond fold for the fourth 007 adventure, *Thunderball*. Meanwhile, Basil Dearden directed Charlton Heston, Laurence Olivier and Ralph

Facing page: *Peter Sellers, Ursula Andress and
Orson Welles lead the cast in* Casino Royale.
The casino sequences were filmed at Pinewood.

Richardson in *Khartoum*. 'That wasn't my first time at Pinewood,' says Charlton Heston, 'because we stopped off there for costume fittings on *Ben-Hur*, and I thought it a wonderful place then. And in my opinion the restaurant was (and still is) the best of any film studio in the world!

'I had a wonderful new Jaguar at the time of *Khartoum* and used to drive myself into the studio. I'll forever remember pulling into my space on one of the first few days, and seeing the great Ralph Richardon pull up in a new Bentley. We hadn't met at this point, so as I was pondering whether or not to go over. I saw him close the door ever so gently, pat the car on the roof and say "Farewell old dear," before trotting off to the stage. I'll never forget that moment!'

Meanwhile, John Mills made his directorial début with *Sky West and Crooked*, which starred Hayley Mills and Ian McShane. 'I took the book to Arthur [Rank] and he agreed to the film on the strength of that alone,' claims Sir John. 'I was very close to Arthur and he was a great personal friend of Mary [Lady Mills] and I. Making the film was an interesting experience, and working with Hayley was sheer joy – she's such a perfectionist. The arguments started, though, when the Rank Organisation wanted the title *Sky West and Crooked*; the story was called *Bats With Baby Faces* and I couldn't understand what *Sky West and Crooked* meant. Anyway, that's the title they insisted on. I rather thought I'd stick to acting thereafter – it's much easier!' Indeed, Mills returned to the other side of the camera for his next venture, Bryan Forbes' comedy *The Wrong Box*, which saw him co-star with Ralph Richardson, Michael Caine, Wilfrid Lawson, Nanette Newman, Peter Cook, Dudley Moore and Peter Sellers.

The studio's 30th birthday was celebrated in 1966, and a publicity brochure of the time proudly proclaimed that 'There are 1,300 people at Pinewood.' Busy times indeed. Work started on two more new stages, to become known as J and K, which were particularly important additions as they provided facilities for both television and feature production. Kip Herren, managing director at the time, explained the evolution of the stages in an article written at the time of the 30th Anniversary. 'We have toured Europe both in front of and behind the Iron Curtain to look at new methods not only of shooting, but even of the initial construction of studios of the future. We have evolved, with our technical friends, stages which will have a completely dual role; stages in which we can continue feature production and also take our place as television film series producers.'

The stages were designed to 'have a carefully landscaped setting in the green acres of the Rank Film Production Division, so that they will skilfully blend in with the current studios and surrounding countryside' and to be the most modern in Europe. However, there was one major difference between film and TV stages of the day – the floors. Kip Heren continued: 'When it came to the problem of the floor of the stages it proved a very tough nut indeed. It is simple to provide a floor for television to allow free rein to their equipment. The floor for feature production is traditionally wood, and the heavy set construction requires braces nailed to the floor. Nails damage the smooth surfaces required for television type mobility. The staff involved in Pinewood came up with many ideas after a great deal of hard work and research, and we think we can combine the benefits of both systems in one type of floor surface.'

The design incorporated the traditional wooden 'feature' floors but underneath lay wonderfully smooth TV production floors which could be accessed very easily. TV productions which took advantage of the new facility later in the year included *The David Niven Story* and *Man in a Suitcase*. The design was adhered to again with the construction of L and M Stages later in the decade.

Other new buildings included an engineering workshop, vehicle maintenance workshops, an extension to the stills department and a new central canteen for the staff. John Davis described Pinewood as 'the finest and most forward-looking studios anywhere. And by enabling television and feature production to share both studios and technicians, they will be more fully employed and offer the best opportunities for modern and economic production.'

Meanwhile, the great star of silent cinema, Charlie Chaplin, unexpectedly returned to features with *A Countess From Hong Kong*, which he wrote, directed and composed the music for. It was an unmitigated disaster. Marlon Brando starred with Sophia Loren, but could do little to help save the film that Chaplin was so passionate about making. When asked why he agreed to appear in it, he replied 'How could you not want to work with Chaplin?' It turned out to be Chaplin's last film and a very uncomfortable and tiring experience for the artists involved, mainly due to the fact that their director insisted on playing every part in rehearsal to show how he wanted them to perform.

Casino Royale was the first of Ian Fleming's Bond novels. The screen rights had been sold at an early stage and thus were not controlled by Broccoli and Saltzman's Eon Productions. The rights ultimately found their way to producer Charles K Feldman at what was the height of Bondmania. Realising that he couldn't emulate Eon's success without Sean Connery, Feldman opted to make a spoof Bond film instead.

'Oh God!' says the film's production accountant, John Collingwood, at the mention of *Casino Royale*. 'You know, I've been involved in hundreds of films in my career and that was the only one ever to go over-budget – but with five directors, three studios and a cast that multiplied daily, it was hardly surprising.'

The production sprawled across several studios, including Pinewood: there were so many sets spread over such a long shoot that no one studio could cope. 'I remember being at MGM, Shepperton, Elstree and Pinewood,' says Val Guest, one of the film's directors. "We were all over the place! It's difficult to remember what was done where really, but I'm sure I did some of the casino scenes at Pinewood. That film is a book in itself!'

'I went on to *Casino Royale* and stayed for 11 months,' says publicist John Willis. 'I'd only usually be on a picture for three or four months. We shot most of the John Huston parts at Pinewood – it was quite crazy! Feldman would phone and say "I've got William Holden for a couple of days next week" and

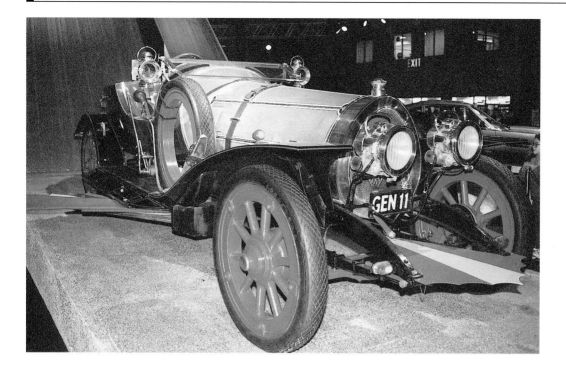

we'd have to change everything – and write new scenes – to bring him in. The script was rewritten almost every day. It didn't matter that a part might not make sense, we just had people who were in town. The publicity side was actually terrific fun because it centred around who was James Bond – was it Woody Allen, Terence Cooper, David Niven? etc – and that was marvellous for someone like me.'

The cast list was indeed a veritable *Who's Who*. In addition to the above-mentioned were Ursula Andress, Jacqueline Bisset, Charles Boyer, John Huston, Deborah Kerr, Derek Nimmo, Peter Sellers, Peter O'Toole, George Raft, Orson Welles ... The list goes on. The five credited directors were Val Guest, Ken Hughes, John Huston, Robert Parrish and Joe McGrath. The film's saving grace was the superb score by Burt Bacharach, which included the Oscar-nominated 'The Look of Love' performed by Dusty Springfield. Although the film was a box-office success, it came nowhere near to rivalling the business generated by Eon's continuing series. The film rights to *Casino Royale* were transferred to MGM/UA (Eon's distributor) as part of the resolution of a law suit with Sony Pictures in February 1999. Whether a 'serious' version of Fleming's novel will ever be produced remains to be seen.

Feature production continued apace with *Funeral in Berlin,* Michael Caine's sequel to *The Ipcress File* – and Michael Anderson's excellent *The Quiller Memorandum* starring George Segal and Alec Guinness, adapted for the screen by Harold Pinter and with a haunting John Barry score. Clive Reed was first assistant director on the film and remembers the location shoot vividly. 'I thought the Berlin locations were extraordinary and our time there was one of remarkable history – the Wall, Checkpoint Charlie, having to wipe your feet on a disinfected mat when stepping from the coach at the checkpoint and the eerie sensation of being at Wanasee at night where on the West side there was music and laughter but across on the East there was only the sound of guard dogs and the sight of searchlights panning across the barbed wire.'

A curious film then made its home at Pinewood: Peter Brook's *Marat/Sade,* or to give it its full title – *The Persecution and Assassination of Jean-Paul Marat as Performed by the Inmates of the Asylum at Charenton Under the Direction of the Marquis de Sade*. Quite a title, and one that pretty much gives the plot away. The film was a stark and disturbing adaptation of the Old Vic production of Peter Weiss's play. Glenda Jackson starred as Charlotte Corday alongside Patrick Magee (Sade) and Ian Richardson (Marat), but had little positive to say about the play or film. 'I loathed and detested doing the play. I couldn't wait for it to end. Then we all did the film and it was a shattering experience. People twitching ... slobber running down their chins ... everyone screaming from nerves and exhaustion!'

Following this was Albert R 'Cubby' Broccoli – fresh from making *You Only Live Twice* – with another of Ian Fleming's stories. Only this was a

Facing page: *The most fantasmogorical car in the world,* Chitty Chitty Bang Bang.

Left: *Bert Luxford puts the finishing touches to the Zeppelin model used in* Chitty Chitty Bang Bang.

children's story: *Chitty Chitty Bang Bang*. Fleming wrote this tale of a phantasmagorical flying car with magical powers while in hospital recuperating from a heart attack. Dick Van Dyke, Sally Ann Howes, Gert Fröbe and Lionel Jeffries starred, while Irwin Kostal's music was complimented by songs from the Sherman Brothers. The title song, in fact, gained an Academy Award nomination.

Production designer Ken Adam came up with some interesting ideas, not least for the car itself. 'When we had to design the airship for the Baron – the Gert Fröbe character – I was quite prepared to design a model which in those days would have cost about £6,000. However, two gentlemen walked into my office – they were balloonists – and they said that they wanted to build us a full-sized airship. I said 'You're joking,' but they came up with some designs and an estimate for about £9,000 – so it wasn't that much more than the model. United Artists and Cubby said that they should go ahead. What we didn't realise, however, was that my original design was based on a French airship – one that never flew! The balloonists were a little nervous about using the engine and one day they crashed into some power lines while on a test flight, and cut off all the electricity in the Hampshire countryside. The farmers were most irate as they couldn't milk their cows and so threatened to sue United Artists!

'It was almost like a period Bond film in many ways, because we had so many gadgets. I designed the car and we built a complete mock-up, which we kept changing, and I found that the period car concept wasn't as easy as I thought it would be. There

were in fact five cars built, by the same people who built the Ford GT, and Cubby had done a deal with Ford to supply the power unit. Other people were called in to build the body, and each car had a specific purpose: for flying sequences, water scenes and ordinary road use. They worked very well.'

All the cars remain in Britain, two in Cumbria's 'Cars of the Stars' Motor Museum, another owned by Pierre Picton, a professional clown who often tours with it, and the fourth with the famous excavator family J C Bamford.

'*Chitty Chitty Bang Bang* is my favourite picture,' says Lionel Jeffries, 'mainly due to the director Ken Hughes. He was great fun and had the secret of making good movies – that was to tell the story and make sure there were no tensions on the floor: I don't remember anyone's voice ever being raised. It was a tough shoot though, and wasn't helped by Dick Van Dyke deciding not to turn up sometimes. In fact, at one point, we all sat on the backlot for two solid weeks as he'd disappeared and we'd run out of things to shoot around him! We found out later that he'd gone to live on the Thames embankment for a week and grown a beard, and the following week he'd gone off to Hollywood to be with Mary Tyler Moore. Meanwhile, the rest of us played darts in our caravans!'

In spring 1968, Freddie Francis returned to Pinewood to direct a horror film for Hammer, the company's first full-length shoot at the studio. *Dracula Has Risen From the Grave* was the third incarnation of Christopher Lee's red-eyed vampire and a proud moment for Hammer: during filming the company was presented with the Queen's Award to Industry on the steps of Pinewood's Castle Dracula.

Guy Hamilton, meanwhile, directed *Battle of Britain* for producer Harry Saltzman. Laurence Olivier, Robert Shaw, Michael Caine, Christopher Plummer and Susannah York headed a star-packed retelling of the famous wartime air battle. The real stars, however, were the historic aeroplanes – Spitfires, Hurricanes and an American Mitchell bomber as camera ship. 'My lingering memory of that film,' unit publicist John Willis points out, 'was seeing literally scores of fibreglass Spitfires pouring out of the workshops at Pinewood. They

were all sent down to the airfields and it's amazing to think that only a few of the planes you see on the fields were actually real!'

One of the last films to shoot in 1968 also proved one of the most controversial: J Lee Thompson's *The Most Dangerous Man in the World*, in which Gregory Peck played an American scientist, recruited by Western intelligence, to go into China and meet Chairman Mao, with a detonator secretly implanted in his head. 'It was probably my biggest film at Pinewood,' said Thompson, 'and was quite a unique story; the idea of an implant was very novel. Greg Peck was very keen on the storyline and was an absolute joy to work with. I think it was his third picture at the studio. We did all of the interiors there but locations were mainly in Wales and Hong Kong.'

On 28 November the *Daily Express* reported that 'Chairman Mao let it be known yesterday that he is very definitely not thinking beautiful thoughts about his début as a ping-pong playing decadent Western film star. An official Communist China newspaper warned that if anybody tried to take shots for the film in Hong Kong there would be "grave consequences". But last night the film company and Gregory Peck were airborne and on their way. Chairman Mao was being "attacked" and the film was highly "anti China" said the *Wen Wei Pai* editorial.'

Twentieth Century-Fox's Arthur P Jacobs said in response: 'We sent a script to the Hong Kong government and had their, and police, approval. There are shots we must have and are going ahead to get them. There are plenty of opportunities for the Chairman to express pro-Chinese views. It is a thriller – not political at all.'

Hong Kong was a free port at the time, without restrictions on the import of film or cameras, so the Hong Kong government vowed not to interfere. Having overcome those problems, however, there were difficulties back at Pinewood in recruiting the many Chinese extras required. Some sequences in the 'House of Exotic Pleasure' called for clusters of nude Chinese girls, but very few of those gathered

Facing page: *The brilliant Baker Street set seen here in* The Private Life of Sherlock Holmes *was used in a number of subsequent productions.*

Left: *Val Guest's* Toomorrow, *starring Olivia Newton-John.*

were prepared to strip off. On top of all that, cinematographer Ted Moore had to be replaced towards the end of shooting by John Wilcox, after one of the large studio lamps hit Moore on the head, rendering him unconscious.

In 1969 Billy Wilder – best known for the classic comedy *Some Like It Hot* – arrived at Pinewood to shoot *The Private Life of Sherlock Holmes*. He cast Robert Stephens as the consulting detective, Colin Blakely as his faithful chronicler Dr Watson and Christopher Lee as Holmes' mysterious brother Mycroft. It was a very personal project for Wilder and proved to be a very ambitious and elaborate undertaking.

The troubles on the shoot grew in scale as it progressed, with filming suspended at one point when Stephens was suddenly taken ill. An impressive Baker Street set was built on the backlot, costing around £80,000 to construct. No expense was spared, according to production runner Gordon Thomsen. 'All the cobbles on that street were real cobbles. They found a street somewhere in the north of England which was being demolished, a real cobbled street, and they brought down lorryloads of cobbles and actually laid them one by one on the set. Each one of those houses had real cellars too. It was dug out so you could walk downstairs below street level. The sash windows weren't made out of cheap wood, they were all proper windows. There were some tremendously good quality materials used in the set building. In fact, I remember one person in the art department saying that Alex Trauner, the production designer, was the last of the Vincent Kordas.'

In fact, Trauner earned the disapproval of some crew members over his extravagant set designs, which were causing practical problems while filming. The director of photography, Christopher Challis, had some arguments with Trauner and later called the designer a 'builder of houses, not sets' who 'didn't know what was required for front projection.'

And Trauner's elaborate and expensive ideas were not confined to the Baker Street set. 'One of the biggest sets was the Diogenes Club,' says Thomsen. 'That was built on E Stage in the north tunnel. It was built for just one shot where they go to see Mycroft Holmes. It was all one composite set on E Stage, but to get extra length they built out into the old projection tunnel, which was left over from the days of Independent Frame. It seemed to take weeks and weeks to build it, just for one walk-through shot!'

Over schedule and over budget, the movie performed badly at the box-office and has since become notorious for the many scenes that United Artists executives demanded cut. The Baker Street set, however, remained a feature of Pinewood's lot for several years (ingeniously recycled in *Carry On At Your Convenience* for example), before being struck after severe flooding in 1973.

Next, Val Guest jetted back to the studio with the barely seen Olivia Newton-John vehicle, *Toomorrow*. 'Aaggh! That was an awful experience!' Guest groans. 'Nobody ever got paid! Harry Saltzman was behind it, and we later discovered that he put up his interests in the Bond films as security on the finance. But he came a cropper with it. He did the same with other projects, and then with his purchase of Technicolor ... That last one went a bit too far, and it led to him and Cubby parting company.'

Pinewood was gearing up, meanwhile, for another action-adventure tale. Anthony Hopkins, Nathalie Delon and Robert Morley starred in Alistair MacLean's *When Eight Bells Toll*, directed by Etienne Perier, and an apparently everyday assignment for one of the studio's production secretaries changed her life. 'Tony and I met on that picture,' says Lady Jenni Hopkins. 'I was working as an assistant at Pinewood and was asked to pick up Tony from the airport and bring him to the studio. We fell for each other there and then!' ∎

12

Left: Ken Russell's The Devils.

Right: Roger Moore and Tony Curtis with their producer Lew Grade on The Persuaders!

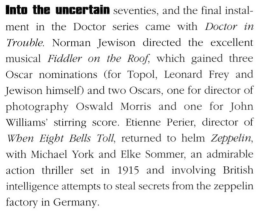

Into the uncertain seventies, and the final instalment in the Doctor series came with *Doctor in Trouble*. Norman Jewison directed the excellent musical *Fiddler on the Roof*, which gained three Oscar nominations (for Topol, Leonard Frey and Jewison himself) and two Oscars, one for director of photography Oswald Morris and one for John Williams' stirring score. Etienne Perier, director of *When Eight Bells Toll*, returned to helm *Zeppelin*, with Michael York and Elke Sommer, an admirable action thriller set in 1915 and involving British intelligence attempts to steal secrets from the zeppelin factory in Germany.

'A garish glossary of sado-masochism ... a taste for visual sensation that makes scene after scene look like the masturbatory fantasies of Roman Catholic boyhood,' was critic Alexander Walker's verdict on Ken Russell's *The Devils*, which starred Vanessa Redgrave and Oliver Reed. With masturbating nuns, demonic possession, burning at the stake, sacrilegious dream sequences – not to mention an abundance of rotting skulls, rats and running sores – the film was pounced on by the Festival of Light and was one of the main 'exhibits' in the censorship controversies which marked the early 1970s. What the devout J Arthur Rank thought is unrecorded.

Back on a family entertainment level, more and more television productions were based at the studio. There were five in 1970 including Gerry and Sylvia Anderson's *UFO* – starring Ed Bishop, Michael Billington and Wanda Ventham – and *The Persuaders!* with Tony Curtis and Roger Moore. 'What you must remember about Pinewood,' says Robert Baker, creator and producer of *The Persuaders!*, 'is that as well as being a first-class facility, there are also some wonderful locations right on the doorstep. We used Black Park [which backs on to the lot] to double for everything from Red China to the south of France and grand country

estates back in England. Apart from the necessary establishing shots we hardly left the locale and used areas around the studio extensively – particularly the house and gardens.'

Stanley Kubrick utilised Pinewood's D Stage in 1971 for his production of *A Clockwork Orange*. The process projection department, headed by Charles Staffell, orchestrated the scene of Alex and his droogs driving recklessly through the London streets.

The same year, director Alfred Hitchcock returned to the studio to make *Frenzy* with Alec McCowen, Jon Finch and Barry Foster in the brutal story of a man framed for rape and murder. The 34 years since *Young and Innocent* had seen Hitchcock achieve incredible success in Hollywood with such movies as *Vertigo*, *Psycho* and *The Birds*. Understandably, his return to British shores was met with excitement and great anticipation, especially given the top-notch cast and the superior script by Anthony Shaffer, adapted from Arthur La Bern's novel *Goodbye Piccadilly, Farewell Leicester Square*. But *Frenzy* met with mixed critical reactions and still makes for uncomfortable viewing today.

The following year was marred with the news of Lord Rank's death. On 29 March 1972, the day of the Rank Organisation's AGM, it was announced that flour and film mogul J Arthur Rank had died. He was

BUST (The 1970s)

Right: The Amazing Mr Blunden.
*(Left to right) Garry Miller, Lynne Frederick,
Laurence Naismith, Rosalyn Landor and
Marc Granger.*

83. Although he had said he didn't want a memorial service, the demand for one was so great that the family organised one at Westminster Central Hall on 24 April. Lords, ladies, politicians, staff from all divisions of his many business empires, and senior Methodist Church officials were among the many who gathered to pay homage to the great businessman and visionary.

His legacy lived on. The Rank Organisation was in a healthy state, the flour business Rank Hovis MacDougal Ltd was going from strength to strength, as was the Lord Rank Research Centre at High Wycombe to which, just before his death, he had donated £1 million. John Davis wrote in the company's annual report: 'It was my good fortune to know Arthur Rank, both as a business colleague and friend, spanning nearly forty years; my relationship with him was both an inspiration and a source of great personal privilege. We have lost the wisdom, friendship and advice of a great and unusual man.'

Pinewood remained very busy. The first production of 1972 was *Sleuth*, with Laurence Olivier and Michael Caine delivering extraordinary, Oscar-nominated performances in Anthony Shaffer's cat-and-mouse mystery thriller. Director Joseph Mankiewicz and composer John Addison also received nominations.

'We had to make the film in a studio,' says production designer Ken Adam. 'We couldn't have done it any other way. We went all over England looking at stately homes, but the geography of the required set was so intimate that we could never have found it – it had to be a set. The whole ground floor of the house was built in one of the wonderful big stages – the cellar and some of the bedrooms were on different stages – and I remember when the director Joseph Mankiewicz arrived to shoot, he said, "Ken you have to allow me two days to live in the set, and I don't want anyone around – just a propman in case I want to change anything around. After that, I'll be ready to shoot.' And he was!'

Fifties sex goddess and blonde bombshell Diana Dors returned to Pinewood for two of the year's productions. *Nothing But the Night* starred Christopher Lee and Peter Cushing, and was the one-and-only production from Lee's company Charlemagne. Dors stayed on afterwards for Lionel

Jeffries' *The Amazing Mr Blunden* with Laurence Naismith and James Villiers, which was adapted by Jeffries himself from Antonia Barber's novel *The Ghosts*. 'We nearly set fire to the admin block on that picture,' observes Jeffries, 'as we double-cladded the back of the building, which the management weren't too keen on, and it caught fire! Thankfully, it was brought under control in time.'

Comedy remained a staple ingredient of Pinewood's output – the *Carry Ons* continued and the big screen treatment was given to TV's popular Hylda Baker vehicle *Nearest and Dearest* and the Jewish sweat-shop hit *Never Mind the Quality, Feel the Width*. 'We used the Baker Street set on that film for one of our main streets,' remembers producer Martin Cahill, 'but dressed it up and modernised it with pubs and bookmakers etc. A wonderful panning shot of the street was going to be used to play the titles and credits over, but when we ran the sequence in rushes, I felt it was a little too short, as it didn't quite extend the full length of the street as I imagined it would. The editor and cameraman told me not to worry, they'd fix it. That was the last I saw of it until the film was completed. The buggers had indeed shot a longer sequence, ending up at the bookmakers. My credit appeared as that shop came into

frame, and to my horror I saw the shop front announcing 'Cahill Bookmakers'. They had it planned right from the start!'

Still with comedy, Frankie Howerd's return to Pinewood came with *The House in Nightmare Park*, which co-starred Ray Milland, Hugh Burden and Kenneth Griffith. Set in 1907, Howerd plays Foster Twelvetrees, a struggling actor engaged for a private performance in a sinister country house. Again, extensive use was made of Black Park while the house itself was the famous Oakley Court next to Bray Studios, immortalised in numerous Hammer horror films and now a luxury hotel.

'I was executive producer on the film,' says Beryl Vertue, 'as well as being agent for both Terry Nation [the writer-producer] and Frankie himself, so I earned my fee plus 10 per cent of theirs. It was very much written with Frankie in mind and he was a real attraction for the other artistes, especially Ray Milland! We didn't have a tremendous amount of money, so Pinewood became everything and every-where, and what we couldn't do at the studio we did in the near vicinity.'

Teddy Joseph was production supervisor on the film and vividly recalls the final sequence, in which Howerd is seen digging up a meadow in search of buried treasure. 'We used Langley Park [adjacent to Black Park, but minus the trees], and had use of a helicopter to achieve the effect of pulling away and revealing just how vast the meadow was. We cleared things with Heathrow and all was set. However, Frankie came over to me, looking quite worried. "Teddy," he said, "nobody knows this, but I wear a toupée." Well, everybody knew that the damn nest on his head was a wig but he sincerely believed he'd succeeded in keeping it a secret. Anyway, rather than upset him, I feigned ignorance. "I'm a bit concerned about this helicopter," he continued. "It'll be going up and down, in and out, and creating a fair bit of wind." "Yes…" I said. "Well, my toupée might blow off." By now I was biting my tongue, and my young son and his friends, who were watching the shooting that day, were in hysterics. But we arranged things so that the helicopter took off down-wind, limiting the "effects" around Frankie. Secretly, though, we were all hoping his piece would blow off and even taking bets on it!'

Into 1973, and television continued to play an increasingly important role, the studio playing host to Peter Hunt's *Gulliver's Travels*, in which Richard Harris shared the screen with cartoon Lilliputians; *Applause*, which teamed American stars Lauren Bacall and Larry Hagman; the ambitious *QB VII*, directed by Tom Gries with an all-star cast including Anthony Hopkins, Ben Gazzara, Leslie Caron, Anthony Quayle and Lee Remick; *Frankenstein: The True Story*, an epic reinterpretation of the horror classic by Christopher Isherwood which played theatrically in the UK, and *The Zoo Gang* series with John Mills, Lilli Palmer, Brian Keith and Barry Morse.

Jack Clayton, meanwhile, was busy preparing *The Great Gatsby*, starring Robert Redford and (substituting for Farrah Fawcett) Mia Farrow. With location shooting in Newport Rhode Island completed, the unit moved to Pinewood on 20 July for interior sequences. The film had been two years in preparation and *Vogue* said the movie 'caused the greatest pre-production excitement since *Gone With the Wind*.'

Sets created at Pinewood by the Oscar-laden production designer John Box included Myrtle's Riverside Drive, her room over the top of her husband's garage, Gatsby's study and bedroom, the

interior of the Buchanan home, and Gatsby's cabana and pool – which survives to this day, aptly dubbed 'The Gatsby Suite'. Attention to detail was minute. A wealth of documents on clothing, furniture, homes, hair styles and jewellery to help create the 'Gatsby look' had been accumulated over the two-year preparation period. The most publicised item was a collection of Cartier jewellery valued at $900,000.

Ten weeks of studio work were completed in October 1973, although the producers were keen that it shouldn't be apparent that a British studio had been utilised for this very American story, hence the omission of the usual 'Made at Pinewood Studios' credit. The film was not well received ('pays its creator the regrettable tribute of erecting a mausoleum over his work,' was one choice response), but Nelson Riddle won an Academy Award for his score.

Freddie Francis kicked off 1974 with *The Ghoul*, a 1920s-set shocker starring Peter Cushing, John Hurt and Alexandra Bastedo which picked up some of the properties left behind by *Gatsby*. Francis followed a few months later with *The Legend of the Werewolf*, again with Peter Cushing. 'I'd made a very successful horror film for Hammer,' says Francis, referring to *Dracula Has Risen From the Grave*, 'and after that all the films I directed were horror! They weren't necessarily brilliant films, but the finished pictures always transcended the script. And that I remain very proud of. Peter Cushing was an absolute joy to work with – such a gentleman. I'll forever remember that I used to meet him at a lovely little tearoom in Charing Cross to talk about the films, and they were often quite gory subjects. Such civilised surroundings for such horrific talk!'

It was a particularly busy year for Roger Moore too. Peter Hunt directed Moore and Susannah York in *Gold*, based on the novel *Goldmine* by Wilbur Smith.

Facing page: *Alan Parker's* Bugsy Malone *presented a mean-looking bunch of pint-sized gangsters.*

Ray Milland, Bradford Dillman and John Gielgud lent support in this spectacular action-thriller with heart-stopping underground sequences. Moore then did a quick change into his tuxedo for his second 007 outing, *The Man With the Golden Gun*, before once again starring with Susannah York, this time in *That Lucky Touch*, a romantic comedy set in Belgium.

Michael Tuchner directed *Mister Quilp*, a musical adaptation of *The Old Curiosity Shop* that brought Anthony Newley back to Pinewood with a Dickens classic 27 years after *Oliver Twist*, while Norman Jewison's choice for his next project couldn't have been more different from his previous Pinewood film *Fiddler on the Roof*. The advertising campaign for *Rollerball* stated that 'In the not too distant future, wars will no longer exist. But there will be Rollerball.' A grim fantasy about major corporations controlling the world in the year 2018 and channelling the public's frustrations into a brutal spectator sport, the film starred James Caan, Ralph Richardson and Maud Adams and went straight to the top of the British box-office charts, where it remained for three weeks before being supplanted by the Robert Redford vehicle *Three Days of the Condor*.

Perhaps inspired by the physical exertion involved in *Rollerball*, the more energetic residents of the studio joined forces in forming a Pinewood football club. Modestly successful, the club became part of the Slough Saturday League and was always cheered on from the touch-line by future managing director, Cyril Howard.

One of the most intriguing films to shoot in 1975, which was a much quieter year for the studio, came from Alan Parker and David Puttnam. The gangster *milieu* of *Bugsy Malone* was a familiar one but in this incarnation it was set to music and all the parts were played by children.

'We decided to make the film at Pinewood,' Parker points out, 'because of (a) sheer logistics – a cast of 200 kids with the need for full-time school (plus a battery of teachers) running parallel with the shoot meant we had to be in a studio situation, and (b), more pragmatically, the film was half-financed by Rank. We built our main set – a huge New York set – inside D Stage. The street was built

to two thirds scale and it was built on 4-foot rostra so that real steam could be squeezed out of the New York cobbles and manholes.

'I had tried to get the film set up for some time, visiting the offices of would-be financiers – the few that there were at the time. I was very successful in TV commercials but had no track record of anything longer than 30 seconds, so they were very suspicious of me. I explained that it was a gangster movie pastiche that would be done in a contemporary way but as a homage to old Hollywood ... er ... er ... oh, and, by the way, it has an entire cast of children. The moment they heard the last bit they used to cough and say politely "Not today thank you". Fortunately, Frank Poole at Rank Film Distributors went with it – 50 per cent anyway – with a little bit of arm twisting of the then Rank chairman Ed Chilton by Evelyn de Rothschild, all orchestrated in his inimitable way by David Puttnam, who was executive producer on the film. And Alan Marshall, who actually produced the film, performed miracles in juggling our tiny budget.

'I remember that Bryan Forbes was at the studio at the same time making *The Slipper and the Rose*. He had the best table in the restaurant and all of the studio's attention, probably because he had real money to spend. We were very much the poor relations. I think most of the studio hierarchy thought that we were nuts!

'One of the things that amused us no end when we first arrived at Pinewood was Rank's "Studio Management" table in the restaurant. At this table sat Kip Herren, a huge Mr Bumble figure, whom we younger filmmakers despised.' [A contentious point, incidentally, as Herren's popularity was formidable.] 'The table was turned around so that it faced the rest of us, like the "high table" in a pompous University dining hall. Anyway, we rented the restaurant for a ballroom set one Sunday when they weren't dining and had the run of the place for the whole day – the lunatics in charge of the asylum. At the end of the day's filming, a gaffer taped a very large Camembert cheese to the underside of the aforementioned table. For many weeks we could all smell it. People would give a wide berth to the top table as they looked towards

the puzzled occupants, wondering why these gentlemen all ponged in such elegant surroundings!

'It was a marvellous restaurant though, and I have wonderful memories of lunching there with people in powdered wigs and crinolines, Christopher Reeve in his Superman costume with a napkin at his neck sitting at my table for a chat after lunch, and David Lean coming up and wondering "Alan, why do you keep making films in America?' He always articulated the word "America" with such disdain, like someone describing the emanation of a leaking sewer.'

The kids, including *Happy Days*' Scott Baio and future Oscar-winner Jodie Foster, all had guns, but not the machine guns associated with traditional gangster pictures. Instead, they had so-called 'splurge' guns that fired custard pies in place of bullets. Attempts to devise a 'working' splurge gun, using compressed air to fire a wax-covered capsule filled with shaving foam, were abandoned when a volunteer special effects man was concussed and needed urgent medical attention. The guns fired table tennis balls instead; as Parker puts it, 'on the cut – trusting to the illusion of editing on film – I would have propmen throw a handful of whipped cream at the poor child's face.' Over 1,000 custard pies were thrown in the film and prop master John Luenberger got through 100 gallons of synthetic cream. The pedal-driven cars in the film managed a respectable 10 mph and were custom-built by hand. In fact, each one cost as much to make as a regular road-going Mini.

Nearly 10,000 children were interviewed for the film and the auditions alone amounted to 20 hours of video tape. Casting ranged from US Air Force bases in England to parochial schools in Brooklyn, the Bronx and Harlem and downtown dancing schools in Hollywood. The dancing girls alone were chosen after seeing and taping over 100 different Christmas shows at dancing schools in Britain. The lucky short-listed ones competed in semi-finals in Leeds and London, but there were only nine that could be picked and producer Alan Marshall had the unenviable job of telling the unsuccessful ones – or, worse still, their mothers.

To cater for all the American visitors,

Pinewood's cafeteria provided some 200 hamburgers a day. Apart from American kids drawn from England, New York and Los Angeles, French and German schools were visited (for journalists), Chinese schools (for laundry workers), Irish schools (for a priest), as well as boxing, drama and stage schools. The paperwork involved was mountainous. Every child had to have a separate working licence and medical approval. Over 33 local councils in England were involved, not to mention their counterparts in New York and Los Angeles.

Parker's company, The Alan Parker Film Company, later based itself at the studio – where it remained for 10 years – in one of the bungalows in the gardens, originally built as a schoolroom. 'Outside it resembled a rather ugly 1950s public lavatory,' Parker recalls, 'but inside we had wonderful views of the gardens and, most importantly, we were completely self-contained. We had, in effect, the equivalent of a bungalow at a Hollywood studio. In fact, the only one in the entire British film industry! Pinewood is a wonderful studio. It's the best studio we've ever had in the UK and hopefully will continue to be so in the future. Every time I drive through the gates I get a tingle. I had many happy years there.'

The Slipper and the Rose was a modern re-telling of the Cinderella story, produced by Stuart Lyons and David Frost and directed by Bryan Forbes. According to production supervisor Peter Manley, 'The picture was set up at Pinewood (after initially starting out at Shepperton) because that was the best situation and studio for a musical of this scale. When the Sherman Brothers first came over with the story outline and the music demo tracks, we spent a long time in development and preparation at the studio. The first location scenes were shot in the winter over in Austria, for about three weeks, and we then came back to Pinewood for some of the interiors, music work etc. When the weather improved, we returned to Austria for some spring sequences. It was then back to the studio and those lovely sets designed by Ray Simm. One of the largest of which was on E Stage, and you must remember the cast were wearing rather heavy period costumes, and under the intense lights it became rather hot to say the least! In fact, it became quite unbearable and we had to arrange to bring in air conditioning.'

It was a particularly memorable film for Bryan Forbes, as it was not only his one and only musical but was also the occasion, while shooting the snow sequences in the Austrian Alps, of a major health scare. Back in London, he had been told that he had multiple sclerosis. The very next day he was scheduled to shoot one of the film's musical numbers in the presence of a Royal party consisting of Her Majesty Queen Elizabeth the Queen Mother, Princess Margaret and her children. The day went without a hitch and Forbes himself refused to accept the inevitable. He battled on and a self-administered treatment – a special diet – has seen him enjoy a period of remission to this day. He continued his work on *The Slipper and the Rose* and was rewarded with the honour of the film being selected as the Royal Film Performance.

At the Earth's Core came from the producer-director team of John Dark and Kevin Connor and kicked off Pinewood's production schedule in 1976. Peter Cushing re-teamed with the duo – their first film together had been *From Beyond the Grave* at Shepperton – and Doug McClure was cast in the first of several adventures he would make with the filmmakers at Pinewood. Based on Edgar Rice Burroughs's novel of the same name, and adapted by Milton Subotsky, the *Boy's Own*-style adventure takes us, appropriately enough, to the centre of the earth by means of a miraculous

giant drill, or geological excavator to give it its technical title. There the intrepid explorers encounter prehistoric people and monsters. Peter Cushing's umbrella helps save the day.

'I first worked at Pinewood as a second assistant editor, on two pictures – *An Alligator Named Daisy* and *Jumping For Joy* – back in 1952,' recalls Kevin Connor, 'and, to be honest, it wasn't a particularly happy experience as the cutting rooms had a very snobbish "old boys" atmosphere and attitude. When I returned to direct my first feature at Pinewood, having moved over from Shepperton (which was being asset-stripped at the time), that atmosphere had gone; mainly, I guess, due to the fact that it wasn't just Rank product and Rank staff anymore; the renters had changed all that. It was a delightful experience this time round and it was the first of many times I returned with a picture.'

By this time the Pinewood-based *Carry On* films were running out of steam. There was also a question mark hanging over the studio's other successful franchise, 007. After lengthy negotiations and legal wrangles over the ownership of Bond –

not to mention a couple of years' absence from the big screen – Cubby Broccoli returned to Pinewood with his most ambitious Bond yet, minus his old partner Harry Saltzman. *The Spy Who Loved Me* was Roger Moore's third, and some say definitive, 007 adventure and also changed the landscape of the studio with the construction of the 007 Stage, described in full in Chapter Ten.

Classic television next came to Pinewood in the shape of *The New Avengers*. One of the most popular series of the 1960s, *The Avengers* had seen Patrick Macnee's sophisticated John Steed partnered in turn by Ian Hendry, Honor Blackman, Diana Rigg and Linda Thorson. The last episode was broadcast in 1969, with Steed and Tara King (Thorson) being unwittingly blasted into outer space. Their boss turned to camera and said 'They'll be back ... you can depend on it!'

The new series came about following a French TV commercial for champagne, for which Macnee and Thorson were engaged to resurrect their *Avengers* characters. The commercial's producer, Rudolph Raffi, then struck a deal with the show's

Facing page: *Peter Cushing as the absent-minded boffin Dr Abner Perry in* At the Earth's Core.

Left: *John Steed (Patrick Macnee) and his new helpers Purdey (Joanna Lumley) and Gambit (Gareth Hunt) in* The New Avengers.

producers, Brian Clemens and Albert Fennell, to make a new series. The original series had been shot at Elstree Studios, and the choice of Pinewood for the new project may well have been influenced by the fact that Fennell's brother Jack was studio manager.

This time, Macnee was to have two assistants; he was now 53 and the producers accordingly introduced a younger male colleague alongside the traditional female. Auditions for the two parts took place at Pinewood on 20 January 1976, with further tests for the short-listed applicants a week later. Among the many hopefuls were Cassandra Harris (later to marry Pierce Brosnan), Jan Harvey, Jan Francis and Diana Quick. The role finally went to Joanna Lumley, who suggested that her character's name be changed from Charlie to Purdey. Gareth Hunt, meanwhile, withstood stiff competition from Lewis Collins, Michael Elphick and John Nettles for the part of Mike Gambit. In the book *The Ultimate Avengers*, Brian Clemens commented: 'The interesting thing about the auditions is that we put a girl and boy opposite each other and it

was purely coincidental that Gareth tested opposite Jo. We took them both.'

Filming commenced in April 1976. The series was to run for 26 episodes, filmed in batches of 13. After the first 13 were completed, a short break was taken during which time the show's French backers indicated that they weren't entirely happy. They complained that Joanna Lumley's character wasn't sexy enough. As fashion and style were an important part of the *Avengers* appeal, Lumley had created the now famous 'Purdey bob' hairstyle, but the French wanted a more sultry look and insisted that she wear French designs in the remaining 13 episodes. Furthermore, they wanted more violence – a controversial point that didn't go down well with either the producers or the fans.

The especially disappointing news for Pinewood, however, was that the French insisted several episodes be filmed in France, and another four in Canada. To help get the series off the ground, Pinewood had done a deal whereby they offered stage space in return for a percentage of the profits, so this new situation was unsatisfactory in the extreme. The changes were implemented nevertheless, but the second series lost out in the ratings, owing to scheduling problems but also to the unpopularity of the new 'look'.

Along with *The New Avengers*, Gerry and Sylvia Anderson's *Space: 1999* helped keep the studio ticking over towards the end of its 40th year, which was not only one of the leanest ever but also the year of managing director Kip Herren's untimely death. The previous year had seen the studio lose some £450,000 and the industry didn't show any signs of picking up, particularly with the double taxation convention with the USA looming large. Taxation had already made life difficult when *Equus* was lost to Canada, after the film had been prepared at Pinewood. Redundancies were unavoidable. Pinewood's labour force was cut from 1,483 to just 700, and rumours were rife that the Rank Organisation was intent on selling off the studio.

When Kip Herren suddenly died, Cyril Howard stepped in as acting managing director at what must have been a very difficult time both on a personal and business level. Soon afterwards he

Right: *Cyril Howard and Pinewood's best customer, Cubby Broccoli. Note his famous number plate.*

Facing page: *David Tomlinson (and friend) in Lionel Jeffries'* **Wombling Free.**

took on the role permanently, having progressed, as he puts it, from general gopher to managing director in 'just 30 years!'

Given the volatile production environment at the time, Howard was horrified when called into the boardroom to see Rank's new chairman Ed Chilton. '"Cyril", he said, "I've decided that we're going back into film financing, and the first project will be *Wombling Free*." I just stood there and thought "You're bloody mad." I honestly couldn't believe what I was hearing.'

There was a big publicity launch detailing how the Organisation was embarking upon a new and exciting production programme. Lionel Jeffries, meanwhile, was brought in to helm *Wombling Free*, based on the children's TV series about cuddly rubbish collectors resident in warrens beneath Wimbledon Common. 'Don't talk to me about that film!' he exclaims. 'It ought to have been flushed down the lavatory. It was a horrible experience and the producer was on the floor every day criticising the set-ups whenever I wasn't looking. It wasn't a happy experience and it was a terrible flop.' Indeed, the film failed to receive a general release.

Ed Chilton used to visit the studio every Friday and on one occasion he blithely asked Cyril Howard to introduce a studio tour. ('That's how he was,' says Howard. 'He was a lovely man, but he'd just think of something and as far as he was concerned that was it.') Plans were set in motion for the tour, which took place over a weekend in July 1977. Howard contacted the local press about the event and took the opportunity of picking their brains as to the sort of turnout the studio could expect.

'They said that similar events usually drew about 5,000 people. In fact, 40,000 turned up! A frightening experience. All we charged was £1 a car. As the day wore on we realised just how overwhelmed we had become. Farmers' fields in the area were opened and duly filled with cars, and the local roads were blocked with parked cars, in fact even the main motorways in the area suffered heavy jams. Many of the special guests, including Roger Moore, couldn't get near the studio and just ended up turning round and going home. It was chaotic

to say the least. Eventually, the police turned up and asked what we were going to do about all the crowds. I was full of abject apologies and informed them that it was our first attempt at this sort of thing – and it was for charity. That sort of swayed them and they left saying "Well, don't do it again!"'

They did do it again, however, in August 1982. Only this time, as Cyril Howard explains, a higher admission price was imposed. "We charged £25 per car, limiting it to 600 cars and everyone received a lunch box in the price. It was glorious weather and we were very fortunate in that respect, because people could wander around and then stroll into the gardens with their picnic lunches and so on. It was certainly better planned and handled than the first time around, but I wouldn't advise any potential managing director keen to make his name to introduce studio tours!"

Kevin Connor and John Dark returned with two productions in 1977, *The People That Time Forgot* and *Warlords of Atlantis*. Meanwhile *The New Avengers* kept the studio ticking over. Times were tough, but Pinewood's fortunes then took a dramatic change for the better when the phone rang and in flew *Superman*. (See Chapter Thirteen for the full story.)

The last film to lens in 1977 came from Bryan Forbes and was a belated sequel to the 1944 classic *National Velvet*. *International Velvet* was the story of how a hostile orphan becomes an accomplished international horsewoman. Tatum O'Neal played the orphan, while Anthony Hopkins,

Nanette Newman, Christopher Plummer and Dinsdale Landen took on the adult roles. O'Neal had been unfairly dubbed 'Tantrum O'Neal' but turned out to be a consummate professional, always on time, knowing all her lines and bursting with enthusiasm. She even performed most of the film's cross-country riding.

For a sequence involving the transportation of five horses by plane, a replica of a cargo jet was built at the studio. Four of the horses were housed in rigid stalls but the fifth was not, for this horse was required to literally kick up a fuss. His stall was made of less rigid material so that it would come apart without hurting him. A jet of compressed air was fired at the stallion's testicles by John Oram, who was concealed in the stall. It did the trick but once the horse had a taste for demolishing his stall, he continued on the rest of the set. Anthony Hopkins, who was on set at the time, jumped to safety and vowed never to return. The horse took some 15 minutes to calm down and, not suprisingly, no second take was called for.

Rank's new production programme continued and in 1978 another remake of *The 39 Steps* went before the cameras. This version starred Robert Powell, John Mills, Eric Porter, David Warner and Karen Dotrice. The steps in this version are the multiple flights of stairs leading to the tower of Big Ben, where the film's climactic scenes take place, for which a full-scale replica of Big Ben's clockface was constructed. Another Rank remake followed, this time of Hitchcock's *The Lady Vanishes*. An international cast was assembled by director Anthony Page, including Cybill Shepherd, Elliot Gould, Angela Lansbury, Herbert Lom and Arthur Lowe, but not even they could save the film from box-office disaster or grant it an American release. This was the last film to date to bear the famous Hammer stamp.

The Rank production programme was abandoned after just a few more films: *Riddle of the Sands*, the Western *Eagle's Wing* and the aptly titled *Bad Timing*. Some £10m had been spent and only a small proportion recouped. Soon afterwards, Ed Chilton resigned as chairman.

Sean Connery's next picture at Pinewood nearly wasn't. *The First Great Train Robbery* was put to Connery after he completed *A Bridge Too Far* but

he turned it down. The film's director and screenwriter, Michael Crichton, then rewrote the script to Connery's satisfaction, but when it was announced that filming was to take place at Pinewood, Connery had to withdraw from the project. The tax laws were such that had he worked in the UK for more than a token number of days he would effectively have been making the film for nothing.

After extensive recces, the production team decided that they couldn't recreate the film's Victorian period in English locations. The answer was found over the Irish Sea and period trains were donated and manned by the Railway Preservation Society. Upon hearing of the move, Connery rejoined the project. Eight weeks in Ireland were followed by carefully scheduled interiors at Pinewood, along with use of the gardens and mansion.

The unfavourable tax laws also saw one of Pinewood's most faithful customers move out. Cubby Broccoli announced that he was relocating to Paris, and along with him he was taking the next Bond film, *Moonraker*. A farewell party was thrown at the studio and emotions were running very high. In the event, Derek Meddings' model department on *Moonraker* utilised the studio considerably.

Superman II was underway at the start of 1979

Facing page: *Cybill Shepherd and Elliott*
Gould in Hammer's 1979 re-make of
The Lady Vanishes.

under the direction of Richard Lester while *Clash of the Titans* was the latest fantasy epic from stop-motion master Ray Harryhausen. Harry Hamlin, now best known for his role in the TV series *LA Law*, was cast as Perseus in this ambitious retelling of the Greek legend. Speaking to *Film Review* magazine, he particularly remembered the lunches at the studio. 'The lunches were daunting. There would be six or seven of us sitting around a table, with Maggie Smith dominating the conversation. She is so fast and witty, and so cutting as well. So with Laurence Olivier also there, I felt very under-staffed in the brainwave department!'

The scenes featuring the Gods – Olivier as Zeus, Ursula Andress as Aphrodite, Maggie Smith as Thetis and Jack Gwillim as Poseidon – were filmed at Pinewood in about a week. No such luxury for Harryhausen and his special effects team, whose patient and painstaking work meant that they were still at the studio in early 1981. Though critically mauled, the film was a box-office success, collecting around $100 million. A sequel, called *Force of the Trojans,* was planned and a production team occupied offices at Pinewood, but a change in management at Columbia-TriStar saw the project scrapped.

British-born Andrew V McLaglen's first film in London had been Euan Lloyd's production, *The Wild Geese* (1978), based at Twickenham Film Studios. His next project, again with Roger Moore, was *North Sea Hijack*, a thriller co-starring Anthony Perkins and James Mason.

'The locations were completed around Galway,' recalls McLaglen, 'and we then pulled back to Pinewood for interiors. The boat which Tony Perkins hijacks, *Ruth*, was supposed to be swishing and swaying around the North Sea, and so to film interiors we set the boat on rockers on one of the stages. It was very effective. All the long and approach shots of the boat and oil rigs were actually achieved with miniatures, as was the helicopter landing on the rig, out on the paddock tank. John Richardson headed the special effects team and I challenge anyone to notice that the rigs were models!' (Keen-eyed viewers will also notice that the Prime Minister's office is actually the Green Room.)

'It was a very enjoyable shoot, and I particularly remember Roger feeling very much at home. But then, with all those baronial lunches in the restaurant, we all felt at home! Regrettably I only returned to the studio with one more picture, and that was for post-production work on *Return to the River Kwai*.'

After dissolving his partnership with Cubby Broccoli, Harry Saltzman made a film which couldn't have been more different from those with which he had been previously associated. Starring Alan Bates and Alan Badel among others, *Nijinsky* was a study of the dancer's complex relationship with his mentor Diaghilev. Saltzman made only one further film, the little seen *Dom Za Vesanje* (1989), before his death in 1994.

David Wickes' *Silver Dream Racer* was one of the last films in which Rank invested before abandoning their new film financing initiative. Like the others before it, it proved less than successful. The story follows a garage mechanic (David Essex) who dreams of becoming a motorcycle racer only to be killed at the peak of his career.

The year in which the studio hosted Rank's last feature also saw the end of its 27-year-old association with Walt Disney. Disney's last Pinewood film was *The Watcher in the Woods*. It was also Bette Davis's last feature at the studio, and one on which she held an unprecedented press conference for all the local papers, whose representatives couldn't believe their luck at being invited to the Green Room to meet the Hollywood superstar. Directed by John Hough, the picture was an unusual departure for Disney in that they tried to combine the family cuteness of earlier films with Hammer-style horror. In an attempt to appeal to a wider audience, they alienated their most loyal. The balance wasn't successfully struck and the film received only a limited release. Two years later, having had additional sequences shot by Vincent McEveety and after some heavy re-editing, the film was re-released (some 15 minutes shorter) but fared just as poorly.

Pinewood ended its fifth decade in a reasonably healthy but somewhat precarious state. One thing was certain, however – the road ahead would not be smooth. ■

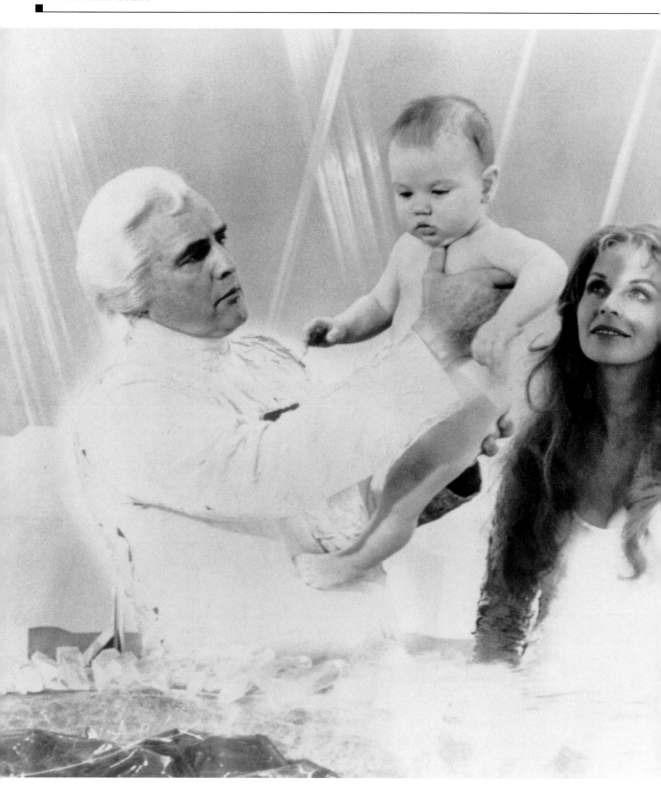

13 SUPERMAN, SAVIOUR O

If there is one fictional character who has come to symbolise the USA, then it is Superman. He has not only come to represent 'the American way' but also, of course, is regularly called upon to save the world. Dubbed 'The Man of Steel', the character was created by Jerry Siegel and Joe Shuster and made his 1938 début in *Action Comics* No.1, which now changes hands at auction for over $50,000. Superman's popularity remained huge and he was certainly king of the comics, with only Batman as a serious rival. And when it was announced in 1974 that Superman was about to get the big screen treatment, it was clear that the producers – Alexander & Ilya Salkind and Pierre Spengler – were aiming to make him king of the movies too.

Up until then, Superman's screen exploits had been largely confined to modestly budgeted outings. Kirk Alyn portrayed the comic book hero in a popular movie serial of 1948 which led to a feature called *Superman and the Mole Men* starring George Reeves. A hugely popular TV series followed in the 1950s, again starring Reeves. Though these remained popular, the notion of a Superman film incorporating all the latest special effects and technology proved extremely exciting to fans. Anticipation was intense.

Getting the film off the ground proved far more complicated than anyone initially imagined. To begin with, there were numerous copyright problems that had to be overcome, with script approval eventually becoming part of the deal with Superman's owners, National Periodical Publications. Then there was the sheer size of the production to think about and, not least, the casting of Superman himself. Fortunately, the producers were riding the crest of a commercial wave with their box-office smash *The Three Musketeers*, and early in pre-production Guy Hamilton was announced as director.

Unfortunately, logistical problems hampered progress in Britain and, at one point, the decision was taken to move the film to Rome. When this proved unsuitable, the team returned to Britain, only for Hamilton to refuse to work there thanks to recently introduced taxation laws. He accordingly left the production but cannily retained his fee. Many other directors were considered, and eventually the producers decided on an American, Richard Donner, who was soon to score a big hit with the supernatural thriller *The Omen*. Steven Spielberg's asking price, incidentally, had been considered too high for a director who had yet to justify such a fee. The release of *Jaws* soon afterwards changed his industry profile considerably.

At last, in 1976, the picture was beginning to take shape. The signing of Marlon Brando to play Superman's father Jor-El, for a reported $3 million, caused a sensation and stories were rife of how such huge fees were likely to sink the production. When Gene Hackman was cast as Lex Luthor, the press began to wonder what would be left to pay the actor playing Superman himself. Big names were considered for the role, including Robert Redford, Clint Eastwood, Steve McQueen, Nick Nolte and Kris Kristofferson. Ilya Salkind's wife even proposed her dentist.

Eventually, a relatively unknown actor, Christopher Reeve, was cast as Superman. Donner initially felt he was too young at 24, but once Reeve had beefed himself up and visited make-up and costume, he was declared the perfect Superman. He could play the dashing hero one moment and then switch deftly to his unsure, bumbling alter ego Clark Kent. 'I didn't find him,' enthused Donner. 'God gave him to me! He looks more like Superman than Superman, and more like Clark Kent than Clark Kent does.'

Superman – The Movie was intended to be the first in a long-running series. In typical Salkind fashion, part of the first sequel was to be filmed

HE WORLD (AND PINEWOOD)

at the same time, which meant existing sets could be utilised and actors' salaries minimised. Salkind had recently done this with the sequel to *The Three Musketeers*, much to the displeasure of certain actors who realised too late that they had unwittingly made two films for the price of one.

The first day of shooting on *Superman* took place at Shepperton Studios on 28 March 1977. But the production had grown in size dramatically and it soon became apparent that Shepperton alone wasn't big enough to accommodate the blockbuster. By May, production had fallen two weeks behind schedule and there was talk of a rift developing between Donner and the producers. The decision was then taken to move everything to Europe's premier studio – Pinewood.

Without a Bond film in the works and nothing else on the horizon, the production came at just the right time for Pinewood, as former MD Cyril Howard recalls. 'We were going down the Swanee and I was paddling the canoe. Then the phone rang and it was *Superman*. We'd turned the film away once before, because of the last Bond film being in. The producers then went off to Italy, and then back to England and Shepperton, but the complex wasn't big enough for their needs. This time I welcomed them with open arms.'

E Stage became the offices of the *Daily Planet*, the newspaper which Clark Kent and Lois Lane (Margot Kidder) work for. It was constructed with such attention to detail that American office equipment was brought in by the ton for realism. Officially the schedule allocated two weeks to complete the scenes on these sets, but the sequences became more complicated than originally envisaged and the shoot stretched to five weeks.

Delays became unavoidable when the casting of the newspaper editor, Perry White, was plunged into turmoil. Jack Klugman pulled out two days before he was due to start and a panic set in to find a replacement. Veteran actor Keenan Wynn was then signed up, but just before shooting the 61-year-old actor collapsed from exhaustion and was rushed to a London hospital. He was declared unfit to resume work and TV star Jackie Cooper took over, literally being thrust straight in front of the cameras.

Furthermore, the huge lights on the stage placed tremendous demands on the studio generators, leading eventually to a power cut on the main line to Iver. The production was granted an extra day free of charge by Pinewood, but the intense heat of the lights then saw temperatures rise to 100 degrees, causing the emergency sprinkler systems to be activated. Not only were the cast and crew doused, but some of the sets and set dressings were damaged. So struck again the so-called 'curse of Superman'.

With the picture falling alarmingly behind schedule, Pierre Spengler blamed Donner's over-attention to detail and a serious argument ensued.

Rumours swept round the studio that Donner was to be replaced, and tensions were not alleviated by the many difficulties experienced by the special effects team in devising the flying sequences – an essential element to the film's success. When the director of *The Three Musketeers*, Richard Lester, was brought in as a producer, it seemed Donner's days were numbered, but Lester's arrival seemed to calm things down, provided a vital neutral ground through which the two parties could communicate. During all this, *Superman II* was already underway and the pressure was on for super-salary stars like Brando and Hackman to complete their scenes early in the schedule.

D Stage was converted into 'Luthor's Lair', an impressive set which was split into five divisions: a sundecked patio area, a study, a major and minor set of control rooms complete with banks of computers and dials, and – the focal point – an indoor swimming pool at the foot of a marble staircase.

Derek Meddings, a leading expert in miniature special effects, was called upon to film complete sequences. Among them he recreated the Golden Gate Bridge on the backlot, and in *American Cinematographer* he explained that 'Our Golden Gate Bridge is 60 feet wide – hardly "miniature" in terms of actual size but decidedly so in comparison to the size of the real thing. In this case the bridge had to partially collapse in an earthquake. We also put Superman up on a wire and flew him towards the bridge as it starts to break up. So Chris [Reeve] was full size but the bridge was miniature – all in the same shot. The camera was set up so that Chris was really a long, long way from the bridge. For the opening sequence, at the climax of which planet Krypton is destroyed, we built a very large miniature which filled F Stage at Pinewood. It was about 20 feet off the ground, because it had deep gullies in it and we had to go down in amongst them and track along the sides of them as the place was falling to pieces.'

Another exciting sequence was the bursting of the Boulder Dam, which was shot on the paddock tank. The set was faithfully recreated from establishing shots of the real dam. 'What I wanted the audience to see were the shots of the dam actually bursting,' Meddings continued. 'What we did was to get about six huge water pumps and we pumped the water from the paddock tank up to the level of the dam, then we constructed a platform made of

Right: *Christopher Reeve as Superman's alter ego, mild-mannered reporter Clark Kent.*

Bottom right: *The crumbling Statue of Liberty prop, abandoned on the Pinewood lot.*

aluminium so that when the dam burst, the water pumped over the edge. It continued to pump a huge volume of water without the level dropping – which meant that we could hold the shot for long enough to show the water bursting through the dam and flooding the valley below.'

The 007 Stage housed the breathtaking – and decidedly cold – Fortress of Solitude, or 'Ice Palace' as some people called it. Production designer John Barry had filled the stage with glaciers and jagged ice peaks. Dendritic dairy salt was used to create the sparkling snowbound effect at a cost of $6,000. A final touch was added with fog machines and mountains of dry ice, providing an appropriately weird and barren atmosphere for the north pole setting. It was, however, an uncomfortable set to work on. A typically cold British autumn, and the long drawn-out process of shooting, made the crew restless and irritable. They demanded additional pay and threatened to walk out if their demands weren't met. Eventually they were appeased when invited to a 30-minute screening in Theatre 7 of the promotional reel. It was the crew's first peek at the footage that had taken seven months to shoot. They left full of enthusiasm and forgot all about the planned walkout.

The crew's belief in the film was justified by its eventual box-office returns. *Superman – The Movie* was a massive success, and the rest of *Superman II* was accordingly lined up for shooting. Although, technically speaking, Donner had directed some of the sequel already, he left the series and was replaced by Richard Lester.

Many of the flying sequences had already been completed, but others proved difficult and dangerous. Stuntman Paul Weston fell 40 feet to the floor on A Stage when one of the wires supporting him snapped, and he missed the mattress. Thankfully he was not seriously injured.

Roy Field was creative supervisor of the optical visual effects and said of the flying, 'It was a combination of many tricks, and the essence of its working is the fact that we have used so many processes. That and always being prepared with another back-up system in case one process looks as though it is going to fail.' Both Roy Field and

Derek Meddings won Oscars for their work on the film. Meddings' statuette takes pride of place in Pinewood's reception hall.

In addition to optical effects, hydraulics, cranes and wires were all used at various points to create the illusion that Superman was flying through the air. Colin Chilvers was the creative director of the special effects. 'We had to use a crane 250 feet high in order to get it out of shot when we were flying Chris on wires. We devised rigs that would give us complete control over Chris while he was up in the air. We built rigs to fly Superman against front and back projection and so on.'

'On one of the many night shoots out on the

Left: *The all-powerful crystals hold the answers in* Superman II.

backlot,' recalls Richard Lester, 'I spent absolutely ages in arranging one of these sequences and was using a large crane when, down below, I noticed one of the food wagons had caught fire. Within seconds, that was the centre of attention and it proved to be far more interesting than my set-up.' Tragedy struck again when a metal worker, Terry Hill, was killed when he was crushed under the wing of a mock-up plane which collapsed. The so-called curse went on to claim yet more victims, as shortly after the first film's release cinematographer Geoffrey Unsworth died of a sudden heart attack.

Pinewood was used extensively for *Superman II* throughout 1979, and a gigantic Manhattan street was built on the backlot – cue car crashes, mass destruction and a huge tanker explosion – but the splendour, spectacle and excitement of the first picture was difficult to match. A third outing was swiftly prepared and went into production in 1982.

'My ever-lasting memory of the Superman films – and I worked on the first three,' says Richard Lester, 'were the sports leagues at the studio. You see, we had up to four units shooting simultaneously and were on most stages. There were competitions set up by each unit for badminton, table tennis, darts ...

and I think it would be fair to say there was more sports activity than filming on some stages!'

Salkind expanded the super-hero franchise further when he brought *Supergirl* to the studio in 1983. Helen Slater portrayed Superman's niece and Faye Dunaway the villain of the piece. Jeannot Szwarc directed – and Derek Meddings and John Evans excelled themselves with the flying sequences, which many critics agreed were the best yet – but the film's mix of fantasy and hocus pocus, hammed up for comic effect, resulted in a disappointing box-office reception.

Production designer Richard Macdonald made the headlines, however, when the *Daily Mail* proclaimed HOW SUPERGIRL CHANGED THE FACE OF BRITAIN. Macdonald had transformed the Pinewood backlot into mid-west America at a cost of £250,000 and the newspaper reported that 'Aerial and ground shots display, quite startlingly, the production designer's art and Pinewood's scope, as "Main Street, Mid Vale, Illinois" stretches across ten acres complete with Popeye's Famous Fried Chicken and Biscuit Parlour and The Little Chapel of The Roses.' It's said that Cyril Howard framed a copy of this article, hanging it on his office wall for many years, so proud was he that Pinewood's expertise had made such big news.

With plans for a third sequel underway, Pinewood was again in the frame for its base. However, in 1986 the Cannon Group (Menahem Golan and Yoram Globus) bought the rights to the franchise and decided to house the fourth outing for Christopher Reeve's super-hero at their newly acquired Elstree Studios in Borehamwood – a great blow to Pinewood. Just as Shepperton had been unable to fully accommodate the first Superman movie, Elstree struggled too, so a substantial part of the production was moved into Pinewood after all. *Superman IV – The Quest For Peace* was the last in the series.

For many of the lean years, Superman helped sustain Pinewood with regular business and almost certainly saved the studio from financial crisis in the late 1970s. And with rumours circulating about a new Superman movie, perhaps the time will come when 'The Man of Steel' flies at Pinewood once more. ■

14 PINEWOOD GOE

1980 kicked off with one of the most disastrous films ever made. An epic 'cattlemen vs immigrants' Western, *Heaven's Gate* was written, produced and directed by Michael Cimino, fresh from the tremendous success of *The Deer Hunter*. He was virtually given a blank cheque to make the film, plus a cast to die for (Kris Kristofferson, Christopher Walken, John Hurt, Sam Waterstone, Joseph Cotten and Jeff Bridges), and the bloated result brought United Artists to its knees.

It wouldn't have been so bad had it been half the success of Cimino's first feature, but the picture was savagely lampooned by the critics and failed miserably. It cost $36m – three times its original budget – after having been re-edited in the wake of a disastrous première. 'The trade must marvel that directors now have such power that no one, in the endless months since work on the picture began, was able to impose some structure and sense,' opined *Variety*. While, according to the *New York Times*, 'It fails so completely that you might suspect Mr Cimino sold his soul to the Devil to obtain the success of *The Deer Hunter*, and the Devil has just come around to collect.'

It is said that *Heaven's Gate* is probably the most talked about and least seen film ever made. Several sequences were shot at Pinewood and, despite the swift burial given the film itself, its effects were still being felt some time later, as Teddy Joseph, then head of UA's production interests in London, can testify. 'I thought it was much better to move the production arm of UA out to Pinewood, rather than being based at Mortimer Street with the distribution people, like Warner Bros were. So in the mid seventies we moved into the old house, next door to Peter Rogers. I thought I was going to retire there! It was absolutely marvellous. However, one day after the *Heaven's Gate* fiasco, I received a phone call from MGM – we'd been told that they were going to take us over – and the head of production told me to clear my desk by Friday. I argued that I had six months to run on my contract, but he didn't care and said MGM were taking over UA and all production was being closed down. And that was that.'

Peter Hyams' *Outland*, one of the next pictures to roll at the studio, starred Sean Connery and was dubbed 'High Noon in Space', much to the displeasure of *High Noon*'s director Fred Zinnemann. Pinewood played host to the entire film, and a spectacular model of Jupiter's moon Io was built by Martin Bower, Bill Pearson and John Stears. Eighteen feet long, it contained more than four miles of fibre optics. Other sets included a gigantic greenhouse and the exterior of a mine camp, which towered above the planet's sands.

Peter Boyle, Frances Sternhagen, Steven Berkoff and John Ratzenberger provided support. Again, however, Connery felt the brunt of British tax laws and was forced to fly out of the country every weekend to comply with the '90-day stay' requirements. 'They seem to be more flexible with villains who break the law,' he said. Towards the end of production, it looked as if he wouldn't have enough time left to finish the film, but his pleas for revision of the laws in respect to people in the film industry met with no sympathy. The film was completed in time, however, and opened to very positive reviews. Its box-office returns were disappointing, though.

The last feature in the lean production year of 1980 was the new Bond adventure, *For Your Eyes Only*, which saw Roger Moore return to a more down-to-earth plotline after *Moonraker*'s sojourn in outer space. A new director, in the shape of former editor and second unit director John Glen, took the reins and made extensive use of the paddock tank (for the *St George*'s sinking sequence) and, just a few miles from the studio, Stoke Poges churchyard (for the grave of Bond's wife Tracy in

OMMERCIAL (The 1980s)

the pre-credit sequence).

1981 fared even worse than the previous year, with only four productions, two of them for TV. First up was Blake Edwards' *Victor/Victoria*, a remake of the 1933 German film *Viktor und Viktoria* by Rheinhold Schünzel and Hans Homburg. Described as 'a musical boudoir farce', Edwards' wife Julie Andrews played a British singer in Paris whose gay friend (Robert Preston) persuades her to take to the stage as a female impersonator, much to the confusion of James Garner's Chicago gangster. The film's production designer, Roger Maus, created some wonderfully colourful sets; particularly impressive was the one contained on E Stage.

Douglas Camfield's version of *Ivanhoe* with James Mason and Anthony Andrews was the first TV movie of the year, swiftly followed by Michael Tuchner's *The Hunchback of Notre Dame* with Anthony Hopkins, Lesley Anne Down and John Gielgud. 'We had a wonderful cast – and I was quite mesmerised by Lesley Anne Down. She was so beautiful!' says Tuchner. 'We recreated part of Notre

Dame cathedral on the backlot, but only to about a third of the way up; the rest was completed with some brilliant matte work. We built the town square there, too, and shot some very moving scenes there with Tony. It was a marvellous experience.'

The other theatrical feature shot at Pinewood in 1981 saw the return of Alan Parker after his success with *Bugsy Malone*. *Pink Floyd The Wall* was a disturbing and blood-spattered musical that starred Bob Geldof, Christine Hargreaves, Bob Hoskins and, of course, the powerful music of Pink Floyd.

'1982 saw the infamous terrorist attack on London's Iranian Embassy hit the headlines all over the world,' observes producer Euan Lloyd. 'I elected to make *Who Dares Wins* to mark the success of Britain's Special Forces in relieving the siege. Reginald Rose's screenplay pictured a terrorist takeover of the American Ambassador's residence, holding 50 or so dinner guests as hostages. In her first film role outside her native Australia, Judy Davis was cast as the terrorist leader. Her motives were eloquently expounded to her captive

Ambassador, played by Richard Widmark. That scene called for a sumptuous set. Equally, the exterior of the Embassy, violently attacked after the Davis-Widmark confrontation, had many critical requirements. After scouring Hertfordshire and the southern counties, production designer Syd Cain

came to me with a lifesaver: "We don't have to build either set, they exist at Pinewood."

'The façade of the old mansion and the studio's main restaurant were dressed to meet director Ian Sharp's needs. The sound of helicopter gunships, the smell of cordite, the fire and smoke did not exactly endear me to other producers at the studio, or the staff who were forced to endure the attack over a week or more. But it was a highlight of the film. In one of his rare letters, Stanley Kubrick complimented me on the realism achieved by the use of Pinewood's major set-pieces, also for the casting of Judy Davis which he described as inspirational. The picture gallery, the backlot and the construction stages all made me thankful for Syd Cain's foresight and to Mr Charles Boot for building my sets back in the 1930s!'

Lewis Collins, Ingrid Pitt, Edward Woodward and Kenneth Griffith also starred in the film and it went on to make a small fortune, according to former Rank Film Distributors MD, Fred Turner. 'Lewis Collins was very big on TV with *The Professionals*

at the time, and was massively popular with the ladies, who flocked into the cinemas. We made our money back in just a few weeks!'

Blake Edwards returned to shoot two of his Pink Panther pictures back-to-back. Sadly, Peter Sellers had died two years earlier, but Edwards decided to make the first film, *The Trail of the Pink Panther*, from previously unseen Sellers footage, with Clouseau 'disappearing' halfway through the film in a plane crash and TV reporter Joanna Lumley piecing together the mystery in his absence. Series regulars Herbert Lom and Burt Kwouk resumed their roles as Inspector Dreyfuss and Cato respectively, while further support came from David Niven and Leonard Rossiter. The second film, *The Curse of the Pink Panther*, saw Dreyfuss select the world's worst detective (Ted Wass) to replace Clouseau. Lumley, Lom, Niven and Kwouk returned along with Robert Wagner. David Niven was very ill and couldn't speak; his voice was dubbed. He died shortly after filming was completed.

Roger Moore made an uncredited appearance in *Curse* as a post-plastic surgery Clouseau. It's almost worth watching the film just to see Moore's mad five minutes.

Burt Kwouk, who got his first taste of acting in *Windom's Way* at Pinewood back in 1957 when he was thrust from being an extra into an artist with one (Malaysian) line, will forever be remembered as Clouseau's manservant Cato. 'That's on the gravestone!' confirms Kwouk. 'The Panthers were quite possibly more fun to make than to watch. I'm always asked if I was ever hurt in those sequences where I leapt out of fridges or cupboards and attacked Peter. I never was, not even a scratch! Peter was great fun. He was a very volatile character, but I always remember the light side of him – the entertaining, amusing, funny guy. He loved dressing up in disguises and putting on different voices and faces and that was always wonderful to see.'

1983 saw a sudden upturn in big television productions, including *The Last Days of Pompeii*, directed by Peter H Hunt and starring Ned Beatty, Ernest Borgnine and Lesley Anne Down with the doomed city recreated on the paddock tank; *The First Modern Olympics – 1896* with David Ogden

Steirs, Angela Lansbury and Honor Blackman; and Kevin Connor's *Master of the Game*. 'The show was based on Sidney Sheldon's book,' says Connor, 'and I directed the first half of the miniseries – Harvey Hart did the second – with Donald Pleasence and Dyan Cannon. It was my first major TV show at the studio.'

Peter Yates' next directorial assignment came with his own production of *The Dresser*, which garnered Academy Award nominations for leads Albert Finney and Tom Courtenay, Yates himself as both director and producer (ie Best Picture) and Ronald Harwood for his screenplay. Finney played the boozy 'Sir', head of a Shakespearean touring company during World War II, who is looked after by his gay dresser Norman (Courtenay). The film carries strong echoes of the famous actor-manager (and Harwood's sometime mentor) Donald Wolfit.

The last film to shoot in the year was certainly the zaniest. *Top Secret!* came from the Jerry and David Zucker/Jim Abrahams stable and, while not in quite the same league as their *Airplane*, is still very funny. Its two genre targets are the spy thriller and teen musical – cue incredible sight gags, bizarre plot twists and brilliant cameo appearances from Peter Cushing and Omar Sharif. Val Kilmer was top-billed in one of his early starring roles as an Elvis impersonator continually bursting into song given the slightest provocation.

Business started to pick up again in 1984, with several large-scale features shooting. However, it was in many ways 'too little too late'. The industry's last fully serviced studio was struggling to keep its head above water and maintain a full staff on the payroll: echoes of the late 1930s when Richard Norton set-up Pinebrook Films. A further nail in the coffin was the Conservative administration's abolition of the Eady Levy. Many foreign producers who

had previously chosen to base themselves in Britain looked elsewhere, and along with them went their films. 'I often wonder which group of "experts" Maggie Thatcher talked to when she decided to scrap the Eady Plan – a plan that had worked well in the past,' growls Bond director John Glen.

Joseph Losey returned in 1984 to direct his last film, *Steaming*, with Vanessa Redgrave, Sarah Miles and Diana Dors. Soon afterwards, Ridley Scott's fairytale sword and sorcery extravaganza *Legend* moved in, marking Tom Cruise's first visit to Pinewood. Although a visually pleasing film (winning an Academy Award nomination for best make-up), it is perhaps most significant (as described in Chapter Ten) as the picture on which the 007 Stage was destroyed just a few months before *A View To A Kill* was to make use of it.

Of the 13 features in the three-year period ending in 1986, there were many large-scale productions: as well as two Bond pictures, there were critically reviled oddities like *Morons From Outer Space* and *Santa Claus the Movie* plus totally forgotten ones like *Gunbus*. *Little Shop of Horrors* was a musical treatment of Roger Corman's 1959 black comedy from director Frank Oz and starred Rick Moranis, James Belushi, John Candy and Steve Martin. Two Oscar nominations were forthcoming,

one for best song ('Mean Green Mother From Outer Space') and the second for Best Visual Effects.

Legendary director Stanley Kubrick then brought his penultimate film, the Vietnam drama *Full Metal Jacket*, to the studio. Location work had been completed at a transformed docklands area in London and the remainder was completed at Pinewood, just under an hour's drive from the reclusive director's St Albans home. As well as taking on directorial duties, Kubrick also produced and co-adapted the screenplay with Michael Herr and Gustav Hasford, for which they received an Oscar nomination. Matthew Modine, Adam Baldwin and Lee Ermey headed an impressive cast.

The studio had been banking on the fourth *Superman* film, but when the franchise was taken over by Menahem Golan and Yoram Globus (who had recently acquired Elstree Studios), Pinewood was plunged into panic. Salvation came in the shape of another big budget film, James Cameron's *Aliens* with star Sigourney Weaver.

At this depressed time, in September 1986, the studio celebrated 50 glorious years and to mark the occasion a special luncheon was held in the grand restaurant with friends, new and old, popping in to pay tribute to the great studio. A special hour-long TV programme was made by Thames TV, which

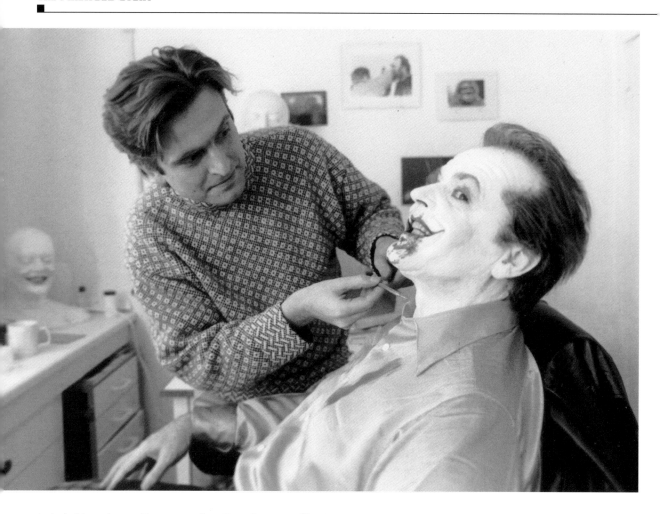

included interviews with everyone from Peter Rogers and some of the *Carry On* team to Cubby Broccoli, Bryan Forbes, Cyril Howard, Dinah Sheridan and Donald Sinden. It was also the year in which Cyril Howard was named a Commander of the British Empire in the Queen's birthday honours, in recognition of his services to the British film industry.

They say that one film does not an industry make. That was especially true post-*Aliens*, for 1987 fared very poorly indeed. A mere handful of features cranked up along with a few TV films. A further blow came when the planned production of *A Fish Called Wanda* moved elsewhere.

'The phone rang one afternoon and it was John Cleese,' recalls Howard. 'And he said "Sorry, Cyril old boy, but I'm afraid I've got some bad news. We've had a better deal offered at Twickenham and so we're having to go with it." I suggested that we could try and match it, but he was adamant that it had to be Twickenham. "Don't worry though," he said. "You're not missing much, it's not much of a film really." So, despite needing the business, I thought at least I had the consolation of knowing it wasn't going to be much of a

film. How wrong we were!'

In October 1987, Howard bit the bullet. Despite his earlier insistence that the only way Pinewood could continue was as a fully serviced studio, he realised he was wrong. 'I was fooling myself really by saying that,' said Howard, 'because deep down knew it couldn't go on. We were losing money, we had a huge staff and there was no product. So one morning I called everyone onto a stage and stood in front of them on a rostrum. I broke the news that we were going "four-wall" [becoming a studio facility, where filmmakers bring in their own labour and staff] and I remember them clapping at the end of my little speech. Of course, then came the negotiations with the unions, but we came to a deal and the staff, or payroll, was reduced from nearly 500 to 145. At least you could sleep a little better and not wake up in the middle of the night wondering how you would meet the next payroll.

'Pinewood was the last film studio to go four-walled,' he adds, 'and I'll never forget that day as long as I live.'

Despite reducing his payroll, Howard was still faced with the fact that there was very little product

Facing page: *Jack Nicholson endured hours in the make-up chair preparing to play the Joker.*

Left: *The Caped Crusader - Michael Keaton as Batman.*

those for Adidas, Argos, AT&T, Barclaycard, BT, Citroën, the *Daily Mirror*, Ford, Guinness, Halifax, Kelloggs, the National Lottery, On Digital, Pepsi, Renault, WH Smith, Tango, Tesco and Visa. Additionally, Simply Red, a-ha, Fatboy Slim and Madonna are just a few of the visiting artistes who have used Pinewood's stages for rehearsals and rock videos. Bill Harrison, or 'Uncle Bill' as he became known, was a mainstay of Pinewood until he retired in 1998. As well as bringing in commercials and TV programmes, he also became the first port-of-call for aspiring filmmakers and college students; he assisted them by offering stage space, materials, encouragement and valuable contacts within the industry.

1988 was, thankfully, somewhat busier than the previous six or seven years with 13 productions of various sizes being based at the studio. Having already played host to one of America's most famous heroes in the shape of *Superman*, another of the country's top comic book heroes came to Pinewood – the 'dark knight' himself, *Batman*.

At a time when the Bond producers decided to move out of the studio because of mounting costs and the UK's unfavourable exchange rate, it was somewhat surprising to find Warner Bros moving in the opposite direction; not that Pinewood was complaining. British co-producer Chris Kenny realised how important the production's arrival in England was, and said at the time: 'I just hope that the film is a success and that Warner Bros want to make more. It could be the start of another series of big pictures to be made in this country.'

Production designer Anton Furst was the man responsible for the gloomy, Gothic look of Gotham City, which was built in its entirety on the backlot. It was truly impressive and worlds away from the camp 1960s TV series. Working flat out with his 14-strong department and a construction team of 200, it took only five months to build. 'There were four stages of construction,' said Furst. 'The buildings were supported by scaffolding and clad in plywood. A plaster, or sometimes fibreglass, covering is added and then finally painted. With a main street which was a quarter of a mile long, I was told that it was the biggest set since *Cleopatra*. It was certainly a massive chal-

coming into the studio. 'If things go wrong on one front, you have to diversify,' he continues. 'It's easy to say "OK, there are no features so let's bring in some more TV," but it doesn't work like that. They're not queuing up to come; they have their own venues. So we decided to hit another market.

'Bill Harrison was our estate manager as well as being a very good friend of mine. I called him up and said "Bill, we're having to get rid of all the heads of department but I've decided to keep you. I want you to start putting the idea around that we're now looking at housing commercials as well as feature films, and you'll be in charge of them." Well, he couldn't get out of the office quick enough. Talk about a dog with two tails! He did an absolutely marvellous job. He had a personality a mile wide and everybody loved him. Commercials and pop promos became very big business and Bill brought in over a hundred per year. Granted, we couldn't survive on them alone, but with those and a few big features every year, we had our bread and butter.'

Among the many hundreds of commercials that have been shot at Pinewood over the years include

lenge, as I no longer had the security of stages. Without the stage rigging to help us at such high levels, massive cranes were brought into service.'

The cathedral was the setting for Batman's (Michael Keaton) final battle with the Joker (Jack Nicholson) and was one of the major buildings in the city. Filming in and around the cathedral was very complicated, and a number of different methods were employed to create the necessary effect. On the lot and in the studio, full-size set-pieces were built to represent the top and bottom of the building, with gigantic bells. Two other scales were used to construct the length in between. Extensive use was made of all studio facilities, not least the restaurant for Billy Dee Williams' political campaign speech.

Director Tim Burton's film heralded the arrival of a new kind of blockbuster. Pinewood had participated in the birth of the 'event' movie. It was hoped that a sequel would return to the complex – to that end, Gotham City remained in place at the studio long after production ceased – but it wasn't to be. A further blow came when Jack Nicholson tore into the British taxation regime, vowing never again to work in Britain after a large chunk of his salary had been withheld by the Exchequer for months on end.

Jack the Ripper, the first of two Michael Caine vehicles, was also shot in 1988. 'We filmed the whole thing at the studio, and had great fun in building those wonderful Victorian sets across, I think, about three stages,' says director David Wickes. 'It was quite something for us, because it was Michael Caine's first TV mini-series and the first British TV show to air prime-time on CBS over

two nights. It was a tremendous ratings winner, both in America and the UK where it knocked *Coronation Street* off the top spot!

'At the same time as us shooting, Dan Curtis was making *War and Remembrance*, and I remember that he and I used to eye each other warily in the corridor, but nothing was ever said. It was all a bit strange. Anyway, one day I went up to him and said "We should have said hello several weeks ago, we keep passing each other in the corridor, I'm David Wickes." "I know who the f*** you are," he snapped and walked off. He then got Jane Seymour, who was my leading lady, into his show and I found out that all this funny eyeing was because my dates had clashed with his, and he couldn't have Jane until three weeks after he'd wanted her. It was a complete misunderstanding and we got along very well once it was cleared up.'

Meanwhile, Wickes was devising another fascinating Pinewood project – no less than the purchase of the studio itself. 'It was at a time when the studio was struggling a bit, and rumours were rife that the Rank Organisation were preparing to sell it off, or something awful like that. I, like many of my colleagues, was horrified and set about wondering what we could do to save the studio. At that time, we had a hotel group called Queen's Moat House and one of my friends happened to know the chairman of the group. There was no hotel of a really high standard between London and Heathrow back then, and it was suggested that if they could get permission to build one beyond the big house in a corner of the gardens – taking a couple of acres out of Pinewood's

Facing page: *One of the impressive sets constructed for* Batman.

Left: *Michelle Pfeiffer on location in Moscow for* The Russia House.

The second visit for Michael Caine came in the shape of *Without a Clue*, in which he starred as a hapless Sherlock Holmes alongside Ben Kingley's superior Dr Watson in an amusing twist on the Conan Doyle characters. It was followed by another lavish period film, the most complete adaptation yet of Dickens' *Great Expectations*, starring Anthony Hopkins as Magwitch, Jean Simmons as Miss Havisham and Anthony Calf as Pip, all ably directed by Kevin Connor. 'It was quite something to think that here we were, 50 years on from David Lean having brought his brilliant production into the studio. So you can just imagine how fascinated I was to be shown photo albums by Charlie Staffell of Lean at work on his version – all the set-ups, the wonderful sets ... wow!'

Five features cranked up in 1989, plus a highly impressive TV version of *Treasure Island*, directed by Charlton's son Fraser C Heston, which was released theatrically in the UK. Clint Eastwood came to the studio for *White Hunter, Black Heart* and David Puttnam's Hollywood-style war epic *Memphis Belle* marked director Michael Caton-Jones' follow-up to the controversial *Scandal*. The *Memphis Belle* was the most celebrated of the US Air Force's B-17 bombers and, as most of the surviving B-17s were based in the USA, the producers had originally planned to make the film there. However, they were unable to find any suitable airfields or even sufficient air space. A huge, empty airbase at Binbrook, Lincolnshire, was accordingly pressed into service as a busy bomber station.

Sean Connery's next Pinewood feature brought him together with Michelle Pfeiffer in Tom Stoppard's adaptation of the John Le Carré espionage novel *The Russia House*, which was intended as the big Christmas picture for 1990. But Fred Schepisi's direction, an admirable supporting cast (Roy Scheider, Klaus Maria Brandauer, even Ken Russell), and some remarkable locations behind the Iron Curtain couldn't save the film from being a major disappointment both critically and commercially. Indeed, in the UK it didn't even manage to come out at Christmas, hanging around instead until February 1991. High hopes and a humbling outcome: an appropriate end for Pinewood's 1980s output. ■

one hundred – the amount of money they would plough into the deal would keep the studio going for a long time. We might have been able to underwrite its losses for five years or more.

'We took the idea to the then chairman of Rank, who was quite interested, and several negotiations followed in South Street with the top brass of the Organisation. Because of the hotel offer, and on the basis of Pinewood's future financial viability, we were able to borrow money from a bank to buy the complex. Obviously, there was a limit as to how high the bank would go, and to our minds it was an extremely fair amount: an awful lot of millions. We went in with our offer and honestly thought it was an offer Rank couldn't refuse. However, we were wrong. They asked for a lot more than we were able to offer. So we had to walk away. It was a very sad day for me, and I was very surprised they turned the offer down. But Pinewood survived. Michael Grade attempted a similar take-over several years later, but on that occasion he was unsuccessful.

15 SE

The 1990s started just as the 1980s had ended: with a modest mixture of TV and features.

Heil Honey I'm Home was a pilot for a projected comedy series for short-lived satellite broadcaster BSB. Starring Sam Kelly as Adolf Hitler, it attempted to show the lighter side of the Führer and his domestic life with Eva Braun, much in the mould of *'Allo 'Allo*, which also featured Kelly. Needless to say, this tasteless concept did not develop into a series and, shortly after its broadcast, BSB was taken over by Rupert Murdoch's Sky Television empire.

The second TV production came with another Fraser Heston project, *The Crucifer of Blood*, in which his father Charlton forsook Long John Silver and became Sherlock Holmes to Richard Johnson's Dr Watson. 'Pinewood lent itself so well to the production,' recalled Charlton Heston, 'as many of the house's rooms fitted in so well with the period. I remember we used the ballroom to great effect in several sequences. The gardens were also used extensively. Fraser came in for some criticism when he said he was going to film a scene which was supposed to represent the Red Fort of Agra in India: "the only structure in the world with a hundred gates," as Holmes describes it. Fray looked at the set and said "All I need to bring it alive is a troop of British lancers riding up the street in the opening shot." Nobody thought it would work – it would cost too much, the set wouldn't stand it – but I'm here to tell you it did. Fray argued for 40 horsemen, and got them; plus one elephant! I will always have a tremendous soft spot for Pinewood, as it's been very kind to me in my career.'

In September 1990 the James Bond Fan Club staged a very special event at Pinewood, and the first such event the studio had permitted. Said club vice-chairman Andrew Pilkington, 'After the première of *Licence To Kill*, we decided the time had come to seriously consider the possibility of holding a convention during 1990. We eventually settled on 29 and 30 September – then we had to find a venue. We considered Pinewood Studios, as the thought of holding a convention at the home of the Bond series was very tempting, but we had no idea of the reaction we would receive from the studio.'

In the event, and after a four-hour meeting at the studio in January 1990, Cyril Howard gave his permission. The studio's franchised catering and special events arm, Location Catering, had previously arranged wedding receptions, product launch parties and conferences, but nothing on the scale of the proposed event. The 1990 Fan Club Convention covered the entire weekend and the club literally took over a large part of the studio. The main house played host to the initial gathering, plus memorabilia stalls and refreshments, while the restaurant was transformed into a cinema for the 200-strong crowd, utilising the window blackouts created for the political rally in *Batman*.

The schedule included two film screenings, a James Bond Mastermind Quiz, a studio tour taking in the gardens, backlot, corridors, and main 'factory', and, to the amazement of those present, a stupendous exhibition on B Stage which represented one of the largest collections of James Bond props and vehicles ever seen before or since. Among the celebrity guests were Desmond ('Q') Llewelyn, Wing Commander Ken Wallis (designer, builder and pilot of 'Little Nellie'), Molly Peters (the masseuse from *Thunderball*), Bond beauty Carole Ashby (*Octopussy* and *A View To a Kill*), production designer Syd Cain, main title designer Maurice Binder, Oscar-winning special effects wizard John Stears and production designer Peter Lamont.

OR THE FUTURE (The 1990s)

Adrian Pasdar and, on top form, Julie Walters. *Patriot Games* was Phillip Noyce's follow-up to *The Hunt for Red October*, with Harrison Ford taking on Alec Baldwin's role as CIA man Jack Ryan. The film left its mark on Pinewood when the boardroom was split in two to represent James Fox's office and anteroom. Such was the skill with which it was done, it remains so to this day, providing Pinewood with a small as well as a large boardroom.

1992 began with the somewhat embarrassing revival of two old series – *Carry On Columbus* and *Son of the Pink Panther*. (The latter went straight-to-video in the UK.) Kevin Connor returned to direct the TV mini-series of Andrew Morton's best-seller *Diana: Her True Story*, with Serena Scott Thomas in the title role. And Agnieszka Holland's wonderfully crafted version of the children's classic *The Secret Garden* made full use of Pinewood's gardens, even boarding over part of the Pinewood pond.

A little bit of history was made that year with Pinewood's first live TV broadcast. The BBC's Saturday morning children's magazine show, *Parallel 9* – set in a distant galaxy – made wonderful use of K Stage in recreating space settings, while out on the backlot sat a little caravan where visiting guest stars needed to stop off in order to be 'transported' to *Parallel 9*. Thankfully, Saturday mornings were reasonably quiet at the studio and broadcasting live from the backlot wasn't a problem. In fact, so happy were the programme makers that they returned for the '93 and '94 seasons, which guaranteed several months' bookings each time.

In an attempt to secure a modest but steady stream of finance, the old props building (located in the covered way) was converted into office space, providing approximately 30 new rooms and 30 new rents from residents. Meanwhile, in a laboratory hidden away in the depths of the studio, evil doings were afoot as Dr Frankenstein continued in his experiments to create the ideal man in another TV *Frankenstein*, 19 years after Pinewood's previous attempt.

'We had a marvellous cast – Patrick Bergin, Randy Quaid, John Hurt – and great fun making it,' remembers director David Wickes. 'But my linger-

The event had been a mammoth undertaking for the club and a leap of faith on Pinewood's behalf. However, after all the fun, the clean-up operation was still to follow and posed a potential problem, as David Seltzer's Michael Douglas vehicle, *Shining Through*, was due to start set-building on B Stage the following Monday. It proved impossible to clear the stage of Bond props in time, but thankfully the construction manager on the picture proved to be very understanding. A lavish 30th anniversary follow-up convention was subsequently staged in 1992 and further events have taken the form of Christmas lunch gatherings.

The second *Alien* sequel, *Alien 3*, kicked off production in 1991 and made extensive, and impressive, use of the 007 Stage and Pinewood's effects and 'creatures' companies, receiving an Oscar nomination for Best Visual Effects. At the other side of the studio was *Year of the Comet* with Penelope Ann Miller, Timothy Daly and Louis Jourdan, an ill-balanced romantic adventure (written by William Goldman) which nevertheless involved a memorable flooding sequence arranged on D Stage.

One of the Rank Organisation's rare forays into British films, in partnership with Zenith and London Weekend Television, was Christopher Monger's *Just Like a Woman*, a transvestite comedy starring

ing memory will have to be the awful accident which resulted in Patrick breaking his arm. The sequence was a fairly simple one, shot on the backlot, where Patrick was on a big sledge being pulled across the snow by a mini-Moke at walking pace. The sledge was very heavy – it took three or four prop men to move it – and very sturdy. All of a sudden, it tipped over. To this day we don't know why. Patrick lost his balance, came off the sledge and landed so heavily that he broke his arm. We still had shooting to complete, and the insurance claim, suspending the movie while Patrick got better, was a nightmare. A court case followed where our insurance company wanted to share the cost of the delay with the sledge manufacturer's insurance company. It dragged on for four years! Our insurance won the case completely, and Patrick and I are still the best of friends.'

In October, cameras were due to start rolling on *Shakespeare In Love*, which was set to star Julia Roberts. Days before principal photography was to start, however, the film was abandoned, along with it 200 crew members and several months of stage space at the studio. Roberts was insistent on Daniel Day-Lewis playing the Bard and, when he declined, she left the production. 'That was a great blow,' says Cyril Howard, who was then in his retirement year,

'as we were depending on that work to keep us going. But here we are seven years later, the film's been made [at Shepperton, with Gwyneth Paltrow and Joseph Fiennes] and it's done so well!'

1993 ushered in several new productions, as well as a new managing director in Steve Jaggs. Formerly manager of Agfa's motion picture division, Jaggs was by no means a stranger to Pinewood or the filmmakers there and, as far as Cyril Howard was concerned, he was the best man for the job. 'I did feel very sorry for Steve though, because I was handing over the reins to him at a time when we weren't doing very well and the studio itself was in quite a bad state of disrepair. In fact, I'm not exaggerating when I say it used to bring me close to tears to look at the place. I might look at a door and realise it needed painting, but I just didn't have the money to do it. It really was that bad.'

'When I joined the studio, on 2 November 1992 for an eight-week hand-over period,' says Jaggs, 'we didn't have very much on at all, which gave me the opportunity to look at the business and at the buildings themselves. I have to tell you, it was a shock – but that's not a criticism of the previous management. There just weren't the monies available. Fortunately, since that time, the Rank Group [the new name for the Rank Organisation]

have been very supportive of what we've wanted to do and a lot of work has been undertaken in picking up many years of neglect. We started looking at the studio from the roof down. It used to leak like a sieve, but it doesn't now!

'We had to bring things up to a standard which would not only be acceptable to ourselves, but to our clients; and doing things for longevity, not just saying "That'll do for now." Then, as business picked up, and the various stages of improvements were completed, we were able to think about expanding.'

Production in 1993 began with Caroline Thompson, screenwriter of *The Secret Garden*, making her directorial bow with another children's classic, *Black Beauty*, starring Sean Bean, David Thewlis, Alun Armstrong and John McEnery and again making considerable use of the gardens at the studio. Actor George Cole made an emotional return to the studio with his tremendously popular TV series *Minder*. Series nine saw the show clock up over 100 episodes. 'It was great to be back,' says Cole. 'I have so many happy memories of working at Pinewood. My first film was in 1943 – the RAF Film Unit's *Journey Together*. If memory serves, it was directed by Fl Lt John Boulting, who had us on the parade ground every morning before shooting.'

May 1993 brought news of the death of Sir John Davis, former Chairman of the Rank Organisation. 'I remember that day very well,' says Dinah Sheridan

with a wry smile. 'Particularly when my son Jeremy came to the telephone singing "Oh what a beautiful morning"!' 'The British film industry needs someone like John Davis now,' counters Daniel Angel, producer of *Carve Her Name With Pride* and *Reach For the Sky*, 'as at least he could make a decision and green-light a picture. No one person can do that nowadays. He may have had his dark side, but at least he made films!'

Meanwhile, Pinewood remained buoyant with Peter Ustinov dropping in for a couple of weeks' work on the children's adventure film *The Phoenix and the Magic Carpet* before David Puttnam commenced production on the ill-fated anthology film *Being Human*. Once in the can, it was left there for at least a year. Given that its main creative team boasted acclaimed director/screenwriter Bill Forsyth and stars Robin Williams, John Turturro and Lorraine Bracco, the film's failure came as quite a surprise to the studio behind it, Warner Bros.

1994, Steve Jaggs' second year in the top job, was a much busier and bigger year than his first. Producers Stephen Woolley and David Geffen, together with director Neil Jordan, turned their attentions to Anne Rice's *Vampire Chronicles* and thus was born *Interview With the Vampire*, starring Tom Cruise and Brad Pitt. Security was very tight, with guards in virtually every corridor and covered walkways erected between trailers and stages, all to keep the innovative make-up a surprise. The picture received two Oscar nomina-

tions: Art Direction (Dante Ferretti) and Original Score (Elliot Goldenthal).

More costume horror followed, though of a more low-key variety. Having been responsible for *Shakespeare In Love* being called off, Julia Roberts returned to Pinewood for *Mary Reilly*, another rendition of Jekyll and Hyde, only this time told through the eyes of Jekyll's maid, Mary Reilly. John Malkovich played Jekyll and Hyde, Stephen Frears directed and Christopher Hampton provided the screenplay. Roberts' capricious behaviour was the talk of the tabloids, but interest in the film fell away sharply when it was completed and delivered. Test screenings were discouraging and re-shoots were

called for, again at Pinewood. Only a limited theatrical release followed, with reviews and returns proving very disappointing for all concerned.

This is where the current author came in. In March 1993, just a few months into his tenure as managing director, Steve Jaggs had been approached by Gareth Owen, a young physics student with a penchant for British films. He'd been creating a bit of a noise in trying to raise government awareness of the need for a thriving British film business, particularly because the early 1990s had witnessed an all-time low in British film production.

The previous month, with a host of celebrity supporters such as Lord Attenborough, Sir Anthony

Hopkins, Alan Rickman and Michael Winner, Owen had staged a successful weekend of British Film in North Wales' Theatr Clwyd. Having been asked to repeat the event nearer London, Owen hit upon Pinewood and, after a year's preparation, British Film Day was held there on 9 April 1994. As well as several high-ranking government officials, celebrity guests included Julian Glover, Liz Fraser, Sylvia Syms, Eunice Gayson, Valerie Leon, Burt Kwouk, Walter Gotell, Jack Douglas and, as guest of honour at the evening dinner, Bryan Forbes and his wife Nanette Newman. The event's success led to Owen forming his own production company and, immediately upon graduation from university, he moved into Pinewood.

1994 also saw the production of Iain Softley's *Hackers*, a fast-moving thriller set in the world of computers and featuring an attractive mix of newcomers including Jonny Lee Miller and Angelina Jolie. Roller blades – used in the film by several of the 'hacker' chums – were the current craze. The young actors could frequently be seen tearing around the studio on their blades. Thankfully, there weren't any reported accidents. Meanwhile, Gerry Anderson's much-hyped *Space Precinct* series began its year-long tenure at Pinewood, marking a welcome return for the producer of such Pinewood shows as *UFO* and *Space: 1999*.

The most expensive science fiction project ever to shoot in the UK, *Space Precinct* had a huge unit, spread across both Pinewood (for live action) and Shepperton (for special effects). The schedule was tough: one 60-minute episode had to be completed every ten days. But in episode one, lead actor Ted Shackleford was hit in the face by a splinter of wood during a special effects sequence of a door being blown open. Shooting was about to start on episode two but the injury couldn't be disguised by make-up. Quick-thinking Gerry Anderson wrote in a scene in which the character's face was grazed by a bullet, thus dispensing with an insurance claim and posing no delay to filming.

Facing page top: *An aerial view of one of the sets constructed for* First Knight.

Facing page bottom: *One of the enchanting sets designed by John Box in Pinewood's orchard for* First Knight.

Above: *The impressive zoo set from* Fierce Creatures, *one of the friendliest productions of the late 1990s.*

Among the directors on the series were Bond regular John Glen and Piers Haggard, who had shot the highly atmospheric horror picture *Blood on Satan's Claw* at the studio back in 1970. Although the financial side of the project had been signed and sealed months earlier, the production was dogged by cashflow problems; by the time episode 18 was underway, huge debts had been run up. Fortunately, the series was completed, but not before its American backers were put into liquidation. Further disappointment followed when the series was scheduled for a 6.00 pm slot on BBC2. Anderson had hoped for an evening slot on BBC1, much like *The X-Files*, but his identification with children's programmes dictated the earlier time. The show did not return for a second series.

Animatronic creatures were also around the studio for *Loch Ness*, the story of 'Nessie', the legendary monster of the Scottish loch (last seen at Pinewood in *The Private Life of Sherlock Holmes*). Ted Danson and Joely Richardson headed the cast, which also boasted Ian Holm. Nessie herself made her home in a wonderful set on A Stage. Then, having loomed on the horizon for some time, Jerry Zucker finally called to say he was on the way over with his next picture, *First Knight*, yet another screen adaptation of the King Arthur legend – this time with a modern living legend in the shape of Sean Connery. Hollywood heart throb Richard Gere was cast as the gallant Sir Lancelot, and intense press speculation about his marriage to supermodel Cindy Crawford overshadowed the shoot.

The backlot once again played host to a splendid set. This time it was Camelot Castle, complete with blue roofs, turrets, flags and Cotswold-style stone. Another section was constructed on the paddock tank for the drawbridge and water dive/chase sequence, as well as one in North

Wales where locations were completed. Production designer John Box was blamed for pushing the production over-budget but set builders working for the Oscar- winning designer threatened to strike in protest at the suggestion.

Bob Anderson, who had worked with Errol Flynn, was the man responsible for bringing Gere's swordmanship up to scratch. He described Gere's swashbuckling talents as superior to Flynn's. 'He'd hardly used a sword before, so he was an absolute novice,' Anderson observes. 'But by the time he came to his first fight in front of the camera, he was brilliant.' It should be pointed out, however, that Gere only held the hilt of the swords in the film's superb fight sequences, the blades being introduced later via computer generated imaging (CGI).

1995 was phenomenally busy for the studio, with both large-scale features and all manner of TV productions. Kicking off the year was the long awaited follow-up to *A Fish Called Wanda*. Originally called *Death Fish 2*, the story was set to reunite *Wanda* stars John Cleese, Jamie Lee Curtis, Kevin Kline and Michael Palin in a zoo-set comedy. *Fierce Creatures*, as the film was eventually retitled, witnessed the construction of one of Pinewood's most delightful and ambitious exterior sets ever – a complete zoo, along with live animal residents. But what of the old adage, never work with children or animals?

'Generally, the animals were brilliant, thanks to our trainer Rona Brown,' says Cleese, 'but we did discover that the ostrich chick was quite alarmed by the kowati because its main diet is eggs and chicks. So in any scene that seems to feature a kowati and ostrich together, the answer is that the kowati was animatronic.'

The smaller animals were not always required on set and resided in their own 'mini-zoo' on the lot, which attracted Tom Cruise and his children as well as the Princess of Wales and the Duchess of York. Once shooting was completed, the sets were destroyed in a matter of days, but a year later most of them had to be rebuilt for further shooting, with a new director, Fred Schepisi, taking over from Robert Young.

'We'd made a couple of mistakes in the script,' explains Cleese. 'I wrote an ending that was a bit

crazy, particularly as it involved Kevin Kline's character being killed off early. The other thing was, I tried to create a little Ealing comedy ensemble with the zoo-keepers but, to my surprise, English audiences just weren't interested in them, only in the main characters. Michael Palin was off around the world and wasn't available for a year, and when we did reunite in 1996 we found the re-shoots were very expensive. With everyone demanding big fees, the budget shot up from the low $20 millions to the very high $20 millions.'

The second big feature to shoot in 1995 came in the shape of an updated 1960s TV series when Tom Cruise, a regular visitor to Pinewood, brought his first movie as producer to the studio. *Mission: Impossible* came with a solid supporting cast (Vanessa Redgrave, Jon Voight, Ving Rhames etc), a $64 million budget and director Brian DePalma, whose previous hits ranged from *Carrie* to *The Untouchables*. To the discomfiture of both stuntmen and insurance people, Cruise did many of his own stunts, including one on the 007 Stage when he was sent flying by an exploding carriage. As he told *Film Review* magazine, 'I was flying across the James Bond Stage at Pinewood Studios and I hit a train. It really hurt and I didn't have to act at all.' The film was a summer box-office smash on both sides of the Atlantic and a sequel was guaranteed, ensuring that Pinewood maintained its global reputation for housing successful blockbusters.

Television continued to play a vital part in the studio's output. Playwright Dennis Potter's final

two shows, *Karaoke* and *Cold Lazarus*, made broadcasting history when the BBC and Channel 4 joined forces to fund and produce the dramas, which aired on both channels later in the year. *Last of the Summer Wine* also made itself comfortable after locations in Yorkshire and other TV shows followed suit – *Annie: A Royal Adventure*, the revived version of *Poldark*, *Deadly Voyage*, *Potamus Park* and, defecting from Shepperton, the lavish game show *You Bet!*

Sir Anthony Hopkins returned to his 'favourite studio' sporting a shaven head and bronze suntan with Merchant-Ivory's production of *Surviving Picasso*, which was shooting on C Stage when pop group Simply Red took up residence on the adjoining B Stage to rehearse for an upcoming tour. Disrupting the period feel of the Picasso biopic, the group was rapidly transferred to A Stage. Shortly afterwards, more music emanated from Pinewood's stages when Alan Parker brought Madonna over to record tracks for *Evita*, his biopic of Eva Peron.

Meanwhile, two further stages were added to Pinewood's already significant facilities. Dubbed N & P Stages, they replaced the former paint shop and electrical maintenance department, adjacent to F Stage. Uniquely among Pinewood's stages, N & P are inter-connected and can be used singly, or if desired, opened up to form one large stage.

1996 was just as busy for Pinewood, with Bruce Willis making two big features: *The Fifth Element* and *The Jackal*. The former was an extravagant futuristic fantasy shrouded in secrecy. It was Luc

Facing page: *Elizabeth Shue and Val Kilmer on the run in the 1996 film* The Saint.

Left: *A scene from* The Apocalypse Watch.

Besson's biggest directorial project and Gaumont's largest ever. With a budget of $70m, the French-backed picture launched the 50th Cannes Film Festival and was the talk of the trade press when Sony stumped up an amazing $25m for the US distribution rights.

The Jackal was originally touted as a remake of Fred Zinnemann's 1972 classic *The Day of the Jackal* but the news was greeted with total disapproval by Zinnemann and novelist Frederick Forsyth. The final film was loosely based, at any rate, on the earlier film in so much as it involved the attempted assassination of a high-ranking political figure. However, although mention was given to Kenneth Ross's 1972 screenplay, Forsyth demanded his name not be used. Michael Caton-Jones directed the picture, which marked the return of both Richard Gere and Sidney Poitier to the studio in a fast-moving, action-packed adventure with not one but two edge-of-the-seat climaxes.

Paramount's thriller *The Saint*, starring Val Kilmer and directed by Phillip Noyce, was another update of a 1960s cult TV show and attracted some bad press thanks to the unlikely casting of Kilmer. Its location shooting made excellent use of Moscow's Red Square but most of the interiors were filmed at Pinewood, perhaps the most outstanding being the villain's mansion. Built on one of the largest stages, the interior was a majestic structure of marble and gold, two-and-a-half storeys high and incorporating a domed roof and an immense chandelier.

Unfortunately, the chandelier (and Pinewood) was involved in the ending that never was. A daring final showdown between Simon Templar (Val Kilmer) and villain Tretiak – brilliantly played by the Croatian actor Rade Serbedzija – was to have taken place high up in the roof of the mansion. It was unusual and elaborate but was cut from the final print after test audiences had objected to the

death of Elizabeth Shue's character, killed by Tretiak's son, Ilya, by means of a poison-tipped cane. The scene was replaced with a mundane exit for the bad guys and a 'happy ending' shot on location in Oxford. All that remains of the chandelier is a one-second view of it being manoeuvred into place when Tretiak enters his home.

Also in 1996, 'creative differences' saw Peter Weller replaced by John Badham as director of *Incognito*, starring Jason Patric and Irene Jacob. *The Apocalypse Watch* was a Hallmark television adaptation of Robert Ludlum's novel about neo-Nazis plotting to take over the world. Directed by Kevin Connor and starring Patrick Bergin and Veronica Hamell, it employed impressive hi-tech sets constructed on the new N & P Stages, as well as using other Pinewood landmarks such as the boardroom and the executive suite (stormed by Bergin), not to mention the construction of part of Downing Street in Car Park One.

Another Hallmark production was an adaptation of Jules Verne's *20,000 Leagues Under the Sea*, starring Richard Crenna and Ben Cross. The production was directed by veteran Michael Anderson and produced by John Davis (no relation), who claims that it was 'Without doubt the most joyous production I've ever worked on. The whole team were brilliant. Nothing was impossible on the shoot, yet much was improbable. Originally, we had intended to shoot with units in the Red Sea and in Malta's giant tank, which has a clear-horizon background. But the logistics and finance didn't really allow. So I decided to bring the picture into Pinewood as I knew with a team like Michael [Anderson] and Alan [Hume, the director of photography] we could recreate those sequences at the studio – and I defy anyone to watch the film and say it was made in Pinewood's paddock tank!

'Our production designer was a wonderful chap named Brian Ackland-Snow and he did some brilliant work, including the magnificent submarine, *Nautilus*. We had decided that rather than use a giant octopus, as in Verne's story, we would have a sea monster that would swallow the Nautilus. Brian designed an ingenious set on one of the stages whereby the monster was on a ramp, and

Right: 20,000 Leagues Beneath the Sea – *or was it a few feet under the paddock tank?*

Facing page top: *John Steed (Ralph Fiennes) and Dr Emma Peel (Uma Thurman) in the ill-fated big-screen version of* The Avengers.

the mechanics of it all allowed it to drop down fast, and towards what would be the submarine, to swallow it. It was very sad when that production came to an end."

1997 got underway with a high-budget space thriller, *Event Horizon*, from the young director-producer team of Paul Anderson and Jeremy Bolt. The spaceship *Event Horizon* mysteriously reappears after becoming lost somewhere beyond Neptune and it soon becomes apparent that something went 'terribly wrong' on the ship. Shot entirely at Pinewood, the film's centrepiece set, on which the final confrontation takes place, was constructed on the 007 Stage.

Stanley Kubrick returned to Pinewood in 1997. He hadn't made a film since *Full Metal Jacket* in 1986, but sometime in the winter of 1995 Tom Cruise and Nicole Kidman flew in by helicopter to the reclusive director's Hertfordshire home to discuss a project called *Eyes Wide Shut*. The film was brought into Pinewood with an estimated six to eight month shoot but with very little else known about it. Such was the secrecy that would surround the film for its entire stay.

The story, it was said in a Warner Bros press release, was to be based on a novella by Arthur Schnitzler which Kubrick had purchased the rights to sometime in the 1960s. Production began in 1997 and, lasting two years, saw changes of cast mid-shoot. The stars had to reschedule other projects and Cruise developed an ulcer.

Like all his later films, *Eyes Wide Shut* was shot entirely in the UK. Kubrick's fear of flying meant that he wouldn't travel to the USA for the New York street scenes, preferring instead to build New York on the backlot – or at least a few blocks of it. And so a little bit of Manhattan could be found in downtown Iver Heath and it really came to life for the night shoots with a haze of sodium street lighting hovering over the studio. You could even hail one of the many yellow cabs that drove around the set to give the impression of a constant traffic flow.

Needless to say, with one of the world's legendary directors helming a much-anticipated film starring two of the business's top names, press interest was immense. And so began the rumours. One

suggested that it was a high-budget porno film, another that it involved necrophilia, still another that in it Tom Cruise wore a dress. Repeated takes were called for, it was reported, sometimes as many as 80, which allegedly drove Tom Cruise to despair. All these rumours proved less than accurate.

In February 1998, 18 months after Cruise and Kidman had started work on the project, they returned home to LA. However, less than two months later, they were recalled as the director wasn't happy with location scenes he'd shot with Jennifer Jason Leigh. Indeed, Leigh had to be recast owing to other filming commitments, and several months of re-shoots ensued. In March 1999, the film was finally completed and a private screening arranged for the stars and studio executives in LA, on 2 March. Five days later, Kubrick died in his sleep, aged 70.

For almost ten years it was mooted that a feature

Below: *Sir August De Wynter (Sean Connery) and John Steed slug it out beneath the Thames in the climactic sequence.*

version of the 1960s series *The Avengers* was on the cards. Rumours persisted and, on 2 June 1997, the cameras finally started rolling. Ralph Fiennes was cast as the debonair John Steed and Uma Thurman as Emma Peel, while Sean Connery portrayed the villain Sir August DeWynter. Patrick Macnee – the original Steed – had a cameo part in the film as 'Invisible Jones'. The picture was filmed entirely in England, utilising Shepperton as well as Pinewood.

Three-time Academy Award winner Stuart Craig was the production designer charged with creating 'Avengerland'. 'One of the economies we made was with the London street, which we built on the back-

lot at Pinewood,' he said. 'We used false perspective to very good effect. We can make a five-yard street look like a 500-yard street – only the first part is full size, with the second in false perspective and the last little bit two dimensional only.'

As well as using the backlot to great effect, the 'snow' sequences were created and filmed in Pinewood's gardens, with gigantic wind machines for the blizzards: a rather strange sight at the height of summer. The production had its share of problems, however, most notably on 13 May. An electrical fault sparked a roof fire on E Stage and, although swiftly brought under control – thanks to dozens of local fire brigades and Pinewood's own fire department – the damage was significant. The stage, which was short-ly due to be renovated in any case, was closed but the film's sets were accommodated on other stages and the production lost very little time as a result. Even so, the movie flopped badly following some of the most savage reviews ever written.

For the big screen début of Rowan Atkinson's Chaplinesque Mr Bean, writer Richard Curtis and actor-turned-director Mel Smith decided to take the disaster-prone Bean to America. However, early scenes in *Bean: The Ultimate Disaster Movie* were London-based, with several shot at Pinewood. The studio's oak-panelled boardroom was actually used as a boardroom for once and the

'board of directors' was chaired by none other than Sir John Mills. 'It's quite fantastic,' he pointed out, 'to think that there I was sitting in the room where 50 years earlier I had sat with J Arthur Rank to sign my contract. He was heading the table then, but in *Bean* it was my turn!'

Before the year was out, Jenny Seagrove and Bill Kenwright brought their production of *Don't Go Breaking My Heart* in: Anthony Edwards' second British film and, indeed, his second at Pinewood. If you look closely, at one point you can catch a glimpse of the restaurant, with the then catering manager showing the characters around it.

1998 kicked off with Dick Clement and Ian La Frenais' *Still Crazy*, a comedy about Strange Fruit, a group of washed-up rockers played by Stephen Rea, Billy Connolly, Timothy Spall, Jimmy Nail and Bill Nighy. One of the early sequences features a wedding party in the Pinewood restaurant and later the garden and admin block are used to great effect as a mental institution. The most interesting set, however, was a gigantic concert hall built on the 007 Stage.

Sean Connery returned with Catherine Zeta Jones and his own production of the slick crime caper

Entrapment. One of the most breathtaking sets ever constructed at Pinewood was on E Stage: the heavily guarded 'mask' room. The room, which had a full ceiling for shots looking up from below ground level, was built from marble, but thanks to the talented and cost-conscious people in the construction department not a stone of real marble was used.

A noticeable change was made to the main entrance in the early summer of 1998 when the 'Man With the Gong' logo was replaced by a large red dot and the brand name 'Deluxe'. In fact, 'Deluxe Entertainment Services' (which had been acquired by Rank some years earlier) was born in May 1998 at the Cannes Film Festival to encompass Rank Film Laboratories, Rank Video Services and Pinewood Studios under a new 'umbrella'. The Rank Group per se was mainly seen as a leisure and holiday business by this time, and by separating the divisions within the Group, the company established its remaining film interests under the Deluxe brand.

Activities remained unaffected. *Old New Borrowed Blue* marked a departure from acclaimed director Michael Winterbottom's more serious fare. Shot on location in London, Liverpool

Facing page: *Sean Connery, producer and star, with Catherine Zeta Jones in* Entrapment.

Below: *Say 'eh-oh' to the* Teletubbies.

Bottom left: *An artist's impression of the new R and S Stages.*

Bottom right: *Christiana Kubrick and Steve Jaggs dedicate the new complex to Stanley Kubrick.*

and Northern Ireland before coming into Pinewood, the feature starred Christopher Eccleston and, making her first film appearance, Dervla Kirwan in a comedy following a Belfast couple's efforts at reproduction.

Having exhausted the supply of cult 1960s TV shows to resuscitate, a cult 1970s TV show, *The Professionals*, was next up for a 1990s makeover as *The New Professionals*, this time for satellite TV under the direction of David Wickes, who had presided over some of the original episodes. Other TV shows included another series of Roy Clarke's long-running *Last of the Summer Wine*, top American comedy series *Friends* for a one-off London-set episode, and the ever popular kids' TV favourite *Teletubbies* called in for a few insert shots, along with its usual post-production work.

Ragdoll Productions' Sue James is no stranger to Pinewood and it was no accident that she set up the London arm of Ragdoll at the studio. 'I grew up here,' she says. 'The family moved to Iver in around 1964 because my father [*Carry On* star Sid James] worked here so much. I used to come up to the studio and ride at the stables where Eon are now based. Captain Taylor would allow me [and other children] to take the ponies out around the complex and into Black Park. Every year we'd hold a gymkhana, usually on the field where they made *Carry On Camping* and in the paddock tank area. It was hysterical, like one of Thelwell's cartoons. They were magical times.'

Late in 1998, work commenced on Pinewood's two new large stages, along with the adjoining office accommodation dubbed The Stanley Kubrick Building, and in the summer of 1999 they opened for business. 'We can cater for the very smallest of productions through to the largest,' says Steve Jaggs. 'However, up until 1999, the studio only had three large stages, plus the 007 Stage, which could very comfortably accommodate any large-scale picture. The problem came when we had two large pictures at the same time. Typically, they would both want at least two large stages – or even three – which made things impossible. That's not a problem any longer with the addition of R and S Stages.

'Fortunately, the studio is laid out quite well, except the area north of our main stages A, B, C, D and E; that needs a lot of work doing to it. The buildings are mainly single storey and the available floor space is not very well used at present. Phase one of our development plan was the addition of R and S Stages, along with the Stanley Kubrick office building, and phase two is to

Right: *Michael Tuchner's* Return to the Secret Garden *utilised Pinewood's ornamental gardens, as did Warner's feature version a few years earlier.*

demolish the area north of the main stages and construct two more large stages plus a medium stage and 70,000 square feet of office space on four floors. Those planned new stages will be 50 feet high, without us building higher than any of the existing buildings. Phases three and four are firmly set in our minds, but having made a multi-million pound investment in R and S, we have to see how things go to a certain extent; but phase two should get underway sometime in 2001.'

Production remained buoyant throughout 1999 with Eon's 19th Bond adventure kick-starting the year. *The World Is Not Enough* marked the return 'proper' to Pinewood of Eon Productions after over ten years' absence. *The Tenth Kingdom* was a collaboration between Sky and Hallmark Productions and saw several stages transformed into a fantasy fairytale land, complete with trolls, goblins and giants. And Ridley Scott's *RKO 281* detailed the making of *Citizen Kane*, rather cheekily transforming Pinewood into RKO studios, complete with a giant sign on the side of E Stage.

It was also the year in which The Really Useful Group brought two of their most successful stage productions to Pinewood to produce full-length videos of them. *Joseph and His Amazing Technicolor Dreamcoat*, starring Donny Osmond, Richard Attenborough and Joan Collins, was first into the studio, closely followed by *Jesus Christ Superstar*. Michael Tuchner's *Return to the Secret Garden* was mainly based in Berlin but also marked a return to the Pinewood gardens for the characters in Agnieszka Holland's 1992 original. The BBC chose Pinewood for its 'Comic Relief' skit *Doctor Who – The Curse of the Fatal Death*, the second series of *Heartburn Hotel* and the children's drama *Nature Boy*. Meanwhile, on 5 August the big-budget period drama *Quills* started shooting under Philip Kaufman's direction and witnessed the return of Michael Caine to his old stamping ground, alongside co-stars Kate Winslet, Geoffrey Rush and Joaquin Phoenix.

The film chronicles the last days of the Marquis de Sade (a character last seen at Pinewood in *Marat/Sade* in 1966) and brought with it a kaleidoscope of technical talent, including Oscar-winning production designer Martin Childs. 'This is actually my first time at Pinewood, as I've worked mainly at Shepperton, Ealing and on location. I started on *Quills* at the beginning of April and by the time we finish it'll have been about 30 weeks. We took two stages, A and F, and also used B Stage very briefly. A Stage was completely taken over by dungeons, cellars and underground rooms. It's proven to be quite a challenge as it's mostly French architecture, which I've never done before, but fortunately for us the wealthy folk of nineteenth-century England built in the style of eighteenth-century Paris. At Luton Hoo, for instance, we added extra roofs and did various things to the inside, and then we moved to Oxford, which we used as Paris.'

As the studio entered the new millennium, the future looked bright for both production and post-production. The latter department won an Oscar for *Fiddler on the Roof* and its corridors are decorated with further nominations from both the American and British Academies, along with a BAFTA award. Under department head Graham Hartstone, the facility no longer offers editors, only editing rooms, but does boast some of the best sound mixers in the business: the last bastion of people employed there.

As well as working on the English versions of films, the department completes the 'FIGS' (French, Italian, German and Spanish) versions, which works particularly well when the whole post-production operation is based at the studio: the same crew mix all the versions.

'The department can accommodate about 60 cutting rooms and has seven theatres in all,' says Hartstone. 'The two large theatres are 1 and 2, the newly refurbished theatres 3 and 4 are for TV along with Theatre 5, which was originally opened for TV mixing on 35mm film. That's where we completed series like *Man in a Suitcase, Space:1999, The*

Below: *Cast members from the BBC's long-running sit-com* The Last of the Summer Wine, *with director-producer Alan J W Bell and writer Roy Clarke.*

Persuaders! and so on. When TV production went over to 16mm film, Rank didn't go down that line because we were doing so well with 35mm features, and so the TV work died out a bit. However, when times were difficult in the early 1990s, I revived it again and now Theatre 6 is equipped to handle digital TV.

'I would say that no more than five per cent of our cutting rooms are occupied by film equipment,' Hartstone adds, 'and to be honest, film and computer cutting are like typewriters and word processors. If you get a word processor, you'll never go back to an old typewriter. The flexibility is wonderful: you can undo everything non-destructively, whereas with film once you've cut it, you've cut it. With big features you do lose something in trying to edit on a TV screen, but for sound the advantages and quality of digital cloning rather than magnetic tracks is brilliant, and the consistency and quality is guaranteed. We sometimes have a hundred soundtracks per reel, and they can all be loaded onto a little disk, whereas years ago it would have been con-

tained in a dozen or so film cans.

'No mention of the department would be complete,' Hartstone concludes, 'without mention of Gordon McCallum. He taught us everything we know and completed 319 films before his death. An amazing record.'

The high standards of the post-production department are typical of the studio as a whole. 'I always use the stills department at the studio,' says Michael Winner, giving just one example of how Pinewood's support services excel, 'for both professional and personal photographic work. It's second to none, and Lofty Rice – who runs the department – has never let me down. He's quite brilliant!'

As the fully self-contained studio – with its own water and power supplies, plus bank, general stores, cinema, restaurant, cafeteria and bars – headed into the 21st century, its facilities and support services were unparalleled, as was its reputation around the world. With an incomparable history behind it, the studio where 'nothing is too much trouble' was very much geared for the future.

16

Throughout the 1990s, the Rank Organisation – latterly known as the Rank Group – moved more towards the holiday and leisure areas of its portfolio, and more and more away from its film-related activities. In fact, the decade saw a massive sell-off of Rank assets: in 1991 the Organisation's roadside service stations were sold for £86 million. The following year a sell-off of hotels raised some £210 million, before a further £66 million was raised through selling Rank Precision Industries. By selling its shares in Shearings Holidays and Kingston Plantation, Rank raised a further £115 million, with £25 million added to that from the sale of many amusement arcade sites. The Organisation was floundering and losing focus.

Under newly appointed chief executive Andrew Teare, 1996 saw the sale of Rank Film Distributors and its impressive library to Carlton Television. This marked the end of Rank's involvement with film financing and distribution. Rank's remaining shares in the massive Rank-Xerox empire were sold for £1.5 billion, and the company was rebranded simply as Xerox. The studios, laboratories and video duplication businesses were then re-branded as part of the Organisation's 'Deluxe Entertainment' group, with rumours rife that the new division had been created solely to make for a clean and tidy sell-off of all remaining film interests.

Rank invested heavily into Butlins and its Hard Rock Café chain, and company debts continued to escalate. Ill conceived investments, such as the purchase of the flagging Tom Cobley pub chain (which was later sold for £90 million – £33 million below what Rank had paid) did little to boost share prices, leading to Teare resigning his position in 1999. A new chief executive was swiftly appointed in Mike Smith, and hopes were raised when he boosted investment within the Deluxe group of companies. However, before the year was out, it was announced that the group had appointed investment bank Goldman Sachs to advise on the company's focus.

In December 1999, it was confirmed that Rank's Odeon cinema chain was for sale. In February 2000 it was revealed that Michael Grade, backed by a city consortium, had once again put in a bid for Pinewood at the suggestion of his old friend and colleague Ivan Dunleavy. By the third week in the month, the 460 screen Odeon chain was sold to Cinven for £280 million. Rank's nightclub chain was sold for £156 million, and Grade clinched Pinewood for £62 million. In one swoop, the Rank Group had divested itself of almost £500 million of assets. In fact, the decade had seen the group raise some £1.8 billion through realisation of assets – later including the Butlins chain and the Organisation's 50 per cent share in Universal Florida Studios too. The empire J Arthur Rank had established is now a shadow of its former self. The famous Gongman logo was dropped, but thankfully reintroduced shortly afterwards in a revamped style and with a new colour scheme.

However, it was very much business as usual at Pinewood under the new ownership. Michael Grade became chairman and Ivan Dunleavy was appointed chief executive. The Pinewood management board remained otherwise unchanged. Grade commented, 'After my attempt to buy-out Rank's film interests – the whole lot from distributors, labs, cinemas to studios – in the '90s failed to come to fruition, I subsequently watched from a distance as, bit by bit, Rank later sold off their film interests – and there finally in late 1999 sat Pinewood. I felt the timing was right. I knew Mike Smith at Rank and within a couple of weeks the deal was signed. In 1934 Heatherden Hall sold to Charles Boot for £35,000. I got to thinking that property prices in Buckinghamshire have soared: by 2000% in fact!'

With new owners at the helm, Pinewood entered the new millennium with a solid programme of film

A NEW ERA

and television productions lined up. Michael Grade was particularly keen to increase the television activity of the studio and announced plans to convert J (and later K) Stages into state-of-the-art, dedicated TV studios. Meanwhile, Pinewood's larger stages were occupied by two big-budget American films: *Tomb Raider* and *Proof of Life*. The former was a big-screen adaptation of the top-selling video game. Its buxom heroine Lara Croft had already achieved unparalleled media status as a sexy, intelligent and take-charge icon for the digital age.

Producers Lawrence Gordon and Lloyd Levin started developing scripts that would realise the potential of the concept and become part of Lara's heritage, rather than merely exploiting it. But, although various draft screenplays of *Tomb Raider* were written, the whole project didn't snap into focus until *ConAir* director Simon West came on board some 18 months later. 'After *The General's Daughter*, I was determined to direct something completely opposite to the dark claustrophobic tone of that picture,' said West, who began his career as a TV director with the BBC. 'I wanted fun, fantasy and imagination, so I could exercise all the other muscles I hadn't used in my movie work so far. I'd heard about *Tomb Raider* on the Hollywood network, but I turned it down twice because I had my own definite ideas about what angles should be explored with it. Then, around Christmas 1999, I was offered the chance to direct the project again. I thought about it more seriously this time, and read the latest commissioned script, which had been written by Patrick

Massett and John Zinman. But I told Larry and Lloyd that I would only direct *Tomb Raider* if I could keep the title and Lara but change everything else and start from scratch. I looked at classic quest movies and big epics like *Dr Zhivago* and *Lawrence of Arabia*, watched every documentary on ancient civilisations and read every book on mysticism, sacred geometry, alchemic artefacts, religious rites, astrology and planet-alignment theories that I could find. The story evolved from all these strands, and I wrote the last screenplay draft in May 2000.'

Despite reports that various actresses from Sandra Bullock to Denise Richards were in the running to play Lara, West only ever wanted Angelina Jolie for the role. 'It was a one-horse race' he said. 'I firmly believed only Angelina would be able to act her way out of tight dramatic corners while never losing Lara's sexual appeal or winning qualities. I also instinctively knew she would satisfy the demands of the game's fans and their preconceived ideas of what Lara looked like. I was ecstatic when she accepted the challenge.'

Six months of principal photography began in July 2000 at Pinewood, on elaborate sets designed by Kirk Petruccelli (*Mystery Men*). After the studio scenes, work continued on location in Hofn, Iceland, and in and around the 12th century temples at Angkor Wat in Cambodia. Indeed, *Tomb Raider* became the first movie since 1963's *Lord Jim* allowed to shoot in the war-torn country.

Proof of Life meanwhile brought together two of the hottest names in the film business, Russell Crowe

Facing page: *Just one of the many elaborate sets designed by Kirk Petruccelli for* Lara Croft: Tomb Raider.

Left: *Rick O'Connell (Brendan Fraser) and his wife Evelyn (Rachel Weiss) battle the resurrected Imhotep in* The Mummy Returns.

inside the corridors and rooms were pretty narrow, so it didn't offer us the cinematic possibilities that building one on a stage here does.'

Meanwhile, over at Shepperton, the sequel to hit film *The Mummy* was in production. *The Mummy Returns* featured the same cast of Brendan Fraser, Rachel Weiss, John Hannah and Arnold Vosloo, though with an extra $18 million in the budget. One sequence, towards the climax of the movie, shows the heroes climbing the outside of a pyramid, and facing the elements thrown at them by a higher power. The pyramid was built on the paddock-tank backlot at Pinewood, and involved some of the most powerful wind fans available – the noise was terrific.

Following his success with *The World Is Not Enough*, director Michael Apted based most of his next film away from Pinewood. The World War II code-breaking drama *Enigma*, based on the Robert Harris novel, was produced by Mick Jagger and Lorne Michaels, and starred Kate Winslet, Dougray Scott and Jeremy Northam. 'Lorne Michaels and Mick Jagger were both bidding for the book when it came out and they knew each other,' explained Apted. 'They realised that they were bidding against each other and so they went halves and bought it. Nobody saw much of Lorne, [but] we saw a bit of Mick. It was a bit weird having one of my heroes as a producer.'

Rather ironically, the finance for the film came from Germany. 'It's ridiculous, isn't' it?' said Apted. 'It's kind of scandalous. We were never going to get American money for the film because we wanted to make it British, with a British cast. But you might have thought it might not be too much to ask for British financiers to step up, since it is entirely a British story. It's ironic that every last cent of the film is German money.'

Kate Winslet donned frumpy garb to play Hester Wallace, a young woman who finds herself falling for a brilliant young code breaker at Bletchley Park. Hester's bespectacled ugly duckling appearance would have put off most young actresses, but Winslet leapt at the chance to appear in the film. 'I was really attracted to the wartime setting of the story,' she enthused. 'It's an adventure set in such a sexy time – with young people determined to live for the moment. In some ways I compare my character

and Meg Ryan, in an Ecuadorian kidnapping thriller. While the film involved extensive location work, the producers opted for Pinewood for the studio-based scenes. Production designer Bruno Rubeo noted that there were no studios in Ecuador, or warehouses big enough or soundproof enough to adapt. 'Plus it is very dangerous there, so we wanted to get in and out as fast as we could and with most of the crew being English, Pinewood was the obvious choice for me. This is my first time at Pinewood, and I love it. It is just like being in Hollywood. In fact I would say that it offers many unique site services. No Hollywood studio has a crèche, for example!'

Proof of Life took over two stages at the studio. On A Stage the Bowman house and garden was recreated – this was the most important set in the movie, as most of the drama unfolds there. 'We themed the design of the house around scorpions, as in the story it was supposedly formerly owned by a drug dealer,' adds Rubeo, 'and he had a thing for scorpions! The house we used in Ecuador was essentially for exteriors only, as it was rather small and

Hester to George in Enid Blyton's *The Famous Five* – she enjoys adventure and won't stop till she gets a result and, in the end, she helps save the day.' The actress was pregnant with her daughter Mia while filming *Enigma*, which called for some tricky camera work from Apted. 'I was five-and-a-half months pregnant at the time and it was very noticeable, so I was filmed mainly from the waist up or behind furniture hiding my stomach.'

Winslet had nothing but praise for producer Mick Jagger. 'He was wonderful. He was very involved and hands-on, but in a very positive way. He was on the set a lot more than I expected him to be. He wasn't just producing because he liked the idea of it – it was very important to him. It was a project he felt really passionate about and it was nice to have him there every day. It was quite funny sometimes when we were standing about in muddy fields and there was Mick Jagger in his wellingtons, too. He was very sweet and what really impressed me was that to help us get into the mood of the film he made up compilation CDs of 1940s music for us. It was fantastic. I thought that was very thoughtful and helpful. Making *Enigma* was a brilliant experience and I had so much fun.'

Another James Bond director, Martin Campbell, based himself at Pinewood for some work on his next film, *Vertical Limit*, starring Chris O'Donnell. This is a story about a climber attempting to rescue his sister from the top of K2. Also part-basing itself at the studio was the harrowing *Last Orders*, starring Michael Caine, Tom Courtenay, David Hemmings, Bob Hoskins and Helen Mirren.

TV production remained buoyant and alongside *One Foot in the Grave*, *Hornblower* and Trevor Nunn's *The Merchant of Venice*, the American Hallmark Productions brought one of the most ambitious TV series of all time to Pinewood early in 2000. Hallmark transformed the backlot for the $80 million epic *Dinotopia*. At the time, Michael Grade quipped, 'I keep my blunderbuss underneath the desk in case one of the dinosaurs should escape.' But Grade was serious about the increasing importance of television to Pinewood. '*Dinotopia* is big. Television is big. As such we are moving towards encompassing TV as a much more important element of Pinewood's business. For instance, we have invested upwards of six figures in transforming J Stage into a state-of-the-art television studio. We're fully equipped for, and on the cutting edge of, the new digital age in production and broadcasting – judging by the level of enquiries we're receiving.'

Meanwhile, another plan was being hatched by Grade. In August 2000 *Screen International* reported:

Facing page: *Code-breakers Hester Wallace (Kate Winslet) and Thomas Jericho (Dougray Scott) investigate the disappearance of a friend in* Enigma.

Right: *Julianne Moore plays pregnant housewife Laura Brown in the 1951 segments of* The Hours.

'Michael Grade and Ridley and Tony Scott are to join forces in running a UK super studio facility combining Pinewood Studios and Shepperton Studios, if current proposals from Grade get the go-ahead. Grade, who became chairman of Pinewood in February after buying the operation from Rank for $93 million (£62 million), confirmed he is close to merging the two studios to create a single company. The combined operation would be worth about $180 million (£120 milion). A deal could be finalised this month, depending on whether private equity company Candover agrees to sell its majority holding in Shepperton. Candover took over Shepperton in 1995 with a consortium which includes the Scott brothers.'

The plan was effectively a takeover of Shepperton Studios, although Grade was quick to say that the individual 'brands' would be kept distinct. Grade maintained that it was hard for any one studio to function at more than 85 per cent capacity. 'If we have three spare sound stages and a production wants to shoot, sod's law, they will want four,' he explained. Grade added that the UK faced increasing competition for large-scale productions from studio facilities in countries such as Australia, the Czech Republic, Spain and Canada. 'The British film industry has always suffered from fragmentation. If we are going to have a substantial UK film production base, it is time we had a little consolidation.' Two months later, the UK government cleared the merger of the two film-making facilities, waved through by Secretary of State for Trade and Industry Stephen Byers as 'the acquisition by Pinewood Studios Holdings of Shepperton Holdings.' Michael Grade stressed that the move was conceived as a merger of the two facilities, not a takeover, and indicated that both Scott brothers would be offered senior positions within the merged operations.

But 2000 ended amid uncertainty. The Screen Actors Guild (SAG) threatened strike action for the following year, which would effectively have precluded US actors from working overseas, as well as stopping Hollywood film production in its tracks. International productions featuring non-US acting talent would have become the world's leading form of movie production for the duration – if the strike

went ahead. Underlining the potential impact of the threatened hiatus, the volume of overseas-financed production in the UK rose 33 per cent in 2000, according to the British Film Commission's annual report. In fact, overseas-backed feature and high-end TV production hit $788 million, eclipsing the previous year's $591 million, with such high-profile studio-backed fare as *Harry Potter and the Philosopher's Stone*, *Band of Brothers*, *The Mummy Returns* and *Tomb Raider*. UK-produced films proved fewer in number (52 compared to 70 in 1999) but bigger in budget (total budgets hit $308 million compared to $248 million in 1999). Overall production volume broke the $1 billion barrier. While the rise gave local companies servicing studio-level projects a cushion, most UK studio facilities and post-production houses were preparing to brace themselves ahead of the threatened strike, and few expected to repeat the previous year's growth.

Further uncertainty was also looming, with the prospect that the UK government would not renew the production tax breaks launched in 1997, which were due to expire in 2002. Janet Anderson, the Minister for Tourism, Film and Broadcasting, stated that the tax incentives had, 'yielded more than $146 million of direct benefit to the film production sector in the UK during the last few years.' Steve Norris, the British Film Commissioner, warned that 2000's success might be 'short-lived' without the tax incentives. He noted that global competition to accommodate US-backed productions was rising, a factor cited by Michael Grade in the proposed merger of Pinewood and Shepperton. Norris hoped that the weakness of the pound against the dollar would continue to help attract US productions to the UK.

2001 began well with the news that Pinewood and Shepperton Studios had finalised their merger. *Screen International* noted: 'Pinewood takes control of Shepperton, which is co-owned by directors Ridley and Tony Scott. Pinewood chief Michael

Grade will become executive chairman of the new group, while the Scotts become co-chairmen.' Further good news followed in the spring, with the Chancellor Gordon Brown's Budget Speech, in which he extended the Section 48 tax break scheme for British film, and filmmaking, for a further three years.

The Hours – with a cast including Nicole Kidman (as Virginia Woolf, complete with prosthetic nose and drab clothing), Julianne Moore and Meryl Streep – was one of the first new productions into the studio. Based on the Pulitzer Prize-winning novel by Michael Cunningham, and adapted by David Hare, it tells of how Woolf wrote her novel *Mrs Dalloway*, and of two subsequent women (in the 1950s and 2001 respectively) who become obsessed by the book. It turns out that of the three women, one is writing it, one is reading it and one is living it. Kidman went on to win the best actress Oscar for her role.

In a year notable for strong female performances, Judi Dench took the title role in *Iris* – the true story of the lifelong romance between novelist Iris Murdoch and her husband John Bayley, from their student days through her battle with Alzheimer's disease. Kate Winslet played the young Iris opposite Hugh Bonneville and, later, opposite Dench, Jim Broadbent turned in an Oscar-winning supporting role as Bayley.

The seeds of *Iris* were first sown three years earlier, when director Richard Eyre was in New York, working with Judi Dench in a production of *Amy's View*. When Dench told Eyre that she had been asked to appear in a film about Iris Murdoch's life, based on two books by John Bayley, he was immediately struck by the project. 'I just thought, oh, what a smart idea of somebody's to get Judi.' When it transpired that the man putting the film project together was an acquaintance, John Calley, Eyre immediately wrote him a letter offering his services as director. But when Calley pitched the script that he and Charles Wood had painstakingly hammered out, the Sony executives looked at him as if he were crazy – 'an English novelist dying of Alzheimer's?' – and immediately pulled out. The disappointed Eyre contacted his friend, the theatrical impresario Robert Fox, and the

Facing page: Director Stephen Daldry on location for The Hours, with Nicole Kidman in full make-up for her role as Virginia Woolf.

Left: Cate Blanchett as the eponymous French Resistance courier in Charlotte Gray.

Hollywood producer Scott Rudin, who put up the quarter of a million pounds it cost to buy the rights. Alan Yentob, from the BBC and Intermediary – the production company started up by Anthony Minghella and Sydney Pollack – then came on board, and together put together the £3.7 million needed. 'By Hollywood standard this was a laughably small amount – Sony's original budget for the project had been somewhere around £20 million,' remembered Eyre. 'But part of the reason why costs were kept so low was that every single one of the actors readily agreed to work for minimum wage. The project, as Robert Fox put it, was "a complete labour of love".'

Judi Dench's husband, Michael Williams, had just died from cancer aged 65 when the final script arrived on her desk. 'It came very, very soon after my husband died and so I simply dreaded doing it,' she said. 'But in fact it was probably one of the best things that could have happened to me because grief generates an incredible energy. It's good if you can use that energy to a purpose and I had the equivalent of a huge amount of stored-up petrol with a long way to go; so that was very, very helpful, because in a

way you can detach yourself.' Dench went on to receive an Oscar nomination.

Charlotte Gray rounded out the three strong female-lead films produced at Pinewood that year. Cate Blanchett starred as a young Scottish woman who joins the French Resistance during World War II to rescue her Royal Air Force boyfriend, who is lost in France. It was the most ambitious project ever put together by the UK's Channel 4 film arm, FilmFour. Ultimately it lost the corporation a fortune, and resulted in it drastically scaling back future production plans. The news broke soon after the film's release in the trade press. FilmFour, after four years of activity, was dismantled. Its distribution and sales arms were closed, and its production capability was reabsorbed into the TV station's drama wing.

Harrison Ford and Liam Neeson came to Pinewood for a little work in the paddock tank and stages for *K:19 – The Widowmaker*. The true story follows a Russian submarine crew on a voyage destined for catastrophe. A radiation leak from the nuclear reactor causes death and disease amongst the sailors and might have started a war had the meltdown not been contained. Director Kathryn Bigelow discovered the story of the K:19 through *National Geographic* when she was looking for true stories to adapt into a film. So moved was she by the efforts of the K:19 crew that she sought their blessing to make the film.

'We were met with some suspicion and some mistrust, especially given how Russians have been handled in Hollywood movies,' Bigelow recalled. 'And it's understandable. Who am I to tell their story? You have to cross that bridge first and that was a process, but one that ended in a lot of very emotional conversations where you're hugged and there are tears in the eyes and you're asked to tell their story. Basically, you're asked to give their lives and that experience meaning. That was a huge request which I did not take lightly.' Harrison Ford also responded to the importance of the story's historical ramifications. 'I think that it's always important to reflect on your history and the choices that you've made as a nation,' Ford said. 'Perhaps now, it's important always to understand what shapes your national will. I think that in the context of the Cold War, we'd

Left: *Tim Roth in Rick Baker's award-winning ape make-up design for his role as General Thade in Tim Burton's* Planet of the Apes.

Facing page: *Q (John Cleese) demonstrates the Aston Martin 'Vanish' to James Bond (Pierce Brosnan) in* Die Another Day.

opened up a Pandora's Box of nuclear potential.'

Tim Burton also made a brief return to Pinewood in 2001, following 1989's *Batman*, and took over D Stage for secret re-shoots on *Planet of the Apes*, which he had recently been working on in the USA. The film was given a false title, to throw people off the scent, though it was quite possibly the worst kept secret at the studio.

Television continued to play an increasingly important part of Pinewood's output. A new head of TV was appointed: Steve Gunn (formerly of Thames, Teddington Studios and Buena Vista Productions). Two huge coups were sealed when Gunn announced that series two of the BBC comedy *My Family* would move to the studio, as would the hugely popular *The Weakest Link* quiz. Pinewood Television was offering more than just the hire of empty studios, offices and workshop areas for the producer to fill with crew, scenery and equipment. Everything a producer needed was there, and if there was something that wasn't, they could rest assured it would be provided quickly. The vast size of the studios (formerly J & K) – 111 x 80 feet and 29 feet 3 inches high – ensured plenty of space for audiences of up to 500, which have been integral to Pinewood TV's output to date. With luxury dressing rooms,

make-up rooms, crowd areas, green rooms and every creature comfort from en-suite bathrooms to televisions, Pinewood quickly attracted plenty of TV business. As well as housing the sitcom *Sam's Game*, the ambitious live-broadcast of *Tomorrow's World Live Lab*, the mammoth *Survivor* and its two hour live final episode, the hit BBC show *The Weakest Link* was a big coup for Gunn and his team. K Stage was converted into a digital studio especially for the show. The show was previously recorded between The Mill studios in East London and (for the prime-time shows) Television Centre. At Pinewood, the set stood permanently, which saved the production a considerable sum. Averaging two shows per day, with audiences being drafted in for the prime time and celebrity editions, the schedule was a demanding one.

Meanwhile, the set for series two of Robert Lindsay's BBC sitcom *My Family* stood for 16 weeks on K Stage. This is unlike most sitcoms, which – for example – build on Monday, record on Tuesday and then move out on Wednesday. The show is also one of the only sitcoms in the UK to have a team of writers, like most of the successful US shows (*Friends*, *Frasier*, *Ally McBeal* and so on) but perhaps that's no surprise when the creator, executive producer and one of the writers is Fred Barron – one of the people behind *The Larry Sanders Show* and *Caroline in the City*. It's a rare case of a distinctive American style and sense of humour working in a British format. So why did the set remain in place on K Stage for the duration? It's important for the writers and cast to have the set to rehearse, and for the writers to be able to move around the set as they polish the scripts and make alterations. The environment is a permanent and practical one, and one which has paid dividends with the cast, who have cited the experience as both exciting and helpful.

During the summer of 2001, Pinewood's film history was showcased in a season of films at London's Barbican Cinema. The posters declared 'Pinewood Studios – Celebrating the best British movies ever made'. The first night gala was attended by scores of actors, directors and producers (many of whom returned during the two-week season to give talks and introduce their movies). Michael Grade

made the welcoming speech, before introducing some vintage newsreel footage of the studio, followed by a special presentation of the first Bond movie, *Dr No*.

The new Bond film, which had been prepping since the summer, was ready to start work at the beginning of 2002. However, the year threatened to be an uncertain one for UK production and Bond. UK actors' union Equity threatened to strike, calling on the 36,000 UK actors that make up its membership to refuse to work on any movie after December 2001 (as their US equivalent SAG had done a year earlier). The dispute concerned a demand by Equity for additional revenue payments for its members, similar to the system of residuals granted to its US counterpart. At that time, British actors received a flat fee for their performances, even if the films they worked on became a huge success in the various ancillary markets. Equity wanted to change that. One of the first casualties could have been the new 007 film, *Die Another Day*, which would have meant very bad news for the studio. Fortunately, the film was cleared to shoot as planned in January, after Eon Productions agreed to give members of UK actors union Equity a royalty payment from video and DVD sales worldwide. The deal, which kicked in after the film's pro-

ducers recouped 30 per cent of its budget from video and DVD sales, was among a string of emergency waiver pacts Equity struck with producers.

Rumours were rife about the female casting in the movie, which was the 20th in the official series and 40 years on from the first, *Dr No*. Pierce Brosnan was returning as Bond for the fourth time … but not much more was known. The world didn't have to wait long, as on 11 January 2002 over 150 journalists descended on D Stage, itself the home to two sets in the new – as then untitled – film. The stage was also shared by two Aston Martin V12 Vanquishes, Bond's mode of transport. It was a welcome return for the British marque, which was first seen in *Goldfinger* (1964).

Producers Barbara Broccoli and Michael G Wilson introduced the New Zealand director Lee Tamahori (*Once Were Warriors*, *Along Came a Spider*), who enthused the assembled journalists with his intention to keep Bond faithful to Fleming's original. 'He will not be turned into a new age guy who goes around visiting shrinks. Bond may seem anachronistic and antediluvian, but it would be wrong to play around with the character too much. It's all very well to reinvent him, but some facets to his character everyone expects.' Despite being unable to offer a title or much

about the plot, Brosnan revealed that although he had fulfilled his contract by starring in a fourth film, he by no means expected to hang up his Walther P99 and call it a day. 'I'd like to do another, and even a sixth. I'm not finished yet!' he said. The supporting cast also lined up to answer questions: Toby Stephens, Halle Berry, and newcomers Rosamund Pike and Rick Yune.

The film was ultimately titled *Die Another Day*. Vic Armstrong returned to the back lot to oversee the action as second unit director. It was the third time that he had fulfilled this role, although his association with the series began when he was a stunt man on *You Only Live Twice* in 1966. 'Most vehicles we drive nowadays have some point of contact with the ground,' he said, describing the unusual pre-credit chase sequence. 'But a hovercraft is literally on this cushion of air being driven by another direction of air behind it. So you have the whole weight on the ground just floating along. When you want to turn it, the whole thing will slide sideways and run down a hillside. You have to think four moves ahead.'

The instability of a hovercraft meant that Armstrong had to develop a new camera system to get the shots. 'I resist it all the way,' he said, explaining the ethos behind Bond action sequences. 'I think it's a cop out in action sequences to go for CG work

– it's almost as if you don't know how to do it any other way. With CG you have much more latitude; with Bond the audience has to think that, "He could have done it." He's Bond after all. My saying for Bond is that you take the truth and stretch it ten per cent.'

Pierce Brosnan was the man with the responsibility of making it all look real on screen. Armstrong was impressed with the manner in which he would launch himself into the action. 'Pierce did very well. We didn't let him loose too much in a hovercraft, but we had him inside one for a while and he was being thrown everywhere. He had the time of life actually

Facing page top: Aston Martin V12 Vanquish versus Jaguar XKR — Die Another Day's ice chase, filmed on location in Iceland.

Facing page bottom: Bond (Pierce Brosnan) attempts to escape from North Korea's Demilitarized Zone in one of Colonel Moon's hovercraft.

Below: The cast and crew of Die Another Day filming on Peter Lamont's Ice Palace set, constructed on the 007 Stage.

– he loves coming down to our unit and getting up to his arms in action.'

Peter Lamont also returned to the series as the production designer. *Die Another Day* required a huge set called the Ice Palace; the exterior was built on the back lot and the interior was built inside the 007 Stage. The structure was inspired by a real 'ice hotel' in Jukkasjarvi, Sweden. This hotel is constructed in ice from December to April and then, in true Bond style, it melts back into the river.

'Tamahori came up with the idea of having a car chase in the ice palace featuring the Aston Martin and the Jaguar with Zao (Rick Yune) trying to prevent Bond from rescuing Jinx (Berry) from a sinking apartment,' recalled Lamont. 'We had to beef up the structure because cars are heavy. We built a composite of the drowning room that sank into a tank beneath the set, and we constructed two upward ramps so that you could drive around to your heart's content within the palace. The biggest problem we had was how to make it look icy. One of my colleagues had worked on Dr Zhivago and they did this whole ice set in candle wax, so we got a paraffin wax and sprayed it on to our finished plaster.'

Once a Bond film is given the green light, there never seems to be enough time no matter how early the start. Team work was vital in this shoot, as Lamont explained: 'All departments involved with the set worked as a team. It was quite miraculous that we got everything ready in time. I started putting the

set together in August 2001 and we started shooting on 14 January 2002.'

The Aston Martin was a welcome sight to 007 fans, but the vehicles required some significant modifications before they could perform the required stunts. Chris Corbould was the special effects supervisor on the film and he explained some of the problems he encountered. 'Vic [Armstrong] and I came to a decision to use four wheel drive versions of the cars, naively thinking we could just trot down to Aston Martin and Jaguar and say "We want to use your cars in a film, can you give us the four wheel drive versions?" Ultimately, they were not in existence, so we then embarked on adapting both versions of the cars into four wheel drive. We felt that it would give the stunt guys the biggest opportunity to get the most out of the cars.'

However, the pressures of working on a Bond film mean a heavy and demanding schedule packed into a relatively short space of time. 'By the end of a Bond you're exhausted both mentally and physically, and all you want to do is go and sit in a dark room,' said Corbould. 'And then two weeks later the first thing you want to do is start on another Bond,' he laughed.

In the series' 40th anniversary year, it was particularly poignant that an anniversary lunch was held at the studio following the press launch with guests from the films going back to the very first: Eunice Gayson who, as Sylvia Trench, prompted Sean Connery's historical introduction as 'Bond, James Bond' in *Dr No*. Golden Girl Shirley Eaton, former Miss Moneypenny Lois Maxwell, 7 foot 4 inch henchman Richard 'Jaws' Kiel and production designers Ken Adam and Syd Cain were amongst a hundred or more other actors, technicians and personnel joining Pierce Brosnan and the cast of 'Bond 20' at the lunch, presided over by the Broccoli family and Michael Grade.

Another favourite returned to the studio in 2002, when Angelina Jolie slipped in to her Lara Croft outfit once again, for *Tomb Raider: The Cradle of Life*. In the film, directed by Jan de Bont, Jolie reprises her role as the sexy explorer, this time battling to stop a madman named Dr Jonathan Reece (Ciarán Hinds) from retrieving Pandora's Box, which is buried in a

mysterious location known only as the Cradle of Life. A Thai town set was built on the backlot at Pinewood, on which many of the film's stunts were performed. Jolie was always keen to get involved in that aspect. 'I like to do as much as I possibly can, and as much as insurance will allow me... I love the opportunity to try something new, and I'm an adrenaline junkie. I think it's part of the character and feels like if you're going to be Lara, then you better be able to back it with skills and guts.'

Finding Neverland was the biopic of Peter Pan creator J M Barrie. Filming principally at Shepperton, the production moved to Pinewood for a little work. The film starred Johnny Depp as Barrie, and he was the director Marc Forster's only choice. 'When I wrote the script, I envisioned Johnny Depp in the part,' he remarked, 'because I felt he would be the right actor to be able to play the dramatic sequences and the playful sequences ... you could say I dreamt of having him in this movie, or of working with him, because I love Johnny Depp. He is a marvellous actor and a marvellous person.' Opposite Depp, Forster cast ten-year-old Freddie Highmore as Peter. 'I think Freddie Highmore is a very gifted child. When he came to audition for me, I was just sitting there and was blown away. He embodies something very truth-

ful. There is nothing fake about him. He projects that onto everybody that is working with him.'

The chemistry between Highmore and Depp on screen is obvious, not least in the last scene where they sit on a park bench together. 'It was very rough,' reveals Depp. 'We had done about a dozen takes or something, with Freddie having to refuel and let go each time, and then we found out there had been a problem with the remote-control camera so we had to go back and re-shoot it. I remember Marc [Forster] approaching Freddie and saying, "I'm really sorry, but I think we have to do this again. Is it okay?" Freddie was really happy. He said, "Great, I don't think I did it so good first time." But doing a scene with a kid like that, you really have to try to hold back the waterworks. My job at that point was just to let Freddie do his thing, because if you start flooding a scene it becomes real messy.'

The film's release was delayed until 2004 because of 2003's *Peter Pan* feature film – the producers didn't want them to be seen as 'rival films'. Depp meanwhile was so impressed with Freddie Highmore that he recommended him to Tim Burton for his next film, *Charlie and the Chocolate Factory* – of which more later.

One of the films that might have lost out when

Facing page left: *Angelina Jolie as the title character in* Lara Croft Tomb Raider: The Cradle of Life.

Facing page right: *JM Barrie (Johnny Depp) and Peter Llewelyn Davies (Freddie Highmore) in* Finding Neverland.

Left: *Bill Paxton as Jeff Tracy and Sophia Myles as Lady Penelope Creighton-Ward in* Thunderbirds.

Dan Akroyd, Jim Broadbent, Simon Callow, Richard E Grant, John Mills, Imelda Staunton and Peter O'Toole. But did Fry the humble actor find himself becoming a tyrant when he climbed into the director's chair? 'There are moments when actors are a bit slow to get onto the set and you think "bloody actors"! But generally speaking, and having been one, I think I retained my sympathy for the profession.' And what did he think Evelyn Waugh would have made of the film? 'God, I wouldn't like to guess. He was a pretty curmudgeonly old sod and he would no doubt have grumbled about it. He hated anything modern, so God knows.'

While 2003 boasted fewer productions at the studio, the scale of the productions was vast. It had long been rumoured, since ITC was taken over by PolyGram in the early 1990s, that the television puppet series *Thunderbirds* would get the big screen treatment, via PolyGram's subsidiary company Working Title Films. A variety of different approaches, including stop-motion animation and digital animation were considered, but media speculation was rife that the project would be filmed in live-action with the actor brothers Alec, William, Daniel and Stephen Baldwin as the Tracy brothers, Sean Connery as Jeff Tracy and Joanna Lumley as Lady Penelope. At the 1997 Cannes Film Festival, Working Title announced that British director Peter Hewitt had been assigned to the film with a budget of $60 million. It was also suggested that the show's original creator Gerry Anderson would be involved, but he was ultimately never engaged. Hewitt developed a script with American screenwriter Karey Kirkpatrick which presented a new, original adventure for the International Rescue team.

Six months of pre-production work began with Hewitt's vision for the production design: a retro vision of the future with big, bright, low-tech, colourful machinery. Then, over the summer of 1998, the massive success of Michael Bay's *Thunderbirds*-style blockbuster *Armageddon* was overshadowed by the devastating failure of two other big-budget feature-film adaptations of the 1960s television series – *Lost in Space* and *The Avengers*. PolyGram was sold to Universal Pictures and the studio's executives got cold feet about *Thunderbirds*, questioning whether

FilmFour all but closed down was Stephen Fry's adaptation of Evelyn Waugh's novel *Vile Bodies*, retitled *Bright Young Things* for the big screen. Fortunately, other partners were found to complete the financing and the film moved onto Pinewood's floors as planned. '*Bright Young Things* is a period film, shot with modern pace and cinematography,' said Fry, who directed as well as adapting the screenplay. 'It deals with fame, sexual scandal, greed, nightclubbing and the frantic glamour of youth...

'After I re-read the book that the movie is based on, *Vile Bodies*, [I realised] that our generation and even generations younger than me somehow believe they invented the party culture and the obsession with celebrity,' continued Fry. 'We all think it's a modern curse. But actually almost everything that defines the way we live today was invented by the young generation in the 1920s. This was the age that invented modern youth. We think it was the fifties when the teenager was born, but actually it was the twenties. You know: no sense of responsibility, damn your parents, to hell with the future ... if it could be sniffed or snorted, then do it!'

Fry was keen to gather a cast of friends and heroes for the movie, and assembled a starry roster including Emily Mortimer, Stephen Campbell-Moore,

■

Right: *The underwater monorail rescue sequence in* Thunderbirds *was filmed 'dry' on a Thames riverbed set using a full-scale prop of the Thunderbird 4 submarine.*

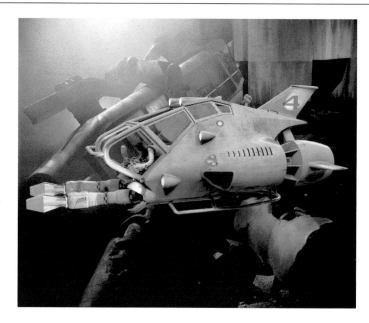

the climate was right for another 1960s TV-to-movie remake – particularly one that was relatively little-known in America. Kirkpatrick left the project, closely followed by Hewitt and, fearing that the cost of *Thunderbirds* would vastly exceed the potential returns, work was suspended.

It was four years before producers Tim Bevan and Eric Fellner were able to revive the production, with an anticipated start date of early 2003. The 1997 Kirkpatrick/Hewitt script was put aside, and an entirely new script commissioned from William Osborne. Re-evaluating the target audience for the film, the producers looked at the success of *Spy Kids* (2001) and *Harry Potter and the Philosopher's Stone* (2001) and decided to pitch *Thunderbirds* for a family audience of under-12s and their parents. With a budget of $70 million, actor Jonathan Frakes – best known for his role as Will Riker in *Star Trek: The Next Generation* – was invited to direct the film. He confirmed that it would appeal to general audiences as well as hardcore *Thunderbirds* fans. But continuity would also be observed. 'We need to honour the look of the series. We've got to make sure the ships resemble very closely the ships from the show.'

Lady Penelope's trademark pink FAB 1 car was built as a full-size working vehicle. Having been refused permission to make the car a futuristic Rolls-Royce similar to the one in the television series, the filmmakers turned to Ford, who immediately came on board to turn FAB 1 into a fantastical pink version of the Ford Thunderbird – a 23-foot-long six-wheeled limousine that transformed into an aircraft and a speedboat for key sequences in the film. Production designer John Beard created the interiors of the Tracys' luxurious multi-level island home on E Stage. A and S Stages were also used extensively for the interior rooms and corridors of Thunderbird 5 and the cockpits of the other Thunderbird vehicles.

Much of the film was acted against green screens to accommodate the many computer-generated effects. The director was undeterred by this. 'We're lucky because we developed a lot of what the movie was going to look like in preproduction,' he said. 'So I was able to share with these guys what would be in the FAB 1, what would be out the window of the spaceship, out of the cockpits, what the silos would

look like. The visual effects team would come to our rehearsals and then come when we were preparing to shoot, and there were visual stimulants that would help us.'

The film was the most expensive ever produced by Working Title. Unfortunately, its box office performance was somewhat disappointing, taking just under $7 million in the US and just over $28 million worldwide.

Another expensive production moving into the studio was *Alexander*. The film was directed by Oliver Stone and headlined Colin Farrell, Angelina Jolie, Val Kilmer and Anthony Hopkins and used Pinewood's largest stages, including the 007 Stage, where the hanging gardens of Babylon were recreated. Stone had been on the trail of the youthful conqueror (who died in 323 BC, at 32 years old) since writing his first *Alexander* script in the mid-eighties. German producer Thomas Schühly approached Stone with his own plans to film *Alexander* in 1989. They combined forces, but it was many years later, and many scripts later, before Stone could move the project into development. The second crucial jigsaw-piece came into place when another German producer, Moritz Borman, hired Stone to write a screenplay about cowboy star Tom Mix's adventures with Pancho Villa. The Mix script was shelved, but the two stayed in touch.

Borman commented on their 2001 meeting: 'Oliver came to me and said, "Maybe it's time, let's figure out if we can find something we can work together on." And I said, "If you come to me with a screenplay, I will, depending on the budget, do that film regardless of what it is.' And he said, "Let me think … Actually, I want to do *Alexander*." And I

Left: *Director Oliver Stone with Colin Farrell on the 007 Stage during the filming of* Alexander.

Below: *For* Alexander, *production designer Jan Roelfs recreated the hanging gardens of Babylon as a magnificent multi-level set on the 007 Stage.*

and Stone needed a major studio to underwrite almost a third of the cost, which was already pegged well north of $100 million. Warners eventually came on board, although they declared Stone's script 'impressive, but costly to shoot'. They needed a major star, or a potent combination of lesser ones, to secure their investment. Stone suggested Colin Farrell: 'I saw him in *Minority Report*, and then I met with him. I ended up screen-testing him, and he was amazing.'

Farrell was signed, followed by Jolie and Kilmer. Then came Anthony Hopkins as Ptolemy. He had worked with Stone last on *Nixon* in 1995, and had received an Oscar nomination. Despite the heady cast and exotic locations, the $155 million production grossed $167 million worldwide, which when taking into account a $40 million marketing spend, wasn't the good news producers hoped for. Stone blamed Warners for insisting key sequences be cut to make a

swallowed deep and thought, "Oh my God, that must be huge"'.

Borman knew it was going to be an uphill struggle when he realised that 'no studio was willing to make a picture of this size – they all kicked us out the front door.' Nevertheless, Stone was determined to continue, and Borman assembled a complex deal from European and Asian rights sales. Ultimately, he

Right: Alexander *courted controversy in Greece where lawyers tried to have the film banned for its depiction of a sexual relationship between Alexander (Colin Farrell) and Hephaistion (Jared Leto).*

Below: *One of production designer Anthony Pratt's Oscar-nominated sets for* The Phantom of the Opera.

certain running time, and has since re-cut it, his way, for the DVD release.

A cheeky French James Bond spoof *Double Zéro* moved onto a couple of stages, while Jude Law's version of *Alfie* completed interiors at the studio following location shooting in Manchester and London (doubling for New York). In September, *The Phantom of the Opera*, thought to be the largest independently-financed UK production ever, cranked up. The long-gestating adaptation of Andrew Lloyd Webber's musical was shot entirely at the studio for 16 weeks under director Joel Schumacher. Gerard Butler, the 33 year-old Scottish actor from *Tomb Raider 2* and Richard Donner's *Timeline*, was cast in the title role of the Phantom, while 17 year-old New York opera singer and acting newcomer Emmy Rossum played Christine.

Producer Andrew Lloyd Webber initially spoke to director Joel Schumacher about making a film of the long running stage musical in the mid 1980s, after he saw *The Lost Boys*. 'I was going to make the movie with Michael Crawford and Sarah Brightman in 1990. We were all set to make it in Munich and Prague,' the director revealed. Unfortunately financing fell through. 'I'd only made four movies when Andrew asked me to do this,' said Schumacher at a BAFTA screening of the movie, 'which is kind of amazing when I think about it. Andrew saw *The Lost Boys*, and he loved the way the music and the visuals were used. I was shocked that he even knew who I was. He brought me to London and offered me the movie. It's hard to even imagine what I would have done then because I'd done four movies and now I've done 18 movies.'

Pinewood's backlot was transformed, with the exterior of the opera house and Parisian landscape in the background, whilst one of the most beautiful sets ever constructed on a Pinewood stage took over E Stage – the interior of the opera house, including the huge glass chandelier, central to the dramatic destruction scene. Production designer Anthony Pratt went on to secure himself an Oscar nomination for his work.

Television regulars *The Weakest Link* and *My Family* were this year supplemented by BBC drama *Spooks* doing a little filming, along with M Stage pro-

viding the home for ITV drama *Henry VIII*, starring Ray Winstone. The pathway from the main administration building into the garden was dug up and gravelled for one sequence of the King walking from his garden at Hampton Court! Another notable TV drama, *Auf Weidersehn Pet*, also made Pinewood its home after completing exteriors in the Dominican Republic. The series returned in 2004 too, for what was to be the final two-part episode of the Geordie builder's adventures. Indeed 2004 proved to be one of the busiest years for TV drama in Pinewood's history. *Spooks* was back, along with *Dead Ringers*, *Last of the Summer Wine*, cookery programme *Planet Cook*, sitcom *My Dad's The Prime Minister*, *BBC Sport Relief* and the Griff Rhys-Jones fronted *Restoration*. However, the biggest TV show was, without doubt, Gerry Anderson's new production of *Captain Scarlet*.

Based on the original 1960s Supermarionation

series *Captain Scarlet and the Mysterons*, Gerry Anderson cut loose his strings and opted for the latest motion-capture system and cutting edge CGI to create his latest production. It was described as one of the most impressive animated series ever seen on children's television, with explosive action, breathtaking settings and dramatic storylines. The 26 x 22-

Dahl's strengths as a storyteller.'

When it came to casting, Burton told his friend Johnny Depp that he was working on the story and asked if he might be interested in the part of Willy Wonka. According to Depp, 'I couldn't wait for him to finish his sentence. I said, "I'm in. Absolutely. I'm there. No question about it."' The supporting cast

minute episodes cost $30 million, raised through private investment. All were produced in high definition with Dolby 5.1 Surround Sound. 'The new *Captain Scarlet* is the most advanced and adventurous production I have ever made, taking family sci-fi action adventure to another level and CGI television animation into a new dimension,' commented Anderson. The series took over the entire top floor of the expansive Kubrick building for over two years.

Just over the way from the Kubrick building, Tim Burton was busy transforming the backlot for his next film, *Charlie and the Chocolate Factory*, based on the story by Roald Dahl. 'One of the interesting aspects of the book,' said Burton, 'is that it's so vivid in mood and feeling and so specific, yet it still leaves room for interpretation ... which, I think, is one of

was impressive: Freddie Highmore as Charlie, at the suggestion of Burton, followed by Helena Bonham Carter, David Kelly, James Fox and Christopher Lee all signing up. The lavish and stunning sets took over seven of Pinewood's stages, and included the impressive and fully-working squirrel room on A Stage (for which trainers spent weeks with real life tame and baby squirrels, training them to perform), Charlie's house on C Stage, and the 'TV room' on D Stage, but most stunning of all was the chocolate river set on the 007 Stage – without doubt the most beautiful set ever constructed. The backlot was dominated by the exterior of the chocolate factory, town and, of course, the bucket house. It was quite something to step onto the backlot in sunny June and find yourself in a snow-strewn city, somewhere between

America and Europe. 'The sets were wonderful,' says David Kelly 'hand-painted, handmade, the kind you rarely see anymore. Going to work every day was endlessly jaw-dropping and magical.'

It had long been rumoured that Pinewood and Shepperton Studios were set for a flotation – enabling Michael Grade to buy out his original backers, while raising significant capital to invest in the two sites. In April this was confirmed when Grade and CEO Ivan Dunleavy announced plans to raise £50 million. The prospectus highlighted the importance of big budget Hollywood movies to the company's trading prospects. This was two months after the Government closed a tax loophole – which it considered a tax abuse – resulting in numerous films collapsing, the most high profile being the Pinewood based *Tulip Fever*, starring Jude Law. Other productions hastily refinanced and relocated (such as *The Libertine* to the Isle of Man). Analysts were therefore a little circumspect about the plans.

'Productions in the UK have doubled since 1997,' Grade said reassuringly, 'and inward investment between 2002 and 2003 rose from £221 million to £410 million.' The company accounts showed that in 2003 a profit of £2.63 million was made against £643,000 the previous year. The time was ripe. A month later, shares floated in Pinewood Shepperton plc at 180p, and soon rose to 200p. The flotation raised £46 million for the company. Grade had also recently been appointed chairman of the BBC, and said that while he had resigned his other director-ships, he would remain as chairman of Pinewood.

Several large scale movies dropped into Pinewood to complete a little filming: *The Chronicles of Riddick, Beyond the Sea, Descent, Revolver, Harry Potter and the Goblet of Fire* and *Stoned*. Then came *Nanny McPhee*, which Emma Thompson both wrote and starred in. Thomson recalled 'I thought that something like this would be easy to adapt. In fact it was more difficult, because there's not in fact a nar-rative in the book. I suddenly discovered that I just agreed to write this and there wasn't a story.

'I had to make a lot of it up, really. My first version of this film had 35 kids in it. Can you imagine? Then I slowly went down to 17, 13, 11, 9, and I absolutely stopped at 9. I said, "I'm not going with any less than

nine. It's not going to make sense and there's not going to be enough kids."' Throwing out the old adage of never working with children or animals, Thompson did both, the animal in question being a dancing donkey. 'That donkey was supposed to be doing things and it just stood there as if it was

Above:

The Round Table set designed by Dan Weil for Antoine Fuqua's King Arthur.

injected with a half pound of heroin. You know that thing that's said at the end of movies where no animal was harmed, accidentally or otherwise? I wanted to harm it. I wanted to have at the end of the film, "Emma Thompson harmed this animal".'

Jerry Bruckheimer's *King Arthur* was shot extensively on location in Ireland and Wales, and headed over to Pinewood for some sequences backing on to Black Park, the paddock tank and interiors, including the impressive 'round table' set. One of the extras involved on the Irish segment of filming, Mick Fitzgerald, described how they moved to Pinewood to film a huge water sequence. 'The lake [in the movie] was replicated in a car park in Pinewood [the paddock tank]. It was a wooden structure covered in the obligatory fake snow, with water underneath. The structure was also designed in such a way that on "action" parts of it split and jutted up like real fractured ice and stuntmen fell into the water.'

2005 was quiet in terms of big budget productions. The uncertainty about replacement tax breaks for UK productions when the current scheme ended (later extended for one more year) coupled with a weak dollar, would be a familar reason given for films to move away from British studios. Meanwhile Pinewood's former parent, Rank, made the announcement in February that the industry had long expected: it was getting out of film – totally – when it unveiled plans to de-merge its only remaining film interests, Deluxe Films, and sell Deluxe Media.

Deluxe Films was to become a separately-listed company valued at $573m (£300m) while Deluxe Media, which makes and distributes DVDs and videos, was expected to be targeted by private equity buyers.

With uncertainty in the film business, Pinewood chose to focus more on its profitable TV arm, and on 1 April Pinewood Shepperton plc announced to the London stock market that it had bought Teddington Studios, which was in administration, as well as the entire share capital of the Studio Broadcasting Company (SBC) for £2.7 million. Teddington, in south-west London, has a long history of film production, stretching back to the silent era. It was Warner Bros' UK base from the 1930s, where its stars such as Tallulah Bankhead, Rex Harrison, Burt Lancaster and Errol Flynn made movies. In the mid 1950s, Teddington was re-customised as a TV studio and became the HQ for ABC Television and their productions of *The Avengers*, *Armchair Theatre* and others, until, in 1968, ABC and Rediffusion Television amalgamated to form Thames TV. Subsequently the studio played host to many top-rated shows including *Benny Hill*, *George and Mildred* and *Man About the House*. In recent years, Teddington has housed some of the UK's top comedy shows – *Birds of a Feather*, *The Office*, *My Hero* and *Harry Hill* among them.

The acquisition came at a time when British studios were beginning to feel the fallout from the uncertainty surrounding the future of UK tax breaks.

Right: *14 years after the original film, Sharon Stone reprised her role as novelist Catherine Tramell in* Basic Instinct 2, *primarily shot on Pinewood's R and S Stages.*

In late March, shares in Pinewood Shepperton fell by 13 per cent. In a statement about the purchase, Ivan Dunleavy commented: 'This is an exciting opportunity for Pinewood Shepperton and is in line with our long-term strategy to diversify our revenue streams in our integrated media businesses. Teddington Studios and SBC, combined with our existing business in television and sound services, significantly enhances our presence in the marketplace. We will be working closely with the management of Teddington Studios and SBC to maximise the benefit of our enlarged television and sound services activities.'

The studio was relieved to hear that the long-gestating follow-up to *Basic Instinct* would be using stages as part of its European shoot, although alas it didn't prove enough. On 20 June the studio issued a profit warning. *Screen International* reported: 'Shares in Pinewood Shepperton have dropped 20 per cent after the studio issued a profit warning. The UK institution has been expanding recently, acquiring Teddington Studios two months ago. But it has been struggling to tie down the big blockbuster movies on which it has built its business and reputation.' In April, the share price had taken a tumble after Paramount's $120 million superhero thriller *Watchmen* abandoned plans to shoot at Pinewood, and that, added to news that the latest Bond looked set to shift to Prague's Barrandov Studios, sent shivers through the City. The company said it expected interim operating profits to be a little below market estimates at £2 million. 'It is proving more difficult to achieve the level of conversion needed to meet market expectations for the full year ended 31 December 2005 and the Board now considers these are unlikely to be met,' the company said in a statement.

Along with *Basic Instinct: Risk Addiction* a number of other productions were attracted to the studio for short stays; four, in particular, to make exclusive use of the new U Stage – Europe's first custom built underwater shooting facility. The tank itself is 65.6 feet long by 32.8 feet wide and is 19.7 feet deep. The water temperature is maintained at a steady 22 degrees C (72 degrees F) and can be raised to 28 degrees C (82 degrees F) within 48 hours. It has fully automated chemical dosing and ultra violet treatment systems. To keep an eye on things, viewing windows are located on the west, south and east sides of the tank. The stage also houses single-sex showers, changing facilities and two offices.

Television production increased. Ricky Gervais' star-studded comedy *Extras* used almost every nook and cranny of the studio. In the garden you could see Jonathan Ross recording links for another series of *Hollywood Greats*, and the old timers from *Last of the Summer Wine* were back too. It was therefore a fitting time for a major refurbishment of Pinewood Television, and the studio re-launched the two 9000 sq ft television studios as 'TV-one' and 'TV-two'. The studios can now accommodate audiences up to 500 strong, and the £100,000 investment in the reception and introduction areas ensure that all will receive a welcome fitting to one of the country's premiere television studio facilities.

One of the most anticipated films of the decade had to be *The Da Vinci Code*. Set in the UK and Europe, director Ron Howard chose to make Shepperton his base for the Tom Hanks-starring drama, though Howard also came over to Pinewood to use the 007 Stage for an impressive recreation of

Instinct 2. It added that 36 films overall began shooting in the UK during the period. Plans to redevelop and rebuild part of the studio were shelved for a year or so, and a number of redundancies were made in the studio workforce, which partly tied in with consolidating the interests of Pinewood, Shepperton and Teddington.

There was a hope that the new Bond film, *Casino Royale*, might base at Pinewood, but this was dashed when director Martin Campbell announced: 'We'll be shooting a little bit at Pinewood but not much. We're going to be in Prague, maybe Italy, Bahamas and places like that. Like everybody, we're heading off to wherever we can get a good exchange rate.' It later transpired that there would be five weeks shooting at Pinewood, primarily on the 007 Stage. Some pre-production work would base at Pinewood but the film unit would move out in January 2006 to Prague. The hot news was in the casting of a new actor to play 007, and many weeks of tests were held on one of Pinewood's stages, under the tightest security. On 14 October 2005 the wait was over and Daniel Craig was unveiled as the new James Bond.

Pinewood's stages saw more activity later in the year with short visits from *Alien Autopsy* (two days), *Stormbreaker, I Could Never Be Your Woman* and some re-shoots for the delayed *V for Vendetta* – postponed from release due to part of the story mirroring the London bomb attacks of July. Then, at the end of the year, 9/11 drama *United 93* moved in. Director Paul Greengrass started shooting *United 93* at Pinewood on 14 November, and shooting continued on location in the UK and the US. The film re-enacts events on United Airlines 93, the last of the four aircraft hijacked on 11 September 2001. The production had the support of family members of flight 93's victims. The story, told in real time, follows events on the plane as well as on the ground with air traffic controllers and military command centres.

'9/11 was unique – the most important event of our lifetime, casting a shadow over all our futures,' said Greengrass. 'It's vital for cinema to begin the task of exploring what it meant, and what it continues to mean today. Hopefully *United 93* will be a worthy contribution to that process.'

Around the same time, Clive Owen's dystopian

the Louvre. But the arrival of *Da Vinci* didn't prove enough to help turn Pinewood's recent fortunes around, and in August the company posted disappointing first half results. Pre-tax losses for the first six months of 2005 were £108,000, compared with £1.63 million profit for the same period of 2004. Revenues tumbled from £20.4 million to £13.3 million.

Ivan Dunleavy explained that it had been difficult to convert provisional film bookings into contracts during the first half of the year. This was, 'principally due to the protracted uncertainty over future UK film fiscal policy and to a lesser extent the adverse dollar/sterling exchange rates.' The studio pointed out that the results reflected a broader picture of reduced film production investment in the UK in the first half of 2005. Overall UK production spend halved to £335 million compared to £668 million in the same period of 2004.

Pinewood added that, 'only two significant Hollywood productions' were shot in the UK in the first half of 2005, both of which were serviced at Pinewood Shepperton: *The Da Vinci Code* and *Basic*

thriller *Children of Men*, based on the book by PD
James, cranked up. The orchard backlot, once the
scene of *Carry On Camping*, was transformed into a
shanty town for director Alfonso Cuarón. The film
follows the story of a radically changed world where
humans can no longer reproduce. When a young
immigrant woman discovers that she has conceived a
child – something no other woman has been able to
do for nearly 20 years – Owen's character is assigned
to protect her life.

When the Government outlined new tax breaks
for the industry, commencing in April 2006, it was felt
that the uncertain times were over. Michael Grade
commented: 'We welcome the Government's com-
mitment to continuing fiscal incentives for the UK
film sector, and the fact that the issue is now on its
way to a positive resolution.' He added: 'The Board
believes the disappointing results for the first half do
not indicate any fundamental shift in the film production business as a whole. Our strategy therefore
remains unchanged and the Board remains confident
in the long-term prospects for the group.'

As Christmas approached, the studio held a
farewell party in honour of managing director Steve
Jaggs, who had run the studio since taking over in
1993 and steered it through the management buy-in
and merger with Shepperton. Hundreds of people
congregated to pay warm tribute to the man they

hold in such high regard. Jaggs said, 'I'd like to think
I'm leaving the studio in a better condition than when
I found it.' No one can deny that he saved the studio
and turned it around in the 1990s, and that is a
legacy that will forever be his.

As the new year was ushered in, welcome news
came when *Stardust*, from British director Matthew
Vaughn, was confirmed as making its home at
Pinewood. Vaughn's £50 million fantasy film, based
on a Neil Gaiman book, 'will shoot at Pinewood and
locations elsewhere in Britain,' according to the
production office. 'I fought for it and insisted on
shooting in England,' Vaughn told the *Daily Mail*.
The fantasy feature is a departure for him. Vaughn is
best known for gritty British gangster movies such as
Lock, Stock and Two Smoking Barrels, which he
produced, and *Layer Cake*, which he produced and
directed.

Meanwhile, eight weeks of principal photography
commenced on 22 January for director Mark
Palansky's offbeat tale, *Penelope*. The film is a
modern-day fable about a young woman, played by
25 year-old Christina Ricci, who has spent her life
under the shadow of the family curse. It is only when
setting out to explore the world about her that she
not only discovers love but also her true self.
Penelope stars (and is produced by) Reese
Witherspoon, taking on the special supporting role of

Facing page: *Theodore Faron (Clive Owen) is reunited with his former lover Julian Taylor (Julianne Moore) on a harrowing mission to save mankind in* Children of Men.

Left: *James Bond (Daniel Craig) falls in love with Treasury agent Vesper Lynd (Eva Green) in Martin Campbell's* Casino Royale.

Annie. Emmy Award-winning actress Catherine O'Hara and Richard E Grant co-star as Jessica and Franklin Wilhern, Penelope's parents. They are joined in the cast by James McAvoy, Peter Dinklage and Simon Woods.

In June the cast and crew of *Casino Royale* returned to Pinewood for about six weeks of filming. Campbell's 'not much at Pinewood' actually equated to about four stages, plus a huge set on the 007 Stage featuring a sinking Venetian house. It was quite possibly one of the most elaborate sets ever constructed by production designer Peter Lamont and required the internal tank of the 007 Stage to be encapsulated and raised about 30 foot in height to accommodate a huge underwater hydraulic-powered set.

Intense speculation surrounded the performance of Daniel Craig, an actor best-known for the violent thriller *Layer Cake*. Campbell denied trying to reinvent Bond as a sort of *Bourne Identity*-inspired character. 'It's easy to fall into the trap of making Bond more of a Jason Bourne, but I think that's wrong,' he said, although he noted that he's a huge fan of both Bourne films. 'I think there are a lot of qualities in Bond – his suaveness, his attitude towards women, his drinking, his great stylishness and sexiness. You've got to have all that. The thing about Jason Bourne is that he's not sexy in that sense. He's a driven man haunted by a past, whereas Bond is a different character entirely.'

Unfortunately Craig suffered an astonishing amount of criticism on being cast as 007. Many Bond fans were unconvinced about his suitability for the role, but Craig had a reassuring message for them all: 'Maybe I'm not the prettiest Bond that's ever been, and maybe I'm not the suavest. All I can say is there are millions of fans and I don't want to let them down. I've worked my butt off for this movie. I'm not going to foul it up.'

Filming wrapped at Pinewood in mid July 2006. On 30 July tragedy struck once again when the alarm was sounded just after 11.00 am. The 007 stage was once again on fire. Within minutes the emergency services were on site and took 90 minutes to bring the blaze under control.

Monday 31 July was a sad day at Pinewood. The once proud 007 Stage stood a blackened, folded wreck on the landscape. The heart of Pinewood had been torn out. Investigations reportedly suggested that the fire could have been caused by a gas cylinder being used by contractors dismantling the *Casino Royale* set. Within hours, Pinewood Shepperton plc moved to reassure its investors, film-making friends and tenants that the jewel in its crown would shine once again. The stage is scheduled to be demolished and rebuilt.

On 13 October 2006, as part of the studio's 70th anniversary celebrations, Film Minister Shaun Woodward joined Michael Grade in burying a time capsule in the studio gardens. Not to be opened for a hundred years, the capsule contains a Pinewood filmography along with scripts and photographs from recent productions *Casino Royale*, *Joe Claus* and *The Bourne Ultimatum*.

Woodward commented: 'Visiting Pinewood is magical. I felt I just had to touch the walls as I entered, much like I did the first time I entered the Palace of Westminster. Long may it continue to produce its magic.'

The film business, as Pinewood knows all too well, is never certain but with a favourable tax break climate, a steady dollar and the very best of facilities, Pinewood is once again poised for success. We will certainly continue to see the legend on screen 'Made at Pinewood Studios, London, England'. ∎

Following the closure of Denham in 1950, Pinewood became the principal studio of the Rank Organisation. Since then, the Buckinghamshire site has been the base for a vast number of producers, directors, actors, actresses and for craftsmen of infinite variety. While Rank remained in production, Pinewood was also, of course, the home of the famed 'Man with the Gong'.

I first went there during the war when the studios were home to a disparate trio of official film units: the Army, Royal Air Force and Crown. Having been given leave from Flying Training Command and seconded to the RAF film unit, I was to appear in a propaganda film written by Flight Lieutenant Terence Rattigan and directed by Flight Lieutenant John Boulting, John Boulting's twin brother, Roy, was a captain in the Army Film Unit and was both the director and supervising editor responsible for the great documentary *Desert Victory.*

One of the UK's greatest documentary film makers, Humphrey Jennings, was also at Pinewood during that time, directing such classics as *Fires Were Started* and *A Diary for Timothy.* Many were the hours I sat in his cutting room enveloped in the clouds billowing from his perpetual cigarettes and marvelling at his seemingly limitless ability to find new ways of juxtaposing factual footage to convey a particular emotion. I admired him enormously and he never seemed to resent my constant questions. Indeed, I felt it pleased him to pass on his knowledge to such an avid novice. His many talents included painting and it is my good fortune now to possess a

number of his wonderfully individual canvases.

I found another unfailing welcome in the nearby cutting rooms assigned to Pat Jackson who made the brilliant *Western Approaches.* There, too, I was able to watch and learn as he worked his wizardry on the Moviola.

It is, however, the Boulting brothers to whom I personally owe the greatest debt of gratitude. The film I appeared in at Pinewood under John's direction in 1943 was *Journey Together.* It not only proved to be a major turning point professionally, but granted me the joy and privilege of acting with the cinema legend, Edward G Robinson. When we were all demobilised John and Roy put me under contract and offered me the wonderful opportunity of playing in two films, *The Guinea Pig* and *Brighton Rock,* which established my career as a screen actor.

Many members of the Army and Royal Air Force film units based at Pinewood were involved in active service during the war. It was they who went into battle, armed only with their cameras, to record for posterity the blood, sweat and tears of an extraordinary period in our history.

In the main corridor of the studios there is a plaque recording the names of those who lost their lives in this way between 1939 and 1945. Many were friends and I am conscious that their sacrifice – and that of millions of others – gave me and all who followed in our industry the peace and the freedom to express ourselves through the medium of film.

I will remember them. ■

Lord Attenborough CBE

AFTERWORD

An Autobiography of British Cinema by Brian McFarlane (Methuen, 1997)
Bryan Forbes: A Divided Life by Bryan Forbes (Heinemann, 1992)
The Carry On Companion by Robert Ross (Batsford, 1996)
David Lean by Kevin Brownlow (Faber and Faber, 1997)
The Films of Sean Connery by Lee Pfeiffer and Philip Lisa (Citadel, 1993)
Gerry Anderson: The Authorised Biography by Simon Archer and Stan Nichols (Legend, 1996)
The Golden Gong by Quentin Falk (Columbus, 1986)
Guinness Box-Office Hits by Phil Swern (Guinness, 1995)
Halliwell's Film Guide (Paladin Grafton, 1989)
Ian Fleming by Andrew Lycett (Weidenfeld & Nicolson, 1995)
J Arthur Rank by Michael Wakelin (Lion, 1996)
J Arthur Rank and the British Film Industry by Geoffrey MacNab (Routledge, 1993)
The James Bond Films by Steven Rubin (Talisman, 1981)
The Kenneth Williams Diaries edited by Russell Davies (HarperCollins, 1994)
The Making of The Avengers by Dave Rogers (Titan, 1998)
The Making of Superman – The Movie by David Michael Petrou (Universal, 1978)
Movies from the Mansion by George Perry (Pavillion, 1986)
Mr Rank by Alan Wood (Hodder and Stoughton, 1952)
Nobody Does It Better by Bob Simmons (Javelin, 1987)
Roger Moore as James Bond 007 by Roger Moore (Pan, 1973)
Superman: The Complete History by Les Daniels (Titan, 1998)
The Ultimate Avengers by Dave Rogers (Boxtree, 1994)
Variety Movie Guide edited by Derek Elley (1999)
The Virgin Film Guide (Virgin, 1992)
When the Snow Melts: The Autobiography of Cubby Broccoli with Donald Zec (Boxtree, 1998)

PERIODICALS

American Cinematographer, Bondage, Daily Renter, Empire, Film Review, Kinematograph Weekly, Movie Collector, Movies, Speedway Gazette, Starburst and *Starlog*. ■

Tranzaqua Developments, and many thanks to the following: Ken Adam OBE, Sir Anthony Havelock-Allan, John Aldred, Gerry Anderson, Daniel Angel, Ken Annakin, Michael Apted, Robert S Baker, Roy Ward Baker, Roy Boulting, Morris Bright, Pierce Brosnan, Sylvia Brookes, Martin Cahill, Martin Childs, John Cleese, George Cole, Kevin Connor, Vivian Cox, Susan d'Arcy, John Davis, Jack Douglas, Ray Flight, Freddie Francis, Jack Gardner, Eunice Gayson, Lewis Gilbert, John Glen, Val Guest, Robert Halmi Jr, Guy Hamilton, Bernard Hanson, Bill Harrison, Graham Hartstone, Cyril Hayden, Roy Hayden, Charlton Heston, Sir Anthony Hopkins CBE, Cyril Howard CBE, Alan Hume, Sue James, Lionel Jeffries, Teddy Joseph, Hardy Kruger, Burt Kwouk, Peter Lamont, John Legard, Richard Lester, Desmond Llewelyn, Euan Lloyd, Bert Luxford, Kay Mander, Elspeth March, Andrew V McLaglen, Hayley Mills, Sir John Mills, Bill Owen, Alan Parker CBE, Muriel Pavlow, Clive Reed, Peter Rogers, Dinah Sheridan, Sir Donald Sinden, Norman Spencer, Anthony Steel, Hugh Stewart, Ralph Thomas, J Lee Thompson, Wendy Toye CBE, John Trumper, Michael Tuchner, Bob Verrall, Beryl Vertue, Kay Walsh, David Wickes, John Willis, Lynn Willis, Michael G Wilson, Michael Winner and Jaz Wiseman.

Special thanks to Meg Simmonds, Amanda Schofield and John Parkinson at Eon Productions for their help and access to their archive; John Herron and Canal + for access to their amazing film library; Lofty Rice in the Pinewood stills department; Hazel Cotton at Allied Marketing Services; Anne Runnecles and Melanie Phillips for their practical help and support; Norman Martlew and his invaluable carrier bag full of Pinewood material, and Geoff Freeman for his help and kindness on the Bond set. Marcus Hearn and Richard Reynolds, for seeing the light.

and
Ian Dickerson
The Saint Club
PO Box 258
Romsey
Hants SO51 6WY

Graham Rye
007 Magazine and Archive Limited
PO Box 007
Addleston
Surrey
KT15 1DY

The Morning After
(ITC/*Persuaders!* Fan Club)
PO Box 1579
Gillingham
Dorset
SP8 4WR

Dave Worrall
James Bond Collector's Club
PO Box 1570
Christchurch
Dorset
BH23 4XS

The publishers wish to thank Chris Bentley, Clive Eardley, Andrew Pixley, Mike Richardson and Jeff Bench for their advice in compiling the filmography. Thanks also to Thai Silkman and Stan Caravan for their help with research, and to Joel Finler for picture research.

EXTRA SPECIAL THANKS TO:

HRH The Princess Royal, Sir Norman Wisdom OBE, Roger Moore CBE, Lord Attenborough CBE, Steve Jaggs and all at Pinewood Studios Ltd, Audrey Skinner, Doris Spriggs and Allan Foenander, without whom…

… and Robin Harbour, who photographed present-day Pinewood on our behalf.

ON A PERSONAL NOTE…

GO: I would like to thank Dick and Noreen Best for inspiring me to set about writing the book, and Steve Jaggs for once again placing his confidence in me, agreeing to let me have a crack at a Pinewood book and for giving me my big break in the film industry all those years ago. Thanks also to Brian Burford for joining me in the adventure, and Peter Manley for his continual guidance, encouragement and corrections. Also, I must thank Peter's late wife Mary for her kindness, support and for allowing me to clutter up her kitchen table.

Robin Harbour deserves more than just a passing thanks too, for without him I'd be a long way from finishing and have mistakes too numerous to mention! And, last but by no means least, thanks to all my family and friends who continually support me in everything I do.

BB: I would like to thank Gareth for inviting me to join him on what was only supposed to be a short adventure, and for his endless interview tapes and quotes to keep me busy. But, most of all, for his patience when the day job got in the way. A special thanks to Carol for letting me leave work early to visit the Bond shoot, and to my Mum for her unstinting support. ■

BIBLIOGRAPHY

ACKNOWLEDGEMENTS

KEY

p: producer sc: screenplay d: director lp: leading players
NB: It has not been possible to obtain full credits for every production on record as having been fully or partly made at Pinewood Studios. Omission of an individual credit signifies that the credit was untraceable at the time of going to press.

1936

London Melody
(US: Girls in the Street)
p: Herbert Wilcox
sc: Florence Tranter,
Monckton Hoffe
d: Herbert Wilcox
lp: Anna Neagle, Tullio Carminati,
Robert Douglas, Horace Hodges

Talk of the Devil
p: Jack Raymond
sc: Carol Reed, Anthony Kimmins,
George Barraud
d: Carol Reed
lp: Ricardo Cortez, Basil Sydney,
Sally Eilers, Randle Ayrton

Splinters in the Air
p: Herbert Wilcox
sc: RP Weston, Bert Lee, Jack Marks,
KRG Browne, Ralph Reader
d: Alfred Goulding
lp: Sydney Howard,
Stuart Robinson, Richard Hearne

The Scarab Murder Case
(aka: Scarlet Murder Mystery)
p: Anthony Havelock-Allan
sc: Selwyn Jepson
d: Michael Hankinson
lp: Wilfred Hyde-White,
Wally Patch, Kathleen Kelly

Our Fighting Navy
(US: Torpedoed)
p: Herbert Wilcox
sc: Gerald Elliott, Harrison Owens,
'Bartimeus'
d: Norman Walker
lp: HB Warner, Noah Beery,
Robert Douglas, Hazel Terry,
Richard Cromwell

The Street Singer
(aka: Interval For Romance)
p: Dora Virva
sc: Reginald Arkell,
Jean de Marguenat, Paul Schiller
d: Jean de Marguenat
lp: Arthur Tracy, Arthur Riscoe,
Margaret Lockwood,
Hugh Wakefield

Cross My Heart
p: Anthony Havelock-Allan
sc: Basil N Keys, Robert Skinner
d: Bernerd Mainwaring
lp: Kathleen Gibson, Tully Comber,
Kenneth Duncan,
Aubrey Fitzgerald, Robert Field

The Gang Show
p: Herbert Wilcox
sc: Ralph Reader, Marjorie Gaffney
d: Alfred Goulding
lp: Ralph Reader, Gina Malo,
Stuart Robinson, Richard Ainley

1937

Midnight Menace
p: Harcourt Templeman
sc: DB Wyndham-Lewis,
GH Moresby-White
d: Sinclair Hill
lp: Fritz Kortner, Charles Farrell,
Margaret Vyner, Danny Green

Holiday's End
p: Anthony Havelock-Allan
sc: Gerald Elliott
d: John Paddy Carstairs
lp: Sally Stuart, Wally Patch,
Rosalyn Boulter, Aubrey Mallalieu

The Frog
p: Herbert Wilcox
sc: Ian Hay, Gerald Elliott
d: Jack Raymond
lp: Gordon Harker, Carol Goodner,
Noah Beery, Jack Hawkins,
Richard Ainley

The Cavalier of the Streets
p: Anthony Havelock-Allan
sc: George Barraud, Ralph Neale
d: Harold French
lp: Margaret Vyner, Patrick Barr,
Carl Barbord, James Craven

Sunset in Vienna
(US: Suicide Legion)
p: Herbert Wilcox
sc: Marjorie Gaffney,
Harrison Owen, Florence Tranter
d: Norman Walker
lp: Tullio Carminati, Lilli Palmer,
John Garrick, Geraldine Hislop

Museum Mystery
p: Anthony Havelock-Allan
sc: Gerald Elliott
d: Clifford Gulliver
lp: Gerald Case, Elizabeth Inglis,
Jock McKay, Tony Wylde

The Fatal Hour
p: Anthony Havelock-Allan
sc: Ralph Neale, Gerald Elliott
d: George Pearson
lp: Edward Rigby, Moira Read,
Dick Hunter, Moore Marriot

Jericho (US: Dark Sands)
p: Walter Futter
sc: George Barraud, Robert N Lee,
Peter Ruric
d: Thornton Freeland
lp: Paul Robeson, Henry Wilcoxon,
Wallace Ford, Princess Kouka
John Laurie, James Carew

Gangway
p: Michael Balcon
sc: Lesser Samuels, Sonnie Hale
d: Sonnie Hale
lp: Barry MacKay, Nat Pendleton,
Alastair Sim, Jessie Mathews,

Night Ride
p: Anthony Havelock-Allan
sc: Ralph Bettinson
d: John Paddy Carstairs
lp: Julien Vedey, Jimmy Hanley,
Wally Patch, Joan Ponsford

Smash and Grab
(US: Larceny Street)
p: Jack Buchanan
sc: Ralph Spence, Jack Buchanan
d: Tim Whelan
lp: Jack Buchanan, Elsie Randolph,
Arthur Margetson, Antony Holles

Young and Innocent
(US: A Girl was Young)
p: Edward Black
sc: Charles Bennett,
Edwin Greenwood,
Anthony Armstrong
d: Alfred Hitchcock
lp: Nova Pilbeam,
Derrick de Marney,
Percy Marmont, Edward Rigby

The Sky's the Limit
p: Jack Buchanan
sc: Ralph Spence, Jack Buchanan,
Douglas Furber
d: Jack Buchanan, Lee Garmes
lp: Jack Buchanan, Mara Losseff,
David Hutcheson, William Kendall

The Last Curtain
p: Anthony Havelock-Allan
sc: AR Rawlinson
d: David MacDonald
lp: Campbell Gullen,
John Wickham, Greta Gynt

Command Performance
p: Harcourt Templeman
sc: George Pearson,
Michael Hankinson, Sinclair Hill
d: Sinclair Hill
lp: Arthur Tracy, Lilli Palmer

Sweet Devil
p: Jack Buchanan
sc: Geoffrey Kerr, Ralph Spence
d: René Guissart
lp: Bobby Howes, Jean Gille,
William Kendal, Syd Walker

Break the News
p: René Clair
sc: Geoffrey Kerr
d: René Clair
lp: Jack Buchanan,
Maurice Chevalier, June Knight,
Marta Labarr, Guy Middleton

Sailing Along
p: Michael Balcon
sc: Sonnie Hale, Lesser Samuels
d: Sonnie Hale
lp: Jessie Matthews, Roland Young,
Barry MacKay, Jack Whiting

Lancashire Luck
p: Anthony Havelock-Allan
sc: AR Rawlinson
d: Henry Cass
lp: George Carney, Muriel George,
Wendy Hiller, Nigel Stock

Follow Your Star
p: Harcourt Templeman
sc: George Pearson,
Stafford Dickens
d: Sinclair Hill
lp: Arthur Tracy, Belle Chrystall,
Mark Daly, Horace Hodges

Kicking the Moon Around
(US: The Playboy, aka:
Millionaire Merry-Go-Round)
p: Howard Welsch
sc: Angus McPhail,
Roland Pertwee, Michael Hogan,
H Fowler Meare, Tom Geraghty
d: Walter Forde
lp: Ambrose and his Orchestra,
Florence Desmond, Evelyn Dall,
Harry Richman, Hal Thompson

Strange Boarders
p: Edward Black
sc: AR Rawlinson, Sidney Gilliat
d: Herbert Mason
lp: Leon M Lion, Ronald Adam,
CV France, Googie Withers

Incident in Shanghai
p: Anthony Havelock-Allan
sc: AR Rawlinson,
John Paddy Carstairs
d: John Paddy Carstairs
lp: Derek Gorst, Rita Davies,
Margaret Vyner, Patrick Barr

FILMOGRAPHY

Mr Smith Carries On
p: Anthony Havelock-Allan
sc: Stephen Clarkson,
John Cousins, Ronald Gow
d: Lister Laurance
lp: Edward Rigby, Julien Mitchell,
HF Maltby, Dorothy Oldfield

Missing, Believed Married
p: Anthony Havelock-Allan
sc: AR Rawlinson
d: John Paddy Carstairs
lp: Julien Vedey, Hazel Terry,
Wally Patch, Peter Coke,
Margaret Rutherford, Charles Paton

1938

Crackerjack
(US: The Man with a Hundred Faces)
p: Edward Black
sc: AR Rawlinson, Basil Mason
d: Albert de Courville
lp: Tom Walls, Lilli Palmer,
Noel Madison, Leon M Lion

Pygmalion
p: Gabriel Pascal
sc: WP Lipscomb, Cecil Lewis,
Ian Dalrymple
d: Anthony Asquith, Leslie Howard
lp: Leslie Howard, Wendy Hiller,
Wilfrid Lawson, Marie Lohr,
Scott Sunderland, Jean Cadell

A Spot of Bother
p: Anthony Havelock-Allan
sc: John Cousins,
Stephen Clarkson, AR Rawlinson
d: David MacDonald
lp: Robertson Hare, Alfred Drayton,
Sandra Storme, Kathleen Joyce

This Man is News
p: Anthony Havelock-Allan
sc: Allan MacKinnon,
Roger MacDougall, Basil Dearden
d: David MacDonald
lp: Barry K Barnes, Edward Lexy,
Alastair Sim, Valerie Hobson

Keep Smiling
p: Robert T Kane
sc: William Conselman,
Rodney Ackland, Val Valentine
d: Monty Banks
lp: Mary Maguire, Gracie Fields,
Roger Livesey, Peter Coke

Stolen Life
p: Anthony Havelock-Allan
sc: George Barraud,
Margaret Kennedy
d: Paul Czinner
lp: Elisabeth Bergner,
Michael Redgrave, Wilfred Lawson,
Mabel Terry Lewis, Richard Ainley

Lightning Conductor
p: Anthony Havelock-Allan
sc: Joseph Jefferson Farjeon,
Lawrence Green, Ivor McLaren,
Evadne Price
d: Maurice Elvey
lp: Gordon Harker, Sally Gray,
John Lodge, Ernest Thesiger

The Mikado
p: Geoffrey Toye, Joseph Somlo
sc: Geoffrey Toye
d: Victor Schertzinger
lp: Kenny Baker, Martyn Green,
Sydney Granville, John Barclay

St Paul: Faith Triumphant
p: Roy Hake
sc: Lawrence Barrett
d: Norman Walker
lp: Neal Arden

St Paul: The Way of Salvation
p: Roy Hake
sc: Lawrence Barrett
d: Norman Walker
lp: Neal Arden, Josephine Wilson

Climbing High
p: Michael Balcon
sc: Lesser Samuels, Marion Dix
d: Carol Reed
lp: Jessie Matthews,
Michael Redgrave, Noel Madison,
Enid Stamp Taylor

So This Is London
p: Robert Kane
sc: William M Conselman,
Ben Travers, Tom Phipps,
Douglas Furber
d: Thornton Freeland
lp: Robertson Hare,
Alfred Drayton, George Sanders,
Berton Churchill, Fay Compton

The Lambeth Walk
p: Anthony Havelock-Allan
sc: John Paddy Carstairs,
Robert Edmunds, Clifford Grey
d: Albert de Courville
lp: Lupino Lane, Sally Gray,
Seymour Hicks, Norah Howard,
Enid Stamp Taylor

Inspector Hornleigh
p: Robert T Kane
sc: Bryan Wallace, Gerald Elliott
d: Eugene Forde
lp: Gordon Harker, Alastair Sim,
Hugh Williams, Gibb McLaughlin

Beyond Our Horizon
p: Roy Hake
sc: Lawrence Barrett
d: Norman Walker
lp: Milton Rosmer,
Josephine Wilson, Mavis Clair

The First Easter
p: Roy Hake
sc: Lawrence Barrett
d: Norman Walker

1941

Listen to Britain
p: Ian Dalrymple
sc: Humphrey Jennings,
Stewart McAllister
d: Humphrey Jennings,
Stewart McAllister

1942

The Silent Village
p: Humphrey Jennings
sc: Humphrey Jennings
d: Humphrey Jennings

Coastal Command
p: Ian Dalrymple
sc: JB Holmes
d: JB Holmes

Malta GC
p: John Monck
sc: Eugeniusz Cekalski,
Derrick De Marney
d: Eugeniusz Cekalski,
Derrick De Marney
lp: Laurence Olivier (narrator)

Left of the Line
d: David MacDonald

1943

Desert Victory
p: David MacDonald
sc: JL Hodson
d: Roy Boulting

Fires Were Started
(aka: I Was a Fireman)
p: Ian Dalrymple
sc: Humphrey Jennings
d: Humphrey Jennings
lp: George Gravett,
Philip Wilson-Dickson,
Fred Griffiths, Loris Rey

Close Quarters
(aka: Up Periscope)
p: Ian Dalrymple
sc: Jack Lee
d: Jack Lee

1944

A Harbour Goes to France
p: Army Film Unit
d: David MacDonald

Why We Fight: Tunisian Victory
p: John Huston, Roy Boulting,
Hugh Stewart, Anthony Veiller,
Frank Capra
sc: Frank Capra, John Huston
d: Frank Capra, John Huston,
Roy Boulting
lp: Anthony Veiller (narration)

Western Approaches
p: Ian Dalrymple
sc: Pat Jackson, Gerard Bryant
d: Pat Jackson
lp: Jack Cardiff, Pat Jackson

1945

Burma Victory
p: David MacDonald
sc: Frank Harvey, Roy Boulting
d: Roy Boulting
lp: David King-Wood, Ivan Brandt,
Norman Claridge

The True Glory
p: US Office of War Information,
UK Ministry of Information
sc: Eric Maschwit, Arthur MacRae,
Gerald Kersh, Guy Trosper,
Jenny Nicholson, Peter Ustinov
d: Carol Reed, Garson Kanin
lp: Dwight D Eisenhower,
Robert Harris (narrator)

A Diary for Timothy
p: Basil Wright
sc: EM Forster
d: Humphrey Jennings
lp: Myra Hess, John Gielgud,
George Woodbridge

Instruments of the Orchestra
p: Alexander Shaw
d: Muir Mathieson
lp: Sir Malcolm Sargent

Journey Together
p: Roy Boulting
sc: John Boulting, Terence Rattigan
d: John Boulting
lp: Richard Attenborough,
Jack Watling, David Tomlinson

They Knew Mr Knight
p: Norman Walker
sc: Victor McClure,
Dorothy Whipple (play)
d: Norman Walker
lp: Mervyn Johns, Nora Swinburne,
Joyce Howard, Joan Greenwood,
Peter Hammond, Marie Ault

1946

Green For Danger
p: Frank Launder, Sidney Gilliat
sc: Sidney Gilliat, Claud Gurney
d: Sidney Gilliat
lp: Sally Gray, Trevor Howard,
Rosamund John, Alastair Sim,
Leo Genn, Judy Campbell

Black Narcissus
p: Michael Powell,
Emeric Pressburger
sc: Michael Powell,
Emeric Pressburger
d: Michael Powell,
Emeric Pressburger
lp: Deborah Kerr, Sabu,
David Farrar, Flora Robson,
Esmond Knight, Jean Simmons

Take My Life
p: Anthony Havelock-Allan
sc: Winston Graham,
Valerie Taylor, Margaret Kennedy
d: Ronald Neame
lp: Hugh Williams, Greta Gynt,
Marius Goring, Francis L Sullivan,
Henry Edwards, Rosalie Crutchley

Captain Boycott
p: Frank Launder, Sidney Gilliat
sc: Frank Launder,
Wolfgang Wilhelm,
Paul Vincent Carroll,
Patrick Campbell
d: Frank Launder
lp: Stewart Granger, Kathleen Ryan,
Alastair Sim, Mervyn Johns,
Noel Purcell, Niall McGinnis

Great Expectations (part)
p: Ronald Neame
sc: David Lean, Ronald Neame,
Anthony Havelock-Allan,
Kay Walsh, Cecil McGivern,
d: David Lean
lp: John Mills, Anthony Wager,
Valerie Hobson, Jean Simmons,
Bernard Miles, Francis L Sullivan,
Finlay Currie, Martita Hunt,
Alec Guinness

1947

The End of the River
p: Michael Powell,
Emeric Pressburger
sc: Wolfgang Wilhelm
d: Derek N Twist
lp: Sabu, Bibi Ferreira,
Esmond Knight, Antoinette Cellier

The Woman in the Hall
p: Ian Dalrymple
sc: Ian Dalrymple, GB Stern,
Jack Lee
d: Jack Lee
lp: Ursula Jeans, Jean Simmons,
Cecil Parker, Joan Miller

Blanche Fury
p: Anthony Havelock-Allan
sc: Audrey Erskine Lindop,
Hugh Mills, Cecil McGivern
d: Marc Allégret
lp: Valerie Hobson,
Stewart Granger, Michael Gough,
Walter Fitzgerald, Suzanne Gibbs

The Red Shoes
p: Michael Powell,
Emeric Pressburger
sc: Michael Powell,
Emeric Pressburger, Keith Winter
d: Michael Powell,
Emeric Pressburger
lp: Anton Walbrook, Marius Goring,
Moira Shearer, Robert Helpmann

Oliver Twist
p: Ronald Neame
sc: David Lean, Stanley Haynes,
Kay Walsh, Eric Ambler
d: David Lean
lp: Robert Newton, Alec Guinness,
Kay Walsh, Francis L Sullivan,
John Howard Davies

Esther Waters
p: Ian Dalrymple, Peter Proud
sc: Michael Gordon, William Rose,
Gerard Tyrrell
d: Ian Dalrymple, Peter Proud
lp: Kathleen Ryan, Dirk Bogarde,
Cyril Cusack, Ivor Barnard,
Fay Compton

London Belongs To Me
(US: Dulcimer Street)
p: Frank Launder, Sidney Gilliat
sc: Sidney Gilliat, JB Williams
d: Sidney Gilliat
lp: Richard Attenborough,
Alastair Sim, Fay Compton,
Stephen Murray, Wylie Watson

1948

The Passionate Friends
p: Ronald Neame
sc: Eric Ambler, David Lean,
Stanley Haynes
d: David Lean
lp: Ann Todd, Claude Rains,
Trevor Howard, Betty Ann Davies

The Blue Lagoon
p: Frank Launder, Sidney Gilliat
sc: Frank Launder, John Baines,
Michael Hogan
d: Frank Launder
lp: Jean Simmons, Donald Houston,
Noel Purcell, Cyril Cusack

Once a Jolly Swagman
p: Ian Dalrymple
sc: William Rose, Jack Lee,
Cliff Gordon
d: Jack Lee
lp: Dirk Bogarde, Bonar Colleano,
Bill Owen, Renée Asherson,
Thora Hird, James Hayter

All Over the Town
p: Ian Dalrymple
sc: Michael Gordon
d: Derek N Twist
lp: Norman Wooland,
Sarah Churchill, Cyril Cusack,
Ronald Adam, Bryan Forbes

Once Upon a Dream
p: Antony Darnborough
sc: Patrick Kirwan, Victor Katona,
Val Guest
d: Ralph Thomas
lp: Googie Withers, Griffith Jones,
Guy Middleton, Raymond Lovell

Fools Rush In
p: Aubrey Baring
sc: Geoffrey Kerr, Kenneth Horne
d: John Paddy Carstairs
lp: Sally Ann Howes,
Nora Swinburne, Guy Rolfe

Dear Mr Prohack
p: Ian Dalrymple
sc: Ian Dalrymple, Donald Bull
d: Thornton Freeland
lp: Cecil Parker, Glynis Johns,
Hermione Baddeley, Dirk Bogarde,
Sheila Sim, Heather Thatcher

Obsession
(US: The Hidden Room)
p: Nat Bronsten
sc: Alec Coppel
d: Edward Dmytryk
lp: Robert Newton, Sally Gray,
Naunton Wayne, Phil Brown

Warning to Wantons
p: Donald B Wilson
sc: Donald B Wilson, James Laver
d: Donald B Wilson
lp: Harold Warrender, Anne Vernon,
David Tomlinson, Sonia Holm

Floodtide
p: Donald B Wilson
sc: George Blake, Donald B Wilson,
Frederick Wilson
d: Frederick Wilson
lp: Gordon Jackson,
Rona Anderson, John Laurie

Kind Hearts and Coronets
(part)
p: Michael Balcon
sc: Robert Hamer, John Dighton
d: Robert Hamer
lp: Dennis Price, Valerie Hobson,
Joan Greenwood, Alec Guinness,
Audrey Fildes, Miles Malleson

1949

Stop Press Girl
p: Donald B Wilson
sc: Basil Thomas, TJ Morrison
d: Michael Barry
lp: Sally Ann Howes,
Gordon Jackson, Basil Radford,
Naunton Wayne

Poet's Pub
p: Donald B Wilson
sc: Diana Morgan
d: Frederick Wilson
lp: Derek Bond, Rona Anderson,
James Robertson Justice,
John McLaren, Barbara Murray

Golden Salamander
p: Alexander Galperson
sc: Lesley Storm, Victor Canning,
Ronald Neame
d: Ronald Neame
lp: Trevor Howard, Anouk Aimée,
Herbert Lom, Walter Rilla
Miles Malleson, Jacques Sernas

Boys in Brown
p: Antony Darnborough
sc: Montgomery Tully
d: Montgomery Tully
lp: Jack Warner,
Richard Attenborough,
Dirk Bogarde, Jimmy Hanley

Madeleine
p: Stanley Haynes
sc: Nicholas Phipps,
Stanley Haynes, Eric Ambler
d: David Lean
lp: Ann Todd, Ivan Desny,
Norman Wooland, Leslie Banks,
Elizabeth Sellars, Jean Cadell

The Spider and the Fly
p: Maxwell Setton, Aubrey Baring
sc: Robert Westerby
d: Robert Hamer
lp: Eric Portman, Guy Rolfe,
Nadia Gray, Edward Chapman

The Astonished Heart
p: Antony Darnborough
sc: Noel Coward
d: Terence Fisher,
Antony Darnborough
lp: Celia Johnson, Noel Coward,
Margaret Leighton, Joyce Carey

So Long at the Fair
p: Betty E Box
sc: Hugh Mills, Anthony Thorne
d: Terence Fisher,
Antony Darnborough
lp: Jean Simmons, Dirk Bogarde,
David Tomlinson, Honor Blackman

Prelude to Fame
p: Donald B Wilson
sc: Robert Westerby, Bridget Boland
d: Fergus McDonell
lp: Guy Rolfe, Kathleen Byron,
Kathleen Ryan, Jeremy Spenser

1950

Waterfront
p: Paul Soskin
sc: John Brophy, Paul Soskin
d: Michael Anderson
lp: Robert Newton,
Kathleen Harrison, Susan Shaw,
Richard Burton, Avis Scott

Tony Draws a Horse
p: Brock Williams
sc: Brock Williams
d: John Paddy Carstairs
lp: Cecil Parker, Anne Crawford,
Derek Bond, Barbara Murray

Trio
p: Antony Darnborough
sc: W Somerset Maugham,
RC Sherriff, Noel Langley
d: Ken Annakin, Harold French,
Antony Darnborough
lp: James Hayter, Kathleen Harrison,
Anne Crawford, Nigel Patrick,
Jean Simmons, Michael Rennie

The Clouded Yellow
p: Betty E Box
sc: Janet Green
d: Ralph Thomas
lp: Jean Simmons, Trevor Howard,
Sonia Dresdel, Barry Jones,
Kenneth More, Geoffrey Keen

The Woman in Question
(US: Five Angles on Murder)
p: Teddy Baird
sc: John Cresswell
d: Anthony Asquith
lp: Jean Kent, Dirk Bogarde,
John McCallum, Susan Shaw,
Hermione Baddeley, Charles Victor

The Adventurers
(US: The Great Adventure)
p: Maxwell Setton, Aubrey Baring
sc: Robert Westerby
d: David MacDonald
lp: Dennis Price, Jack Hawkins,
Siobhan McKenna, Peter Hammond

Highly Dangerous
p: Antony Darnborough
sc: Eric Ambler
d: Roy Baker
lp: Margaret Lockwood,
Dane Clark, Marius Goring,
Naunton Wayne

Blackmailed
p: Harold Huth
sc: Hugh Mills, Roger Vadim
d: Marc Allégret
lp: Mai Zetterling, Dirk Bogarde,
Fay Compton, Robert Flemyng,
Michael Gough

The Browning Version
p: Teddy Baird
sc: Terence Rattigan
d: Anthony Asquith
lp: Michael Redgrave, Jean Kent,
Nigel Patrick, Ronald Howard

Night Without Stars
p: Hugh Stewart
sc: Winston Graham
d: Anthony Pélissier
lp: David Farrar, Nadia Gray,
Maurice Teynac, Gilles Quéant

White Corridors
p: Joseph Janni, John Croydon
sc: Jan Read, Pat Jackson
d: Pat Jackson
lp: James Donald, Googie Withers,
Godfrey Tearle, Jack Watling,
Petula Clark, Moira Lister

1951

Hotel Sahara
p: George H Brown
sc: Patrick Kirwan, George H Brown
d: Ken Annakin
lp: Yvonne De Carlo, Peter Ustinov,
David Tomlinson, Roland Culver

High Treason
p: Paul Soskin
sc: Frank Harvey, Roy Boulting
d: Roy Boulting
lp: Liam Redmond, André Morell,
Anthony Bushell, Kenneth Griffith

Valley of Eagles
p: Nat Bronsten
sc: Terence Young, Paul Tabori,
Nat Bronsten
d: Terence Young
lp: Jack Warner, Nadia Gray,
John McCallum, Anthony Dawson

Appointment with Venus
(US: Island Rescue)
p: Betty E Box
sc: Nicholas Phipps, Jerrard Tickell
d: Ralph Thomas
lp: David Niven, Glynis Johns,
George Calouris, Barry Jones,
Kenneth More, Noel Purcell

Encore
p: Antony Darnborough
sc: TEB Clarke, Arthur MacRae,
Eric Ambler
d: Pat Jackson, Anthony Pélissier,
Harold French
lp: Nigel Patrick, Roland Culver,
Kay Walsh, Noel Purcell,
Glynis Johns, Terence Morgan

Hunted
p: Julian Wintle
sc: Jack Whittingham
d: Charles Crichton
lp: Dirk Bogarde, Jon Whitely,
Elizabeth Sellars, Kay Walsh,
Frederick Piper, Julian Somers

The Card
(US: The Promoter)
p: John Bryan
sc: Eric Ambler
d: Ronald Neame
lp: Alec Guinness, Glynis Johns,
Valerie Hobson, Petula Clark,
Edward Chapman

The Importance of Being Earnest
p: Teddy Baird
sc: Oscar Wilde (play),
Anthony Asquith
d: Anthony Asquith
lp: Michael Redgrave,
Richard Wattis, Michael Denison,
Walter Hudd, Edith Evans,
Joan Greenwood, Dorothy Tutin,
Margaret Rutherford

1952

Penny Princess
p: Val Guest
sc: Val Guest
d: Val Guest
lp: Yolande Donlan, Dirk Bogarde,
AE Mathews, Reginald Beckwith

The Planter's Wife
(US: Outpost in Malaya)
p: John Stafford
sc: Peter Proud, Guy Elmes
d: Ken Annakin
lp: Claudette Colbert,
Jack Hawkins, Anthony Steel,
Ram Gopal, Jeremy Spenser

Something Money Can't Buy
p: Joseph Janni
sc: Pat Jackson,
James Lansdale Hodson
d: Pat Jackson
lp: Anthony Steel, Patricia Roc,
AE Matthews, Moira Lister,
David Hutcheson

Venetian Bird
(US: The Assassin)
p: Betty E Box
sc: Victor Canning
d: Ralph Thomas
lp: Richard Todd, Eva Bartok,
John Gregson, George Coulouris

Meet Me Tonight
p: Anthony Havelock-Allan
sc: Noel Coward
d: Anthony Pélissier
lp: Valerie Hobson, Nigel Patrick,
Kay Walsh, Ted Ray,
Stanley Holloway, Betty Ann Davies

It Started in Paradise
p: Sergei Nolbandov, Leslie Parkyn
sc: Marghanita Laski, Hugh Hastings
d: Compton Bennett
lp: Jane Hylton, Ian Hunter,
Terence Morgan, Muriel Pavlow,
Brian Worth, Martita Hunt

The Long Memory
p: Hugh Stewart
sc: Robert Hamer, Frank Harvey
d: Robert Hamer
lp: John Mills, John McCallum,
Elizabeth Sellars, Eva Bergh
Geoffrey Keen

The Net
(US: Project M7)
p: Antony Darnborough
sc: William Fairchild
d: Anthony Asquith
lp: Phyllis Calvert, James Donald,
Robert Beatty, Herbert Lom,
Muriel Pavlow, Noel Willman

Top of the Form
p: Paul Soskin
sc: Patrick Kirwan, Ted Willis
John Paddy Carstairs
d: John Paddy Carstairs
lp: Ronald Shiner,
Anthony Newley, Harry Fowler,
Jacqueline, Pierreux, Alfie Bass

Genevieve
p: Henry Cornelius
sc: William Rose
d: Henry Cornelius
lp: Dinah Sheridan, John Gregson,
Kay Kendall, Kenneth More,
Geoffrey Keen, Reginald Beckwith,
Arthur Wontner, Joyce Grenfell

Desperate Moment
p: George H Brown
sc: Patrick Kirwan, George H Brown
d: Compton Bennett
lp: Dirk Bogarde, Mai Zetterling,
Philip Friend, Albert Lieven

The Final Test
p: RJ Minney
sc: Terence Rattigan
d: Anthony Asquith
lp: Jack Warner, Robert Morley,
George Relph, Adrianne Allen

Turn the Key Softly
p: Maurice Cowan
sc: Jack Lee, Maurice Cowan
d: Jack Lee
lp: Yvonne Mitchell,
Terence Morgan, Joan Collins,
Kathleen Harrison, Thora Hird

Malta Story
p: Peter de Sarigny
sc: William Fairchild, Nigel Balchin
d: Brian Desmond Hurst
lp: Alec Guinness, Jack Hawkins,
Anthony Steel, Muriel Pavlow,
Renee Asherson, Hugh Burden

The Sword and the Rose
p: Perce Pearce
sc: Laurence E Watkin
d: Ken Annakin
lp: Richard Todd, Glynis Johns,
James Robertson Justice,
Michael Gough, Jane Barrett

Made in Heaven
p: George H Brown
sc: George H Brown,
William Douglas-Home
d: John Paddy Carstairs
lp: David Tomlinson, Petula Clark,
Sonja Ziemann, AE Matthews,
Charles Victor, Sophie Stewart

1953

Always a Bride
p: Robert Garrett
sc: Ralph Smart, Peter Jones
d: Ralph Smart
lp: Peggy Cummins,
Terence Morgan, Ronald Squire

Personal Affair
p: Antony Darnborough
sc: Lesley Storm
d: Anthony Pélissier
lp: Pamela Binns, Gene Tierney,
Leo Genn, Pamela Brown

Hell Below Zero
p: Irving Allen, Albert R Broccoli
sc: Alec Coppel, Max Trell,
Richard Maibaum
d: Mark Robson
lp: Alan Ladd, Joan Tetzel,
Basil Sydney, Stanley Baker,
Joseph Tomelty, Niall MacGinnis

A Day to Remember
p: Betty E Box
sc: Robin Estridge
d: Ralph Thomas
lp: Stanley Holloway, Joan Rice
Odile Versois, Donald Sinden,
James Hayter, Bill Owen

The Million Pound Note
(US: Man with a Million)
p: John Bryan
sc: Jill Craigie
d: Ronald Neame
lp: Gregory Peck, Ronald Squire,
Joyce Grenfell, AE Matthews

The Kidnappers
(US: The Little Kidnappers)
p: Sergei Nolbandov, Leslie Parkyn
sc: Neil Patterson
d: Philip Leacock
lp: Duncan Macrae, Jean Anderson
Theodore Bikel, Adrienne Corri

You Know What Sailors Are!
p: Peter Rogers, Julian Wintle
sc: Peter Rogers
d: Ken Annakin
lp: Akim Tamiroff, Donald Sinden,
Sarah Lawson, Naunton Wayne

Trouble in Store
p: Maurice Cowan
sc: John Paddy Carstairs,
Maurice Cowan, Ted Willis
d: John Paddy Carstairs
lp: Norman Wisdom,
Margaret Rutherford, Moira Lister,
Derek Bond, Lana Morris

Fast and Loose
p: Teddy Baird
sc: AR Rawlinson, Ben Travers
d: Gordon Parry
lp: Stanley Holloway, Kay Kendall,
Brian Reece, Joan Young

Doctor in the House
p: Betty E Box
sc: Nicholas Phipps,
Richard Gordon
d: Ralph Thomas
lp: Dirk Bogarde, Muriel Pavlow,
Kenneth More, Donald Sinden,
Kay Kendall

The Seekers
(US: Land of Fury)
p: George H Brown
sc: William Fairchild
d: Ken Annakin
lp: Jack Hawkins, Glynis Johns,
Noel Purcell, Inia Te Wiata,
Kenneth Williams, Laya Raki

Forbidden Cargo
p: Sydney Box
sc: Sydney Box
d: Harold French
lp: Nigel Patrick, Elizabeth Sellars,
Terence Morgan, Greta Gynt

The Beachcomber
p: William MacQuitty
sc: Sydney Box
d: Muriel Box
lp: Glynis Johns, Robert Newton,
Donald Sinden, Walter Crisham
Michael Hordern, Paul Rogers

The Black Knight
p: Irving Allen, Albert R Broccoli
sc: Alec Coppel, Dennis O'Keeffe,
Bryan Forbes
d: Tay Garnett
lp: Alan Ladd, Patricia Medina,
André Morell, Harry Andrews,
Peter Cushing, Anthony Bushell

1954

The Young Lovers
(US: Chance Meeting)
p: Anthony Havelock-Allan
sc: Robin Estridge
d: Anthony Asquith
lp: Odile Versois, David Knight,
Joseph Tomelty, Theodore Bikel

Up To His Neck
p: Hugh Stewart
sc: Patrick Kirwan, Ted Willis
John Paddy Carstairs, Peter Rogers
d: John Paddy Carstairs
lp: Ronald Shiner, Brian Rix

The Purple Plain
p: John Bryan
sc: Eric Ambler
d: Robert Parrish
lp: Gregory Peck, Win Min Than,
Maurice Denham, Lyndon Brook,
Brenda de Banzie, Bernard Lee

Simba
p: Peter de Sarigny
sc: John Baines, Robin Estridge
d: Brian Desmond Hurst
lp: Dirk Bogarde, Donald Sinden,
Virginia McKenna, Basil Sydney,
Marie Ney, Joseph Tomelty

Mad About Men
p: Betty E Box
sc: Peter Blackmore
d: Ralph Thomas
lp: Glynis Johns, Donald Sinden,
Anne Crawford,
Margaret Rutherford, Dora Bryan

One Good Turn
p: Maurice Cowan
sc: Maurice Cowan,
John Paddy Carstairs, Ted Willis,
Sid Collin, Talbot Rothwell
d: John Paddy Carstairs
lp: Norman Wisdom, Joan Rice,
Shirley Abicair, Thora Hird

To Paris, With Love
p: Antony Darnborough
sc: Robert Buckner
d: Robert Hamer
lp: Alec Guinness, Odile Versois,
Vernon Gray, Elina Labourdette

As Long As They're Happy
p: Raymond Stross
sc: Alan Melville
d: J Lee-Thompson
lp: Jack Buchanan, Janette Scott,
Jean Carson, Brenda de Banzie

Passage Home
p: Julian Wintle
sc: William Fairchild
d: Roy Baker
lp: Anthony Steel, Peter Finch,
Diane Cilento, Cyril Cusack,
Geoffrey Keen, Hugh Griffith

Above Us the Waves
p: William MacQuitty
sc: Robin Estridge
d: Ralph Thomas
lp: John Mills, John Gregson,
Donald Sinden, Michael Medwin
James Robertson Justice

The Prisoner
p: Vivian A Cox
sc: Bridget Boland
d: Peter Glenville
lp: Alec Guinness, Jack Hawkins,
Wilfred Lawson, Kenneth Griffith

1955

Value for Money
p: Sergei Nolbandov
sc: RF Delderfield, William Fairchild
d: Ken Annakin
lp: John Gregson, Diana Dors,
Susan Stephen, Derek Farr

Doctor At Sea
p: Betty E Box
sc: Nicholas Phipps, Jack Davies,
Richard Gordon
d: Ralph Thomas
lp: Dirk Bogarde, Brigitte Bardot,
Brenda de Banzie,
James Robertson Justice

The Woman for Joe
p: Leslie Parkyn
sc: Neil Paterson
d: George More O'Ferrall
lp: Diane Cilento, George Baker

Man of the Moment
p: Hugh Stewart
sc: Vernon Sylvaine,
John Paddy Carstairs
d: John Paddy Carstairs
lp: Norman Wisdom, Lana Morris

An Alligator Named Daisy
p: Raymond Stross
sc: Jack Davies
d: J Lee-Thompson
lp: Donald Sinden, Diana Dors,
Jean Carson, Stanley Holloway,
James Robertson Justice

Simon and Laura
p: Teddy Baird
sc: Peter Blackmore
d: Muriel Box
lp: Peter Finch, Kay Kendall,
Muriel Pavlow, Hubert Gregg

All for Mary
p: Paul Soskin
sc: Peter Blackmore, Paul Soskin,
Alan Melville
d: Wendy Toye
lp: Nigel Patrick, Kathleen Harrison,
David Tomlinson, Jill Day

A Town Like Alice
p: Joseph Janni
sc: WP Lipscomb, Richard Mason
d: Jack Lee
lp: Virginia McKenna, Peter Finch,
Marie Löhr, Renee Huston,
Eileen Moore, Jean Anderson

**Lost
(US: Tears for Simon)**
p: Vivian A Cox
sc: Janet Green
d: Guy Green
lp: David Farrar, David Knight,
Julia Arnall, Anthony Oliver

The Black Tent
p: William MacQuitty
sc: Robin Maugham, Bryan Forbes
d: Brian Desmond Hurst
lp: Anthony Steel, Donald Sinden,
Anna Maria Sandri, André Morell

Reach For the Sky
p: Daniel M Angel
sc: Lewis Gilbert, Vernon Harris
d: Lewis Gilbert
lp: Kenneth More, Muriel Pavlow,
Lyndon Brook, Lee Patterson

Jumping For Joy
p: Raymond Stross
sc: Jack Davies, Henry E Blyth
d: John Paddy Carstairs
lp: Frankie Howerd,
Stanley Holloway, AE Matthews,
Tony Wright, Alfie Bass

**The Battle of the River Plate
(US: Pursuit of the Graf Spee)**
p: Michael Powell,
Emeric Pressburger
sc: Michael Powell,
Emeric Pressburger
d: Michael Powell,
Emeric Pressburger
lp: John Gregson, Anthony Quayle,
Ian Hunter, Jack Gwillim,
Bernard Lee, Lionel Murton

1956

The Iron Petticoat
p: Betty E Box
sc: Ben Hecht
d: Ralph Thomas
lp: Bob Hope, Katherine Hepburn,
Noelle Middleton,
James Robertson Justice

Jacqueline
p: George H Brown
sc: Patrick Kirwan, Liam O'Flaherty,
Patrick Campbell,
Catherine Cookson
d: Roy Baker
lp: John Gregson, Kathleen Ryan,
Jacqueline Ryan, Noel Purcell,
Cyril Cusack, Marie Kean

Eyewitness
p: Sydney Box
sc: Janet Green
d: Muriel Box
lp: Donald Sinden, Muriel Pavlow,
Belinda Lee, Nigel Stock,
Michael Craig, Ada Reeve

The Big Money
p: Joseph Janni
sc: John Baines, Patrick Campbell
d: John Paddy Carstairs
lp: Ian Carmichael, Belinda Lee,
Kathleen Harrison,
Robert Helpmann, James Hayter

The Spanish Gardener
p: John Bryan
sc: Lesley Storm, John Bryan
d: Philip Leacock
lp: Dirk Bogarde, Jon Whitely,
Michael Hordern, Cyril Cusack,
Maureen Swanson, Geoffrey Keen

**House of Secrets
(US: Triple Deception)**
p: Julian Wintle, Vivan A Fox
sc: Robert Buckner, Bryan Forbes
d: Guy Green
lp: Michael Craig, Julia Arnall,
Brenda de Banzie, Barbara Bates,
David Kossoff, Gérard Oury

Checkpoint
p: Betty E Box
sc: Robin Estridge
d: Ralph Thomas
lp: Anthony Steel, Odile Versois,
Stanley Baker, Maurice Denham,
James Robertson Justice

Tiger in the Smoke
p: Leslie Parkyn
sc: Anthony Pélissier
d: Roy Baker
lp: Donald Sinden, Muriel Pavlow,
Tony Wright, Bernard Miles,
Alec Clunes, Laurence Naismith

The Secret Place
p: John Bryan
sc: Linette Perry
d: Clive Donner
lp: Belinda Lee, Ronald Lewis

True as a Turtle
p: Peter de Sarigny
sc: Jack Davies, John Coates,
Nicholas Phipps
d: Wendy Toye
lp: John Gregson, June Thorburn,
Cecil Parker, Keith Michell

Up in the World
p: Hugh Stewart
sc: Jack Davies, Henry Blyth,
Peter Blackmore
d: John Paddy Carstairs
lp: Norman Wisdom,
Jerry Desmonde, Maureen Swanson,
Colin Gordon, Michael Caridia

**Ill Met By Moonlight
(US: Night Ambush)**
p: Michael Powell,
Emeric Pressburger
sc: Michael Powell,
Emeric Pressburger
d: Michael Powell,
Emeric Pressburger
lp: Dirk Bogarde, Marius Goring,
David Oxley, Demitri Andreas,
Cyril Cusack, Laurence Payne

The Prince and the Showgirl
p: Laurence Olivier
sc: Terence Rattigan
d: Laurence Olivier
lp: Laurence Olivier,
Marilyn Monroe, Sybil Thorndike,
Jeremy Spenser, Richard Wattis

High Tide at Noon
p: Julian Wintle
sc: Neil Paterson
d: Philip Leacock
lp: Betta St John, William Sylvester,
Michael Craig, Flora Robson

Doctor at Large
p: Betty E Box
sc: Nicholas Phipps
d: Ralph Thomas
lp: Dirk Bogarde, Muriel Pavlow,
James Robertson Justice,
Donald Sinden, Shirley Eaton

1957

Hell Drivers
p: S Benjamin Fisz
sc: John Kruse, Cy Endfield
d: Cy Endfield
lp: Stanley Baker, Herbert Lom,
Peggy Cummins, William Hartnell,
Patrick McGoohan

Miracle in Soho
p: Emeric Pressburger
sc: Emeric Pressburger
d: Julian Aymes
lp: John Gregson, Belinda Lee,
Cyril Cusack, Peter Illing

Across the Bridge
p: John Stafford
sc: Guy Elmes, Denis Freeman
d: Ken Annakin
lp: Rod Steiger, David Knight,
Noel Willman, Marla Landi

Robbery Under Arms
p: Joseph Janni
sc: Alexander Baron, WP Lipscomb
d: Jack Lee
lp: Peter Finch, David McCallum,
Ronald Lewis, Maureen Swanson,
Laurence Naismith, Jill Ireland

The One That Got Away
p: Julian Wintle
sc: Howard Clewes
d: Roy Baker
lp: Hardy Kruger, Colin Gordon,
Michael Goodliffe,
Terence Alexander, Jack Gwillim

Seven Thunders
(US: The Beasts of Marseilles)
p: Daniel M Angel
sc: John Baines
d: Hugo Fregonese
lp: Stephen Boyd, Tony Wright,
James Robertson Justice,
Anna Gaylor, Kathleen Harrison

Campbell's Kingdom
p: Betty E Box
sc: Robin Estridge, Hammond Innes
d: Ralph Thomas
lp: Dirk Bogarde, Stanley Baker,
Michael Craig, Barbara Murray,
James Robertson Justice

Dangerous Exile
p: George H Brown
sc: Robin Estridge, Patrick Kirwan
d: Brian Desmond Hurst
lp: Louis Jourdan, Belinda Lee,
Keith Michell, Richard O'Sullivan

Just My Luck
p: Hugh Stewart
sc: Alfred Shaughnessy,
Peter Blackmore
d: John Paddy Carstairs
lp: Norman Wisdom, Jill Dixon,
Leslie Phillips, Delphi Lawrence

Windom's Way
p: John Bryan
sc: Jill Craigie
d: Ronald Neame
lp: Peter Finch, Mary Ure,
Natasha Parry, Robert Flemyng

The Gypsy and the Gentleman
p: Maurice Cowan
sc: Janet Green
d: Joseph Losey
lp: Melina Mercouri, Keith Michell,
Flora Robson, Patrick McGoohan,
June Laverick, Lyndon Brook

A Tale of Two Cities
p: Betty E Box
sc: TEB Clarke
d: Ralph Thomas
lp: Dirk Bogarde, Dorothy Tutin,
Cecil Parker, Stephen Murray,
Athene Seyler, Paul Guers

Violent Playground
p: Michael Relph
sc: James Kennaway
d: Basil Dearden
lp: Stanley Baker, Anne Heywood,
David McCallum, Peter Cushing

Carve Her Name with Pride
p: Daniel M Angel
sc: Vernon Harris, Lewis Gilbert
d: Lewis Gilbert
lp: Virginia McKenna,
Paul Scofield, Jack Warner,
Denise Grey, Maurice Ronet

Innocent Sinners
p: Hugh Stewart
sc: Neil Paterson, Rumer Godden
d: Philip Leacock
lp: Flora Robson, David Kossoff,
Barbara Mullen, Catherine Lacey

Rooney
p: George H Brown
sc: Patrick Kirwan
d: George Pollock
lp: John Gregson, Muriel Pavlow,
Barry Fitzgerald, June Thorburn,
Noel Purcell, Marie Kean

A Night to Remember
p: William MacQuitty
sc: Eric Ambler
d: Roy Baker
lp: Kenneth More,
Laurence Naismith,
Michael Goodliffe,
David McCallum, Honor Blackman

The Wind Cannot Read
p: Betty E Box
sc: Richard Mason
d: Ralph Thomas
lp: Dirk Bogarde, Yoko Tani,
Ronald Lewis, John Fraser,
Anthony Bushell, Henry Okawa

The Naked Truth
(US: Your Past is Showing)
p: Mario Zampi
sc: Michael Pertwee
d: Mario Zampi
lp: Terry-Thomas, Peter Sellers,
Peggy Mount, Shirley Eaton,
Dennis Price, Geogina Cookson

Heart of a Child
p: Alfred Shaughnessy
sc: Leigh Vance
d: Clive Donner
lp: Jean Anderson,
Donald Pleasence

The Abominable Snowman
(US: The Abominable Snowman
of the Himalayas) *(part)*
p: Aubrey Baring
sc: Nigel Kneale
d: Val Guest
lp: Forrest Tucker, Peter Cushing,
Maureen Connell, Richard Wattis

1958

Nor the Moon By Night
(US: Elephant Gun)
p: John Stafford
sc: Guy Elmes
d: Ken Annakin
lp: Belinda Lee, Michael Craig,
Patrick McGoohan, Anna Gaylor

Sea Fury
p: Benjamin Fisz
sc: John Kruse, Cy Endfield
d: Cy Endfield
lp: Stanley Baker, Victor McLagen,
Luciana Paluzzi, Grégoire Aslan

Rockets Galore!
p: Basil Dearden
sc: Monja Danischewsky
d: Michael Relph
lp: Jeannie Carson, Donald Sinden,
Roland Culver, Catherine Lacey,
Noel Purcell, Ian Hunter

Passionate Summer
p: Kenneth Harper,
George Willoughby
sc: Joan Henry
d: Rudolph Cartier
lp: Bill Travers, Virginia McKenna,
Yvonne Mitchell, Alexander Knox

Floods of Fear
p: Sydney Box
sc: Charles Crichton
d: Charles Crichton
lp: Howard Keel, Anne Heywood,
Cyril Cusack, Harry H Corbett

Sea of Sand
(US: Desert Patrol)
p: Robert S Baker, Monty Berman
sc: Robert Westerby
d: Guy Green
lp: Richard Attenborough,
John Gregson, Michael Craig,
Vincent Ball, Percy Herbert

The Square Peg
p: Hugh Stewart
sc: Jack Davies, Henry Blyth,
Norman Wisdom, Eddie Leslie
d: John Paddy Carstairs
lp: Norman Wisdom,
Honor Blackman,
Edward Chapman, Campbell Singer

The Captain's Table
p: Joseph Janni
sc: John Whiting, Bryan Forbes,
Nicholas Phipps
d: Jack Lee
lp: John Gregson, Peggy Cummins,
Donald Sinden, Nadia Gray
Maurice Denham, Richard Wattis

Operation Amsterdam
p: Maurice Cowan
sc: Michael McCarthy,
John Eldridge
d: Michael McCarthy
lp: Peter Finch, Eva Bartok,
Tony Britton, Alexander Knox

Too Many Crooks
p: Mario Zampi
sc: Michael Pertwee
d: Mario Zampi
lp: Terry-Thomas, George Cole,
Brenda de Banzie,
Bernard Bresslaw, Sidney James

Whirlpool
p: George Pitcher
sc: Lawrence P Bachmann
d: Lewis Allen
lp: Juliette Gréco, OW Fischer,
Marius Goring, Muriel Pavlow,
William Sylvester, Richard Palmer

The 39 Steps
p: Betty E Box
sc: Frank Harvey
d: Ralph Thomas
lp: Kenneth More, Taina Elg,
Brenda de Banzie, Barry Jones,
Reginald Beckwith, Faith Brook

Ferry to Hong Kong
p: George Maynard
sc: Vernon Harris, Lewis Gilbert,
John Mortimer
d: Lewis Gilbert
lp: Curt Jurgens, Orson Welles,
Sylvia Syms, Jeremy Spenser,
Noel Purcell, Margaret Withers

Sapphire
p: Michael Relph
sc: Janet Green, Lukas Heller
d: Basil Dearden
lp: Nigel Patrick, Yvonne Mitchell,
Michael Craig, Paul Massie,
Bernard Miles, Olda Lindo

Carry On Sergeant
p: Peter Rogers
sc: Norman Hudis
d: Gerald Thomas
lp: William Hartnell, Shirley Eaton,
Eric Barker, Dora Bryan,
Bill Owen, Charles Hawtrey
Kenneth Connor, Kenneth Williams

The Sheriff of Fractured Jaw
p: Daniel M Angel
sc: Arthur Dales
d: Raoul Walsh
lp: Kenneth More, Jayne Mansfield,
Henry Hull, Bruce Cabot

Carry On Nurse
p: Peter Rogers
sc: Norman Hudis
d: Gerald Thomas
lp: Kenneth Connor, Shirley Eaton,
Charles Hawtrey, Hattie Jacques,
Terence Longdon, Bill Owen,
Leslie Phillips, Joan Sims

Interpol Calling
(TV series, 39 episodes)
p: Anthony Perry,
Connery Chappell
sc: David Chantler, Brain Clemens,
Lewis Davidson, Leonard Fincham,
Larry Forrester, John Kruse,
Robert Banks Stewart and others
d: Charles Frend, Bill Lewthwaite,
Robert Lynn, George Pollock,
CM Pennington-Richards,
Max Varnel and others
lp: Charles Korvin, Edwin Richfield

1959

The Heart of a Man
p: Anna Neagle
sc: Jack Trevor Story, Pamela Bower
d: Herbert Wilcox
lp: Frankie Vaughan,
Anne Heywood, Tony Britton

Upstairs and Downstairs
p: Betty E Box
sc: Frank Harvey
d: Ralph Thomas
lp: Michael Craig, Anne Heywood,
Mylène Demongeot,
James Robertson Justice

North West Frontier
(US: Flame Over India)
p: Marcel Hellman
sc: Robin Estridge, Frank Nugent
d: J Lee-Thompson
lp: Kenneth More, Lauren Bacall,
Herbert Lom, Wilfrid Hyde-White.
IS Johar, Ursula Jeans

SOS Pacific
p: John Nasht,
Patrick Filmer-Sankey
sc: Robert Westerby
d: Guy Green
lp: Richard Attenborough,
Pier Angeli, John Gregson

Kidnapped
p: Walt Disney, Hugh Attwooll
sc: Robert Stevenson
d: Robert Stevenson
lp: Peter Finch, James MacArthur,
Bernard Lee, John Laurie

The Savage Innocents
p: Maleno Malenotti
sc: Nicholas Ray
d: Nicholas Ray, Baccio Bandini
lp: Anthony Quinn, Yoko Tani,
Marie Yang, Peter O'Toole

Sink the Bismarck!
p: John Brabourne
sc: Edmund H North
d: Lewis Gilbert
lp: Kenneth More, Dana Wynter,
Carl Mohner, Laurence Naismith

Conspiracy of Hearts
p: Betty E Box
sc: Robert Presnell Jr, Dale Pitt
d: Ralph Thomas
lp: Lilli Palmer, Sylvia Syms,
Yvonne Mitchell, Ronald Lewis

Follow a Star
p: Hugh Stewart
sc: Jack Davies, Henry Blyth,
Norman Wisdom
d: Robert Asher
lp: Norman Wisdom, June Laverick,
Jerry Desmonde, Hattie Jacques

Please Turn Over
p: Peter Rogers
sc: Norman Hudis
d: Gerald Thomas
lp: Julia Lockwood, Jean Kent,
Ted Ray, Leslie Phillips, Joan Sims,
Dilys Laye, Lionel Jeffries

Dentist in the Chair
p: Bertram Ostrer
sc: Val Guest, Bob Monkhouse,
George Wadmore
d: Don Chaffey
lp: Bob Monkhouse,
Peggy Cummins, Kenneth Connor

Carry On Teacher
p: Peter Rogers
sc: Norman Hudis
d: Gerald Thomas
lp: Kenneth Connor,
Charles Hawtrey, Leslie Phillips,
Joan Sims, Kenneth Williams

Peeping Tom
p: Michael Powell
sc: Leo Marks
d: Michael Powell
lp: Carl Boehm, Moira Shearer,
Anna Massey, Maxine Audley

Carry On Constable
p: Peter Rogers
sc: Norman Hudis
d: Gerald Thomas
lp: Sidney James, Eric Barker,
Kenneth Connor, Charles Hawtrey,
Kenneth Williams, Leslie Phillips

The League of Gentlemen
p: Michael Relph
sc: Bryan Forbes
d: Basil Dearden
lp: Jack Hawkins, Nigel Patrick,
Richard Attenborough,
Roger Livesey, Bryan Forbes

The 3 Worlds of Gulliver (part)
p: Charles H Schneer
sc: Arthur A Ross, Jack Sher
d: Jack Sher
lp: Kerwin Matthews, Jo Morrow,
June Thorburn, Lee Patterson,
Grégoire Aslan, Basil Sydney

1960

Make Mine Mink
p: Hugh Stewart
sc: Michael Pertwee,
Peter Blackmore
d: Robert Asher
lp: Terry-Thomas, Athene Seyler,
Hattie Jacques, Billie Whitelaw

Sons and Lovers
p: Jerry Wald
sc: Gavin Lambert, TEB Clarke
d: Jack Cardiff
lp: Dean Stockwell, Trevor Howard,
Wendy Hiller, Mary Ure,
Heather Sears, William Lucas

Doctor in Love
p: Betty E Box
sc: Nicholas Phipps
d: Ralph Thomas
lp: Michael Craig, Virginia Maskell,
James Robertson Justice,
Carole Lesley, Leslie Phillips,

The Professionals
p: Norman Priggen
sc: Peter Barnes
d: Don Sharp
lp: William Lucas, Stratford Johns,
Charles Vance, Edward Cast

Piccadilly Third Stop
p: Norman Williams
sc: Leigh Vance
d: Wolf Rilla
lp: Terence Morgan, Yoko Tani,
Mai Zetterling, William Hartnell,
John Crawford, Ann Lynn

Man in the Moon
p: Michael Relph
sc: Michael Relph, Bryan Forbes
d: Basil Dearden
lp: Kenneth More,
Shirley Anne Field, Norman Bird,
Michael Hordern, John Glyn-Jones

The Singer Not the Song
p: Roy Baker
sc: Nigel Balchin
d: Roy Baker
lp: Dirk Bogarde, John Mills,
Mylène Demongeot,
Laurence Naismith, John Bentley

There Was a Crooked Man
p: John Bryan
sc: Reuben Ship
d: Stuart Burge
lp: Norman Wisdom, Alfred Marks,
Andrew Cruickshank,
Reginald Beckwith, Susannah York

Watch Your Stern
p: Peter Rogers
sc: Alan Hackney, Vivian A Cox
d: Gerald Thomas
lp: Kenneth Connor, Eric Barker,
Leslie Phillips, Joan Sims,
Noel Purcell, Hattie Jacques

The Hellfire Club
p: Robert S Baker, Monty Berman
sc: Jimmy Sangster, Leon Griffiths
d: Robert S Baker, Monty Berman
lp: Keith Michell, Adrienne Corri,
Peter Arne, Kai Fischer,
Peter Cushing, Bill Owen

No Kidding
(US: Beware of Children)
p: Peter Rogers
sc: Norman Hudis, Robin Estridge
d: Gerald Thomas
lp: Leslie Phillips,
Geraldine McEwan,
Julia Lockwood, Noel Purcell,
Irene Handl, Joan Hickson

Cleopatra
(Pinewood filming abandoned)
p: Walter Wanger
sc: Joseph L Mankiewicz,
Ranald MacDougall,
Sidney Buchman, Ben Hecht
d: Rouben Mamoulien
lp: Elizabeth Taylor, Peter Finch,
Stephen Boyd, Harry Andrews

The Impersonator
p: Anthony Perry
sc: Alfred Shaughnessy,
Kenneth Cavander
d: Alfred Shaughnessy
lp: John Crawford, Jane Griffiths,
Patricia Burke, John Salew

The Treasure of Monte Cristo
(US: The Secret of Monte Cristo)
p: Robert S Baker, Monty Berman
sc: Leon Griffiths
d: Robert S Baker
lp: Rory Calhoun, Patricia Bredin,
Peter Arne, Gianna Maria Canale

Carry On Regardless
p: Peter Rogers
sc: Norman Hudis
d: Gerald Thomas
lp: Sidney James, Kenneth Connor,
Charles Hawtrey, Joan Sims,
Kenneth Williams, Bill Owen

Flame in the Streets
p: Roy Baker
sc: Ted Willis
d: Roy Baker
lp: John Mills, Sylvia Syms,
Brenda de Banzie, Earl Cameron

No Love for Johnnie
p: Betty E Box
sc: Nicholas Phipps,
Mordecai Richler
d: Ralph Thomas
lp: Peter Finch, Stanley Holloway,
Mary Peach, Donald Pleasence

The Boy Who Stole a Million
p: George H Brown
sc: John Eldridge, Charles Crichton
d: Charles Crichton
lp: Vergilio Teixeira, Maurice Rayna,
Marianne Benet, Harold Kasket,
Curt Christian, Bill Nagy

The Bulldog Breed (part)
p: Hugh Stewart
sc: Jack Davies, Henry Blyth,
Norman Wisdom
d: Robert Asher
lp: Norman Wisdom, Ian Hunter,
David Lodge, Robert Urquhart

1961

Victim
p: Michael Relph
sc: Janet Green, John McCormick
d: Basil Dearden
lp: Dirk Bogarde, Sylvia Syms,
Dennis Price, Nigel Stock

Whistle Down the Wind
p: Richard Attenborough
sc: Keith Waterhouse, Willis Hall
d: Bryan Forbes
lp: Hayley Mills, Bernard Lee,
Alan Bates, Norman Bird,
Diane Clare, Patricia Heneghan

No, My Darling Daughter
p: Betty E Box
sc: Frank Harvey
d: Ralph Thomas
lp: Michael Redgrave,
Michael Craig, Roger Livesey,
Rad Fulton, Juliet Mills

Raising the Wind
p: Peter Rogers
sc: Bruce Montgomery
d: Gerald Thomas
lp: James Robertson Justice,
Leslie Phillips, Paul Massie,
Kenneth Williams, Liz Fraser

The Long Shadow
p: John Pellatt
sc: Manning O'Brine
d: Peter Maxwell
lp: John Crawford,
Susan Hampshire, Bill Nagy

What a Whopper
p: Teddy Joseph
sc: Terry Nation
d: Gilbert Gunn
lp: Adam Faith, Sidney James,
Carol Lesley, Terence Longdon

In the Doghouse
p: Hugh Stewart
sc: Michael Pertwee
d: Darcy Conyers
lp: Leslie Phillips, Peggy Cummins,
Hattie Jacques, James Booth,
Dick Bentley, Colin Gordon

All Night Long
p: Michael Relph, Basil Dearden
sc: Nel King, Peter Achilles
d: Basil Dearden
lp: Patrick McGoohan,
Keith Michell, Betsy Blair,
Paul Harris, Marti Stevens,
Richard Attenborough

Waltz of the Toreadors
p: Peter de Sarigny
sc: Wolf Mankowitz
d: John Guillermin
lp: Peter Sellers, Dany Robin,
Margaret Leighton, John Fraser,
Cyril Cusack, Prunella Scales

In Search of the Castaways
p: Walt Disney, Hugh Attwooll
sc: Lowell S Hawley
d: Robert Stevenson
lp: Maurice Chevalier,
Hayley Mills, George Sanders,
Wilfrid Hyde-White

Tiara Tahiti
p: Ivan Maxwell
sc: Geoffrey Cotterell,
Ivan Foxwell, Mordecai Richler
d: Ted Kotcheff
lp: James Mason, John Mills,
Rosenda Monteros, Herbert Lom

A Pair of Briefs
p: Betty E Box
sc: Nicholas Phipps
d: Ralph Thomas
lp: Michael Craig, Mary Peach,
Brenda de Banzie,
James Robertson Justice

Twice Round the Daffodils
p: Peter Rogers
sc: Norman Hudis
d: Gerald Thomas
lp: Juliet Mills, Donald Sinden,
Donald Houston,
Kenneth Williams, Ronald Lewis

Der Rosenkavalier
p: Paul Czinner
sc: Hugo von Hofmannstal,
Richard Strauss
d: Paul Czinner
lp: Elisabeth Schwarzkopf,
Otto Edelmann, Sena Jurinac,
Erich Kunz

The Johnny Leyton Touch
p: Robert Stigwood
d: Norman Harrison
lp: Johnny Leyton, Iain Gregory

1962

**Life For Ruth
(US: Condemned to Life)**
p: Michael Relph
sc: Janet Green, John McCormick
d: Basil Dearden
lp: Michael Craig,
Patrick McGoohan, Janet Munro,
Paul Rogers, Malcolm Keen

Carry On Cruising
p: Peter Rogers
sc: Norman Hudis
d: Gerald Thomas
lp: Sidney James, Kenneth Williams,
Kenneth Connor, Liz Fraser,
Dilys Laye, Esma Cannon

Play it Cool
p: David Deutsch, Dennis Holt
sc: Jack Davies Jr
d: Michael Winner
lp: Billy Fury, Michael Anderson Jr,
Dennis Price, Helen Shapiro

Dr. No
p: Harry Saltzman, Albert R Broccoli
sc: Richard Maibaum,
Johanna Harwood, Berkely Mather,
d: Terence Young
lp: Sean Connery, Ursula Andress,
Joseph Wiseman, Jack Lord,
Bernard Lee, Anthony Dawson,
John Kitzmiller, Zena Marshall

Masters of Venus
(serial, 8 episodes)
p: A. Frank Bundy
sc: Michael Barnes,
Mary Cathcart Borer
d: Ernest Morris
lp: Norman Wooland,
Amanda Coxell, Robin Stewart

The Traitors
p: Jim O'Connelly
sc: Jim O'Connelly
d: Robert Tronson
lp: Patrick Allen, Jacqueline Ellis,
James Maxwell, Zena Walker

Band of Thieves
p: Lance Comfort
sc: Lyn Fairhurst
d: Peter Bezencenet
lp: Acker Bilk, Colin Smith,
Jonathan Mortimer, Ron McKay

The Primitives
p: Negus Fancey
sc: Alfred Travers, Moris Farhi
d: Alfred Travers
lp: Jan Holden, Bill Edwards,
Rio Fanning, George Mikell

**Lancelot and Guinevere
(US: Sword of Lancelot)**
p: Bernard Luber
sc: Richard E Schayer,
Jefferson Pascal
d: Cornel Wilde
lp: Cornel Wilde, Jean Wallace,
Brian Aherne, George Baker,
Michael Meacham, Adrienne Corri

The Horse without a Head
p: Walt Disney, Hugh Attwooll
sc: TEB Clarke
d: Don Chaffey
lp: Jean-Pierre Aumont,
Herbert Lom, Leo McKern,
Pamela Franklin, Vincent Winter

**The Wild and the Willing
(US: Young and Willing)**
p: Betty E Box
sc: Nicholas Phipps,
Mordecai Richler
d: Ralph Thomas
lp: Virginia Maskell, Paul Rogers,
Ian McShane, Samantha Eggar,
Catherine Wooville, David Sumner

Stranglehold
p: David Henley
sc: Guy Elmes, Joy Garrison
d: Lawrence Huntington
lp: MacDonald Carey,
Barbara Shelley, Philip Friend,
Nadja Regin, Leonard Sachs

The Mind Benders
p: Michael Relph
sc: James Kennaway
d: Basil Dearden
lp: Dirk Bogarde, Mary Ure,
John Clements, Michael Bryant,
Wendy Craig, Harold Goldblatt

On the Beat
p: Hugh Stewart
sc: Norman Wisdom, Jack Davies,
Eddie Leslie
d: Robert Asher
lp: Norman Wisdom,
Jennifer Jayne, Raymond Huntley,
David Lodge, Esma Cannon

**The Iron Maiden
(US: The Swinging Maiden)**
p: Peter Rogers
sc: Vivian Cox, Leslie Bricusse
d: Gerald Thomas
lp: Michael Craig, Ann Helm,
Jeff Donnell, Alan Hale,
Noel Purcell, Cecil Parker

The Three Lives of Thomasina
p: Walt Disney, Hugh Attwooll
sc: Robert Westerby
d: Don Chaffey
lp: Patrick McGoohan,
Susan Hampshire,
Laurence Naismith, Jean Anderson

The Mouse on the Moon
p: Walter Shenson
sc: Michael Pertwee
d: Richard Lester
lp: Margaret Rutherford,
Bernard Cribbins, Ron Moody,
David Kossoff, Terry-Thomas

Bitter Harvest
p: Albert Fennell
sc: Ted Willis
d: Peter Graham Scott
lp: Janet Munro, John Stride,
Alan Badel, Anne Cunningham,
Terence Alexander, Richard Thorp

The Party's Over
p: Anthony Perry
sc: Marc Behm
d: Guy Hamilton
lp: Oliver Reed, Clifford David,
Catherine Woodville, Ann Lynn,
Louise Sorel, Eddie Albert

Call Me Bwana
p: Albert R Broccoli
sc: Nate Monaster,
Johanna Harwood
d: Gordon Douglas
lp: Bob Hope, Anita Ekberg,
Edie Adams, Lionel Jeffries,
Percy Herbert, Paul Carpenter

The Informers
p: William MacQuitty
sc: Alun Falconer, Paul Durst
d: Ken Annakin
lp: Nigel Patrick, Margaret Whiting,
Catherine Woodville, Colin Blakely,
Derren Nesbitt, Harry Andrews

Nurse on Wheels
p: Peter Rogers
sc: Norman Hudis
d: Gerald Thomas
lp: Juliet Mills, Ronald Lewis,
Joan Sims, Noel Purcell,
Esma Cannon, Raymond Huntley

1963

The Bay of Saint Michel
p: John Ainsworth
sc: Christopher Davis
d: John Ainsworth
lp: Keenan Wynn, Mai Zetterling,
Ronald Howard, Rona Anderson

80,000 Suspects
p: Val Guest
sc: Val Guest
d: Val Guest
lp: Claire Bloom, Richard Johnson,
Yolande Donlan, Cyril Cusack

Farewell Performance
p: Jim O'Connolly
sc: Aileen Burke, Leone Stuart,
Jim O'Connolly
d: Robert Tronson
lp: Delphi Lawrence, David Kernan

The Switch
p: Lance Comfort, Philip Ridgeway
sc: Philip Ridgeway, Colin Fraser
d: Peter Maxwell
lp: Anthony Steel, Zena Marshall,
Conrad Phillips, Dermot Walsh

Bomb in the High Street
p: Theodore Zichy
sc: Ben Simcoe
d: Terence Egan Bishop,
Peter Bezencenet,
lp: Ronald Howard, Terry Palmer,
Suzanna Leigh, Jack Allen

Doctor in Distress
p: Betty E Box
sc: Nicholas Phipps,
Ronald Scott Thorn
d: Ralph Thomas
lp: Dirk Bogarde, Samantha Eggar,
James Robertson Justice,
Donald Houston, Barbara Murray

Dr Syn – Alias the Scarecrow
p: Walt Disney, Bill Anderson
sc: Robert Westerby
d: James Neilson
lp: Patrick McGoohan,
George Cole, Tony Britton,
Michael Hordern, Geoffrey Keen

Carry On Cabby
p: Peter Rogers
sc: Talbot Rothwell
d: Gerald Thomas
lp: Sidney James, Hattie Jacques,
Kenneth Connor, Charles Hawtrey,
Esma Cannon, Liz Fraser

From Russia With Love
p: Harry Saltzman, Albert R Broccoli
sc: Richard Maibaum,
Johanna Harwood
d: Terence Young
lp: Sean Connery, Daniela Bianchi,
Pedro Armendariz, Lotte Lenya,
Robert Shaw, Bernard Lee,
Eunice Gayson, Walter Gotell

Live it Up
p: Lance Comfort
sc: Lyn Fairhurst
d: Lance Comfort
lp: David Hemmings, Jennifer Moss,
John Pike, Heinz Burt

A Stitch in Time
p: Hugh Stewart
sc: Jack Davies, Norman Wisdom,
Henry Blyth, Eddie Leslie
d: Robert Asher
lp: Norman Wisdom,
Edward Chapman, Jeanette Sterke,
Jerry Desmonde, Jill Melford

Séance on a Wet Afternoon
p: Richard Attenborough,
Bryan Forbes, Jack Rix
sc: Bryan Forbes
d: Bryan Forbes
lp: Kim Stanley,
Richard Attenborough,
Nanette Newman, Patrick Magee

This is My Street
p: Jack Hanbury, Peter Rogers
sc: Bill MacIlwraith
d: Sidney Hayers
lp: Ian Hendry, June Ritchie,
Avice Landon, Meredith Edwards,
Madge Ryan, John Hurt

Woman of Straw
p: Michael Relph
sc: Robert Muller, Stanley Mann,
Michael Relph
d: Basil Dearden
lp: Gina Lollobrigida, Sean Connery,
Ralph Richardson, Alexander Knox

Carry On Jack
p: Peter Rogers
sc: Talbot Rothwell
d: Gerald Thomas
lp: Kenneth Williams,
Bernard Cribbins, Juliet Mills,
Charles Hawtrey, Donald Houston

The Moon-Spinners
p: Bill Anderson, Hugh Attwooll
sc: Michael Dyne
d: James Neilson
lp: Hayley Mills, Eli Wallach,
Peter McEnery, Joan Greenwood,
Irene Papas, John Le Mesurier

Hot Enough for June
p: Betty E Box
sc: Lukas Heller
d: Ralph Thomas
lp: Dirk Bogarde, Sylva Koscina,
Robert Morley, Leo McKern,
Roger Delgado, Derek Fowlds

The Beauty Jungle
(US: Contest Girl)
p: Val Guest
sc: Robert Muller, Val Guest
d: Val Guest
lp: Ian Hendry, Janette Scott,
Ronald Fraser, Edmund Purdom,
Jean Claudio, Tommy Trinder

Blind Corner
p: Tom Blakeley
sc: James Kelley, Peter Miller
d: Lance Comfort
lp: William Sylvester,
Barbara Shelley

1964

Topo Gigio (TV Pilot)
p: Jolly Film, Sullivan Enterprises
sc: Federico Caldura,
Mario Faustinelli
d: Federico Caldura, Luca De Rico

The Magnificent Showman
(US: Circus World) (part)
p: Samuel Bronston
sc: Ben Hecht, Julian Halevy,
James Edward Grant
d: Henry Hathaway
lp: John Wayne, Claudia Cardinale,
Rita Hayworth, Lloyd Nolan,
Richard Conte, John Smith

Carry On Spying
p: Peter Rogers
sc: Talbot Rothwell, Sid Colin
d: Gerald Thomas
lp: Kenneth Williams,
Barbara Windsor, Bernard Cribbins,
Charles Hawtrey, Eric Barker

Guns at Batasi
p: George H Brown
sc: Robert Holles,
CM Pennington-Richards
d: John Guillermin
lp: Richard Attenborough,
Flora Robson, John Leyton,
Mia Farrow, Jack Hawkins

Goldfinger
p: Harry Saltzman, Albert R Broccoli
sc: Richard Maibaum, Paul Dehn
d: Guy Hamilton
lp: Sean Connery, Honor Blackman,
Gert Frobe, Shirley Eaton,
Tania Mallet, Harold Sakata,
Bernard Lee, Martin Benson

Devils of Darkness
p: Tom Blakeley
sc: Lyn Fairhurst
d: Lance Comfort
lp: William Sylvester, Hubert Noel,
Carole Gray, Tracy Reed,
Diana Decker, Rona Anderson

Those Magnificent Men in
Their Flying Machines, or How
I Flew from London to Paris in
25 Hours 11 Minutes
p: Stan Marguilies
sc: Jack Davies, Ken Annakin
d: Ken Annakin
lp: Stuart Whitman, Sarah Miles,
James Fox, Alberto Sordi,
Robert Morley, Gert Frobe,
Jean-Pierre Cassel, Irina Demick

Masquerade
p: Michael Relph
sc: Michael Relph,
William Goldman
d: Basil Dearden
lp: Cliff Robertson, Jack Hawkins,
Marisa Mell, Michel Piccoli
Bill Fraser, Charles Gray

The High Bright Sun
(US: McGuire Go Home)
p: Betty E Box
sc: Ian Stuart Black
d: Ralph Thomas
lp: Dirk Bogarde, George Chakiris,
Susan Strasberg, Denholm Elliott

A High Wind in Jamaica
p: John Croydon
sc: Stanley Mann, Ronald Harwood,
Denis Cannan
d: Alexander Mackendrick
lp: Anthony Quinn, James Coburn,
Dennis Price, Lila Kedrova,
Nigel Davenport, Isabel Dean

Carry On Cleo
p: Peter Rogers
sc: Talbot Rothwell
d: Gerald Thomas
lp: Sidney James, Kenneth Williams,
Kenneth Connor, Charles Hawtrey,
Joan Sims, Jim Dale, Amanda Barrie

Court Martial
(TV series, 26 episodes)
p: Robert Douglas, Bill Hill
sc: Milton S. Gelman, Bill Strutton,
Julian Bond and others
d: Seth Holt, Robert Douglas,
Alvin Rakoff, Peter Maxwell,
Peter Medak, Sam Wanamaker
and others
lp: Bradford Dillman, Peter Graves

The Legend of Young
Dick Turpin
p: Bill Anderson, Hugh Attwooll
sc: Robert Westerby
d: James Neilson
lp: David Weston, Bernard Lee,
George Cole, Maurice Denham

The Ipcress File
p: Harry Salztman
sc: Bill Canaway, James Doran
d: Sidney J Furie
lp: Michael Caine, Nigel Green,
Guy Doleman, Sue Lloyd,
Gordon Jackson, Aubrey Richards

The Intelligence Men
(US: Spylarks)
p: Hugh Stewart
sc: Sidney C Green, Richard M Hills
d: Robert Asher
lp: Eric Morecambe, Ernie Wise,
William Franklyn, April Olrich,
Gloria Paul, Richard Vernon

The City under the Sea
(US: War-Gods of the Deep)
p: George Willoughby
sc: Charles Bennett,
Louis M Heyward, David Whittaker
d: Jacques Tourneur
lp: Vincent Price, David Tomlinson,
Tab Hunter, Susan Hart,
John Le Mesurier, Harry Oscar

The Heroes of Telemark
p: S Benjamin Fisz
sc: Ivan Moffat, Benjamin Barzman
d: Anthony Mann
lp: Kirk Douglas, Richard Harris,
Ulla Jacobsson, Michael Redgrave,
David Weston, Anton Diffring

1965

The Big Job
p: Peter Rogers
sc: Talbot Rothwell
d: Gerald Thomas
lp: Sidney James, Sylvia Syms,
Dick Emery, Lance Percival,
Joan Sims, Jim Dale

Thunderball
p: Kevin McClory
sc: Richard Maibaum,
John Hopkins, Jack Whittingham
d: Terence Young
lp: Sean Connery, Claudine Auger,
Adolfo Celi, Luciana Paluzzi,
Rik Van Nutter, Bernard Lee,
Martine Beswick, Guy Doleman,
Molly Peters

Arabesque
p: Stanley Donen
sc: Julian Mitchell, Stanley Price,
Pierre Marton
d: Stanley Donen
lp: Gregory Peck, Sophia Loren,
Alan Badel, Kieron Moore,
Carl Duering, John Merivale

Sky West and Crooked
p: Jack Hanbury
sc: Mary Hayley Bell, John Prebble
d: John Mills
lp: Hayley Mills, Ian McShane,
Laurence Naismith,
Geoffrey Bayldon, Annette Crosbie

The Early Bird
p: Hugh Stewart
sc: Jack Davies, Norman Wisdom,
Eddie Leslie, Henry Blyth
d: Robert Asher
lp: Norman Wisdom,
Edward Chapman, Jerry Desmonde,
Paddie O'Neil, Bryan Pringle

Carry On Cowboy
p: Peter Rogers
sc: Talbot Rothwell
d: Gerald Thomas
lp: Sidney James, Kenneth Williams,
Jim Dale, Charles Hawtrey,
Joan Sims, Angela Douglas

Khartoum
p: Julian Blaustein
sc: Robert Ardrey
d: Basil Dearden
lp: Charlton Heston,
Laurence Olivier, Richard Johnson,
Ralph Richardson, Alexander Knox

The Fighting Prince of Donegal
p: Walt Disney, Bill Anderson
sc: Robert Westerby
d: Michael O'Herlihy
lp: Peter McEnery,
Susan Hampshire, Tom Adams,
Gordon Jackson, Andrew Keir

The Wrong Box
p: Bryan Forbes
sc: Larry Gelbart, Burt Shevelove
d: Bryan Forbes
lp: John Mills, Ralph Richardson,
Michael Caine, Peter Cook,
Dudley Moore, Nanette Newman

Romeo and Juliet
p: Paul Czinner
sc: Kenneth MacMillan
d: Paul Czinner
lp: Margot Fonteyn,
Rudolph Nureyev, David Blair,
Desmond Doyle, Anthony Dowell

Doctor in Clover
p: Betty E Box
sc: Jack Davies
d: Ralph Thomas
lp: Leslie Phillips,
James Robertson Justice,
Shirley Anne Field, John Fraser

That Riviera Touch
p: Hugh Stewart
sc: Sidney C Green, Richard M Hills,
Peter Blackmore
d: Cliff Owen
lp: Eric Morecambe, Ernie Wise,
Suzanne Lloyd, Paul Stassino

Stop the World –
I Want to Get Off
p: Ted Lloyd
sc: Leslie Bricusse, Anthony Newley
David Donabie, Al Ham,
Marilyn Bergman, Alan Bergman
d: Philip Saville,
Michael Lindsay-Hogg
lp: Tony Tanner, Millicent Martin

Island of Terror
p: Tom Blakeley
sc: Edward Andrew Mann,
Alan Ramsen
d: Terence Fisher
lp: Peter Cushing, Edward Judd,
Carole Gray, Eddie Byrne

Runaway Railway
p: George H Brown
sc: Michael Barnes
d: Jan Darnley-Smith
lp: John Moulder-Brown,
Kevin Bennett, Leonard Brockwell,
Roberta Tovey, Sydney Tafler,
Ronnie Barker

Three Hats for Lisa
p: Jack Hanbury
sc: Talbot Rothwell, Leslie Bricusse
d: Sidney Hayers
lp: Joe Brown, Sophie Hardy,
Sidney James, Una Stubbs,
Dave Nelson, Peter Bowles

Dateline Diamonds
p: Harry Benn
sc: Tudor Gates
d: Jeremy Summers
lp: William Lucas, Kenneth Cope,
George Mikell, Conrad Phillips,
Patsy Rowlands, Burnell Tucker

The Vulture
p: Lawrence Huntington
sc: Lawrence Huntington
d: Lawrence Huntington
lp: Robert Hutton, Akim Tamiroff,
Broderick Crawford, Diane Clare,
Philip Friend, Annette Carell

1966

Carry On Screaming!
p: Peter Rogers
sc: Talbot Rothwell
d: Gerald Thomas
lp: Harry H Corbett,
Kenneth Williams, Jim Dale,
Charles Hawtrey, Fenella Fielding,
Joan Sims, Angela Douglas

Fahrenheit 451
p: Lewis M Allen
sc: François Truffaut,
Jean-Louis Richard, David Rudkin,
Helen Scott
d: François Truffaut
lp: Oskar Werner, Julie Christie,
Cyril Cusack, Anton Diffring,
Jeremy Spenser, Bee Duffell

Kaleidoscope
p: Elliott Kastner
sc: Robert Carrington,
Jane-Howard Carrington
d: Jack Smight
lp: Warren Beatty, Susannah York,
Clive Revill, Eric Porter,
Murray Melvin, George Sewell

A Countess from Hong Kong
p: Jerome Epstein
sc: Charles Chaplin
d: Charles Chaplin
lp: Marlon Brando, Sophia Loren,
Sydney Chaplin, Tippi Hedren,
Patrick Cargill, Michael Medwin

Casino Royale
p: Charles K Feldman, Jerry Bresler
sc: Wolf Mankowitz, John Law,
Michael Sayers and others
d: John Huston, Kenneth Hughes,
Val Guest, Robert Parrish,
Joseph McGrath
lp: David Niven, Deborah Kerr,
Orson Welles, Peter Sellers,
Ursula Andress, Woody Allen

Funeral in Berlin
p: Charles Kasher
sc: Evan Jones
d: Guy Hamilton
lp: Michael Caine, Paul Hubschmid,
Oscar Homolka, Eva Renzi,
Guy Doleman, Hugh Burden

The Quiller Memorandum
p: Ivan Foxwell
sc: Harold Pinter
d: Michael Anderson
lp: George Segal, Alec Guinness,
Max Von Sydow, Senta Berger,
George Sanders, Robert Helpmann

The Whisperers
p: Michael S Laughlin,
Ronald Shedlo
sc: Bryan Forbes
d: Bryan Forbes
lp: Edith Evans, Eric Portman,
Nanette Newman, Gerald Sim,
Avis Bunnage, Ronald Fraser

**The Persecution and
Assassination of Jean-Paul
Marat as performed by the
inmates of the Asylum of
Charenton under the direction
of the Marquis de Sade
(aka: Marat/Sade)**
p: Michael Birkett
sc: Adrian Mitchell
d: Peter Brook
lp: Ian Richardson, Patrick Magee,
Glenda Jackson, Michael Williams,
Robert Lloyd, Clifford Rose

Deadlier than the Male
p: Betty E Box
sc: Jimmy Sangster, David Osborn,
Liz Charles-Williams
d: Ralph Thomas
lp: Richard Johnson, Elke Sommer,
Sylva Koscina, Nigel Green,
Steve Carlson, Suzanna Leigh

To Sir With Love
p: James Clavell
sc: James Clavell
d: James Clavell
lp: Sidney Poitier, Christian Roberts,
Judy Geeson, Suzy Kendall, Lulu,
Faith Brook, Geoffrey Bayldon

Finders Keepers
p: George H Brown
sc: Michael Pertwee
d: Sidney Hayers
lp: Cliff Richard, Robert Morley,
Peggy Mount, Viviane Ventura,
Graham Stark, John Le Mesurier

You Only Live Twice
p: Harry Saltzman, Albert R Broccoli
sc: Roald Dahl, Harold Jack Bloom
d: Lewis Gilbert
lp: Sean Connery, Donald Pleasence,
Akiko Wakabayashi, Tetsuro Tamba,
Mie Hama, Teru Shimada,
Karin Dor, Bernard Lee

Maroc-7
p: John Gale, Leslie Phillips,
Martin C. Schute
sc: David Osborn
d: Gerry O'Hara
lp: Gene Barry, Elsa Martinelli,
Leslie Phillips, Cyd Charisse,
Denholm Elliott, Alexandra Stewart

Man in a Suitcase
(TV series, 30 episodes)
p: Sidney Cole
sc: Philip Broadley, Bernie Cooper,
Morris Farhi, Wilfred Greatorex,
Donald Jonson, Francis Megahy,
Jan Read and others
d: Charles Crichton, Peter Duffell,
Freddie Francis, Charles Frend,
John Glen, Pat Jackson,
Robert Tronson and others
lp: Richard Bradford

**Don't Lose Your Head
(aka: Carry On ... Don't Lose
Your Head)**
p: Peter Rogers
sc: Talbot Rothwell
d: Gerald Thomas
lp: Sidney James, Kenneth Williams,
Jim Dale, Charles Hawtrey,
Peter Butterworth, Joan Sims

The Magnificent Two
p: Hugh Stewart
sc: Sidney C Green, Richard M Hills,
Michael Pertwee, Peter Blackmore
d: Cliff Owen
lp: Eric Morcambe, Ernie Wise,
Margit Saad, Vergilio Texeira
Cecil Parker, Isobel Black

The Long Duel
p: Ken Annakin
sc: Peter Yeldham
d: Ken Annakin
lp: Yul Brynner, Trevor Howard,
Harry Andrews, Andrew Keir,
Charlotte Rampling,
Virginia North, Laurence Naismith

The Avengers
*(TV series, two episodes filmed
at Pinewood)*
p: Albert Fennell, Brian Clemens
sc: Philip Levene
d: Gordon Flemyng, John Krish
lp: Patrick Macnee, Diana Rigg,
Patrick Cargill, Brian Wilde,
Peter Bowles, Geoffrey Bayldon

1967

Charlie Bubbles
p: Michael Medwin, George Pitcher
sc: Shelagh Delaney
d: Albert Finney
lp: Albert Finney, Billie Whitelaw,
Colin Blakely, Liza Minnelli,
Timothy Garland, Richard Pearson

Billion Dollar Brain
p: Harry Saltzman
sc: John McGrath
d: Ken Russell
lp: Michael Caine, Karl Malden,
Ed Begley, Oscar Homolka,
Francoise Dorléac, Guy Doleman

Work is a Four-Letter Word
p: Thomas Clyde
sc: Jeremy Brooks
d: Peter Hall
lp: David Warner, Cilla Black,
Zia Mohyeddin, David Waller,
Elizabeth Spriggs, Tony Church

**Pretty Polly
(US: A Matter of Innocence)**
p: George W George, Frank Granat
sc: Keith Waterhouse, Willis Hall
d: Guy Green
lp: Hayley Mills, Trevor Howard,
Shashi Kapoor, Brenda de Banzie

**Night of the Big Heat
(US: Island of the Burning
Damned)**
p: Tom Blakeley
sc: Ronald Liles
d: Terence Fisher
lp: Christopher Lee, Patrick Allen,
Peter Cushing, Jane Merrow,
Sarah Lawson, William Lucas

A Challenge for Robin Hood
p: Clifford Parkes
sc: Peter Bryan
d: CM Pennington-Richards
lp: Barrie Ingham, James Hayter,
Leon Greene, Gay Hamilton,
Peter Blythe, Jenny Till

**Follow That Camel
(aka: Carry On ... Follow That
Camel)**
p: Peter Rogers
sc: Talbot Rothwell
d: Gerald Thomas
lp: Phil Silvers, Kenneth Williams,
Jim Dale, Charles Hawtrey,
Joan Sims, Angela Douglas

Deadfall
p: Paul Monash, Jack Rix
sc: Bryan Forbes
d: Bryan Forbes
lp: Michael Caine, Giovanna Ralli,
Eric Portman, Nanette Newman,
David Buck, Leonard Rossiter

Prudence and the Pill
p: Kenneth Harper, Ronald Kahn
sc: Hugh Mills
d: Fielder Cook, Ronald Neame
lp: Deborah Kerr, David Niven,
Robert Coote, Irina Demick
Joyce Redman, Judy Geeson

Chitty Chitty Bang Bang
p: Albert R Broccoli
sc: Roald Dahl, Ken Hughes,
Richard Maibaum
d: Ken Hughes
lp: Dick Van Dyke,
Sally Ann Howes, Lionel Jeffries,
Gert Frobe, Anna Quayle,
Benny Hill, Robert Helpmann,
James Robertson Justice,
Heather Ripley, Adrian Hall

Carry On Doctor
p: Peter Rogers
sc: Talbot Rothwell
d: Gerald Thomas
lp: Frankie Howerd, Sidney James,
Charles Hawtrey, Kenneth Williams,
Jim Dale, Barbara Windsor,
Joan Sims, Bernard Bresslaw

The Limbo Line
p: Frank Bevis
sc: Donald James
d: Samuel Gallu
lp: Craig Stevens, Kate O'Mara,
Vladek Sheybal, Eugene Deckers,
Moira Redmond, Yolande Turner
Jean Marsh, Rosemary Rogers

Nobody Runs Forever
(US: The High Commissioner)
p: Betty E Box
sc: Wilfred Greatorex
d: Ralph Thomas
lp: Rod Taylor,
Christopher Plummer, Lilli Palmer,
Camilla Sparv, Daliah Lavi

1968

The Assassination Bureau
p: Michael Relph
sc: Michael Relph, Wolf Mankowitz
d: Basil Dearden
lp: Oliver Reed, Diana Rigg,
Telly Savalas, Curt Jurgens,
Philippe Noiret, Warren Mitchell,
Beryl Reid, Clive Revill

Carry On ... Up the Khyber
p: Peter Rogers
sc:Talbot Rothwell
d: Gerald Thomas
lp: Sidney James, Kenneth Williams,
Charles Hawtrey, Roy Castle,
Joan Sims, Bernard Bresslaw,
Peter Butterworth, Terry Scott

Dracula Has Risen From
the Grave
p: Aida Young
sc: John Elder
d: Freddie Francis
lp: Christopher Lee, Rupert Davies,
Veronica Carlson, Barbara Ewing,
BarryAndrews, Ewan Hooper

Battle of Britain
p: Harry Saltzman, S Benjamin Fisz
sc: James Kennaway,
Wilfrid Greatorex
d: Guy Hamilton
lp: Laurence Olivier, Robert Shaw,
Christopher Plummer,
Susannah York, Ian McShane,
Michael Caine, Kenneth More,
Trevor Howard, Ralph Richardson,
Curt Jurgens, Michael Redgrave

The Prime of Miss Jean Brodie
p: Robert Fryer
sc: Jay Presson Allen
d: Ronald Neame
lp: Maggie Smith, Robert Stephens,
Pamela Franklin, Gordon Jackson,
Celia Johnson, Diane Grayson,
Jane Carr, Shirley Steedman

Some Girls Do
p: Betty E Box
sc: David Osborn,
Liz Charles-Williams
d: Ralph Thomas
lp: Richard Johnson, Daliah Lavi,
Beba Loncar, James Villiers,
Sydne Rome, Ronnie Stevens

Doppelgänger
(US: Journey to the Far Side of
the Sun)
p: Gerry Anderson, Sylvia Anderson
sc: Gerry Anderson,
Sylvia Anderson, Donald James
d: Robert Parrish
lp: Ian Hendry, Roy Thinnes,
Patrick Wymark, Lynn Loring,
Loni Von Friedl, Franco Derosa,
George Sewell, Edward Bishop

Strange Report
(TV series, 16 episodes)
p: Robert Buzz Berger
sc: Don Brinkley,
Edward DeBlasio, Brian Degas,
Morris Farhi, Tudor Gates,
John Kruse, Roger Parkes,
Jan Read, Leigh Vance and others
d: Robert Asher, Charles Crichton,
Peter Duffell, Peter Medak,
Daniel Petrie, Brian Smedley-Aston
lp: Anthony Quayle, Kaz Garas,
Anneke Wills, Charles Lloyd Pack

The Most Dangerous Man in
the World (US: The Chairman)
p: Mort Abrahams
sc: Ben Maddow
d: J Lee-Thompson
lp: Gregory Peck, Anne Heywood,
Arthur Hill, Conrad Yama,
Francisca Tu, Keye Luke

Foreign Exchange *(TV)*
p: Jimmy Sangster
sc: Jimmy Sangster
d: Roy Ward Baker
lp: Robert Horton, Sebastian Cabot,
Jill St John, Dudley Foster

Carry On Camping
p: Peter Rogers
sc: Talbot Rothwell
d: Gerald Thomas
lp: Sidney James, Charles Hawtrey,
Joan Sims, Kenneth Williams,
Terry Scott, Barbara Windsor

Guns in the Heather
p: Ron Miller, Hugh Attwooll
sc: Herman Groves
d: Robert Butler
lp: Glenn Corbett, Alfred Burke,
Kurt Russell, Patrick Dawson,
Patrick Barr, Hugh McDermott

1969

On Her Majesty's Secret Service
p: Harry Saltzman, Albert R Broccoli
sc: Richard Maibaum
d: Peter Hunt
lp: George Lazenby, Diana Rigg,
Telly Savalas, Gabriele Ferzetti,
Ilse Steppat, Angela Scoular,
Lois Maxwell, Catherina Von Schell,
George Baker, Bernard Lee

Connecting Rooms
p: Harry Field
sc: Franklin Gollings
d: Franklin Gollings
lp: Bette Davis, Michael Redgrave,
Alexis Kanner, Kay Walsh

Carry On Again Doctor
p: Peter Rogers
sc: Talbot Rothwell
d: Gerald Thomas
lp: Sidney James, Kenneth Williams,
Charles Hawtrey, Jim Dale,
Joan Sims, Barbara Windsor

The Private Life of
Sherlock Holmes
p: Billy Wilder
sc: Billy Wilder, IAL Diamond
d: Billy Wilder
lp: Robert Stephens, Colin Blakely,
Genevieve Page, Christopher Lee,
Tamara Toumanova, Clive Revill

Anne of the Thousand Days
(part)
p: Hal B Wallis
sc: John Hale, Bridget Boland,
Richard Sokolove
d: Charles Jarrott
lp: Richard Burton,
Geneviève Bujold, Irene Papas,
Anthony Quayle, John Colicos

David Copperfield
p: Frederick H. Brogger
sc: Jack Pulman
d: Delbert Mann
lp: Robin Phillips, Susan Hampshire,
Edith Evans, Michael Redgrave,
Ralph Richardson, Wendy Hiller

Toomorrow
p: Don Kirshner, Harry Saltzman
sc: Val Guest
d: Val Guest
lp: Olivia Newton-John,
Benny Thomas, Vic Cooper,
Karl Chambers, Roy Dotrice

Tam Lin
(US: The Devil's Widow)
p: Alan Ladd Jr, Stanley Mann
sc: William Spier
d: Roddy McDowall
lp: Ava Gardner, Ian McShane,
Richard Wattis, Cyril Cusack,
Stephanie Beacham

Perfect Friday
p: Jack Smith
sc: Anthony Greville-Bell,
C Scott Forbes
d: Peter Hall
lp: Ursula Andress, Stanley Baker,
David Warner, Patience Collier,
TP McKenna, David Waller

When Eight Bells Toll
p: Elliott Kastner
sc: Alistair MacLean
d: Étienne Périer
lp: Anthony Hopkins,
Nathalie Delon, Robert Morley,
Jack Hawkins, Corin Redgrave

Carry On Up The Jungle
p: Peter Rogers
sc: Talbot Rothwell
d: Gerald Thomas
lp: Frankie Howerd, Sidney James,
Charles Hawtrey, Joan Sims,
Terry Scott, Kenneth Connor

From A Bird's Eye View
(TV series, 15 episodes)
p: Jack Greenwood
sc: TEB Clarke, Pat Dunlop
and others
d: Peter Duffell, Ralph Levy,
John Robins
lp: Millicent Martin, Patte Finley,
Peter Jones

Run A Crooked Mile *(TV)*
p: Ian Lewis
sc: Trevor Wallace
d: Gene Levitt
lp: Louis Jourdan, Mary Tyler Moore,
Wilfrid Hyde-White,
Stanley Holloway, Alexander Knox

Destiny of a Spy *(TV)*
p: Jack Laird
sc: John Blackburn,
Stanford Whitmore
d: Boris Sagal
lp: Lorne Green, Rachel Roberts,
Anthony Quayle, James Donald

Mister Jerico
p: Julian Wintle
sc: Philip Levene
d: Sidney Hayers
lp: Patrick Macnee, Connie Stevens,
Herbert Lom, Marty Allen

The Firechasers
p: Julian Wintle
sc: Philip Levene
d: Sidney Hayers
lp: Chad Everett, Anjanette Comer,
Keith Barron, Joanne Dainton,
Rupert Davies, James Hayter

1970

Doctor in Trouble
p: Betty E Box
sc: Jack Davies
d: Ralph Thomas
lp: Leslie Phillips, Harry Secombe,
Angela Scoular, Irene Handl,
Robert Morley, Simon Dee

Carry On Loving
p: Peter Rogers
sc: Talbot Rothwell
d: Gerald Thomas
lp: Sidney James, Kenneth Williams,
Charles Hawtrey, Joan Sims,
Hattie Jacques, Terry Scott

Jane Eyre
p: Frederick H Brogger,
James Franciscus
sc: Jack Pulman
d: Delbert Mann
lp: George C Scott, Susannah York,
Ian Bannen, Jack Hawkins,
Nyree Dawn Porter

UFO
(TV series, nine episodes
made at Pinewood)
p: Gerry Anderson, Reg Hill
sc: Tony Barwick, Bob Bell,
Terence Feely, Dennis Spooner, David Tomblin
d: Cyril Frankel, David Lane,
Jeremy Summers, David Tomblin,
Ken Turner
lp: Ed Bishop, Michael Billington,
Wanda Ventham, Vladek Sheybal

The Persuaders!
(TV series, 24 episodes)
p: Robert S Baker
sc: Brian Clemens, Terence Feely,
Donald James, John Kruse,
Val Guest, Terry Nation and others
d: Roy Ward Baker, Basil Dearden,
Val Guest, Sidney Hayers,
Roger Moore and others
lp: Roger Moore, Tony Curtis,
Laurence Naismith

Assault
p: George H Brown
sc: John Kruse
d: Sidney Hayers
lp: Suzy Kendall, Frank Finlay,
Freddie Jones, James Laurenson

Zeppelin
p: Owen Crump
sc: Arthur Rowe, Donald Churchill
d: Etienne Perier
lp: Michael York, Elke Sommer,
Peter Carsten, Marius Goring,
Anton Diffring, Andrew Keir

Fiddler on the Roof
p: Norman Jewison
sc: Joseph Stein
d: Norman Jewison
lp: Topol, Norma Crane,
Leonard Frey, Molly Picon

Countess Dracula
p: Alexander Paal
sc: Jeremy Paul
d: Peter Sasdy
lp: Ingrid Pitt, Nigel Green,
Sandor Elès, Maurice Denham

The Devils
p: Robert H Solo, Ken Russell
sc: Ken Russell
d: Ken Russell
lp: Vanessa Redgrave, Oliver Reed,
Dudley Sutton, Max Adrian,
Gemma Jones, Murray Melvin

Carry On Henry
p: Peter Rogers
sc: Talbot Rothwell
d: Gerald Thomas
lp: Sidney James, Kenneth Williams,
Charles Hawtrey, Joan Sims,
Terry Scott, Barbara Windsor

Revenge
p: George H Brown
sc: John Kruse
d: Sidney Hayers
lp: Joan Collins, James Booth,
Ray Barrett, Sinead Cusack

The Beast in the Cellar
p: Tony Tenser, Graham Harris
sc: James Kelly
d: James Kelly
lp: Beryl Reid, Flora Robson,
John Hamill, Tessa Wyatt,
TP McKenna, John Kelland

**Blood on Satan's Claw
(US: Satan's Skin)**
p: Malcolm B Heyworth,
Peter L Andrews
sc: Robert Wynne-Simmons
d: Piers Haggard
lp: Patrick Wymark, Linda Hayden,
Barry Andrews, Michele Dotrice

Quest For Love
p: Peter Eton
sc: Terence Feely
d: Ralph Thomas
lp: Tom Bell, Joan Collins,
Denholm Elliott, Laurence Naismith

1971

The Odessa File
p: John Woolf, John R Sloan
sc: Kenneth Ross, George Markstein
d: Ronald Neame
lp: Jon Voight, Maximilian Schell,
Maria Schell, Mary Tamm,
Derek Jacobi, Peter Jeffrey

A Clockwork Orange *(part)*
p: Stanley Kubrick
sc: Stanley Kubrick
d: Stanley Kubrick
lp: Malcolm McDowall,
Patrick Magee, Adrienne Corri,
Miriam Karlin, Warren Clarke,
James Marcus, Michael Tarn

200 Motels
p: Herb Cohen, Jerry D Good
sc: Tony Palmer, Frank Zappa
d: Tony Palmer, Frank Zappa
lp: Theodore Bikel, Mark Volman,
Howard Kaylan, Ian Underwood

Hands of the Ripper
p: Aida Young
sc: LW Davidson
d: Peter Sasdy
lp: Eric Porter, Angharad Rees,
Jane Merrow, Keith Bell

Nobody Ordered Love
p: John Lightfoot
sc: Robert Shearer
d: Robert Hartford-Davis
lp: Ingrid Pitt, Judy Huxtable,
John Ronane, Tony Selby

Carry On At Your Convenience
p: Peter Rogers
sc: Talbot Rothwell
d: Gerald Thomas
lp: Sidney James, Kenneth Williams,
Charles Hawtrey, Joan Sims
Hattie Jacques, Bernard Bresslaw

Twins of Evil
p: Harry Fine, Michael Style
sc: Tudor Gates
d: John Hough
lp: Peter Cushing, Dennis Price,
Mary Collinson,
Madeleine Collinson, Isobel Black,
Kathleen Byron, Damien Thomas

**The Magnificent Seven
Deadly Sins**
p: Graham Stark
sc: Bob Larbey, John Esmonde,
Dave Freeman, Barry Cryer,
Graham Chapman, Graham Stark,
Marty Feldman, Alan Simpson,
Ray Galton, Spike Milligan
d: Graham Stark
lp: Bruce Forsyth, Joan Sims,
Roy Hudd, Harry Secombe,
Geoffrey Bayldon, Leslie Phillips,
Julie Ege, Harry H Corbett,
Ian Carmichael, Alfie Bass,
Spike Milligan, Ronald Fraser

All Coppers Are…
p: George H Brown
sc: Allan Prior
d: Sidney Hayers
lp: Nicky Henson, Martin Potter,
Julia Foster, Robin Askwith,
David Essex, Ian Hendry

Please Sir!
p: Andrew Mitchell
sc: John Esmonde, Bob Larbey
d: Mark Stuart
lp: John Alderton, Deryck Guyler,
Noel Howlett, Joan Sanderson,
Richard Davies, Eric Chitty

Kidnapped
p: Frederick H Brogger,
James Franciscus
sc: Jack Pulman
d: Delbert Mann
lp: Michael Caine,
Lawrence Douglas, Vivien Heilbron,
Trevor Howard, Jack Hawkins

Diamonds Are Forever
p: Harry Saltzman, Albert R Broccoli
sc: Richard Maibaum,
Tom Mankiewicz
d: Guy Hamilton
lp: Sean Connery, Jill St John,
Charles Gray, Lana Wood,
Jimmy Dean, Bruce Cabot,
Lois Maxwell, Joseph Furst,
Putter Smith, Bernard Lee

Rentadick
p: Ned Sherrin, Terry Glinwood
sc: John Cleese, Graham Chapman
d: Jim Clark
lp: James Booth, Richard Briers,
Julie Ege, Ronald Fraser,
Donald Sinden, Tsai Chin

Frenzy
p: Alfred Hitchcock
sc: Anthony Shaffer
d: Alfred Hitchcock
lp: Jon Finch, Alec McCowen,
Barry Foster, Billie Whitelaw,
Anna Massey, Barbara Leigh-Hunt

Madame Sin
p: Lew Grade, Lou Morheim,
Robert Wagner, Julian Wintle
sc: David Greene, Barry Oringer
d: David Greene
lp: Bette Davis, Robert Wagner,
Denholm Elliott, Gordon Jackson
Dudley Sutton, Catherine Schell

Vampire Circus
p: Wilbur Stark
sc: Judson Kinberg
d: Robert Young
lp: Adrienne Corri, Thorley Walters,
Anthony Higgins, Laurence Payne

Baffled! *(TV)*
p: Philip Leacock
sc: Theordore Apstein
d: Philip Leacock
lp: Leonard Nimoy,
Susan Hampshire, Rachel Roberts

Lady Caroline Lamb
p: Fernando Ghia
sc: Robert Bolt
d: Robert Bolt
lp: Sarah Miles, Jon Finch,
Richard Chamberlain, John Mills,
Margaret Leighton, Pamela Brown
Ralph Richardson, Laurence Olivier

Carry On Matron
p: Peter Rogers
sc: Talbot Rothwell
d: Gerald Thomas
lp: Sidney James, Kenneth Williams,
Charles Hawtrey, Joan Sims
Hattie Jacques, Bernard Bresslaw

Doomwatch
p: Tony Tenser
sc: Clive Exton
d: Peter Sasdy
lp: Ian Bannen, Judy Geeson,
George Sanders, Geoffrey Keen

Shirley's World
(TV series, 17 episodes)
p: Barry Delmaine
sc: Peter Miller, Lew Schwartz
and others
d: Ray Austin, Charles Crichton,
Ralph Levy and others
lp: Shirley MacLaine, John Gregson

Two English Girls
p: Marcel Berbert, Claude Miler
sc: Henri Pierre Roché,
Francois Truffaut
d: Francois Truffaut
lp: Jean-Piere Léaud,
Kika Markham, Stacey Tendeter

Hamlet *(TV)*
p: BBC, Prospect Theatre
sc: William Shakespeare
d: David Giles
lp: Ian McKellen, Susan Fleetwood

The Challenge
p: Religious Films
sc: Lawrence Barratt
d: Norman Walker
lp: David Blagdon, Duncan Lamont,
Alan Lee, Michael Robbins

1972

Sleuth
p: Morton Gottlieb
sc: Anthony Shaffer
d: Joseph L Mankiewicz
lp: Laurence Olivier, Michael Caine

Innocent Bystanders
p: George H Brown
sc: James Mitchell
d: Peter Collinson
lp: Stanley Baker, Geraldine Chaplin,
Donald Pleasence, Dana Andrews

A Warm December
p: Melville Tucker
sc: Lawrence Roman
d: Sidney Poitier
lp: Sidney Poitier, Esther Anderson,
Yvette Curtis, George Baker,
Johnny Sekka, Earl Cameron

Carry On Abroad
p: Peter Rogers
sc: Talbot Rothwell
d: Gerald Thomas
lp: Sidney James, Kenneth Williams,
Charles Hawtrey, Joan Sims,
Bernard Bresslaw, Barbara Windsor

Nothing But The Night
p: Anthony Nelson Keys
sc: Brian Hayles
d: Peter Sasdy
lp: Christopher Lee, Peter Cushing,
Diana Dors, Georgia Brown

That's Your Funeral
p: Michael Carreras
sc: Peter Lewis
d: John Robins
lp: Bill Fraser, Raymond Huntley,
David Battley, Dennis Price

Nearest and Dearest
p: Michael Carreras
sc: Tom Brennard, Roy Bottomley
d: John Robins
lp: Hylda Baker, Jimmy Jewel,
Eddie Malin, Madge Hindle

The Amazing Mr Blunden
p: Barry Levinson
sc: Lionel Jeffries
d: Lionel Jeffries
lp: Laurence Naismith, Diana Dors,
Lynne Frederick, Garry Miller

Diamonds On Wheels
p: Ron Miller
sc: William R. Yates
d: Jerome Courtland
lp: Patrick Allen, George Sewell
Derek Newark, Dudley Sutton

Bless This House
p: Peter Rogers
sc: Dave Freeman
d: Gerald Thomas
lp: Sid James, Diana Coupland,
Sally Geeson, Peter Butterworth,
Terry Scott, June Whitfield

The Day of the Jackal
p: John Woolf, David Deutsch,
Julien Derode
sc: Kenneth Ross
d: Fred Zinnemann
lp: Edward Fox, Michel Lonsdale,
Alan Badel, Cyril Cusack,
Derek Jacobi, Eric Porter

Phase IV
p: Paul B Radin
sc: Mayo Simon
d: Saul Bass
lp: Nigel Davenport,
Michael Murphy, Lynne Frederick

The 14
(US: The Wild Little Bunch)
p: Frank Avianca, Robert Mintz
sc: Roland Starke
d: David Hemmings
lp: Jack Wild, June Brown

Go For A Take
p: Roy Simpson
sc: Alan Hackney
d: Harry Booth
lp: Reg Varney, Norman Rossington,
Sue Lloyd, Dennis Price, Julie Ege

The Belstone Fox
p: Sally Shuter
sc: James Hill
d: James Hill
lp: Eric Porter, Rachel Roberts,
Jeremy Kemp, Bill Travers

The Mackintosh Man
p: John Huston
sc: Walter Hill
d: John Huston
lp: Paul Newman, James Mason,
Dominique Sanda, Harry Andrews,
Nigel Patrick, Ian Bannen

The House in Nightmare Park
p: Clive Exton, Terry Nation,
Beryl Virtue
sc: Clive Exton, Terry Nation
d: Peter Sykes
lp: Frankie Howerd, Ray Milland,
Hugh Burden, Kenneth Griffith

**Never Mind The Quality,
Feel The Width** *(TV)*
p: Martin Cahill
sc: Vince Powell, Harry Driver
d: Ronnie Baxter
lp: John Bluthal, Joe Lynch,
Ann Beech, David Kelly

Live and Let Die
p: Harry Saltzman, Albert R Broccoli
sc: Tom Mankiewicz
d: Guy Hamilton
lp: Roger Moore, Yaphet Kotto,
Jane Seymour, Clifton James,
Julius W Harris, Gloria Hendry,
Geoffrey Holder, David Hedison,
Lois Maxwell, Bernard Lee

Anoop and the Elephant
p: Hugh Stewart
sc: Gerard Bryant, Owen Holder
d: David Eady
lp: Anoop Singh, Linda Robson,
Jimmy Edwards, Julian Orchard

Miss Julie
p: Martin C Schute,
Peter J Thompson
sc: August Strindberg (play)
d: John Glenister, Robin Phillips
lp: Helen Mirren, Donal McCann,
Heather Canning

Juggernaut *(part)*
p: Richard De Koker
sc: Richard De Koker, Alan Plater
d: Richard Lester
lp: Richard Harris, Omar Sharif,
David Hemmings, Ian Holm
Anthony Hopkins, Shirley Knight

1973

Gulliver's Travels
p: Josef Shaftel
sc: Don Black
d: Peter R Hunt
lp: Richard Harris, Catherine Schell,
Norman Shelley, Meredith Edwards

Penny Gold
sc: Liz Charles-Williams,
David D Osborn
d: Jack Cardiff
lp: Francesca Annis, James Booth,
Nicky Henson, Sue Lloyd

No Sex Please – We're British
p: John R Sloan
sc: Anthony Marriott,
Johnnie Mortimer, Brian Cooke
d: Cliff Owen
lp: Ronnie Corbett, Beryl Reid,
Arthur Lowe, Ian Ogilvy

Carry On Girls
p: Peter Rogers
sc: Talbot Rothwell
d: Gerald Thomas
lp: Sidney James, Barbara Windsor,
Joan Sims, Kenneth Connor,
Bernard Bresslaw, June Whitfield,
Peter Butterworth, Jack Douglas

The Abdication
p: Robert Fryer, James Cresson
sc: Ruth Wolff
d: Anthony Harvey
lp: Peter Finch, Liv Ullmann,
Cyril Cusack, Paul Rogers

The Great Gatsby
p: David Merrick
sc: Francis Ford Coppola
d: Jack Clayton
lp: Robert Redford, Mia Farrow,
Bruce Dern, Karen Black,
Scott Wilson, Sam Waterston,
Lois Chiles, Howard Da Silva

You'd Better Go In Disguise
(unfinished)
p: Martin Cahill
sc: Eric Sykes
d: Eric Sykes
lp: Eric Sykes

11 Harrowhouse
p: Elliott Kastner
sc: Jeffrey Bloom
d: Aram Avakian
lp: Charles Grodin, Candice Bergen,
James Mason, Trevor Howard,
John Gielgud, Helen Cherry

Cat And Mouse (US: Mousey)
p: Aida Young
sc: John Peacock
d: Daniel Petrie
lp: Kirk Douglas, Jean Seberg,
John Vernon, Bessie Love,
Beth Porter, Sam Wanamaker

Applause *(TV)*
p: Richard M Rosenbloom,
Lawrence Kasha, Joseph Kipness
sc: Betty Comden, Adolph Green
lp: Lauren Bacall, Larry Hagman

QBVII *(TV)*
p: Douglas Kramer
sc: Edward Anhalt
d: Tom Gries
lp: Ben Gazzara, Anthony Hopkins,
Leslie Caron, Lee Remick,
Juliet Mills, Dan O'Herlihy,
Robert Stephens, Anthony Quayle

Frankenstein: The True Story
(TV)
p: Hunt Stromberg Jr
sc: Christopher Isherwood,
Don Bachardy
d: Jack Smight
lp: James Mason, Leonard Whiting,
David McCallum, Jane Seymour,
Nicola Pagett, Michael Sarrazin

The Zoo Gang
(TV series, 6 episodes)
p: Herbert Hirschman
sc: Peter Yeldham, Sean Graham,
Reginald Rose, Howard Dimsdale,
John Kruse, William Fairchild
d: Sidney Hayers, John Hough
lp: Brian Keith, John Mills,
Lilli Palmer, Barry Morse

The Glass Menagerie *(TV)*
p: David Susskind
sc: Tennessee Williams
d: Anthony Harvey
lp: Katharine Hepburn,
Sam Waterston, Joanna Miles,
Michael Moriarty

Space: 1999
(TV series, 24 episodes)
p: Sylvia Anderson
sc: George Bellak, Johnny Byrne,
David Weir, Edward di Lorenzo,
Anthony Terpiloff, Jesse Lasky Jr.,
Christopher Penfold and others
d: Lee H Katzin, Charles Crichton,
Ray Austin, David Tomblin,
Bob Kellett
lp: Martin Landau, Barbara Bain,
Barry Morse, Prentis Hancock,
Nick Tate, Zienia Merton,
Clifton Jones, Anton Phillips

1974

The Ghoul
p: Kevin Francis
sc: John Elder
d: Freddie Francis
lp: Peter Cushing, John Hurt,
Alexandra Bastedo, Gwen Watford,
Veronica Carlson, Don Henderson

Gold
p: Michael Klinger
sc: Wilbur Smith, Stanley Price
d: Peter R Hunt
lp: Roger Moore, Susannah York,
Ray Milland, Bradford Dillman,
John Gielgud, Tony Beckley

Carry On Dick
p: Peter Rogers
sc: Talbot Rothwell
d: Gerald Thomas
lp: Sidney James, Barbara Windsor,
Kenneth Williams, Hattie Jacques,
Bernard Bresslaw, Joan Sims

**Mister Quilp
(US: The Old Curiosity Shop)**
p: Helen M Strauss
sc: Louis Kamp, Irene Kamp
d: Michael Tuchner
lp: Anthony Newley,
David Hemmings, Jill Bennett,
Sarah-Jane Varley, Michael Hordern,
David Warner, Peter Duncan

The Man With the Golden Gun
p: Harry Saltzman, Albert R Broccoli
sc: Richard Maibaum,
Tom Mankiewicz
d: Guy Hamilton
lp: Roger Moore, Christopher Lee,
Britt Ekland, Maud Adams,
Hervé Villechaize, Clifton James,
Richard Loo, Soon-Taik Oh

The Wilby Conspiracy
p: Stanley Sopel
sc: Rod Amateau, Harold Nebenzal
d: Ralph Nelson
lp: Sidney Poitier, Michael Caine,
Nicol Williamson, Prunella Gee

One of Our Dinosaurs Is Missing
p: Bill Walsh
sc: Bill Walsh
d: Robert Stevenson
lp: Peter Ustinov, Helen Hayes,
Clive Revill, Derek Nimmo,
Joan Sims, Bernard Bresslaw

Brief Encounter *(TV)*
p: Cecil Clarke, Carlo Ponti
sc: Noel Coward (play),
John Bowen
d: Alan Bridges
lp: Richard Burton, Sophia Loren

Legend of the Werewolf
p: Kevin Francis
sc: John Elder (Anthony Hinds)
d: Freddie Francis
lp: Peter Cushing, Ron Moody,
Hugh Griffith, Roy Castle

**What Changed Charley Farthing?
(US: The Bananas Boat)**
p: Tristam Cones
sc: David Pursall, Jack Seddon
d: Sidney Hayers
lp: Doug McClure, Lionel Jeffries,
Hayley Mills, Warren Mitchell

Rollerball
p: Norman Jewison
sc: William Harrison
d: Norman Jewison
lp: James Caan, John Houseman,
Maud Adams, John Beck,
Moses Gunn, Pamela Hensley,
Barbara Trentham,
Ralph Richardson, Shane Rimmer

Hennessey
p: Peter Snell
sc: John Gay
d: Don Sharp
lp: Rod Steiger, Lee Remick,
Richard Johnson, Trevor Howard,
Peter Egan, Eric Porter

**I Don't Want To Be Born
(US: The Devil Within Her)**
p: Norma Corney
sc: Stanley Price
d: Peter Sasdy
lp: Joan Collins, Eileen Atkins,
Ralph Bates, Donald Pleasence

That Lucky Touch
p: Dimitri de Grunwald
sc: John Briley
d: Christopher Miles
lp: Roger Moore, Susannah York,
Shelley Winters, Lee J Cobb,
Jean-Pierre Cassel, Raf Vallone

Love Among the Ruins (TV)
p: Allan Davis
sc: James Costigan
d: George Cukor
lp: Katharine Hepburn,
Laurence Olivier, Colin Blakely
Richard Pearson, Joan Sims

1975

The Human Factor
p: Frank Avianca, Lou Peraino
sc: Thomas Hunter, Peter Powell
d: Edward Dmytryk
lp: George Kennedy, John Mills,
Raf Vallone, Barry Sullivan,
Rita Tushingham, Shane Rimmer

Carry On Behind
p: Peter Rogers
sc: Dave Freeman
d: Gerald Thomas
lp: Elke Sommer, Kenneth Williams,
Bernard Bresslaw, Kenneth Connor,
Jack Douglas, Joan Sims,
Windsor Davies, Peter Butterworth

**The Bawdy Adventures
of Tom Jones**
p: Robert Sadoff
sc: Jeremy Lloyd
d: Cliff Owen
lp: Nicky Henson, Trevor Howard,
Terry-Thomas, Arthur Lowe,
Georgia Brown, Joan Collins

The Slipper and the Rose
p: Stuart Lyons
sc: Bryan Forbes, Robert B Sherman,
Richard M Sherman
d: Bryan Forbes
lp: Richard Chamberlain,
Gemma Craven, Annette Crosbie,
Edith Evans, Christopher Gable,
Michael Hordern,
Margaret Lockwood, Kenneth More

Bugsy Malone
p: David Puttnam, Alan Marshall
sc: Alan Parker
d: Alan Parker
lp: Scott Baio, Florrie Dugger,
Jodie Foster, John Cassisi

**The Day After Tomorrow:
Into Infinity** (TV pilot)
p: Gerry Anderson
sc: Johnny Byrne
d: Charles Crichton
lp: Brian Blessed, Joanna Dunham,
Nick Tate, Katharine Levy,
Martin Lev, Don Fellows

The Incredible Sarah
p: Helen M Strauss
sc: Ruth Wolff
d: Richard Fleischer
lp: Glenda Jackson, Daniel Massey,
Yvonne Mitchell, Douglas Wilmer,
David Langton, Simon Williams

The Seven-Per-Cent Solution
p: Herbert Ross
sc: Nicholas Meyer
d: Herbert Ross
lp: Nicol Williamson, Robert Duvall,
Alan Arkin, Laurence Olivier,
Vanessa Redgrave, Joel Grey

**Escape from the Dark
(US: The Littlest Horse Thieves)**
p: Ron Miller, Hugh Attwooll
sc: Rosemary Anne Sisson
d: Charles Jarrott
lp: Alastair Sim, Peter Barkworth,
Maurice Colbourne, Susan Tebbs,
Geraldine McEwan, Prunella Scales

God Told Me To
p: Larry Cohen
sc: Larry Cohen
d: Larry Cohen
lp: Tony Lo Bianco, Deborah Raffin,
Sandy Dennis, Sylvia Sidney,
Sam Levene, Robert Drivas

1976

Space:1999
(TV series, 24 episodes)
p: Fred Freiberger
sc: Johnny Byrne, Donald James,
Tony Barwick, Charles Woodgrove,
Terence Feely and others
d: Charles Crichton, Ray Austin,
Tom Clegg, Bob Brooks, Val Guest,
Robert Lynn, Kevin Connor,
Peter Medak
lp: Martin Landau, Barbara Bain,
Catherine Schell, Tony Anholt,
Nick Tate, Zienia Merton

At the Earth's Core
p: John Dark
sc: Milton Subotsky
d: Kevin Connor
lp: Doug McClure, Peter Cushing,
Caroline Munro, Cy Grant,
Godfrey James, Sean Lynch

Carry On England
p: Peter Rogers
sc: David Pursall, Jack Seddon
d: Gerald Thomas
lp: Kenneth Connor,
Windsor Davies, Judy Geeson,
Patrick Mower, Jack Douglas,
Joan Sims, Melvyn Hayes

**The Prince and the Pauper
(US: Crossed Swords)**
p: Pierre Spengler
sc: George MacDonald Fraser,
Berta Dominguez, Pierre Spengler
d: Richard Fleischer
lp: Mark Lester, Oliver Reed,
Raquel Welch, Ernest Borgnine,
George C Scott, Rex Harrison

Candleshoe
p: Ron Miller, Hugh Attwooll
sc: David Swift,
Rosemary Anne Sisson
d: Norman Tokar
lp: Jodie Foster, Helen Hayes,
David Niven, Leo McKern

The Spy Who Loved Me
p: Albert R Broccoli
sc: Christopher Wood,
Richard Maibaum
d: Lewis Gilbert
lp: Roger Moore, Barbara Bach,
Curt Jurgens, Richard Kiel,
Caroline Munro, Geoffrey Keen,
Edward de Souza, George Baker

The New Avengers
(TV series, 13 episodes)
p: Albert Fennell, Brian Clemens
sc: Brian Clemens, Dennis Spooner,
Terence Feely
d: Desmond Davis, Robert Fuest,
Ray Austin, James Hill, John Hough,
Sidney Hayers, Graeme Clifford
lp: Patrick Macnee, Gareth Hunt,
Joanna Lumley

1977

The People That Time Forgot
p: John Dark
sc: Patrick Tilley
d: Kevin Connor
lp: Patrick Wayne, Doug McClure,
Sarah Douglas, Dana Gillespie,
Thorley Walters, Shane Rimmer

The New Avengers
(TV series, 9 episodes made at
Pinewood)
p: Albert Fennell, Brian Clemens
sc: Brian Clemens, Terence Feely,
Dennis Spooner, John Goldsmith
d: Sidney Hayers, Ray Austin,
Ernest Day, Yvon Marie Coulais
lp: Patrick Macnee, Gareth Hunt,
Joanna Lumley

The Medusa Touch
p: Anne V Coates, Jack Gold
sc: John Briley
d: Jack Gold
lp: Richard Burton, Lino Ventura,
Lee Remick, Harry Andrews,
Alan Badel, Marie-Christine Barrault

That's Carry On
p: Peter Rogers
sc: Tony Church
d: Gerald Thomas
lp: Kenneth Williams,
Barbara Windsor

Wombling Free
p: Ian Shand
sc: Lionel Jeffries
d: Lionel Jeffries
lp: David Tomlinson,
Frances de la Tour, Bonnie Langford

Meetings with Remarkable Men
p: Stuart Lyons
sc: Peter Brook,
Jeanne DeSalzmann
d: Peter Brook
lp: Dragan Maksimovic,
Terence Stamp, Athol Fugard

Superman
p: Pierre Spengler
sc: Mario Puzo, David Newman,
Leslie Newman, Robert Benton,
Tom Mankiewicz
d: Richard Donner
lp: Marlon Brando, Gene Hackman,
Christopher Reeve, Margot Kidder,
Ned Beatty, Jackie Cooper,
Glenn Ford, Trevor Howard,
Jack O'Halloran, Valerie Perrine,
Maria Schell, Terence Stamp,
Phyllis Thaxter, Susannah York

Death on the Nile
p: John Brabourne,
Richard Goodwin
sc: Anthony Shaffer
d: John Guillermin
lp: Peter Ustinov, Jane Birkin,
Lois Chiles, Bette Davis, Mia Farrow,
Jon Finch, Olivia Hussey, IS Johar,
George Kennedy, Angela Lansbury,
Simon McCorkindale, David Niven,
Maggie Smith, Jack Warden

Warlords of Atlantis
p: John Dark
sc: Brian Hayles
d: Kevin Connor
lp: Doug McClure, Peter Gilmore,
Shane Rimmer, Lea Brodie,
Michael Gothard, Hal Galili,
Cyd Charisse, Daniel Massey

International Velvet
p: Bryan Forbes
sc: Bryan Forbes
d: Bryan Forbes
lp: Tatum O'Neal,
Christopher Plummer,
Anthony Hopkins, Nanette Newman

The Professionals
(TV series, 13 episodes)
p: Sidney Hayers
sc: Brian Clemens, Anthony Read,
Dennis Spooner, James McAteer
d: David Wickes, William Brayne
Charles Crichton and others
lp: Gordon Jackson, Martin Shaw,
Lewis Collins

1978

The Thirty Nine Steps
p: Greg Smith
sc: Michael Robson
d: Don Sharp
lp: Robert Powell, David Warner,
Eric Porter, Karen Dotrice,
John Mills, George Baker,
Ronald Pickup, Donald Pickering

Carry On Emmannuelle
p: Peter Rogers
sc: Lance Peters
d: Gerald Thomas
lp: Kenneth Williams,
Kenneth Connor, Joan Sims,
Jack Douglas, Peter Butterworth,
Larry Dann, Suzanne Danielle

Absolution
p: Danny O'Donovan,
Elliott Kastner
sc: Anthony Shaffer
d: Anthony Page
lp: Richard Burton, Dominic Guard,
Dai Bradley, Billy Connolly,
Andrew Keir, Willoughby Gray

**The First Great Train Robbery
(US: The Great Train Robbery)**
p: John Foreman
sc: Michael Crichton
d: Michael Crichton
lp: Sean Connery,
Donald Sutherland,
Lesley-Anne Down, Alan Webb

Ike: The War Years *(TV)*
p: Melville Shavelson
sc: Melville Shavelson
d: Melville Shavelson
lp: Robert Duvall, Lee Remick

**The Spaceman and King Arthur
(US: Unidentified Flying Oddball)**
p: Ron Miller
sc: Don Tait
d: Russ Mayberry
lp: Dennis Dugan, Jim Dale,
Ron Moody, Kenneth More,
John Le Mesurier, Rodney Bewes

Arabian Adventure
p: John Dark
sc: Brian Hayles
d: Kevin Connor
lp: Christopher Lee, Milo O'Shea,
Oliver Tobias, Emma Samms,
Peter Cushing, Mickey Rooney

Moonraker *(part)*
p: Albert R Broccoli
sc: Christopher Wood
d: Lewis Gilbert
lp: Roger Moore, Lois Chiles,
Michael Lonsdale, Richard Kiel,
Corinne Clery, Emily Bolton,
Toshiro Suga, Irka Bochenko

The Lady Vanishes
p: Michael Carreras, Tom Sachs
sc: George Axelrod
d: Anthony Page
lp: Elliott Gould, Cybill Shepherd,
Angela Lansbury, Herbert Lom,
Arthur Lowe, Ian Carmichael

The Shout
p: Jeremy Thomas
sc: Michael Austin, Jerzy
Skolimowski
d: Jerzy Skolimowski
lp: Alan Bates, Susannah York,
John Hurt, Robert Stephens,
Tim Curry, Julian Hough

1979

Superman II
p: Pierre Spengler
sc: Mario Puzo, David Newman,
Leslie Newman
d: Richard Lester
lp: Gene Hackman,
Christopher Reeve, Ned Beatty,
Jackie Cooper, Sarah Douglas,
Margot Kidder, Jack O'Halloran,
Valerie Perrine, Susannah York,
Clifton James, Terence Stamp

Bear Island
p: Peter Snell
sc: David Butler, Don Sharp
d: Don Sharp
lp: Donald Sutherland,
Vanessa Redgrave,
Richard Widmark, Christopher Lee,
Barbara Parkins, Lloyd Bridges

Bad Timing
p: Jeremy Thomas
sc: Yale Udoff
d: Nicholas Roeg
lp: Art Garfunkel, Theresa Russell,
Harvey Keitel, Denholm Elliott,
Daniel Massey, Dana Gillespie

Clash of the Titans
p: Charles H Schneer,
Ray Harryhausen
sc: Beverley Cross
d: Desmond Davis
lp: Harry Hamlin, Judi Bowker,
Burgess Meredith, Maggie Smith,
Ursula Andress, Claire Bloom,
Laurence Olivier

North Sea Hijack (US: ffolkes)
p: Elliott Kastner
sc: Jack Davies
d: Andrew V McLaglen
lp: Roger Moore, James Mason,
Anthony Perkins, Michael Parks,
David Hedison, Jack Watson

McVicar
p: Bill Curbishley, Roy Baird,
Roger Daltrey
sc: Tom Clegg, John McVicar
d: Tom Clegg
lp: Roger Daltrey, Adam Faith,
Cheryl Campbell, Billy Murray,
Georgina Hale, Steven Berkoff

Rough Cut
p: David Merrick
sc: Francis Burns (Larry Gelbart)
d: Don Siegel
lp: Burt Reynolds,
Lesley-Anne Down, David Niven,
Timothy West, Patrick Magee

Silver Dream Racer
p: Rene Dupont
sc: David Wickes
d: David Wickes
lp: David Essex, Beau Bridges,
Cristina Raines, Clarke Peters,
Harry H Corbett, Diane Keen

There Goes the Bride
p: Martin C Schute, Ray Cooney
sc: Terence Marcel, Ray Cooney
d: Terence Marcel
lp: Tom Smothers, Twiggy,
Sylvia Syms, Martin Balsam

The Watcher in the Woods
p: Ron Miller
sc: Brian Clemens, Harry Spalding,
Rosemary Anne Sisson
d: John Hough, Vincent McEveety
lp: Bette Davis, Carroll Baker,
David McCallum,
Lynn-Holly Johnson, Kyle Richards

Why Not Stay for Breakfast
p: Alan Cluer, Martin C Schute
sc: Ray Cooney, Terence Marcel
d: Terence Marcel
lp: George Chakiris, Gemma Craven

The World is Full of Married Men
p: Malcolm Fancey, Oscar Lerman
sc: Jackie Collins
d: Robert Young
lp: Anthony Franciosa,
Carroll Baker, Sherrie Lee Cron,
Paul Nicholas, Gareth Hunt

The Kids are Alright
p: Bill Curbishley, Tony Klinger
sc: Jeff Stein
d: Jeff Stein
lp: Roger Daltry, John Entwhistle,
Keith Moon, Pete Townshend

1980

Heaven's Gate
p: Joann Carelli
sc: Michael Cimino
d: Michael Cimino
lp: Kris Kristofferson,
Christopher Walken, John Hurt,
Sam Waterston, Brad Dourif,
Isabelle Huppert, Joseph Cotton

Hawk the Slayer
p: Harry Robertson
sc: Terry Marcel, Harry Robertson
d: Terry Marcel
lp: Jack Palance, John Terry,
Bernard Bresslaw, Ray Charleson,
Peter O'Farrell, Morgan Sheppard

Outland
p: Richard A Roth
sc: Peter Hyams
d: Peter Hyams
lp: Sean Connery, Peter Boyle,
Francis Sternhagen, James B Sikking,
Kika Markham, Clarke Peters

Dragonslayer
p: Hal Barwood
sc: Hal Barwood, Matthew Robbins
d: Matthew Robbins
lp: Peter MacNicol, Caitlin Clarke,
Ralph Richardson, John Hallam,
Peter Eyre, Albert Salmi

For Your Eyes Only
p: Albert R Broccoli
sc: Richard Maibaum,
Michael G Wilson
d: John Glen
lp: Roger Moore, Carole Bouquet,
Topol, Lynn-Holly Johnson,
Julian Glover, Cassandra Harris,
Jill Bennett, Michael Gothard,
Jack Hedley, Walter Gotell

1981

Victor/Victoria
p: Blake Edwards, Tony Adams
sc: Blake Edwards
d: Blake Edwards
lp: Julie Andrews, James Garner,
Robert Preston, Lesley Anne Warren,
Alex Karras, John Rhys-Davies

Ivanhoe *(TV)*
p: Norman Rosemont
sc: John Gay
d: Douglas Camfield
lp: James Mason, Anthony Andrews,
Sam Neill, Michael Hordern,
Olivia Hussey, Lysette Anthony,
Julian Glover, George Innes

The Hunchback of Notre Dame
(TV)
p: Norman Rosemont
sc: John Gay
d: Michael Tuchner
lp: Anthony Hopkins, Derek Jacobi,
David Suchet, Gerry Sundquist,
Tim Piggott-Smith, John Gielgud,
Robert Powell, Lesley-Anne Down

Pink Floyd The Wall
p: Alan Marshall
sc: Roger Waters
d: Alan Parker
lp: Bob Geldof,
Christine Hargreaves,
James Laurenson, Eleanor David

1982

**Who Dares Wins
(US: The Final Option)**
p: Euan Lloyd
sc: Reginald Rose
d: Ian Sharp
lp: Lewis Collins, Judy Davis,
Richard Widmark,
Edward Woodward, Robert Webber

Krull
p: Ron Silverman
sc: Stanford Sherman
d: Peter Yates
lp: Ken Marshall, Lysette Anthony,
Freddie Jones, Francesca Annis,
Alun Armstrong, David Battley

Trail of the Pink Panther
p: Blake Edwards, Tony Adams
sc: Frank Waldman, Tom Waldman,
Blake Edwards, Geoffrey Edwards
d: Blake Edwards
lp: Peter Sellers, David Niven,
Herbert Lom, Richard Mulligan,
Joanna Lumley, Capucine

Curse of the Pink Panther
p: Blake Edwards, Tony Adams
sc: Blake Edwards,
Geoffrey Edwards
d: Blake Edwards
lp: Ted Wass, David Niven,
Robert Wagner, Herbert Lom,
Joanna Lumley, Capucine

Superman III
p: Pierre Spengler
sc: David Newman, Leslie Newman
d: Richard Lester
lp: Christopher Reeve,
Richard Pryor, Jackie Cooper,
Marc McClure, Annette O'Toole
Robert Vaughn, Margot Kidder

Octopussy
p: Albert R Broccoli
sc: George MacDonald Fraser,
Richard Maibaum, Michael G Wilson
d: John Glen
lp: Roger Moore, Maud Adams,
Louis Jourdan, Kristina Wayborn,
Kabir Bedi, Steven Berkoff,
Vijay Amritraj

Witness for the Prosecution *(TV)*
p: Norman Rosemont
sc: John Gay
d: Alan Gibson
lp: Ralph Richardson, Deborah Kerr,
Diana Rigg, Beau Bridges,
Donald Pleasence, Wendy Hiller

1983

Slayground
p: John Dark, Gower Frost
sc: Trevor Preston
d: Terry Bedford
lp: Peter Coyote, Mel Smith,
Billie Whitelaw, Philip Sayer

Supergirl
p: Timothy Burrill
sc: David Odell
d: Jeannot Szwarc
lp: Faye Dunaway, Helen Slater,
Peter O'Toole, Mia Farrow,
Brenda Vaccaro, Peter Cook

The Dresser
p: Peter Yates, Ronald Harwood
sc: Ronald Harwood
d: Peter Yates
lp: Albert Finney, Tom Courtenay,
Edward Fox, Zena Walker,
Eileen Atkins, Michael Gough

The Last Days of Pompeii *(TV)*
p: William Hill, Richard Irving
sc: Carmen Culver
d: Peter R Hunt
lp: Ned Beatty, Brian Blessed,
Ernest Borgnine, Nicholas Clay,
Lesley-Anne Down, Franco Nero

Master of the Game *(TV)*
p: Norman Rosemont
sc: John Nation, Alvin Boretz,
d: Kevin Connor, Harvey Hart
lp: Dyan Cannon, Harry Hamlin,
Ian Charleson, Cliff DeYoung

Squaring the Circle *(TV)*
sc: Tom Stoppard
d: Mike Hodges
lp: Alex McCowan, Bernard Hill,
Don Henderson, John Woodvine

**The First Modern Olympics –
Athens 1896** *(TV)*
p: William Hill
sc: Gary Allison, William Bast
d: Alvin Rakoff
lp: David Ogden Stiers, Hunt Block,
David Caruso, Alex Hyde-White

Top Secret!
p: Jon Davison, Hunt Lowry
sc: Jim Abrahams, David Zucker,
Jerry Zucker, Martyn Burke
d: Jim Abrahams, David Zucker,
Jerry Zucker
lp: Val Kilmer, Lucy Gutteridge,
Peter Cushing, Jeremy Kemp,
Christopher Villiers, Warren Clarke

1984

Steaming
p: Paul Mills
sc: Patricia Losey
d: Joseph Losey
lp: Vanessa Redgrave, Sarah Miles,
Diana Dors, Patti Love,
Brenda Bruce, Felicity Dean

King David
p: Martin Elfand
sc: Andrew Birkin, James Costigan
d: Bruce Beresford
lp: Richard Gere,
Edward Woodward, Alice Krige,
Denis Quilley, Niall Buggy

Legend
p: Arnon Milchan
sc: William Hjortsberg
d: Ridley Scott
lp: Tom Cruise, Mia Sara, Tim Curry,
David Bennent, Alice Playten

Dream Lover
p: Alan J Pakula, Jon Boorstin
sc: Jon Boorstin
d: Alan J Pakula
lp: Kristy McNichol, Ben Masters,
Paul Shenar, Justin Deas

Morons from Outer Space
p: Barry Hanson
sc: Griff Rhys Jones, Mel Smith
d: Mike Hodges
lp: Mel Smith, Griff Rhys Jones,
James B Sikking, Dinsdale Landen

Santa Claus
p: Ilya Salkind, Pierre Spengler
sc: David Newman, Leslie Newman
d: Jeannot Szwarc
lp: Dudley Moore, John Lithgow,
David Huddleston,
Burgess Meredith, Judy Cornwell

A View to a Kill
p: Albert R Broccoli,
Michael G Wilson
sc: Richard Maibaum,
Michael G Wilson
d: John Glen
lp: Roger Moore, Tanya Roberts,
Grace Jones, Patrick Macnee,
Christopher Walken,
Patrick Bachau, David Yip

The Corsican Brothers *(TV)*
p: David A Rosemont
sc: Robin Miller
d: Ian Sharp
lp: Trevor Eve, Margaret Tyzack,
Patsy Kensit, Olivia Hussey

1985

Deceptions *(TV)*
p: William Hill
sc: Robert Chenault,
Melville Shavelson
d: Robert Chenault,
Melville Shavelson
lp: Stefanie Powers, Barry Bostwick,
Jeremy Brett, Gina Lollobrigida

D.A.R.Y.L.
p: John Heyman, Burtt Harris,
Gabrielle Kelly
sc: David Ambrose, Allan Scott,
Jeffrey Ellis
d: Simon Wincer
lp: Mary Beth Hurt, Barret Oliver
Michael McKean, Kathryn Walker

Spies Like Us
p: Brian Grazer, George Folsey Jr
sc: Dan Aykroyd, Lowell Ganz,
Babaloo Mandel
d: John Landis
lp: Chevy Chase, Dan Aykroyd,
Steve Forrest, Donna Dixon

Murder Elite
p: Jeffrey Broom
sc: NJ Crisp
d: Claude Whatham
lp: Ali MacGraw, Billie Whitelaw,
Hywel Bennett, Ray Lonnen

**Gunbus
(US: Sky Bandits)**
p: Richard Herland
sc: Thom Keyes
d: Zoran Perisic
lp: Scott McGinnis, Jeff Osterhage,
Ronald Lacey, Miles Anderson

Little Shop of Horrors
p: David Geffen
sc: Howard Ashman
d: Frank Oz
lp: Rick Moranis, Ellen Greene,
Vincent Gardenia, Steve Martin

Aliens
p: Gale Anne Hurd
sc: James Cameron, Walter Hill,
David Giler
d: James Cameron
lp: Sigourney Weaver, Carrie Henn,
Michael Biehn, Lance Henriksen,
Paul Reiser, Bill Paxton,
William Hope, Jenette Goldstein

The Second Victory
p: Gerald Thomas
sc: Morris L West
d: Gerald Thomas
lp: Anthony Andrews,
Helmut Griem, Max Von Sydow

1986

The Living Daylights
p: Albert R Broccoli,
Michael G Wilson
sc: Richard Maibaum,
Michael G Wilson
d: John Glen
lp: Timothy Dalton, Maryam d'Abo,
Joe Don Baker, Art Malik,
John Rhys-Davies, Jeroen Krabbé,
Andreas Wisniewski,
Thomas Wheatley, Julie T Wallace

Still Crazy Like a Fox *(TV)*
p: William Hill
sc: Frank Cardea, George Schenk
d: Paul Krasny
lp: Jack Warden, John Rubinstein,
Graham Chapman, James Faulkner

Full Metal Jacket
p: Stanley Kubrick
sc: Stanley Kubrick, Michael Herr,
Gustav Hasford
d: Stanley Kubrick
lp: Matthew Modine,
Adam Baldwin, Vincent D'Onofrio,
R Lee Ermey, Dorian Harewood

Mio in the Land of Faraway
p: Ingemar Ejve
sc: William Aldridge
d: Vladimir Grammatikov
lp: Timothy Bottoms,
Susannah York, Christopher Lee,
Nicholas Pickard, Christian Bale

**Superman IV:
The Quest for Peace**
p: Yoram Globus, Menahem Golan
sc: Lawrence Konner,
Mark Rosenthal, Christopher Reeve
d: Sidney J Furie
lp: Christopher Reeve,
Gene Hackman, Jackie Cooper,
Sam Wanamaker, Marc Pillow,
Mariel Hemingway, Margot Kidder

1987

Paperhouse
p: Tim Bevan, Sarah Radclyffe
sc: Matthew Jacobs
d: Bernard Rose
lp: Charlotte Burke, Elliott Spiers,
Glenne Headly, Ben Cross,
Gemma Jones, Sarah Newbold

Consuming Passions
p: William P Cartlidge
sc: Paul D Zimmerman,
Andrew Davies
d: Giles Foster
lp: Tyler Butterworth,
Jonathan Pryce, Freddie Jones,
Vanessa Redgrave, Prunella Scales

Pack of Lies *(TV)*
p: Robert Halmi Sr
sc: Ralph Gallup (Hugh Whitemore)
d: Anthony Page
lp: Ellen Burstyn, Teri Garr,
Sammi Davis, Ronald Hines,
Clive Swift, Daniel Benzali

Hazard of Hearts (TV)
p: Albert Fennell, John Hough
sc: Terence Feely
d: John Hough
lp: Diana Rigg, Edward Fox,
Helena Bonham Carter,
Fiona Fullerton, Neil Dickson,
Christopher Plummer

The Dressmaker
p: Ronald Shedlo
sc: John McGrath
d: Jim O'Brien
lp: Joan Plowright, Billie Whitelaw,
Peter Postlethwaite, Jane Horrocks

Hawks
p: Steve Lanning
sc: Roy Clarke
d: Robert Ellis Miller
lp: Timothy Dalton,
Anthony Edwards, Janet McTeer,
Camille Coduri, Jill Bennett

1988

Hellbound: Hellraiser II
p: Christopher Figg
sc: Peter Atkins
d: Tony Randel
lp: Clare Higgins, Ashley Laurence,
Kenneth Cranham,
Imogen Boorman, Sean Chapman,
William Hope, Doug Bradley

Slipstream
p: Gary Kurtz, Steve Lanning
sc: Tony Kayden
d: Steven Lisberger
lp: Mark Hamill, Bob Peck,
Bill Paxton, Kitty Aldridge,
F Murray Abraham, Ben Kingsley

Batman
p: Jon Peters, Peter Guber
sc: Sam Hamm, Warren Skaaren
d: Tim Burton
lp: Michael Keaton, Jack Nicholson,
Kim Basinger, Robert Wuhl,
Pat Hingle, Billy Dee Williams,
Michael Gough, Jack Palance

Dealers
p: William P Cartlidge
sc: Andrew MacLear
d: Colin Bucksey
lp: Paul McGann,
Rebecca De Mornay,
Derrick O'Connor, John Castle

The Lady and the Highwayman
(TV)
p: Albert Fennell, John Hough
sc: Terence Feely
d: John Hough
lp: Lysette Anthony, Hugh Grant,
Michael York, Emma Samms,
Oliver Reed, Claire Bloom

Without a Clue
p: Marc Stirdivant
sc: Gary Murphy, Larry Strawther
d: Thom Eberhardt
lp: Michael Caine, Ben Kingsley,
Jeffrey Jones, Lysette Anthony

**The Adventures of
Baron Munchausen** *(part)*
p: Thomas Schühly
sc: Charles McKeown,
Terry Gilliam
d: Terry Gilliam
lp: John Neville, Eric Idle,
Sarah Polley, Oliver Reed

A Man for All Seasons *(TV)*
p: Fraser Clarke Heston
sc: Robert Bolt
d: Charlton Heston
lp: Charlton Heston, John Gielgud,
Vanessa Redgrave

War and Remembrance *(TV)*
p: Barbara Steele
sc: Dan Curtis, Earl W Wallace,
Herman Wouk
d: Dan Curtis
lp: Robert Mitchum, Jane Seymour,
Hart Bochner, Victoria Tennant,
Ralph Bellamy, John Gielgud

A Dry White Season
p: Paula Weinstein
sc: Colin Welland, Euzhan Palcy
d: Euzhan Palcy
lp: Donald Sutherland,
Janet Suzman, Zakes Mokae,
Jurgen Prochnow, Susan Sarandon,
Marlon Brando, Winston Ntshona

Strike It Rich
p: Graham Easton,
Christine Oestreicher
sc: James Scott
d: James Scott
lp: Robert Lindsay, Molly Ringwald,
John Gielgud, Frances de la Tour

Great Expectations *(TV)*
p: Greg Smith
sc: John Goldsmith
d: Kevin Connor
lp: Jean Simmons, John Rhys-Davies,
Anthony Calf, Anthony Hopkins

The Return of the Musketeers
p: Pierre Spengler
sc: George MacDonald Fraser
d: Richard Lester
lp: Michael York, Oliver Reed,
Frank Finlay, C Thomas Howell,
Kim Cattrall, Geraldine Chaplin,
Roy Kinnear, Christopher Lee,
Richard Chamberlain

1989

Nightbreed
p: Gariella Martinelli
sc: Clive Barker
d: Clive Barker
lp: Craig Sheffer, Anne Bobby,
David Cronenberg, Charles Haid,
Hugh Quarshie, Hugh Ross

Outpost *(TV pilot)*
p: Patrick Dromgoole,
Johnny Goodman
sc: Jeff Melvoin, Michael Bryant
d: Tommy Lee Wallace
lp: Joanna Going, Ben Marley,
Jeremy Flynn, David Robb,
Marissa Dunlop, Joseph Marcell

Act of Will *(TV)*
p: Victor Glynn, Ian Warren
sc: Jill Hyem
d: Don Sharp
lp: Victoria Tennant, Peter Coyote,
Elizabeth Hurley, Kevin McNally

Press Gang
(TV series, 12 episodes)
p: Sandra C Hastie
sc: Steven Moffat
d: Colin Nutley, Bob Spiers,
Lorne Magory,
lp: Julia Sawalha, Dexter Fletcher,
Lee Ross, Kelda Holmes,
Paul Reynolds, Mmoloki Chystie,
Lucy Benjamin

Treasure Island *(TV)*
p: Peter Snell, Ted Lloyd
sc: Fraser Clarke Heston
d: Fraser Clarke Heston
lp: Charlton Heston, Christian Bale,
Oliver Reed, Christopher Lee,
Richard Johnson, Julian Glover

Memphis Belle
p: David Puttnam, Catherine Wyler
sc: Monte Merrick
d: Michael Caton-Jones
lp: Matthew Modine, Eric Stoltz,
Tate Donovan, DB Sweeney,
Billy Zane, Sean Astin

Chicago Joe and the Showgirl
p: Tim Bevan
sc: David Yallop
d: Bernard Rose
lp: Kiefer Sutherland, Emily Lloyd,
Patsy Kensit, Keith Allen

The Russia House
p: Paul Maslansky, Fred Schepisi
sc: Tom Stoppard
d: Fred Schepisi
lp: Sean Connery, Michelle Pfeiffer,
Roy Scheider, James Fox,
John Mahoney, Michael Kitchen

The Gravy Train *(TV)*
p: Ian Warren, Philip Hinchcliffe
sc: Malcolm Bradbury
d: David Tucker
lp: Christoph Waltz, Ian Richardson,
Almanta Suska, Alexei Sayle

White Hunter, Black Heart
p: Clint Eastwood
sc: Peter Viertel, James Bridges,
Burt Kennedy
d: Clint Eastwood
lp: Clint Eastwood, Jeff Fahey,
Charlotte Cornwell

1990

Air America
p: Daniel Melnick
sc: John Eskow, Richard Rush
d: Roger Spottiswoode
lp: Mel Gibson, Robert Downey Jr,
Nancy Travis, Ken Jenkins,
David Marshall Grant, Lane Smith

King Ralph
p: Jack Brodsky
sc: David S Ward
d: David S Ward
lp: John Goodman, Peter O'Toole,
John Hurt, Camille Coduri,
Richard Griffiths, Leslie Phillips

Buddy's Song
p: Bill Curbishley, Roy Baird,
Roger Daltrey
sc: Nigel Hinton
d: Claude Whatham
lp: Roger Daltrey, Chesney Hawkes,
Sharon Duce, Michael Elphick,
Douglas Hodge, Paul McKenzie

Heil Honey I'm Home
(TV series, 8 episodes)
p: Paul Jackson, Harry Waterson
sc: Geoff Atkinson
d: Juliet May
lp: Neil McCaul, Denica Fairman

Let Him Have It
p: Luc Roeg, Robert Warr
sc: Neal Purvis, Robert Wade
d: Peter Medak
lp: Christopher Ecclestone,
Paul Reynolds, Tom Courtenay,
Tom Bell, Eileen Atkins

Crucifer of Blood *(TV)*
p: Fraser Clarke Heston
sc: Fraser Clarke Heston
d: Fraser Clarke Heston
lp: Charlton Heston,
Richard Johnson, Susannah Harker,
Edward Fox, John Castle

Shining Through
p: Howard Rosenman, Carol Baum
sc: David Seltzer
d: David Seltzer
lp: Michael Douglas,
Melanie Griffith, Liam Neeson,
Joely Richardson, John Gielgud

1991

Alien³
p: Gordon Carroll, David Giler,
Walter Hill
sc: David Giler, Walter Hill,
Larry Ferguson
d: David Fincher
lp: Sigourney Weaver,
Charles S Dutton, Charles Dance,
Paul McGann, Brian Glover,

The Camomile Lawn *(TV)*
p: Sophie Balhetchet,
Glenn Wilhide
sc: Kenneth Taylor
d: Peter Hall
lp: Felicity Kendal, Paul Eddington,
Oliver Cotton, Claire Bloom,
Rosemary Harris, Richard Johnson,
Virginia McKenna

Year of the Comet
p: Nigel Wooll, Peter Yates
sc: William Goldman
d: Peter Yates
lp: Penelope Ann Miller,
Timothy Daly, Louis Jourdan,
Art Malik, Ian Richardson

Project Shadowchaser
p: John Eyres
sc: Stephen Lister
d: John Eyres
lp: Martin Kove, Meg Foster,
Frank Zagarino, Paul Koslo,
Joss Ackland, Ricco Ross

Kafka
p: Harry Benn, Stuart Cornfeld
sc: Lem Dobbs
d: Steven Soderbergh
lp: Jeremy Irons, Theresa Russell,
Joel Grey, Ian Holm, Jeroen Krabbé,
Armin Mueller-Stahl, Alec Guinness

Just Like a Woman
p: Nick Evans
sc: Nick Evans
d: Christopher Monger
lp: Julie Walters, Adrian Pasdar,
Paul Freeman, Susan Wooldridge,
Gordon Kennedy, Ian Redford

City of Joy
p: Jake Eberts, Roland Joffé
sc: Mark Medoff
d: Roland Joffé
lp: Patrick Swayze, Om Puri,
Pauline Collins, Art Malik

Jeeves and Wooster
(TV series, 6 episodes)
p: Brian Eastman
sc: Clive Exton
d: Simon Langton
lp: Stephen Fry, Hugh Laurie

Patriot Games
p: Mace Neufeld, Robert Rehme
sc: Peter Iliffe, Donald Stewart
d: Phillip Noyce
lp: Harrison Ford, Anne Archer,
Patrick Bergin, Sean Bean

Bye Bye Baby *(TV)*
p: Linda Agran, Christopher Neame
sc: Jack Rosenthal
d: Jack Rosenthal, Edward Bennett
lp: Ben Chaplin, Jason Flemyng

Prisoner of Honor *(TV)*
p: Richard Dreyfuss, Judith James
sc: Ron Hutchinson
d: Ken Russell
lp: Richard Dreyfuss, Oliver Reed,
Peter Firth, Brian Blessed,
Jeremy Kemp, Peter Vaughan

Red Fox *(TV)*
p: Adrian Bate, Ian Toynton
sc: James MacManus
d: Ian Toynton
lp: John Hurt, Jane Birkin,
Brian Cox, Didier Flamand,
Francois Negret, Marc Samuel

Inspector Morse: Dead on Time
(TV)
p: Deirdre Keir
sc: Daniel Boyle
d: John Madden
lp: John Thaw, Joanna David,
Samantha Bond, Kevin Whatley

My Friend Walter *(TV)*
p: Gavin Millar
sc: Michael Morpurgo, Gavin Millar
d: Gavin Millar
lp: Ronald Pickup, Prunella Scales,
Polly Grant, James Hazeldine,
Louise Jameson

Don't Get Me Started
p: Steve Clark-Hall,
Michael Smeaton
sc: Arthur Ellis
d: Arthur Ellis
lp: Trevor Eve, Steven Waddington,
Marion Bailey, Nathan Grower

Tales from the Poop Deck
(TV series, 6 episodes)
p: Adrian Bate, Chris Langham
sc: Lenny Barker, Vicki Stepney
d: John Birkin
lp: Helen Atkinson-Wood,
Nicholas Pritchard, Paul Shearer,
Dudley Sutton, Colin McFarlane,
Mike Grady, Griff Rhys Jones

1992

Carry On Columbus
p: John Goldstone
sc: Dave Freeman
d: Gerald Thomas
lp: Jim Dale, Bernard Cribbins,
Maureen Lipman, Peter Richardson,
Alexei Sayle, Sara Crowe

Diana: Her True Story *(TV)*
p: Martin Poll
sc: Stephen Zito
d: Kevin Connor
lp: Serena Scott Thomas,
David Threlfall, Elizabeth Garvie

Son of the Pink Panther
p: Tony Adams
sc: Blake Edwards,
Madeline Sunshine, Steven Sunshine
d: Blake Edwards
lp: Robert Benigni, Herbert Lom,
Debrah Farentino, Robert Davi
Claudia Cardinale, Burt Kwouk

The Secret Garden
p: Fred Fuchs, Tom Luddy,
Fred Roos
sc: Caroline Thompson
d: Agnieszka Holland
lp: Kate Maberly, Heydon Prowse,
Andrew Knott, Maggie Smith

Great Moments in Aviation *(TV)*
p: Phillippa Giles
sc: Jeanette Winterson
d: Beeban Kidron
lp: Vanessa Redgrave, John Hurt,
Jonathan Pryce, Dorothy Tutin

Parallel 9 *(TV series)*
p: Glyn Edwards
d: Graham C Williams
lp: Lucinda Crowden

Lipstick on Your Collar
(TV series, 6 episodes)
p: Alison Barnett,
Rosemarie Whitman
sc: Dennis Potter
d: Renny Rye
lp: Giles Thomas, Louise Germaine,
Ewan McGregor, Peter Jeffrey

Frankenstein *(TV)*
p: David Wickes
sc: David Wickes
d: David Wickes
lp: Patrick Bergin, Randy Quaid,
John Mills, Lambert Wilson

Lady Chatterley *(TV)*
p: Michael Haggiag
sc: Ken Russell
d: Ken Russell
lp: Joely Richardson, Sean Bean,
James Wilby, Shirley Ann Field

Head Over Heels
(TV series, 7 episodes)
p: Brian Eastman, Jane Prowse
sc: Jane Prowse, Simon Baker,
Patrick Gale
d: Chris King, Graham Theakston
lp: Ann Bell, Jackie Morrison,
Sally Geoghegan, Diana Morrison,
Kathy Kiera Clarke, Elena Ferrari,
Jessica Lloyd, Gemma Page

1993

Black Beauty
p: Peter Macgregor-Scott,
Robert Shapiro
sc: Caroline Thompson
d: Caroline Thompson
lp: Sean Bean, David Thewlis,
Jim Carter, Peter Davison

Death Machine
p: Dominic Anciano, Ray Burdis
sc: Stephen Norrington
d: Stephen Norrington
lp: Brad Dourif, Ely Pouget

Minder *(TV series, 10 episodes)*
p: Ian Toynton
sc: Bernard Dempsey,
Kevin Sperring, William Ivory,
Tony Hoare, Arthur Ellis
d: Charles Beeson, Ken Hannam,
Gordon Flemyng and others
lp: George Cole, Gary Webster

U.F.O.
p: Simon Wright
sc: Roy 'Chubby' Brown, Richard
Hall, Simon Wright
d: Tony Dow
lp: Roy 'Chubby' Brown,
Sara Stockbridge, Amanda Symonds

**The Phoenix and the Magic
Carpet**
p: Zoran Perisic, Peter Waller
sc: Florence Fox
d: Zoran Perisic
lp: Peter Ustinov, Dee Wallace

Spender: The French Collection
(TV)
p: Steve Lanning
sc: Jimmy Nail
d: Matt Forrest
lp: Jimmy Nail, Sammy Johnson,
Tom Bell, Laurie Killing

Being Human
p: Robert F Colesberry,
David Puttnam
sc: Bill Forsyth
d: Bill Forsyth
lp: Robin Williams, Maudie Johnson,
Max Johnson, Robert Carlyle

The Borrowers *(TV)*
p: Grainne Marmion
sc: Richard Carpenter
d: John Henderson
lp: Ian Holm, Penelope Wilton,
Rebecca Callard, Paul Cross,
Daniel Newman, Sian Phillips

Moving Story
(TV series, 13 episodes)
p: Linda Agran
sc: Jack Rosenthal, Bill Gallagher,
Willis Hall, Michael Russell,
Bernard Dempsey, Ron Rose
d: Roger Bamford, Andrew Grieve,
Philip Davis, Dave Richards
lp: Warren Clarke, Phil Davis,
Con O'Neill, Ronny Jhutti,
Kenneth Colley

Sister My Sister
p: Norma Heyman
sc: Wendy Kesselman
d: Nancy Meckler
lp: Julie Walters, Joely Richardson

Parallel 9 *(TV series)*
p: Glyn Edwards
d: Graham C Williams
lp: Lucinda Crowden

Left Hand Drive *(TV)*
p: Tim Field
sc: Peter Chiang, Tim Field,
Christopher Fowler
d: Peter Chiang
lp: Alex Richardson,
Jonathan Copestake, Juliet Bond

Tomorrow Calling *(TV)*
p: Polly Tapson
sc: Tim Leandro
d: Tim Leandro
lp: Colin Salmon, Toyah Willcox,
Don Henderson, Sara Stockbridge,
Jack Raymond

Alice in Russialand *(TV)*
p: Ronaldo Vasconcellos
sc: Ken Russell, Hetty Baynes
d: Ken Russell
lp: Amanda Ray-King, Hetty Baynes

Raging Earth
p: Rene L Ash, Ethel C Ash,
Roland Giustini
sc: J Frank James
d: Vic Armstrong
lp: Helen Mirren, Joss Ackland,
John Rhys-Davies, Patrick Bergin

A Martial Kind of Men *(TV)*
p: Charles Steel
sc: Tim Willocks
d: Devon Dickson
lp: Paul Whitby, Richard Standing,
Marc Warren, Sean McKenzie

Dirtysomething (TV)
p: Peter Salmi
sc: Peter Salmi, Carl Prechezer
d: Carl Prechezer
lp: Paul Reynolds, Rachel Weisz,
Bernard Hill, Rufus Sewell,
Susannah Doyle, Walter Sparrow

1994

Interview with the Vampire
p: David Geffen, Stephen Woolley
sc: Anne Rice
d: Neil Jordan
lp: Tom Cruise, Brad Pitt,
Kirsten Dunst, Stephen Rea
Antonio Banderas, Christian Slater

Jack & Sarah
p: Simon Channing-Williams,
Pippa Cross, Janette Day
sc: Tim Sullivan
d: Tim Sullivan
lp: Richard E Grant,
Samantha Mathis, Judi Dench,
Eileen Atkins, Cherie Lunghi

Middleton's Changeling
p: Marcus Thompson
sc: Marcus Thompson
d: Marcus Thompson
lp: Ian Dury, Amanda Ray-King,
Colm O'Maonlaí, Billy Connolly

Space Precinct
(TV series, 24 episodes)
p: Gerry Anderson
sc: Steve Brown, J Larry Carroll,
David Bennett Carren,
Arthur Sellers, Marc Scott Zicree
and others
d: Colin Bucksey, John Glen,
Sidney Hayers, Alan Birkinshaw,
Jim Goddard, Peter Duffell,
Piers Haggard
lp: Ted Shackleford,
Rob Youngblood, Simone Bendix,
Nancy Paul, Jerome Willis

Mary Reilly
p: Norma Heyman,
Nancy Graham Tanen, Ned Tanen
sc: Christopher Hampton
d: Stephen Frears
lp: Julia Roberts, John Malkovich,
George Cole, Michael Gambon,
Kathy Staff, Glenn Close

Parallel 9 *(TV series)*
p: Vanessa Hill
d: Claire Winyard
lp: Lucinda Crowden

Chandler & Co
(TV series, 6 episodes)
p: Ann Skinner
sc: Paula Milne, Bill Gallagher
Jacqueline Holborough
d: Renny Rye, Robert Marchand
lp: Catherine Russell,
Barbara Flynn, Peter Capaldi

**The Englishman Who Went Up
a Hill, But Came Down a
Mountain**
p: Sarah Curtis
sc: Christopher Monger
d: Christopher Monger
lp: Hugh Grant, Tara Fitzgerald,
Colm Meaney, Ian McNeice,
Ian Hart, Kenneth Griffith

Scarlett *(TV)*
p: John Erman
sc: William Hanley
d: John Erman
lp: Joanne Whalley-Kilmer,
Timothy Dalton, Barbara Barrie,
Stephen Collins, Annabeth Gish

Poirot (*TV series, 4 episodes*)
p: Brian Eastman
sc: Clive Exton, Anthony Horowitz, Douglas Watkinson
d: Edward Bennett, Andrew Grieve
lp: David Suchet, Hugh Fraser, Philip Jackson, Pauline Moran, Vernon Dobtcheff, Damian Lewis, Diane Fletcher, Patrick Ryecart

First Knight
p: Hunt Lowry, Jerry Zucker
sc: William Nicholson, Lorne Cameron, David Hoselton
d: Jerry Zucker
lp: Sean Connery, Richard Gere, Julia Ormond, Ben Cross

Hackers
p: Michael Peyser, Ralph Winter
sc: Rafael Moreu
d: Iain Softley
lp: Jonny Lee Miller, Angelina Jolie, Jesse Bradford, Matthew Lillard

The Vacillations of Poppy Carew (*TV*)
p: Brian True-May
sc: William Humble
d: James Cellan Jones
lp: Tara Fitzgerald, Daniel Massey, Samuel West, Edward Atterton

Blue Juice
p: Peter Salmi, Simon Relph
sc: Peter Salmi, Carl Prechezer
d: Peter Salmi
lp: Sean Pertwee, Catherine Zeta-Jones, Ewan McGregor, Peter Gunn

Loch Ness
p: Tim Bevan, Eric Fellner, Stephen Ujlaki
sc: John Fusco
d: John Henderson
lp: Ted Danson, Joely Richardson, Iam Holm, Harris Yulin

Scavengers (*TV*)
p: John Paul Chappell, Geoff Wilson
sc: Duncan McLachlan
d: Chema Quero, John Rooney
lp: John Leslie, Anna Galvin

The Spooks of Bottle Bay (*TV series*)
p: Ray Burdis, John Thirtle
sc: Ian Allen
d: Paul Cole
lp: John Thirtle, Nigel Plaskitt, Richard Coombs, Ian Allen, Heather Tobias, Lousie Gold

Strike It Lucky (*TV series*)
p: Maurice Leonard
d: Paul Kirrage
lp: Michael Barrymore

1995

Screen Two: Mrs Hartley and the Growth Centre (*TV*)
p: Debbie Shewell
sc: Philippa Gregory
d: Noella Smith
lp: Pam Ferris, Peter Blythe, Charlotte Coleman, David Ryall, Ken Christiansen, Danny Webb, Constance Chapman, Jim Carter

Karaoke (*TV series, 4 episodes*)
p: Kenith Trodd, Rosemarie Whitman
sc: Dennis Potter
d: Renny Rye
lp: Albert Finney, Richard E Grant, Julie Christie, Alison Steadman

The Turn of the Screw (*TV*)
p: Martin Pope
sc: Nick Dear
d: Ben Bolt
lp: Jodhi May, Pam Ferris, Colin Firth, Joe Sowerbutts

Cold Lazarus
(*TV series, 4 episodes*)
p: Kenith Trodd, Rosemarie Whitman
sc: Dennis Potter
d: Renny Rye
lp: Albert Finney, Grant Masters, Ciarán Hinds, Ganiat Kasumu, Frances de la Tour

Chandler & Co
(*TV series, 6 episodes*)
p: Ann Skinner
sc: Paula Milne, Bill Gallagher, Alma Cullen, Jacqueline Holborough,
d: Christopher King, Diana Patrick
lp: Catherine Russell, Susan Fleetwood, Adrian Lukis

Class Act
(*TV series, 7 episodes*)
p: Sharon Bloom
sc: Michael Aitkens, Sam Lawrence
d: Herbert Wise, Rick Stroud
lp: Joanna Lumley, John Bowe, Nadine Garner, Richard Vernon, James Gaddas

The Final Cut
(*TV series, 4 episodes*)
p: Ken Riddington
sc: Andrew Davies
d: Mike Vardy
lp: Ian Richardson, Diane Fletcher, Nick Brimble, Nickolas Grace, Andrew Seear

The Canterville Ghost (*TV*)
p: Robert Benedetti
sc: Robert Benedetti
d: Sydney Macartney
lp: Patrick Stewart, Neve Campbell, Joan Sims, Donald Sinden

Mission: Impossible
p: Tom Cruise, Paula Wagner
sc: David Koepp, Steven Zaillian, Robert Towne
d: Brian De Palma
lp: Tom Cruise, Jon Voight, Emmanuelle Béart, Henry Czerny, Jean Reno, Ving Rhames, Kristin Scott Thomas, Vanessa Redgrave

Attack of the Hawkmen (*TV*)
p: Rick McCallum
sc: Matthew Jacobs, Rosemary Anne Sisson, Ben Burtt
d: Ben Burtt
lp: Sean Patrick Flanery, Ronny Couteure, Patrick Toomey, Marc Warren, Craig Kelly, Daniel Kash, Ewan Bailey

Fierce Creatures
p: John Cleese, Michael Shamberg
sc: John Cleese, Iain Johnstone
d: Fred Schepisi, Robert Young
lp: John Cleese, Jamie Lee Curtis, Kevin Kline, Robert Lindsay, Michael Palin, Ronnie Corbett

The Darkening
p: Michael Collins, John G Jones, Victoria Parker, Joshua Culp, Nick Davis
sc: John G Jones, Victoria Parker
d: William Mesa
lp: Jeff Rector, George Saunders, Rebecca Kyler Downs

CutThroat Island (*part*)
p: James Gorman, Renny Harlin, Laurence Mark, Joel B Michaels
sc: Robert King, Mark Norman, Michael Frost Beckner, James Gorman, Bruce A Evans, Raynold Gideon
d: Renny Harlin
lp: Geena Davis, Matthew Modine, Frank Langella, Maury Chaykin

Emma
p: Patrick Cassavetti, Steven Haft
sc: Douglas McGrath
d: Douglas McGrath
lp: Gwyneth Paltrow, James Cosmo, Greta Scacchi, Alan Cumming

Just Cause (*part*)
p: Arne Glimcher, Steve Perry, Lee Rich
sc: Jeb Stuart, Peter Stone
d: Arne Glimcher
lp: Sean Connery, Laurence Fishburne, Kate Capshaw, Blair Underwood, Ed Harris

Ken Russell's Treasure Island (*TV*)
p: Maureen Murray
sc: Ken Russell
d: Ken Russell
lp: Hetty Baynes, Gregory Hall, Michael Elphick

Last of the Summer Wine: A Leg Up for Christmas (*TV*)
p: Alan JW Bell
sc: Roy Clarke
d: Alan JW Bell
lp: Bill Owen, Peter Sallis, Brian Wilde, Kathy Staff, Jane Freeman

Annie: A Royal Adventure (*TV*)
p: Wendy Dytman, Ruth Slawson
sc: Trish Soodik
d: Ian Toynton
lp: Ashley Johnson, Joan Collins, George Hearn, Ian McDiarmid

Poldark (*TV*)
p: Sally Haynes
sc: Winston Graham (novel)
d: Richard Laxton
lp: John Bowe, Mel Martin, Michael Attwell, Ioan Gruffudd

Surviving Picasso
p: Ismail Merchant, David L Wolper
sc: Ruth Prawer Jhabvala
d: James Ivory
lp: Anthony Hopkins, Natascha McElhone, Julianne Moore

White Squall
p: Mimi Polk Gitlin, Rocky Lang
sc: Todd Robinson
d: Ridley Scott
lp: Jeff Bridges, Caroline Goodall, Scott Wolf, John Savage, Jeremy Sisto, Ryan Phillippe

You Bet! (*TV series*)
p: Linda Beale
d: Sue McMahon
lp: Matthew Kelly

Evita
p: Alan Parker, Robert Stigwood, Andrew G Vajna
sc: Alan Parker, Oliver Stone
d: Alan Parker
lp: Madonna, Antonio Banderas, Jonathan Pryce, Jimmy Nail

Firelight
p: Brian Eastman
sc: William Nicholson
d: William Nicholson
lp: Sophie Marceau, Stephen Dillane, Dominique Belcourt

Deadly Voyage (*TV*)
p: Bradley Adams, John Goldschmidt
sc: Stuart Urban
d: John Mackenzie
lp: Omar Epps, Joss Ackland, Sean Pertwee

Potamus Park (*TV series*)
p: Paul Cole, John Lee, Chris Noulton
sc: Paul Cole
d: Paul Cole
lp: Atalanta Harmsworth, Nigel Plaskitt, Simon Buckley

1996

The Fifth Element
p: Patrice Ledoux, Iain Smith
sc: Luc Besson, Robert Mark Kamen
d: Luc Besson
lp: Bruce Willis, Gary Oldman, Ian Holm, Milla Jovovich, Chris Tucker, Luke Perry

The Saint
p: David Brown, Robert Evans, William J MacDonald, Mace Neufeld
sc: Jonathan Hensleigh, Wesley Strick
d: Phillip Noyce
lp: Val Kilmer, Elizabeth Shue, Rade Serbedzija, Valery Nikolaev

Fairytale – A True Story
p: Bruce Davey, Wendy Finerman
sc: Ernie Contreras, Albert Ash, Tom McLoughlin
d: Charles Sturridge
lp: Florence Hoath, Elizabeth Earl, Paul McGann, Phoebe Nicholls

Incognito
p: James G Robinson
sc: Jordan Katz
d: John Badham
lp: Jason Patric, Irène Jacob, Thomas Lockyer, Ian Richardson

The Apocalypse Watch *(TV)*
p: Steven North
sc: John Goldsmith,
Christopher Canaan
d: Kevin Connor
lp: Patrick Bergin, John Shea,
Virginia Madsen, Benedick Blyth

Ivanhoe *(TV series, 6 episodes)*
p: Jeremy Gwilt
sc: Deborah Cook
d: Stuart Orme
lp: Steven Waddington,
Ciarán Hinds, Victoria Smurfitt,
James Cosmo, Ralph Brown

20,000 Leagues Under the Sea
(TV)
p: John Davis
sc: Joe Wiesenfeld
d: Michael Anderson
lp: Richard Crenna, Ben Cross,
Julie Cox, Michael Jayston

The Preventers *(TV)*
p: Nick Symons
sc: Morwenna Banks,
Robert Harley, Chris England
d: Liddy Oldroyd
lp: Morwenna Banks,
Robert Harley, Chris England,
William Gaunt, Ed Devereaux

Potamus Park 2 *(TV series)*
p: Paul Cole, John Lee,
Chris Noulton
sc: Paul Cole
d: Paul Cole
lp: Atalanta Harmsworth,
Nigel Plaskitt, Simon Buckley

Hostile Waters *(TV)*
p: Tony Garnett
sc: Troy Kennedy-Martin
d: David Drury
lp: Rutger Hauer, Martin Sheen,
Max von Sydow, Colm Feore

Born to Run
(TV series, 6 episodes)
p: Laura Mackie
sc: Debbie Horsfield
d: Jean Stewart
lp: Billie Whitelaw, Keith Allen,
Marian McLoughlin, Linda Henry,
Terence Rigby

Mirad *(TV)*
p: Michael Kelk
sc: Ad de Bont
d: Jeremy Irons
lp: Sinead Cusak, Jeremy Irons,
Jamie Yeates

The Designated Mourner
p: Donna Grey, David Hare,
Mike Nichols
sc: Wallace Shawn
d: David Hare
lp: Mike Nichols,
Miranda Richardson,
David De Keyser

Jonathan Creek
(TV series 5 episodes)
p: Susan Belbin
sc: David Renwick
d: Marcus Mortimer, Sandy Johnson
lp: Alan Davies, Caroline Quentin

The Jackal
p: Michael Caton-Jones,
Sean Daniel, James Jacks,
Kevin Jarre
sc: Kenneth Ross, Chuck Pfarrer
d: Michael Caton-Jones
lp: Bruce Willis, Richard Gere,
Sidney Poitier, Diane Venora

Eyes Wide Shut
p: Stanley Kubrick, Brian W Cook
sc: Stanley Kubrick,
Frederic Raphael
d: Stanley Kubrick
lp: Tom Cruise, Nicole Kidman,
Madison Eginton, Jackie Sawiris,
Sydney Pollack, Leslie Lowe

Event Horizon
p: Lawrence Gordon, Lloyd Levin,
Jeremy Bolt
sc: Philip Eisner
d: Paul Anderson
lp: Laurence Fishburne, Sam Neill,
Kathleen Quinlan, Joely Richardson

1997

Tomorrow Never Dies *(part)*
p: Michael G Wilson,
Barbara Broccoli
sc: Bruce Feirstein
d: Roger Spottiswoode
lp: Pierce Brosnan, Jonathan Pryce,
Michelle Yeoh, Teri Hatcher,
Joe Don Baker, Ricky Jay,
Götz Otto, Judi Dench

Crime Traveller
(TV series, 8 episodes)
p: Brian Eastman
sc: Anthony Horowitz
d: Brian Farnham, Rick Stroud
lp: Michael French, Chloe Annett,
Sue Johnson, Paul Trussell,
Richard Dempsey

Love Bites: Perfect Blue *(TV)*
p: Elinor Day
sc: Nick Collins
d: Kieron J Walsh
lp: Inday Ba, Michele Austin,
Philip Glenister, Ruth Gemmell,
James Lennie

The Avengers
p: Jerry Weintraub
sc: Don MacPherson
d: Jeremiah Chechik
lp: Ralph Fiennes, Uma Thurman,
Sean Connery, Patrick Macnee,
Jim Broadbent, Fiona Shaw

The IMAX Nutcracker
p: Olivier Stockman, Lorne Orleans
sc: Christine Edzard
d: Christine Edzard
lp: Miriam Margolyes,
Heathcote Williams, Lotte Johnson,
Benjamin Hall, Harriet Thorpe

The Governess
p: Sarah Curtis
sc: Sandra Goldbacher
d: Sandra Goldbacher
lp: Minnie Driver, Tom Wilkinson,
Harriet Walter, Jonathan Rhys Myers

The Jasper Carrott Trial
(TV series, 6 episodes)
p: Nic Phillips
sc: Jasper Carrott and others
d: Nic Phillips
lp: Jasper Carrot, Robert Lang,
Richard Cordery, Caroline Webster

Tom's Midnight Garden
p: Charles Salmon, Adam Shapiro
sc: Willard Carroll
d: Willard Carroll
lp: Anthony Way, Nigel Le Vaillant,
Greta Scacchi, James Wilby

Jonathan Creek
(TV series 6 episodes)
p: Verity Lambert
sc: David Renwick
d: Sandy Johnson,
Keith Washington
lp: Alan Davies, Caroline Quentin,
Stuart Milligan

Potamus Park 3 *(TV series)*
p: Paul Cole, John Lee,
Chris Noulton
sc: Paul Cole
d: Paul Cole
lp: Atalanta Harmsworth,
Nigel Plaskitt, Simon Buckley

Bean
p: Peter Bennet-Jones, Tim Bevan,
Eric Fellner
sc: Richard Curtis, Robin Driscoll
d: Mel Smith
lp: Rowan Atkinson, Peter MacNicol,
John Mills, Pamela Reed,
Harris Yulin, Burt Reynolds

Invasion Earth
(TV series, 6 episodes)
p: Jed Mercurio, Chrissy Skinns
sc: Jed Mercurio
d: Patrick Lau, Richard Laxton
lp: Vincent Regan, Maggie O'Neill,
Fred Ward, Phyllis Logan

**Star Wars: Episode I –
The Phantom Menace** *(part)*
p: Rick McCallum
sc: George Lucas
d: George Lucas
lp: Liam Neeson, Ewan McGregor,
Natalie Portman, Jake Lloyd,
Pernilla August, Frank Oz,
Ian McDiarmid, Oliver Ford Davies

Sliding Doors
p: Sydney Pollack, William
Horberg, Philippa Braithwaite
sc: Peter Howitt
d: Peter Howitt
lp: Gwyneth Paltrow, John Hannah,
John Lynch, Jeanne Tripplehorn

The Vanishing Man
(TV series, 6 episodes)
p: Linda Agran
sc: Tony Jordan, David Richard Fox
d: Rick Stroud, Roger Bamford
lp: Neil Morrissey, Lucy Akhurst,
Mark Womack, John Castle

Merlin *(TV)*
p: Damian Lee
sc: Tom Richards,
Christoper A Woosen
d: David Winning
lp: Jason Connery, Deborah Moore,
Gareth Thomas, Graham McTavish

Rogue Trader
p: James Dearden, Paul Raphael,
Janette Day
sc: James Dearden
d: James Dearden
lp: Ewan McGregor, Anna Friel,
Yves Beneyton, Betsey Brantley

Don't Go Breaking My Heart
p: Bill Kenwright
sc: Geoff Morrow
d: Willi Patterson
lp: Anthony Edwards,
Jenny Seagrove, Charles Dance,
Jane Leeves. Tom Conti

1998

Still Crazy
p: Amanda Marmot
sc: Dick Clement, Ian La Frenais
d: Brian Gibson
lp: Stephen Rea, Billy Connolly,
Jimmy Nail, Timothy Spall,
Bill Nighy, Juliet Aubrey

Entrapment
p: Sean Connery,
Michael Hertzberg,
Rhonda Tollefson
sc: Ronald Bass, William Broyles,
Michael Hertzberg
d: Jon Amiel
lp: Sean Connery,
Catherine Zeta-Jones, Ving Rhames,
Will Patton, Maury Chaykin

Little White Lies *(TV)*
p: Jack Emery
sc: Trevor Preston
d: Philip Saville
lp: Tara Fitzgerald, Cherie Lunghi,
Peter Bowles, Gerard Butler

Hornblower
(TV series, 3 episodes)
p: Andrew Benson
sc: Russell Lewis, Mike Cullen,
Patrick Harbinson
d: Andrew Grieve
lp: Ioan Gruffudd, Robert Lindsay,
Paul Copley, Sean Gilder,
Simon Sherlock, Jamie Bamber

A Perfect Murder *(part)*
p: Arnold Kopelson,
Anne Kopelson,
Christopher Mankiewicz,
Peter Macgregor-Scott
sc: Patrick Smith Kelly
d: Andrew Davis
lp: Michael Douglas,
Gwyneth Paltrow, Viggo Mortensen

Plunkett & Macleane
p: Tim Bevan, Eric Fellner,
Rupert Harvey
sc: Robert Wade, Neil Purvis,
Charles McKeown, Selwyn Roberts
d: Jake Scott
lp: Robert Carlyle, Jonny Lee Miller,
Liv Tyler, Ken Stott,
Michael Gambon, Alan Cumming

With or Without You
p: Andrew Eaton, Gina Carter
sc: John Forte
d: Michael Winterbottom
lp: Christopher Eccleston,
Dervla Kirwan, Yvan Attal,
Julie Graham, Alun Armstrong

CI5: The New Professionals
(TV series, 13 episodes)
p: David Wickes
David Bainbridge, Peter Hitchen
sc: Brian Clemens, Steven Whitney,
Duncan Gould, Jeremy Burnham,
Colin Brake, David Wickes
d: Christopher King, David Wickes
Ray Austin, John Davies,
Harley Cokeliss, Ken Grieve,
Colin Bucksey, Sidney Hayers
lp: Edward Woodward, Kal Webber,
Colin Wells, Lexa Doig

The Last Yellow
p: Jolyon Symonds
sc: Paul Tucker
d: Julian Farino
lp: Mark Addy, Samntha Morton,
Kenneth Cranham, Alan Atherall

Last of the Summer Wine
(TV series, 10 episodes)
p: Alan JW Bell
sc: Roy Clarke
d: Alan JW Bell
lp: Bill Owen, Peter Sallis,
Frank Thornton, Kathy Staff,
Jane Freeman

The Dark Room (TV)
p: Tony Redston
sc: Niall Leonard
d: Graham Theakston
lp: Dervla Kirwan, James Wilby

Roger Roger
(TV series, 7 episodes)
p: Gareth Gwenlan
sc: John Sullivan
d: Roger Bamford, Tony Dow
lp: Robert Daws, Pippa Guard,
David Ross, Philip Glenister,
Terence Maynard

Midsomer Murders
(TV series, 4 episodes)
p: Brian True-May, Betty Willingale
sc: Anthony Horowitz,
Douglas Watkinson
d: Jeremy Silberston,
Moira Armstrong
lp: John Nettles, Daniel Casey

Lighthouse
p: Tim Dennison, Mark Leake
sc: Simon Hunter, Graeme Scarfe
d: Simon Hunter
lp: James Purefoy, Rachel Shelley

Great Expectations (TV)
p: David Snodin
sc: Tony Marchant
d: Julian Jarrold
lp: Charlotte Rampling,
Ioan Gruffudd, Bernard Hill,
Justine Waddell, Gabriel Thomson,
Gemma Gregory, Clive Russell

Mrs Merton & Malcolm
(TV series, 6 episodes)
p: Glenn Wilhide
sc: Caroline Aherne, Craig Cash,
Henry Normal
d: John Birkin
lp: Caroline Aherne, Craig Cash,
Brian Murphy

Harbour Lights
(TV series, 9 episodes)
p: Steve Lanning
sc: Lizzie Mickery, Stephen Clarke,
Gil Brailey and others
d: Keith Boak, Tim Dowd,
Gary Love, Terry Bedford
lp: Nick Berry, Matilda Ziegler,
Tina Hobley, Paola Dionisotti

French & Saunders: Titanic (TV)
p: Janice Thomas
d: Edgar Wright
sc: Jennifer Saunders, Dawn French
lp: Jennifer Saunders,
Dawn French, Joanna Lumley,
Adrian Edmondson, Helen Lederer

**Friends: The One with
Ross's Wedding**
(TV series, 2 episodes)
p: Todd Stevens
sc: Michael Borkow, Scott Silveri,
Shana Goldberg-Meehan,
Jill Condon, Amy Toomin
d: Kevin S Bright
lp: Jennifer Anniston,
Courteney Cox, Lisa Kudrow,
Matt LeBlanc, Matthew Perry,
David Schwimmer, Tom Conti,
Jennifer Saunders, June Whitfield

Mansfield Park
p: Sarah Curtis
sc: Patricia Rozema
d: Patricia Rozema
lp: Embeth Davidtz,
Jonny Lee Miller, Alessandro Nivola,
Frances O'Connor, Harold Pinter,
Lindsay Duncan, Sheila Gish

Teletubbies (TV series)
p: Anne Wood
sc: Andrew Davenport
d: Vic Finch, David G Hillier
lp: Tim Whitnall, John Simmit,
Nikki Smedley, Pui Fan Lee,
Simon Shelton

The Dance of Shiva
sc: Joseph Miller
d: Jamie Payne
lp: Sanjeev Bhaskar,
Kenneth Branagh, Julian Glover,
Paul McGann, Samuel West

1999

The World is Not Enough
p: Michael G Wilson,
Barbara Broccoli
sc: Neal Purvis, Robert Wade,
Bruce Feirstein
d: Michael Apted
lp: Pierce Brosnan, Sophie Marceau,
Robert Carlyle, Denise Richards,
Robbie Coltrane, Judi Dench,
Desmond Llewelyn,
Vincent Schiavelli, Geoffrey Palmer

The 10th Kingdom
(TV series, 9 episodes)
p: Brian Eastman, Simon Moore,
Jane Prowse
sc: Simon Moore
d: David Carson, Herbert Wise
lp: Kimberly Williams, John
Larroquette, Scott Jared Cohen,
Daniel LaPaine, Dianne Wiest

RKO 281 (TV)
p: Su Armstrong
sc: Richard Ben Cramer,
Thomas Lennon, John Logan
d: Benjamin Ross
lp: Liev Schreiber, James Cromwell,
Melanie Griffith, John Malkovitch,
Brenda Blethyn, Roy Scheider

Birthday Girl
p: Steve Butterworth, Diana Phillips
sc: Jez Butterworth,
Tom Butterworth
d: Jez Butterworth
lp: Nicole Kidman, Ben Chaplin,
Vincent Cassel, Mathieu Kassovitz

**Joseph and the Amazing
Technicolor Dreamcoat** (TV)
p: Andrew Lloyd Webber
sc: Tim Rice, Andrew Lloyd Webber
d: David Mallet
lp: Donny Osmond, Maria Friedman,
Joan Collins, Richard Attenborough

Jesus Christ Superstar (TV)
p: Dusty Symonds
sc: Tim Rice, Andrew Lloyd Webber
d: Gale Edwards, Nick Morris
lp: Glenn Carter, Jérôme Pradon,
Renee Castle, Fred Johanson

Jonathan Creek
(TV series 6 episodes)
p: Verity Lambert
sc: David Renwick
d: Keith Washington,
Richard Holthouse
lp: Alan Davies, Caroline Quentin,
Stuart Milligan

Longitude (TV)
p: Selwyn Roberts
sc: Charles Sturridge
d: Charles Sturridge
lp: Michael Gambon, Jeremy Irons,
Peter Vaughan, Anna Chancellor,
Stephen Fry, Nigel Davenport

Return to the Secret Garden
p: Steve Thompson, Don A Judd,
Jeff T Miller
sc: Steve Thompson
d: Scott Featherstone
lp: Mercedes Kastner,
Michelle Horn, Josh Zuckerman,
Booth Colman, Guy Siner

**Doctor Who – The Curse of the
Fatal Death** (TV)
p: Sue Vertue
sc: Steven Moffat
d: John Henderson
lp: Rowan Atkinson, Julia Sawalha,
Jonathan Pryce

Heartburn Hotel
(TV series, 6 episodes)
p: Gareth Gwenlan
sc: John Sullivan, Steve Glover
d: Gareth Gwenlan
lp: Tim Healy, Clive Russell,
Peter Gunn, Rina Mahony

Nature Boy
(TV series, 4 episodes)
p: Catherine Wearing
sc: Brian Elsley
d: Joe Wright
lp: Lee Ingleby, Paul McGann,
Mark Benton, Lesley Sharp,
Joanne Frogatt, Andrew Woodall

The Golden Bowl
p: Ismail Merchant
sc: Ruth Prawer Jhabvala
d: James Ivory
lp: Kate Beckinsale, James Fox,
Anjelica Huston, Nick Nolte

Vertical Limit
p: Lloyd Phillips, Robert King,
Martin Campbell
sc: Robert King, Terry Hayes
d: Martin Campbell
lp: Chris O'Donnell, Robin Tunney,
Scott Glenn, Izabella Scorupco,
Bill Paxton, Nicholas Lea,
Alexander Siddig, Robert Taylor

Quills
p: Julia Chasman, Peter Kaufman,
Nick Wechsler
sc: Doug Wright
d: Philip Kaufman
lp: Geoffrey Rush, Kate Winslet,
Joaquin Phoenix, Michael Caine,
Billie Whitelaw, Patrick Malahide

The Man Who Cried
p: Christopher Sheppard,
Simona Benzakein
sc: Sally Potter
d: Sally Potter
lp: Christina Ricci, Cate Blanchett,
John Turturro, Johnny Depp,
Harry Dean Stanton

Snatch
p: Matthew Vaughn
sc: Guy Ritchie
d: Guy Ritchie
lp: Benicio Del Toro,
Dennis Farina, Vinnie Jones,
Brad Pitt, Rade Sherbedgia,
Jason Statham, Alan Ford

2000

Proof of Life
p: Taylor Hackford,
Charles Mulvehill
sc: Tony Gilroy
d: Taylor Hackford
lp: Meg Ryan, Russell Crowe,
David Morse, Pamela Reed,
David Caruso, Anthony Heald

The Sleeper (TV)
p: Joy Spink
sc: Gwenyth Hughes
d: Stuart Orme
lp: Eileen Atkins, Anna Massey,
Elizabeth Spriggs, George Cole,
Ciarán Hinds, Annabelle Apsion

Enigma (part)
p: Lorne Michaels, Mick Jagger
sc: Tom Stoppard
d: Michael Apted
lp: Dougray Scott, Kate Winslet,
Jeremy Northam, Saffron Burrows,
Nikolaj Coster Waldau,
Tom Hollander, Corin Redgrave,
Matthew Macfadyen

The Mummy Returns (part)
p: James Jacks, Sean Daniel
sc: Stephen Sommers
d: Stephen Sommers
lp: Brendan Fraser, Rachel Weisz,
John Hannah, Arnold Vosloo,
Oded Fehr, Patricia Velasquez

The Merchant of Venice (TV)
p: Richard Price, Chris Hunt
sc: William Shakespeare
d: Chris Hunt, Trevor Nunn
lp: Henry Goodman, David Bamber,
Derbhle Crotty, David Burt,
Andrew French, Peter de Jersey

Lara Croft: Tomb Raider
p: Lawrence Gordon, Lloyd Levin,
Colin Wilson
sc: Patrick Massett, John Zinman,
Simon West, Sara B Cooper,
Mike Werb, Michael Colleary
d: Simon West
lp: Angelina Jolie, Jon Voight,
Noah Taylor, Iain Glen,
Daniel Craig, Christopher Barrie,
Julian Rhind-Tutt, Leslie Phillips

Wit (TV)
p: Simon Bosanquet
sc: Mike Nichols, Emma Thompson
d: Mike Nichols
lp: Emma Thompson,
Christopher Lloyd, Eileen Atkins,
Audra McDonald, Harold Pinter

Dinotopia (TV series, 3 episodes)
p: William P Cartlidge,
Dusty Symonds
sc: Simon Moore
d: Marco Brambilla
lp: Tyrone Leitso, Wentworth Miller,
Katie Carr, Jim Carter,
David Thewlis, Stuart Wilson,
Alice Krige, Colin Salmon

Last Orders
p: Fred Schepisi, Elisabeth Robinson
sc: Fred Schepisi
d: Fred Schepisi
lp: Michael Caine, Tom Courtenay,
David Hemmings, Bob Hoskins,
Helen Mirren, Ray Winstone

Ma Femme est une Actrice
p: Claude Berri
sc: Yvan Attal
d: Yvan Attal
lp: Charlotte Gainsbourg, Yvan Attal,
Terence Stamp, Noémie Lvovsky,
Laurent Bateau, Ludivine Sagnier

Revelation
p: Jonathan Woolf, Stuart Urban
sc: Stuart Urban
d: Stuart Urban
lp: Terence Stamp, James D'Arcy,
Natasha Wightman,
Liam Cunningham, Derek Jacobi
Heathcote Williams

Mrs Caldicot's Cabbage War
p: Andy Birmingham
sc: Malcolm Stone
d: Ian Sharp
lp: Pauline Collins, John Alderton,
Isla Blair, Paul Freeman,
Martin Jarvis, Tony Robinson,
Terence Rigby, Wanda Wentham

**Jack and the Beanstalk:
The Real Story** (TV)
p: Thomas G Smith
sc: Jim V Hart
d: Brian Henson
lp: Matthew Modine,
Vanessa Redgrave, Mia Sara,
Daryl Hannah, Jon Voight

Thursday the 12th (TV)
p: Paula Milne
sc: Paula Milne
d: Charles Beeson
lp: Ciarán Hinds, Maria Doyle,
Elizabeth McGovern, Peter Vaughan

Play
p: Tim Bricknell, Michael Colgan,
Alan Moloney
sc: Samuel Beckett
d: Anthony Minghella
lp: Alan Rickman,
Kristin Scott Thomas,
Juliet Stevenson

Hornblower
(TV series, 2 episodes)
p: Andrew Benson
sc: TR Bowen
d: Andrew Grieve
lp: Ioan Gruffudd, Robert Lindsay,
David Warner, Nicholas Jones,
Paul McGann, Jamie Bamber

One Foot in the Grave
(TV series, part)
p: Jonathan P Llewellyn
sc: David Renwick
d: Christine Gernon
lp: Richard Wilson, Annette Crosbie

Queen of Swords (TV series, part)
p: Steve Roberts, Ken Gord
sc: Scott Kraft, James Thorpe
d: Norma Bailey, Paolo Barzman
lp: Tessie Santiago, Paulina Galvez,
Valentine Pelka, Anthony Lemke,
Peter Wingfield, Elsa Pataky

2001

Charlotte Gray
p: Sarah Curtis, Douglas Rae
sc: Jeremy Brock
d: Gillian Armstrong
lp: Cate Blanchett, Billy Crudup,
Michael Gambon,
Rupert Penry-Jones,
James Fleet, Abigail Cruttenden

K-19: The Widowmaker
p: Kathryn Bigelow,
Joni Sighvatsson, Christine Whitaker,
Edward S Feldman
sc: Christopher Kyle, Tom Stoppard,
Louis Nowra
d: Kathryn Bigelow
lp: Harrison Ford, Liam Neeson,
Peter Sarsgaard, Joss Ackland,
John Shrapnel, Donald Sumpter

Miranda
p: Laurence Bowen
sc: Rob Young, Abi Morgan
d: Marc Munden
lp: Christine Ricci, John Simm,
Kyle MacLachlan, John Hurt

Below
p: Sue Baden-Powell,
Darren Aronononofsky, Eric Watson
sc: Susan Sussman,
Darren Aronononofsky, David Twohy
d: David Twohy
lp: Matt Davis, Bruce Greenwood,
Olivia Williams, Holt McCallany,
Jason Flemyng, Dexter Fletcher

The Hours
p: Scott Rudin, Robert Fox
sc: David Hare
d: Stephen Daldry
lp: Nicole Kidman, Julianne Moore,
Meryl Streep, Stephen Dillane,
Miranda Richardson, George Loftus

Iris
p: Robert Fox, Scott Rudin
sc: Richard Eyre, Charles Wood
d: Richard Eyre
lp: Judi Dench, Jim Broadbent,
Kate Winslet, Hugh Bonneville,
Penelope Wilton, Juliet Aubrey

Planet of the Apes (part)
p: Richard D Zanuck
sc: William Broyles Jr,
Lawrence Konner,
Mark Rosenthal, Charles Wicker
d: Tim Burton
lp: Mark Wahlberg, Tim Roth,
Helena Bonham Carter,
Michael Clarke Duncan,
Kris Kristofferson, Estella Warren,
Paul Giamatti, Charlton Heston

Stranded (TV)
p: Dyson Lovell
sc: Greg Dinner, Dominic Minghella,
Chris Harrald, Anton Diether
d: Charles Beeson
lp: Liam Cunningham, Brana Bajic,
Roger Allam, Jesse Spencer

The Seventh Stream (TV)
p: David A Rosemont
sc: John Gray
d: John Gray
lp: Scott Glenn, Saffron Burrows,
Eammon Morrissey, Joseph Kelly,
John Lynch, Fiona Shaw

Lenny Henry in Pieces
(TV series, 6 episodes)
p: Lucy Robinson
d: Ed Bye
lp: Lenny Henry, Omid Djalili,
Tony Gardner, Roger Griffiths

**Jonathan Creek:
Satan's Chimney** (TV)
p: Verity Lambert
sc: David Renwick
d: Sandy Johnson
lp: Alan Davies, Julia Sawalha,
Stuart Milligan, Steven Berkoff,
Mary Tamm, Bill Bailey

The Lost World (TV)
p: Christopher Hall
sc: Tony Mulholland, Adrian Hodges
d: Stuart Orme
lp: Bob Hoskins, James Fox,
Tom Ward, Matthew Rhys,
Elaine Cassidy, Peter Falk

Sirens (TV)
d: Nicholas Laughland
sc: Christopher Lang
lp: Daniela Nardini, Greg Wise,
Robert Glenister, Sarah Parish

The Queen's Nose
(TV series, 6 episodes)
p: Clive Parsons, Davina Belling,
Carol Wiseman
sc: Graham Alborough
d: Carol Wiseman, Clive Parsons
lp: Ella Jones, Dominique Moore,
Pablo Duarte, Scott Charles

Sam's Game
(TV series, 6 episodes)
p: Sue Birbeck
sc: Paul Waite
d: Tristram Shapeero
lp: Davina McCall, Ed Byrne,
Tristan Gemmill, Tameka Empson

My Family
(TV series, 13 episodes)
p: John Bartlett
sc: James Hendrie, Ian Brown,
Steve Armogida, Jim Armogida,
Andrea Solomons, Fred Barron
d: Dewi Humphries
lp: Robert Lindsay, Zoë Wanamaker,
Kris Marshall, Daniela Denby-Ashe,
Gabriel Thomson

The Car Man (TV)
p: Gordon Baskerville
sc: Matthew Bourne
d: Matthew Bourne,
Ross MacGibbon
lp: Alan Vincent, Saranne Curtin,
Will Kemp, Etta Murfitt

Dog Eat Dog (TV series)
p: Mike Agnew
d: Mick Thomas
lp: Ulrika Jonsson

The Weakest Link (TV series)
p: Eileen Herlihy, Dee Todd,
Alexandra McLeod
d: Sue McMahon, Richard Valentine
lp: Anne Robinson

Tomorrow's World Live Lab
(TV)
p: Marshall Corwin
lp: Peter Snow, Philippa Forrester

Shafted (TV series)
p: Phil Parsons
d: Mick Thomas
lp: Robert Kilroy-Silk

Survivor (TV series, 20 episodes)
p: Nigel Lythgoe
d: Nigel Lythgoe
lp: Mark Austin

2002

Die Another Day
p: Michael G Wilson,
Barbara Broccoli
sc: Neal Purvis, Robert Wade
d: Lee Tamahori
lp: Pierce Brosnan, Halle Berry,
Toby Stephens, Rosamund Pike,
Rick Yune, Kenneth Tsang,
Will Yun Lee, Judi Dench

The Water Giant
p: Barry Authors, Rainer Mockert
sc: Barry Authors
d: John Henderson
lp: Bruce Greenwood, Rena Owen,
Daniel Magder, Phyllida Law,
Shane Rimmer, Tom Jackson

What a Girl Wants
p: Denise Di Novi, Bill Gerber,
Hunt Lowry
sc: Jenny Bicks, Elizabeth Chandler
d: Dennie Gordon
lp: Amanda Byrnes, Colin Firth,
Kelly Preston, Eileen Atkins

Finding Neverland (part)
p: Richard N Gladstein,
Nellie Bellflower
sc: David Magee
d: Marc Foster
lp: Johnny Depp, Kate Winslet,
Julie Christie, Radha Mitchell,
Dustin Hoffman, Freddie Highmore

**Lara Croft: Tomb Raider –
The Cradle of Life**
p: Lawrence Gordon, Lloyd Levin
sc: Dean Georgaris,
Steven E De Souza, James V Hart
d: Jan de Bont
lp: Angelina Jolie, Gerard Butler,
Ciarán Hinds, Christopher Barrie,
Noah Taylor, Djimon Hounsou

LD50
p: Alistair MacLean-Clark,
Basil Stephens
sc: Matthew McGuchan
d: Simon de Selva
lp: Katherine Towne,
Melanie Brown, Tom Hardy,
Leo Bill, Philip Winchester

Bright Young Things
p: Gina Carter, Miranda Davis
sc: Stephen Fry
d: Stephen Fry
lp: Emily Mortimer,
Stephen Campbell Moore,
James McAvoy, Michael Sheen,
David Tennant, Fenella Woolgar

My Family
(TV series, 14 episodes)
p: John Bartlett
sc: James Hendrie, Ian Brown,
Steve Armogida, Jim Armogida,
Andrea Solomons, Fred Barron
d: Dewi Humphries
lp: Robert Lindsay, Zoë Wanamaker,
Kris Marshall, Daniela Denby-Ashe,
Gabriel Thomson

Hornblower
(TV series, 2 episodes)
p: Andrew Benson
sc: Niall Leonard, Stephen Churchett
d: Andrew Grieve
lp: Ioan Gruffudd, Robert Lindsay,
Paul McGann, Lorcan Cranitch,
Tony Haygarth, Julia Sawalha,
Barbara Flynn, Paul Copley

Trial and Retribution
(TV series, 4 episodes)
p: Lynda La Plant
sc: Lynda La Plant
d: Aisling Walsh, Ferdinand Fairfax
lp: David Hayman, Kate Buffery,
Dorian Lough, Dermot Crowley,
Sean Chapman, Jacqueline Tong

Wild West (TV series, 6 episodes)
p: Paul Schlesinger
sc: Simon Nye
d: Jonathan Gershfield
lp: Dawn French, Catherine Tate,
Ann Marie Duff, Richard Mylan

Jeffrey Archer – The Truth (TV)
p: Chrissy Skinns
sc: Guy Jenkin
d: Guy Jenkin
lp: Damian Lewis, Greta Scacchi,
Richard Wilson, Ben Miller,
Emily Mortimer, Polly Walker,
Richard Griffiths, Gary Lineker

The Weakest Link (TV series)
p: Eileen Herlihy, Dee Todd,
Alexandra McLeod
d: Sue McMahon, Richard Valentine
lp: Anne Robinson

Dog Eat Dog (TV series)
p: Mike Agnew
d: Mick Thomas
lp: Ulrika Jonsson

The Chair (TV series)
p: Suzy Lamb
d: Jonathan Glazer
lp: John McEnroe

2003

Cargo
p: Andi Reiss, Karen Vaughan
sc: Andi Reiss, Tudor Jones
d: Andi Reiss
lp: Daniela Nardini,
Heathcote Williams, Velibor Topic

Thunderbirds
p: Tim Bevan, Eric Fellner,
Mark Huffam
sc: William Osborne,
Michael McCullers, Peter Hewitt
d: Jonathan Frakes
lp: Bill Paxton, Anthony Edwards,
Sophia Myles, Ron Cook,
Lex Shrapnel, Philip Winchester,
Brady Corbet, Ben Kingsley

Tooth
p: Susie Brooks-Smith,
Zygi Kamasa, Simon Franks
sc: Edouard Nammour,
Piers Fletcher, Simon Franks,
Zygi Kamasa
d: Edouard Nammour
lp: Harry Enfield, Vinnie Jones,
Stephen Fry, Jim Broadbent,
Tim Dutton, Sally Phillips,
Jerry Hall, Richard E Grant

New Captain Scarlet
(TV series, 13 episodes)
p: Gerry Anderson
sc: Phil Ford, John Brown,
Brian Finch
d: David Lane, Mark Woollard,
Dominic Lavery
lp: Wayne Forester, Emma Tate,
Robbie Stevens, Mike Hayley,
Jules de Jongh, Nigel Plaskitt,
Julia Brahms, Jeremy Hitchen

Chasing Liberty
p: Broderick Johnson,
Andrew A Kosove, David Parfitt
sc: Derek Guiley,
David Schneiderman
d: Andy Cadiff
lp: Mandy Moore, Matthew Goode,
Jeremy Piven, Annabella Sciorra,
Caroline Goodall, Mark Harmon

Double Zéro
p: Thomas Langmann
sc: Matt Alexander
d: Gérard Pirès
lp: Éric Judor, Ramsy Bedia,
Édouard Baer,
Georgianna Robertson,
François Chattot, Didier Flamand

King Arthur
p: Jerry Bruckheimer
sc: David Franzoni,
John Lee Hancock
d: Antoine Fuqua
lp: Clive Owen, Keira Knightley,
Ioan Gruffudd, Stellan Skarsgard,
Stephen Dillane, Ray Winstone

Ripley Under Ground
p: Michael Ohoven, William Vince,
Marco Mehlitz, Stephen Ujlaki,
Antoine de Cermont Tonnerre
sc: William Blake Herron,
Donald E Westlake
d: Roger Spottiswoode
lp: Barry Pepper, Jacinda Barrett,
Tom Wilkinson, Willem Dafoe

The Phantom of the Opera
p: Andrew Lloyd Webber
sc: Andrew Lloyd Webber,
Joel Schumacher, Richard Stilgoe
d: Joel Schumacher
lp: Gerard Butler, Emmy Rossum,
Patrick Wilson, Miranda Richardson,
Simon Callow, Ciarán Hinds

Ladies in Lavender
p: Nicolas Brown,
Elizabeth Karlsen, Nik Powell
sc: Charles Dance
d: Charles Dance
lp: Judi Dench, Maggie Smith,
Natascha McElhone,
Miriam Margolyes, David Warner,
Daniel Brühl, Freddie Jones

Alexander
p: Thomas Schühly, Jon Kilik,
Iain Smith, Moritz Borman
sc: Oliver Stone, Christopher Kyle,
Laeta Kalogridis
d: Oliver Stone
lp: Colin Farrell, Angelina Jolie,
Val Kilmer, Christopher Plummer,
Jared Leto, Rosario Dawson,
Anthony Hopkins, Brian Blessed

Alfie
p: Charles Shyer, Elaine Pope
sc: Elaine Pope, Charles Shyer
d: Charles Shyer
lp: Jude Law, Marisa Tomei,
Omar Epps, Nia Long,
Jane Krakowski, Sienna Miller,
Susan Saranson, Renée Taylor

Spooks (TV series, 10 episodes)
p: Simon Crawford Collins
sc: David Wolstencroft,
Howard Brenton, Matthew Graham,
Simon Mirren, Steve Bailie,
Ben Richards
d: Bharat Nalluri, Rob Bailey,
Justin Chadwick, Ciaran Donnelly,
Sam Miller
lp: Matthew Macfadyen,
Keeley Hawes, David Oyelowo,
Peter Firth, Hugh Simon,
Nicola Walker

My Family
(TV series, 14 episodes)
p: John Bartlett
sc: James Hendrie, Ian Brown,
Steve Armogida, Jim Armogida,
Fred Barron and others
d: Dewi Humphries
lp: Robert Lindsay, Zoë Wanamaker,
Kris Marshall, Daniela Denby-Ashe,
Gabriel Thomson

Auf Wiedersehen, Pet
(TV series, 6 episodes)
p: Chrissy Skinns
sc: Dick Clement, Ian La Frenais
d: Maurice Phillips,
David Innes Edwards
lp: Tim Healy, Kevin Whatley,
Timothy Spall, Jimmy Nail,
Christopher Fairbank, Pat Roach

Dead Ringers
(TV series, 8 episodes)
p: Bill Dare, Caroline Norris,
Gareth Edwards
sc: Tom Jamieson, Nev Fountain,
Jon Holmes and others
d: Jonathan Gershfield, Pati Marr
lp: Jon Culshaw, Jan Ravens,
Mark Perry, Kevin Connelly,
Phil Cornwell

The Catherine Tate Show
(TV series, 6 episodes)
p: Geoffrey Perkins
sc: Catherine Tate, Aschlin Ditta
Derren Litten and others
d: Gordon Anderson
lp: Catherine Tate, Derren Litten,
Mathew Horne, Ella Kenion,
Jonathan McGuinness, Niky Wardley

The Weakest Link (TV series)
p: Eileen Herlihy, Dee Todd,
Alexandra McLeod
d: Sue McMahon, Richard Valentine
lp: Anne Robinson

Henry VIII (TV)
p: Francis Hopkinson
sc: Pete Morgan
d: Pete Travis
lp: Joss Ackland, Sid Mitchell,
Ray Winstone, Assumpta Serna,
David Suchet, Charles Dance

Rescue Robots
(TV series, 6 episodes)
p: Mentorn Barraclough Carey
lp: Anna Williamson

2004

Beyond the Sea (part)
p: Arthur E Friedman,
Andy Paterson, Jan Fantl,
Kevin Spacey
sc: Kevin Spacey, Lewis Colick
d: Kevin Spacey
lp: Kevin Spacey, Kate Bosworth,
John Goodman, Bob Hoskins,
Brenda Blethyn, Greta Scacchi

The Chronicles of Riddick (part)
p: Steve Kroopf, Vin Diesel
sc: David Twohy
d: David Twohy
lp: Vin Diesel, Colm Feore,
Thandie Newton, Judi Dench,
Karl Urban, Alexa Davalos,
Linus Roache, Keith David

Nanny McPhee
p: Lindsay Doran, Tim Bevan,
Eric Fellner
sc: Emma Thompson
d: Kirk Jones
lp: Emma Thompson, Colin Firth,
Kelly Macdonald, Derek Jacobi,
Patrick Barlow, Celia Imrie,
Imelda Staunton, Angela Lansbury

**Charlie and the
Chocolate Factory**
p: Brad Grey, Richard D Zanuck
sc: John August
d: Tim Burton
lp: Johnny Depp, Freddie Highmore,
David Kelly, Helena Bonham Carter,
Noah Taylor, Missi Pile, James Fox,
Deep Roy, Christopher Lee

**Harry Potter and the
Goblet of Fire** *(part)*
p: David Heyman
sc: Steve Kloves
d: Mike Newell
lp: Daniel Radcliffe, Rupert Grint,
Emma Watson, Robbie Coltrane,
Ralph Fiennes, Michael Gambon

Stoned *(part)*
p: Finola Dwyer, Stephen Woolley
sc: Neal Purvis, Robert Wade,
Frank Budgen
d: Stephen Woolley
lp: Leo Gregory, Paddy Considine,
David Morrissey, Tuva Novotny

Revolver *(part)*
p: Luc Besson, Virginie Silla
sc: Guy Ritchie, Luc Besson
d: Guy Ritchie
lp: Jason Statham, Ray Liotta,
Vincent Pastore, André Benjamin

Kinky Boots *(part)*
p: Nicholas Barton,
Suzanne Mackie, Peter Ettedgui
sc: Geoff Deane, Tim Firth
d: Julian Jarrold
lp: Joel Edgerton, Chiwetel Ejiofor,
Sarah-Jane Potts, Nick Frost

The Descent
p: Christian Colson
sc: Neil Marshall
d: Neil Marshall
lp: Sarah MacDonald,
Natalie Mendoza, Alex Reid,
Saskia Mulder, Nora Jane Noone

The Fete
p: Jack Arbuthnott
sc: Paul Farrell
d: Ville Jankerri
lp: Jane Gurnett, Nicky Henson

Road to Damascus
p: John Parr
sc: Chris Munro, John Parr
d: Chris Munro
lp: Paul Bigley, Max Cane

Spooks *(TV series, 10 episodes)*
p: Andrew Woodhead
sc: Howard Brenton, Rupert Walters,
Ben Richards, David Wolstencroft,
Raymond Koury
d: Jonny Campbell, Cilla Ware,
Justin Chadwick, Bill Anderson,
Alrick Riley
lp: Rupert Penry-Jones,
Matthew Macfadyen, Keeley Hawes,
David Oyelowo, Peter Firth,
Hugh Simon, Nicola Walker

Jonathan Creek
(TV series, 6 episodes)
p: Verity Lambert
sc: David Renwick
d: Christine Gernon, Sandy Johnson
lp: Alan Davies, Julia Sawalha,
Adrian Edmonson, Stuart Milligan

My Family
(TV series, 14 episodes)
p: John Bartlett
sc: James Hendrie, Ian Brown,
Steve Armogida, Jim Armogida,
Andrea Solomons, Darin Henry,
James Cary, Sophie Hetherington
d: Dewi Humphries
lp: Robert Lindsay, Zoë Wanamaker,
Kris Marshall, Daniela Denby-Ashe,
Gabriel Thomson

My Dad's the Prime Minister
(TV series, 7 episodes)
p: Matthew Francis
sc: Ian Hislop, Nick Newman
d: Juliet May
lp: Robert Bathurst, Carla Mendonca,
Joe Prospero, Emma Sackville,
Jasper Britton, Marcia Warren

Auf Wiedersehen, Pet
(TV series, 2 episodes)
p: Joy Spink
sc: Dick Clement, Ian La Frenais
d: Sandy Johnson
lp: Tim Healy, Kevin Whatley,
Timothy Spall, Jimmy Nail,
Christopher Fairbank, Noel Clarke

Dead Ringers
(TV series, 6 episodes)
p: Bill Dare, Caroline Norris
sc: Tom Jamieson, Nev Fountain,
Jon Holmes and others
d: Jonathan Gershfield, Pati Marr
lp: Jon Culshaw, Jan Ravens,
Mark Perry, Kevin Connelly,
Phil Cornwell

Brainiac: Science Abuse
(TV series, 13 episodes)
p: Mike Griffiths, Lindsay Keith,
Grant Shearer, Tom Thompson
d: Peter Eyre, Mike Griffiths,
Lindsay Keith, Grant Shearer,
Tom Thompson
lp: Richard Hammond, Jon Tickle,
Tom Pringle, Charlotte Hudson

The Weakest Link *(TV series)*
p: Eileen Herlihy, Dee Todd,
Alexandra McLeod
d: Sue McMahon, Richard Valentine
lp: Anne Robinson

According to Bex
(TV series, 6 episodes)
p: Alex Walsh-Taylor
sc: Fred Barron, Julia Barron,
Katie Douglas, Danny Robins,
Dan Tetsell
d: Dewi Humphries
lp: Jessica Stevenson, Greg Wise,
Raquel Cassidy, Oliver Chris

All About Me
(TV series, 8 episodes)
p: Richard Boden
sc: Steven Knight, Gary Lawson,
John Phelps and others
d: Richard Boden
lp: Jasper Carrott, Amanda Root,
Jamil Dhillon, Ryan Cartwright

Planet Cook *(TV series)*
p: Nigel Stone
sc: Tommy Donbavand,
Simon Grover
d: Iain McLean
lp: Kevin Woodford

X-Perimental
(TV series, 13 episodes)
p: Martyn Day
d: Martyn Day
lp: Simon Grant, Jane Farnham

Restoration *(TV series)*
p: Paul Couselant
d: Paul Couselant
lp: Griff Rhys Jones,
Marianne Suhr, Ptolemy Dean

20th Century Roadshow
*(TV series, 1 episode recorded
at Pinewood)*
p: John Miller
d: Mark Ashton, Amanda Fidler,
Liz Igoe, Alex Parkinson
lp: Alan Titchmarsh

Strictly Ice Dancing *(TV)*
p: Izzie Pick
d: Alex Rudzinski
lp: Bruce Forsyth, Tess Daly

2005

New Captain Scarlet
(TV series, 13 episodes)
p: Gerry Anderson
sc: Phil Ford, John Brown
d: David Lane, Mark Woollard,
Dominic Lavery
lp: Wayne Forester, Emma Tate,
Robbie Stevens, Mike Hayley,
Jules de Jongh, Nigel Plaskitt,
Julia Brahms, Jeremy Hitchen

Goal! *(part)*
p: Mike Jefferies, Matt Barrelle,
Mark Huffam
sc: Dick Clement, Ian La Frenais
d: Danny Cannon
lp: Kuno Becker, Alessandro Nivola,
Anna Friel, Stephen Dillane,
Gary Lewis, Kieran O'Brien,
Sean Pertwee, Marcel Iures

Marie Antoinette
p: Sofia Coppola, Ross Katz
sc: Sofia Coppola
d: Sofia Coppola
lp: Kirsten Dunst, Marianne Faithfull,
Steve Coogan, Clara Braiman,
Mélodie Berenfeld, Judy Davis

Extras *(TV series, 6 episodes)*
p: Charlie Hanson
sc: Stephen Merchant, Ricky Gervais
d: Ricky Gervais, Stephen Merchant
lp: Ricky Gervais, Ashley Jensen,
Stephen Merchant,
Shaun Williamson

Basic Instinct 2
p: Mario F Kassar, Andrew G Vajna,
Joel B Michaels
sc: Leora Barish, Henry Bean
d: Michael Caton-Jones
lp: Sharon Stone, David Morrissey,
Charlotte Rampling, David Thewlis,
High Dancy, Flora Montgomery

Alien Autopsy *(part)*
p: William Davies,
Barnaby Thompson
sc: William Davies
d: Jonny Campbell
lp: Declan Donnelly, Ant McPartlin,
Bill Pullman, Harry Dean Stanton,
Omid Djalili, Jimmy Carr

V for Vendetta *(part)*
p: Joel Silver, Andy Wachowski,
Larry Wachowski, Grant Hill
sc: Andy Wachowski,
Larry Wachowski
d: James McTeigue
lp: Natalie Portman, Hugo Weaving,
Stephen Rea, Stephen Fry,
John Hurt, Tim Pigott-Smith

I Could Never Be Your Woman
p: Cerise Hallam, Alan Latham,
Philippe Martinez
sc: Amy Heckerling
d: Amy Heckerling
lp: Michelle Pfeiffer, Paul Rudd,
Tracey Ullman, Fred Willard,
Henry Winkler, Saoirse Ronan

The Da Vinci Code *(part)*
p: Brian Grazer, John Calley
sc: Akiva Goldsman
d: Ron Howard
lp: Tom Hanks, Audrey Tautou,
Ian McKellen, Jean Reno,
Paul Bettany, Alfred Molina

Stormbreaker *(part)*
p: Steve Christian, Andreas Grosch,
Marc Samuelson, Peter Samuelson
sc: Anthony Horowitz
d: Geoffrey Sax
lp: Alex Pettyfer, Mickey Rourke,
Bill Nighy, Alicia Silverstone,
Stephen Fry, Damian Lewis

Last of the Summer Wine
(TV series, 9 episodes)
p: Alan JW Bell
sc: Roy Clarke
d: Alan JW Bell
lp: Peter Sallis, Frank Thornton,
Jane Freeman, Kathy Staff

The Line of Beauty
(TV series, 3 episodes)
p: Kate Lewis
sc: Andrew Davies
d: Saul Dibb
lp: Dan Stevens, Hayley Atwell,
Tim McInnerny, Alice Krige,
Alex Wyndham, Oliver Coleman

Children of Men
p: Marc Abraham, Eric Newman,
Hilary Shor, Iain Smith, Tony Smith
sc: Alfonso Cuarón,
Timothy J. Sexton, David Arata,
Mark Fergus, Hawk Ostby
d: Alfonso Cuarón
lp: Clive Owen, Julianne Moore,
Michael Caine, Chiwetal Ejiofor,
Charlie Hunnam, Pam Ferris,
Claire-Hope Ashitey, Danny Huston

United 93 *(part)*
p: Tim Bevan, Eric Fellner,
Lloyd Levin
sc: Paul Greengrass
d: Paul Greengrass
lp: Christian Clemenson,
Trish Gates, David Alan Basche,
Cheyenne Jackson, Opal Alladin

Cashback
p: Sean Ellis, Lene Bausager
sc: Sean Ellis
d: Sean Ellis
lp: Sean Biggerstaff, Emilia Fox,
Shaun Evans, Michelle Ryan

Sixty Six (part)
p: Tim Bevan, Eric Fellner,
Elizabeth Karlsen
sc: Bridget O'Connor,
Peter Straughan
d: Paul Weiland
lp: Eddie Marsan,
Helena Bonham Carter,
Stephen Rea, Catherine Tate

Hibernation
p: Andy Gordon, Christos Michaels
sc: John Williams
d: John Williams
sc: Adam Paroussos, Peter Reynolds,
Sonny Rooney

Lights2
p: Marcus Dillstone
sc: Marcus Dillstone
d: Marcus Dillstone
lp: John Mills, Oreke Mosheshe

Zoltan the Great
p: Thomas Benski
sc: Robert Samuels
d: Robert Samuels
lp: Paul Conway, Jenny Foulds,
Niall Greig Fulton, Saeed Jaffrey

Footprints in the Snow (TV)
p: Mark Bentley
sc: Nigel Williams
d: Richard Spence
lp: Caroline Quentin,
Kevin Whatley, Philip Davis,
Kerry Fox, Annette Crosbie

Riot at the Rite (TV)
p: David Snodin
sc: Kevin Elyot
d: Andy Wilson
lp: Adam Garcia, Alex Jennings,
Aiden McArdle, Rachael Sterling

Fantabulosa! (TV)
p: Ben Evans
sc: Martyn Hesford
d: Andy de Emmony
sc: Michael Sheen, Cheryl Campbell,
Peter Wright, Beatie Edney

To the Ends of the Earth
(TV series, 3 episodes)
p: Lynn Horsford
sc: Tony Bagsgallop, Leigh Jackson
d: David Attwood
lp: Benedict Cumberbatch,
Jared Harris

Dead Ringers
(TV series, 6 episodes)
p: Bill Dare, Caroline Norris
sc: Tom Jamieson, Nev Fountain,
Jon Holmes and others
d: Jonathan Gershfield, Pati Marr
lp: Jon Culshaw, Jan Ravens,
Mark Perry, Kevin Connelly,
Phil Cornwell

A Bear's Tail
(TV series, 6 episodes)
p: Ben Palmer
sc: Leigh Francis
d: Ben Palmer
lp: Leigh Francis, Patsy Kensit,
Sean Pertwee, Yasmin Kerr

Hollywood Greats (TV series)
d: Hans Petch
p: Pauline Law
lp: Jonathan Ross

**Two Pints of Lager
and a Packet of Crisps**
(TV series, 10 episodes)
p: Helen Williams
sc: Susan Nickson, Daniel Peak
d: Gareth Carrivick
lp: Ralf Little, Will Mellor,
Natalie Casey, Sheridan Smith,
Kathryn Drysdale

Planet Cook (TV series)
d: Iain McLean
sc: Tommy Donbavand,
Simon Grover
p: Nigel Stone
lp: Kevin Woodford

Brainiac: Science Abuse
(TV series, 9 episodes)
d: Peter Eyre, Mike Griffiths,
Lindsay Keith, Grant Shearer,
Tom Thompson
p: Mike Griffiths, Lindsay Keith,
Grant Shearer, Tom Thompson
lp: Richard Hammond, Jon Tickle

Foyle's War: Bad Blood
(TV, part)
p: Jill Green, Simon Passmore
sc: Anthony Horowitz
d: Jeremy Silberston
lp: Michael Kitchen,
Anthony Howell,
Honeysuckle Weeks, Philip Franks

Little Britain (TV series, part)
p: Myfanwy Moore, Geoff Posner
sc: Matt Lucas, David Walliams
d: Declan Lowney
lp: Matt Lucas, David Walliams

Avid Merrion's XXXmas Special
(TV)
p: Ben Palmer
sc: Leigh Francis, Ben Palmer
d: Ben Palmer
lp: Leigh Francis,
Barunka O'Shaughnessy

2006

Penelope
p: Jennifer Simpson,
Scott Steindorff, Reese Witherspoon
sc: Leslie Caveny
d: Mark Palansky
lp: Christina Ricci, James McAvoy,
Catherine O'Hara,
Reese Witherspoon,
Peter Dinklage, Richard E Grant

**Doctor Who: The Impossible
Planet/The Satan Pit**
(TV series, part)
p: Phil Collinson
sc: Matt Jones
d: James Strong
lp: David Tennant, Billie Piper,
Will Thorp, MyAnna Buring

X-Men – The Last Stand (part)
p: Lauren Schuler Donner,
Ralph Winter
sc: Zac Penn, Simon Kinberg
d: Brett Ratner
lp: Hugh Jackman, Halle Berry,
Ian McKellan, Famke Janssen,
Anna Paquin, Kelsey Grammer,
James Marsden, Patrick Stewart

Death Wish Live
(TV series, 5 episodes)
p: Anthony Owen, Justin Gorman,
Paul Hupfield, Simon Mills
d: Ben Cohen
lp: Alex Zane

The Walker
p: Deepak Nayar
sc: Paul Schrader
d: Paul Schrader
lp: Woody Harrelson,
Kristin Scott Thomas, Lauren Bacall,
Ned Beatty, Moritz Bleibtreu,
Willem Dafoe, Lily Tomlin

Stardust
p: Lorenzo de Bonaventura,
Michael Dreyer, Neil Gaiman,
Matthew Vaughn
sc: Jane Goldman, Matthew Vaughn
d: Matthew Vaughn
lp: Charlie Cox, Claire Danes,
Robert De Niro, Sienna Miller,
Michelle Pfeiffer, Jason Flemyng,
Henry Cavill, Rupert Everett

Casino Royale
p: Michael G Wilson,
Barbara Brocolli
sc: Robert Wade, Neal Purvis,
Paul Haggis
d: Martin Campbell,
lp: Daniel Craig, Eva Green,
Mads Mikkelsen, Judi Dench,
Caterina Murino, Jeffrey Wright,
Giancarlo Gianini, Ivana Milicevic

Atonement
p: Tim Bevan, Eric Fellner,
Paul Webster
sc: Christopher Hampton
d: Joe Wright
lp: Keira Knightley, James McAvoy,
Romola Garai, Saoirse Ronan,
Brenda Blethyn, Vanessa Redgrave

Extras (TV series, 6 episodes)
p: Charlie Hanson
sc: Stephen Merchant, Ricky Gervais
d: Ricky Gervais, Stephen Merchant
lp: Ricky Gervais, Ashley Jensen,
Stephen Merchant

1408
p: Lorenzo de Bonaventura
sc: Scott Alexander,
Matt Greenberg, Larry Karaszewski
d: Mikael Hafström
lp: John Cusack, Samuel L Jackson,
Mary McCormack, Len Cariou,
Andrew Lee Potts, Walter Lewis

Last of the Summer Wine
(TV series, 5 episodes)
p: Alan JW Bell
sc: Roy Clarke
d: Alan JW Bell
lp: Peter Sallis, Frank Thornton,
Jane Freeman, Kathy Staff

Eragon (part)
p: John Davis, Wyck Godfrey,
Adam Goodman
sc: Peter Buchman,
Lawrence Konner, Mark Rosenthal,
Jesse Wigutow
d: Stefen Fangmeier
lp: Edward Speleers,
Sienne Guillory, Garrett Hedlund,
Djimon Hounsou, Jeremy Irons,
John Malkovich, Robert Carlyle

Back in Business
p: Neil Gardiner
sc: Chris Munro
d: Chris Munro
lp: Martin Kemp, Chris Barrie,
Dennis Waterman, Brian Blessed,
Stefan Booth, Joanna Taylor

Life & Lyrics
p: Esther Douglas, Fiona Neilson
sc: Ken Williams
d: Richard Laxton
lp: Ashley Walters, Louise Rose,
Christopher Steward, Cat Simmons,
Akemnji Ndifornyen, Beau Baptiste,
Patrick Regis, Alexis Rodney

**Windkracht 10 –
Koksijde Rescue** (part)
p: Hilde De Laere, Erwin Provoost
sc: Pierre De Clercq
d: Hans Herbots
lp: Rick Symons, Veerle Baetens,
Koen de bouw, Stan Van Samang,
Warre Borgmans, Ludo Busschots,
Jelle Cleymans, Axel Daeseleire

My Family (TV series, 7 episodes)
p: John Bartlett
sc: Fred Barron, Andrea Solomons,
Tom Leopold, Steve Armogida,
Jim Armogida and others
d: Dewi Humphries
lp: Robert Lindsay, Zoë Wanamaker,
Kris Marshall, Daniela Denby-Ashe,
Gabriel Thomson

The Weakest Link (TV series)
p: Eileen Herlihy, Dee Todd,
Alexandra McLeod
d: Sue McMahon, Richard Valentine
lp: Anne Robinson

The Apprentice
(TV series, 12 episodes, titles)
p: James Bainbridge,
Daniel Adamson
d: James Bainbridge,
Andy Devonshire, Beth Dicks,
Danielle Graham, Alf Lawrie
lp: Alan Sugar

Brainiac: Science Abuse
(TV series, 9 episodes)
d: Peter Eyre, Mike Griffiths,
Lindsay Keith, Grant Shearer,
Tom Thompson
p: Mike Griffiths, Lindsay Keith,
Grant Shearer, Tom Thompson
lp: Richard Hammond, Jon Tickle

The Bourne Ultimatum
p: Patrick Crowley, Frank Marshall,
Paul Sandberg
sc: Tony Gilroy, Tom Stoppard
d: Paul Greengrass
lp: Matt Damon, Julia Stiles,
Joan Allen, David Strathairn,
Paddy Considine, Edgar Ramirez

Fred Claus
p: David Dobkin, Jessie Nelson
sc: Dan Fogelman, Jessie Nelson
d: David Dobkin
lp: Vince Vaughn, Paul Giametti,
John Michael Higgins,
Kevin Spacey, Minja Filipovic

Abdication, The 218
Abicair, Shirley 66
Abominable Snowman, The 211
Above Us the Waves 97, 210
Abrahams, Jim 158
Absolution 220
According to Bex (TV series) 229
Ackland, Noreen 36-37, 87
Ackland-Snow, Brian 173
Across the Bridge 79
Act of Will (TV) 222
Action Comics (periodical) 149
Adam and Evil 71
Adam, Ken 110, 112-113, 114-115, 117, 119, 131, 136, 191
Adams, Maud 139
Addison, John 136
Adler, Larry 53
Adventurers, The 208
Adventures of Baron Munchausen, The 222
Agent 8 3/4 125
Air America 222
Airplane 158
Alan Parker Film Company 140
Alcott, Arthur 49
Aldred, John 27-28, 29, 30, 31
Alexander 194, 228
Alexander, Terence 69
Alfie 196, 228
Alice in Russialand (TV) 223
Alien Autopsy 229
Alien 3 166, 222
Aliens 159, 160, 221
All About Me (TV series) 229
All Coppers Are... 217
All For Mary 60-61, 210
All Night Long 212
All Over the Town 208
Allen, Irving 55-56, 109
Allen, Woody 130
Allied Film-Makers 87, 90, 93
Alligator Named Daisy, An 59, 142, 210
'Allo 'Allo (TV series) 165
Always a Bride 209
Alwyn, William 31
Alyn, Kirk 149
Amazing Mr Blunden, The 136, 218
Ambler, Eric 45
American Academy 70th anniversary 57
American Academy Awards (Oscars)
  Adam, Ken 119
  Barry Lyndon 119
  Black Narcissus 35
  Boulting, Roy 30
  Box, John 171
  Bullitt 30
  Childs, Martin 178
  Craig, Stuart 175
  Desert Victory 30
  Easdale, Brian 36
  Fiddler on the Roof 135, 178
  Field, Roy 152
  Foster, Jodie 140
  Keller, Frank P 30
  Lamont, Peter 113, 122
  Madness of King George, The 119
  Meddings, Derek 152
  Morris, Oswald 135
  Red Shoes, The 36
  Riddle, Nelson 138
  Staffell, Charles 41
  Titanic 113
  Williams, John 135
  Winter, Vincent 57
American Academy nominations
  Adam, Ken 119
  Addison, John 136
  Aldred, John 30
  Alien 3 166
  Annakin, Ken 127
  Bacharach, Burt 130
  Caine, Michael 136
  Chitty Chitty Bang Bang 131

Courtenay, Tom 158
Dresser, The 158
Ferretti, Dante 169
Finney, Albert 158
Frey, Leonard 135
Goldenthal, Elliot 169
Harwood, Ronald 158
Hasford, Gustav 159
Herr, Michael 159
Interview With the Vampire 168-169
Jewison, Norman 135
Kim, Stanley 125
Legend 159
Little Shop of Horrors 159
Mankiewicz, Joseph 136
Mary Queen of Scots 30
Mathieson, Muir 53
Olivier, Laurence 136
Pygmalion 24
Red Shoes, The 36
Topol 135
Wisdom, Norman 71
Yates, Peter 158
Anderson, A F B 15
Anderson, Bob 171
Anderson, Gerry 135, 143, 170, 196-7
Anderson, Janet 185
Anderson, Michael 130, 173
Anderson, Paul 174
Anderson, Rona 45
Anderson, Sylvia 135, 143
Andress, Ursula 130, 147, 156
Andrews, Harry 71
Andrews, Julie 156
Androcles and the Lion 71
Angel, Daniel 168
Anglo-Amalgamated 93, 98, 102
Angry Silence, The 93
Annakin, Ken 47, 48, 49, 51-52, 54, 57, 59, 79, 127
Anne of the Thousand Days 216
Année dernière, L' 110
Annie: A Royal Adventure (TV) 172, 224
Anoop and the Elephant 218
Anouilh, Jean 92
Apocalypse Watch, The (TV) 173, 218
Applause (TV) 137, 218
Appointment With Venus 51, 209
Apprentice, The (TV series) 230
Apted, Michael 122-123, 183
Arabesque 214
Arabian Adventure 220
Archibald, George 33, 47, 61
Armendariz, Pedro 110-111
Armstrong, Alun 168
Armstrong, Vic 190-1
Army Film and Photography Unit 27, 28, 29
Army Film Unit 31, 204
As Long As They're Happy 58-59, 210
Asher, Robert 67, 68, 69, 71, 127
Askwith, Robin 105
Asquith, Anthony 24-25, 49, 51, 54, 85
Assassination Bureau, The 216
Assault 216
Associated British Pictures Corporation 65
Aston Martin 112-113
Astonished Heart, The 208
At the Earth's Core 141-142, 219
Atkinson, Rowan 175
Atonement 230
Attack of the Hawkmen (TV) 224
Attenborough, Lord [Richard] 31, 87, 125, 126, 178, 204
Attwooll, Hugh 51, 57
Auf Wiedersehen, Pet (TV series) 196, 228, 229
autogyro 115, 127
Avengers, The 175, 225
Avengers, The (TV series) 142, 215
Avid Merrion's XXXmas Special (TV) 230

B picture industry 43
Bacall, Lauren 137

Bacharach, Burt 130
Back in Business 230
Bad Timing 146, 220
Badel, Alan 147
Badham, John 173
Baffled! (TV) 217
BAFTA awards 66, 178
Baio, Scott 140
Baker, Hylda 136
Baker, Robert 135
Baker, Roy 61-62, 79-81, 82-83, 89, 90
Baker, Stanley 61, 62, 79
Balcon, Michael 22, 32, 52
Baldwin, Adam 159
Baldwin, Alec 166
Bambi 41
Bamford, J C 131
Band of Brothers (TV series) 185
Band of Thieves 213
Barber, Antonia 136
Bardot, Brigitte 76
Barker, Eric 69
Barnes, Alan 92
Barr, Patrick 21
Barry, John 130, 152
Basic Instinct 2 200-1, 229
Bass, Alfie 55
Bastedo, Alexandra 138
Bates, Alan 91, 147
Batman 161-162, 165, 221
Bats With Baby Faces 128
Battle of Britain 131-132, 216
Battle of the River Plate, The 59, 210
Bawdy Adventures of Tom Jones, The 219
Bax, Sir Arnold 31
Bay of Saint Michel, The 213
Beachcomber, The 209
Beaconsfield Studios 32
Bean 175-176, 225
Bean, Sean 168
Bear Island 220
Bear's Tail, A (TV series) 230
Beast in the Cellar, The 217
Beatty, Ned 158
Beatty, Robert 54
Beau Geste 102
Beauty Jungle, The 214
Beckwith, Reginald 84
Being Human 168, 223
Bell, Mary Hayley (Lady Mills) 91, 128
Below 227
Belstone Fox, The 218
Belushi, James 159
Ben-Hur 128
Bennett, Compton 54
Bentine, Michael 71
Bergin, Patrick 166-167, 173
Berkoff, Steven 155
Besson, Luc 172-173
Best British Film 1953 53
Best, Richard 19, 28, 29, 30
Bevan, Tim 194
Beyond Our Horizon 207
Beyond the Sea 228
Big Job, The 214
Big Money, The 210
Bigelow, Kathryn 187
Billington, Michael 135
Billion Dollar Brain 215
Bird, Norman 91
Birthday Girl 226
Bishop, Ed 135
Bisset, Jacqueline 130
Bitter Harvest 94, 213
Black Beauty 168, 223
Black Knight, The 55-56, 209
Black Narcissus 33, 35, 207
Black Tent, The 210
Blackmailed 208
Blackman, Honor 142, 158
Blakely, Colin 133
Blanche Fury 208
Blanchett, Cate 187
Bless This House 218

Blind Corner 214
Blockbusters (TV series) 109
Blood on Satan's Claw 171, 217
Blue Juice 224
Blue Lagoon, The 45, 208
Blue Lamp, The 75
Boehm, Carl 87
Bogarde, Sir Dirk 39, 54, 73, 74, 75-77, 79, 85, 89-90, 93, 107, 125
Bolt, Jeremy 174
Bomb in the High Street 213
Bond films 39, 93, 108-123
  changing Bond 123
  EON Bond films 123
  gadgets 111-113, 114, 116
Bond, Samantha 123
Boot, Charles 9, 11, 13, 16, 82, 157, 181
Borgnine, Ernest 158
Born to Run (TV series) 225
Borrowers, The (TV) 223
Boulting, John 29, 31, 168, 204
Boulting, Roy 29, 30, 204
Bourne Ultimatum, The 230
Bower, Martin 155
Box, Betty 49, 51, 55, 73-74, 77, 79, 85, 87, 89, 97, 106, 107, 109,125
Box, John 137, 171
Box, Muriel 59, 60, 61
Box, Sydney 49, 73, 97
Boy Who Stole a Million, The 212
Boyd, Stephen 87
Boyer, Charles 130
Boyle, Peter 155
Boys in Brown 208
Bracco, Lorraine 168
Brainiac: Science Abuse (TV series) 229, 230
Brandauer, Klaus Maria 163
Brando, Marlon 90, 129, 149, 151
Bray Studios 137
Beaconsfield Studios 98
Break the News 206
Bresslaw, Bernard 99
Bridge Too Far, A 146
Bridges, Jeff 155
Brief Encounter (TV) 218
Bright, Morris 106
Bright Young Things 193, 228
Brighton Rock 204
British & Dominion Film Corporation 18
British Comedy Awards 106
British Comedy Society 106, 107
British Federation of Women Zionists 28
British Film Day 170
British Film Institute 92
British Film Production Fund 49-50
British Lion 92
British National Films 10, 22
British/American film distribution 44
Britten, Benjamin 32
Broccoli, Albert R 55, 56, 94, 109-110, 113, 114, 117, 119, 120, 122, 130-131, 133, 142, 146, 147
Broccoli, Barbara 122, 189
Broccoli, Dana 119
Brook, Peter 130
Brosnan, Pierce 121, 190
Brown, Chip 114
Brown, Michael 117, 120
Brown, Rona 171
Browning Version, The 49, 208
Bryan, John 37-39, 68, 69
Buchanan, Jack 58-59
Buddy's Song 222
Bugsy Malone 139, 156, 219
Bull Boys, The (novel) 97
Bulldog Breed, The 69, 212
Burden, Hugh 137
Burge, Stuart 68
Burgin, Leslie 19
Burma Victory 29, 31, 207
Burroughs, Edgar Rice 141
Burton, Peter 111
Burton, Richard 89

Burton, Tim 162, 188, 192, 197
Bush Radio 51, 55
Bye Bye Baby (TV) 222
Byers, Stephen 185

Caan, James 139
Caesar and Cleopatra 25
Cahill, Martin 136
Cain, Syd 110, 157, 191
Caine, Michael 69, 126, 128, 130, 131, 136, 162, 163, 178
Calf, Anthony 163
Call Me a Cab 99
Call Me Bwana 94-95, 213
Call My Bluff (TV series) 109
Calley, John 186
Calvert, Phyllis 54
Cameron, James 159
Cameron, Ken 32
Camfield, Douglas 156
Camomile Lawn, The (TV) 222
Campbell, Martin 184, 201, 203
Campbell's Kingdom 75, 79, 211
Campus Capers 74
Candleshoe 219
Candy, John 159
Cannon Group 153
Cannon, Dyan 158
Canterbury Tale, A 33
Capra, Frank 28, 30
Captain Boycott 207
Captain Scarlet (TV series) 196-7, 228, 229
Captain's Table, The 84-85, 211
Car Man, The (TV) 227
Card, The 209
Cardiff, Jack 63
Cargill, Patrick 69
Cargo 228
Carlton Television 181
Caron, Leslie 137
Carrie 172
Carry On films 39, 57, 73, 85, 96-107, 136, 142, 177
    awards 106
    compilations 105
    dinner party scene 102-104
    exteriors at Pinewood 97
    40th anniversary gala reunion 107
    list 107
    Rogers, Peter 97
    spoofs on other films 101, 102
    title decisions 99
Carry On Abroad 217
Carry On Again Doctor 216
Carry On At Your Convenience 133, 217
Carry On Behind 218
Carry On Cabby 99, 213
Carry On Camping 104-105, 177, 216
Carry On Cleo 101-102, 214
Carry On Columbus 105-106, 166, 223
Carry On Constable 99, 212
Carry On Cowboy 99, 102, 214
Carry On Cruising 99, 213
Carry On Dallas 105
Carry On Dick 105, 218
Carry On Doctor 215
Carry On ... Don't Lose Your Head 102, 215
Carry On Down Under 105
Carry On Emmannuelle 105, 218
Carry On England 218
Carry On ... Follow That Camel 102, 215
Carry On Girls 105, 218
Carry On Henry 217
Carry On Jack 99, 214
Carry On Loving 216
Carry On Matron 217
Carry On Nurse 98-99, 211
Carry On Regardless 89, 99, 212
Carry On Screaming! 102, 215
Carry On Sergeant 98, 211
Carry On Spying 101, 214
Carry On Teacher 99, 212
Carry On Up the Jungle 216
Carry On ... Up the Khyber 102-104, 105, 216
Carstairs, John Paddy 55, 65-66, 67, 68
Carve Her Name With Pride 48, 81-82, 168, 211
Cashback 229
Casino Royale (1967) 129-130, 215
Casino Royale (2006) 201, 203, 230
Casino Royale (novel) 109, 129

Cat and Mouse 218
Catherine Tate Show, The (TV series) 228
Caton-Jones, Michael 163, 173
Cavalier of the Street, The 206
censorship controversy 135
Chaffey, Don 93
Chair, The (TV series) 228
Challenge, The 217
Challenge for Robin Hood, A 215
Challis, Christopher 133
Chandler & Co. (TV series) 223, 224
Chaplin, Charles 129
Chapman, Edward 67, 69, 77
Charlemagne (company) 136
Charles, HRH Prince 85, 87, 121
Charlie and the Chocolate Factory 192, 197, 229
Charlie Bubbles 215
Charlotte Gray 187, 227
Chasing Liberty 228
Checkpoint 61, 210
Chevalier, Maurice 92
Chicago Joe and the Showgirl 222
Children of Men 202, 229
Children's Film Foundation 44, 97
Childs, Martin 178
Chilton, Ed 139, 144, 146
Chilvers, Colin 152
Chitty Chitty Bang Bang 131, 215
Chronicles of Riddick, The 228
Churchill, Odette 81-82
CI5: The New Professionals (TV series) 226
Cimino, Michael 155
Cineguild 33, 35, 37, 45
cinema closures 51, 95
Cinema-Television concept 50-51
CinemaScope 58
Cinematograph Films Act 1927 21
Cinven 181
Circus Friends 97
Circus World (TV show) 126
Citizen Kane 178
City of Joy 222
City Under the Sea, The 214
Clair, René 52
Clark, Petula 65
Clarke, Frank 29
Clarke, Roy 177
Clary, Julian 106
Clash of the Titans 147, 220
Class Act (TV series) 224
Clayton, Jack 137
Cleese, John 123, 160, 171-172
Clemens, Brian 143
Clement, Dick 176
Cleopatra 87-89, 92, 101, 212
Clifford, Fred 15
Climbing High 207
Clockwork Orange, A 135, 217
Close Quarters 31, 207
Clouded Yellow, The 49, 73, 208
Coastal Command 31, 207
Cohen, Nat 93, 94, 102
Cohn, Harry 56
Colbert, Claudette 54
Cold Lazarus (TV series) 172, 224
Cole, George 125, 168
Collingwood, John 129
Collins, Joan 42, 89, 178
Collins, Lewis 143, 157
Columbia-TriStar 147
Command Performance 206
commercials 161
Company of Youth 42
computer generated imaging 171
Confessions films 105
Connecting Rooms 216
Connery, Sean 79, 94, 97, 110, 113-114, 115, 126, 146, 155, 163, 171, 175, 176
Connolly, Billy 176
Connor, Kenneth 98
Connor, Kevin 141-142, 144, 158, 163, 166, 173
Conspiracy of Hearts 85, 87, 212
Constellation Films 45
Consuming Passions 221
Cook, Peter 128
Cooper, Jackie 150
Cooper, Terence 130
Corbett, Harry H 102
Corbould, Chris 191
Corfield, John 10, 22
Corman, Roger 159

Cornelius, Henry 52-53
Corri, Adrienne 57
Corsican Brothers, The (TV) 221
Cotten, Joseph 155
Countess Dracula 217
Countess From Hong Kong, A 129, 215
Court Martial (TV series) 126, 214
Courtenay, Tom 158
Courville, Albert de 23
Cowan, Maurice 65, 66, 67
Coward, Noel 71
Crackerjack 207
Craig, Daniel 201, 203
Craig, Michael 77, 79, 87, 93
Craig, Stuart 175
Craigie, Jill 57, 65
Crawford, Cindy 171
Crenna, Richard 173
Cribbins, Bernard 94, 105
Crichton, Michael 146
Crime Traveller (TV series) 225
Cross, Ben 173
Cross My Heart 206
Crowe, Russell 182
Crowe, Sara 106
Crown Film Unit 27, 28, 29, 31, 32
Croydon, John 43
Crucifer of Blood (TV) 165, 222
Cruikshank, George 37
Cruise, Tom 159, 168, 171, 172, 174
Cuarón, Alfonso 202
Culley, Cliff 69
Cummins, Peggy 84
Curse of the Pink Panther 158, 220
Curtis, Dan 162
Curtis, Jamie Lee 171
Curtis, Richard 175
Curtis, Tony 135
Cushing, Peter 56, 136, 138, 141-142, 158
CutThroat Island 224

D and P Studios Ltd 25
Da Vinci Code, The 200-1, 229
Daisy (alligator) 59
Daldry, Stephen 186
Dale, Jim 99, 105
Dalrymple, Ian 31, 33, 45
Dalton, Timothy 120-121
Daly, Timothy 166
Dambusters, The 19
Dance of Shiva, The 226
Dangerous Exile 210
Daniels, Penny 91
Danson, Ted 171
Dark, John 141, 144
Dark Room, The (TV) 226
Darkening, The 224
Darnborough, Antony 73
D.A.R.Y.L. 221
Dateline Diamonds 215
David Copperfield 216
David Niven Story, The 128
Davidson, Lionel 125
Davies, Jack 37, 67, 69
Davies, John Howard 37
Davis, Bette 147
Davis, Jeremy 168
Davis, John (not Sir John) 173-174
Davis, Judy 156-157
Davis, Sir John
    progress 33
    Independent Frame 41
    cost cutting approach 47, 49
    reminiscences of colleagues 47-48
    Cinema-Television concept 50-51
    meeting Dinah Sheridan 54
    production involvement 62
    The One That Got Away 81
    cinema closures 95
    move away from films 95
    on Lord Rank 136
    death 168
Day After Tomorrow, The (TV pilot) 219
Day of the Jackal, The 173
Day to Remember, A 209
Day-Lewis, Daniel 167
de Bont, Jan 191
Dead Ringers (TV series) 228, 229, 230
Deadfall 215
Deadlier than the Male 215
Deadly Voyage (TV) 172, 224
Dealers 222
Dear Mr Prohack 45, 208

Dearden, Basil 87, 93, 126, 127
Death Fish 2 171
Death Machine 223
Death on the Nile 219
Death Wish Live (TV series) 230
Deceptions (TV) 221
Deer Hunter, The 155
Delderfield, R F 97
Delon, Nathalie 133
Delta Doric 119
Deluxe Entertainment Services 176, 181
Deluxe Films 199
Deluxe Media 199
Dench, Dame Judi 71, 123, 186
Denham Studios 22, 25, 47, 51, 204
Denham, Maurice 84, 85
Dentist in the Chair 212
DePalma, Brian 172
Depp, Johnny 192, 197
Descent, The 229
Desert Victory 29, 30, 31, 204, 207
Designated Mourner, The 225
Desmonde, Jerry 66, 68, 69
Desperate Moment 109
Destiny of a Spy (TV) 216
Deutsch, David 93
Deutsch, Oscar 25, 32, 44
Devils, The 135, 217
Devils of Darkness 214
Diamonds Are Forever 115, 217
Diamonds on Wheels 218
Diana, Princess of Wales 121, 171
Diana: Her True Story (TV) 166, 223
Diary for Timothy, A 29, 31, 204, 207
Dickens, Charles 33, 35, 37, 139, 163
Die Another Day 189-191, 227
Dillman, Bradford 139
Dillon, Carmen 51
Dinotopia (TV series) 184, 227
Dirtysomething (TV) 223
Disney, Walt 41, 51, 57, 92, 93, 125, 127, 147
Dixon, Jill 82
Doctor films 55, 72-77, 107
Doctor at Large 61, 76-77, 210
Doctor at Sea 75-76, 210
Doctor in Clover 77, 215
Doctor in Distress 77, 125, 213
Doctor in Love 77, 89, 212
Doctor in the House 55, 73-75, 77, 209
Doctor in Trouble 77, 135, 216
Doctor Who (TV series) 98, 230
Doctor Who – The Curse of Fatal Death 178, 226
documentaries, wartime 29-30, 32, 204
Dodds, Olive 42
Dog Eat Dog (TV series) 227, 228
Dolores (dog) 79
Dom Za Vesanje 147
Don't Get Me Started 223
Don't Go Breaking My Heart 176, 225
Don't Lose Your Head 102, 215
Donald, James 54
Donlan, Yolande 54
Donner, Richard 149, 150-151, 152
Doomwatch 217
Doppelgänger 216
Dors, Diana 42, 58, 59, 136, 159
Dotrice, Karen 146
007 Stage 117-120
Double X 71
Double Zéro 196, 228
Douglas, Jack 99, 105
Douglas, Kirk 127
Douglas, Michael 166
Down, Lesley Anne 156, 158
Dr No 94, 109, 110, 114, 189, 213
Dr Syn Alias The Scarecrow 125, 213
Dr Zhivago 191
Dracula Has Risen From the Grave 131, 138, 216
Dragonslayer 220
Drayton, Alfred 23
Dream Lover 221
Dresdel, Sonia 49
Dresser, The 158, 221
Dressmaker, The 221
Drew, Hon George 87
Dry White Season, A 221
Dunaway, Faye 153
Dunleavy, Ivan 181, 198, 201

Eady Fund or Eady Levy 50, 55, 87, 158-159

Eady, Sir Wilfrid 50
Eagle's Wing 146
Ealing comedies 53
Ealing Studios 52
Early Bird, The 69, 214
Easdale, Brian 36
Eastwood, Clint 149, 163
Easy, Bert 35
Eaton, Shirley 77, 99, 107, 191
Eccleston, Christopher 177
Edwards, Anthony 176
Edwards, Blake 156, 158
80,000 Suspects 213
Ekberg, Anita 94, 95
Ekland, Britt 71
Elephant Boy 22
11 Harrowhouse 218
Elizabeth II, Her Majesty Queen 85, 87
Elizabeth, Her Majesty the Queen Mother 141
Ellenshaw, Peter 51
Elliott, Denholm 71
Elphick, Michael 143
Elstree Studios 32, 153, 159
Emma 224
Encore 49, 209
End of the River, The 36, 208
Endfield, Cy 79
Englishman Who Went Up a Hill, But Came Down a Mountain, The 223
Enigma 183, 226
Entertainer, The 109
Entrapment 176, 225
Eon Productions 94, 109-110, 114, 121, 123, 126, 129, 177, 178
Equus 143
Eragon 230
Ermey, Lee 159
Escape from the Dark 219
Essex, David 147
Esther Waters 39, 208
Evans, Dame Edith 51
Evans, John 153
Event Horizon 174, 225
Evita 172, 224
extras, five thousand 89
Extras (TV series) 229, 230
Eyes Wide Shut 174, 225
Eyewitness 61, 210
Eyre, Richard 186

Fahrenheit 451 215
Fairytale – A True Story 224
Faith, Adam 92
Fantabulosa! (TV) 230
Farewell Performance 213
Farrell, Charles 23
Farrell, Colin 194-5
Farrow, Mia 137
Fast and Loose 209
Fatal Hour, The 206
Fawcett, Farrah 137
Feldman, Charles K 129
Fellner, Eric 194
Fennell, Albert 143
Fennell, Jack 143
Ferretti, Dante 169
Ferry to Hong Kong 211
Fete, The 229
Fiddler on the Roof 135, 139, 178, 217
Field, D P 28
Field, Mary 44
Field, Roy 152
Fiennes, Joseph 167
Fiennes, Ralph 175
Fierce Creatures 171, 224
Fifth Element, The 172, 224
Fighting Prince of Donegal, The 214
FIGS versions 178
Film Artistes Association 58
Films Act 1938 23
Final Cut, The (TV series) 224
Final Test, The 209
Finch, Jon 135
Finch, Peter 59-60, 81, 87, 89
Finders Keepers 215
Finding Neverland 192, 228
Finney, Albert 158
Firechasers, The 216
Firelight 224
Fires Were Started 31, 204, 207
First Easter, The 207
First Great Train Robbery, The 146, 220

First Knight 171, 224
First Modern Olympics, The (TV) 158, 221
Fish Called Wanda, A 160, 171
Fisher, Terence 73
Fitzgerald, Geraldine 10
Fitzgerald, Mick 199
Flame in the Streets 90, 212
Fleming, Ian 109, 110, 129, 130-131
Floods of Fear 211
Floodtide 45, 208
Flynn, Errol 33
Follow a Star 68, 212
Follow That Camel 102, 215
Follow Your Star 206
Fools Rush In 208
Footprints in the Snow (TV) 230
For Your Eyes Only 119, 120, 155, 220
Forbes, Bryan 56, 84, 87, 91-92, 125, 128, 141, 144, 170
Forbidden Cargo 209
Force of the Trojans 147
Ford, Harrison 166
Ford, John 159
Foreign Exchange 216
Forster, Marc 192
Forsyth, Bill 168
Forsyth, Frederick 173
14, The 218
1408 229
49th Parallel 39
Foster, Barry 135
Foster, Jodie 140
Four Feathers, The 22
Fowler, Harry 55
Fox, James 127
Fox, Robert 186-7
Foyle's War: Bad Blood (TV) 230
Frakes, Jonathan 194
Francis, Freddie 21-22, 131, 138
Francis, Jan 143
Francis, Teddy 137
Frankenstein (TV) 166-167, 223
Frankenstein: The True Story 137, 218
Fraser, Liz 99
Frears, Stephen 71, 169
Fred Claus 230
Freeborn, Stuart 37
French, Harold 49
French & Saunders: Titanic 226
Frenzy 135, 217
Freud, Clement 62
Frey, Leonard 135
Friedkin, William 71
Friends (TV series) 177, 226
Frog, The 22, 206
Frogmore studio 122
From a Bird's Eye View (TV series) 216
From Beyond the Grave 141
From Russia With Love 69, 95, 110, 111, 213
Frost, David 141
Fröbe, Gert 127, 131
Fry, Stephen 193
Full Metal Jacket 159, 174, 221
Funeral in Berlin 130, 215
Furse, Roger 63
Furst, Anton 161
Fury, Billy 93

Gainsborough 22, 47, 49, 73
Gang Show, The 25, 206
Gangway 206
Gardner, Jack 66, 99, 101
Garner, James 156
Garnett, Tay 55-56
Gaumont-British 22, 32, 41
Gayson, Eunice 191
Gazzara, Ben 137
Geddes, Sir Auckland 11
Geeson, Sally 71
Geffen, David 168
Geldof, Bob 156
General Cinema Finance Corporation 44
General Film Distributors 11, 22
Genevieve 52-53, 209
Genn, Leo 31
Gere, Richard 171, 173
Ghosts, The (novel) 136
Ghoul, The 138, 218
Gielgud, John 139, 156
Gilbert, Lewis 47-48, 61, 81, 85, 114, 115
Gilliatt, Sidney 33, 35, 45
Girl on the Boat, The 69

Glass Menagerie, The (TV) 218
Glen, John 120, 155, 159, 171
Globus, Yoram 153, 159
Go For a Take 218
Goal! 229
God Save The King (National Anthem) 99
God Told Me To 219
Going Gently (TV play) 71
Golan, Menahem 71, 153, 159
Gold 138-139, 218
Golden Bowl, The 226
GoldenEye 121
Golden Salamander 208
Goldenthal, Elliot 169
Goldfinger 111-113, 114, 120, 126, 214
Goldman Sachs 181
Goldman, William 166
Goldmine (novel) 138
Goldstone, John 105
Gone With the Wind 33
Goodbye Piccadilly, Farewell Leicester Square (novel) 135
Gopal, Ram 54
Gordon, Lawrence 182
Gordon, Richard 73, 84
Goring, Marius 35, 36-37
Gough, Michael 51
Gould, Elliot 71, 146
Governess, The 225
Grade, Lew 87
Grade, Michael 163, 181-2, 184-5, 188, 198, 203
Grand Fenwick, Duchy of 94
Granger, Stewart 49
Grant, Cary 54
Grantley, Lord (Richard Norton) 18-19, 23, 24, 49, 158
Gravy Train, The (TV) 222
Gray, Sally 23, 35
Great Expectations 33, 35, 37, 207
Great Expectations (TV, 1988) 163, 222
Great Expectations (TV, 1998) 226
Great Gatsby, The 137-138, 218
Great Moments in Aviation (TV) 223
Green for Danger 35, 207
Green, Guy 87, 91
Green, Martyn 24
Green, Nigel 60-61
Greene, Graham 22, 79
Greengrass, Paul 201
Gregson, John 53, 59, 62, 84
Grenfell, Joyce 57
Gribble, Bernard 28
Gries, Tom 137
Griffith, Jane 57
Griffith, Kenneth 137, 157
Grosvenor Sound Films 22
Guest, Val 54, 129-130, 133
Guilaroff, Sydney 88-89
Guinea Pig, The 204
Guinness advertisement 74
Guinness, Sir Alec 37, 130
Gulliver's Travels 137, 218
Gunbus 159, 221
Gunn, Steve 188
Guns at Batasi 126, 214
Guns in the Heather 216
Guthridge, Johnny 29
Gwillim, Jack 147
Gynt, Greta 21, 35
Gypsy and the Gentleman, The 211

Hackers 170, 224
Hackman, Gene 149, 151
Haggard, Piers 171
Hagman, Larry 137
Hallmark Productions 173, 178
Hamell, Veronica 173
Hamilton, Guy 41, 111, 131, 149
Hamlet 217
Hamlin, Harry 147
Hammer Films 131, 146
Hampton, Christopher 169
Hamshere, Keith 92-93
Hand, David 41
Hands of the Ripper 217
Hanley, Jimmy 21
Hanson, Bernard 39, 41
Happy Days 140
Harbour Goes to France, A 30, 207
Harbour Lights (TV series) 226
Hare, Robertson 23
Hargreaves, Christine 156

Harker, Gordon 23
Harris, Cassandra 143
Harris, Richard 127, 137
Harrison, Bill 161
Harrison, Rex 21, 28-29, 89
Harry Potter and the Goblet of Fire 198, 229
Harry Potter and the Philosopher's Stone 185, 194
Harryhausen, Ray 147
Hart, Harvey 158
Hartford-Davis, Robert 71
Hartnell, William 98
Hartstone, Graham 178-179
Harvey, Jan 143
Harwood, Ronald 158
Hasford, Gustav 159
Havelock-Allan, Sir Anthony 14, 19, 21, 23, 33, 35-36, 45
Hawk the Slayer 220
Hawkins, Jack 54, 57, 62, 87
Hawks 221
Hawtrey, Charles 98, 101
Hayden, Cyril 50
Hazard of Hearts (TV) 221
Head Over Heels (TV series) 223
Heart of a Child 211
Heart of a Man, The 211
Heartburn Hotel (TV series) 178, 226
Heath Farm 14, 15
Heatherden Hall 11-15, 181
Heaven's Gate 155, 220
Heil Honey, I'm Home (TV) 165, 222
Hell Below Zero 55, 209
Hell Drivers 79, 210
Hellbound: Hellraiser II 221
Hellfire Club, The 212
Hellman, Marcel 33
Hendry, Ian 142
Hennessey 219
Hennessey, Peggy 33
Hennessey, Peter 54
Henry, Sir John 11
Henry VIII (TV) 196, 228
Hepburn, Katharine 62
Heroes of Telemark, The 127, 214
Herr, Michael 159
Herren, Kip 128, 139, 143
Hess, Myra 31, 32
Heston, Charlton 127-128, 165
Heston, Fraser C 163, 165
Heywood, Anne 87
Hibernation 230
High Bright Sun, The 214
High Tide at Noon 210
High Treason 209
High Wind in Jamaica, A 214
Highbury Studios 42, 43, 47
Highly Dangerous 208
Highmore, Freddie 192, 197
Hill, Bernard 71
Hill, Bill 126
Hill, Derek 87
Hill, Sinclair 22
Hill, Terry 153
Hiller, Dame Wendy 21, 22, 24-25
Hird, Dame Thora 107
Hitchcock, Alfred 22, 135, 146
Hobson, Valerie 19
Hobson's Choice (play) 71
Hodson, J L 31
Holden, William 129-130
Holding, Ernie 88
Holgate, Diane 92
Holiday Camp 97
Holiday's End 206
Holland, Agnieszka 166, 178
Holloway, Stanley 59
Hollywood Greats (TV series) 230
Holm, Ian 171
Holmes, Jack 29, 31
Holness, Bob 109
Homburg, Hans 156
Home Guard 27
Homes For All 41
homosexuality 90
Hope, Bob 62, 94
Hopkins, Lady Jenni 133
Hopkins, Sir Anthony 133, 137, 144, 145, 156, 163, 172
Hordern, Michael 85
Hornblower (TV series) 184, 225, 227, 228
Horse Without a Head, The 93, 213

horses, not stolen by Alan Ladd 56-57
Hoskins, Bob 156
Hostile Waters (TV) 225
Hot Enough for June 125, 214
Hotel Sahara 208
Hough, John 147
Hours, The 186, 227
House in Nightmare Park, The 137, 218
House of Secrets 210
Houston, Donald 74
Howard, Cyril 52-53, 95, 119, 120, 139, 143-144, 150, 153, 160, 165, 167
Howard, Leslie 24-25, 33
Howard, Ron 200
Howard, Trevor 35, 49
Howell, John 29
Howerd, Frankie 59, 137
Howes, Sally Ann 131
Hudis, Norman 98, 107
Hughes, Ken 130, 131
Human Factor, The 219
Hume, Alan 39, 41, 99, 101, 102, 105, 173
Hunchback of Notre Dame, The (TV) 156, 220
Hunt for Red October, The 166
Hunt, Gareth 143
Hunt, Peter 111, 137, 138
Hunt, Peter H 158
Hunted 209
Hunter, Ian 59, 109
Huntley, Raymond 69
Hurt, John 138, 155, 166
Huston, John 130
Hyams, Peter 155
Hylton, Jane 39

I Could Never Be Your Woman 229
I Don't Want To Be Born 219
Ice Cold in Alex 19
ice cream sales 51
Ike: The War Years (TV) 220
Ill Met By Moonlight 210
IMAX Nutcracker, The 225
Impersonator, The 212
Importance of Being Earnest, The 51, 209
In Search of the Castaways 92-93, 213
In the Doghouse 212
Incident in Shanghai 206
Incognito 173, 224
Incredible Sarah, The 219
Independent Frame (IF) 39, 41, 45, 85, 133
Independent Producers Ltd 33, 47
industrial product, film-making as 36
Infamy! Infamy! 101
Informers, The 213
Innes, Hammond 55
Innocent Bystanders 217
Innocent Sinners 211
Inspector Hornleigh 207
Inspector Morse: Dead on Time (TV) 222
Instruments of the Orchestra 32, 207
Intelligence Men, The 127, 214
International Velvet 144-145, 219
Interpol Calling (TV series) 213
Interview With the Vampire 168-169, 223
Invasion Earth (TV series) 225
Ipcress File, The 126, 130, 214
Ireland, Jill 42, 79, 82
Iris 186, 227
Irish Free State treaty 1921 12
Iron Maiden, The 213
Iron Petticoat, The 62, 210
Isherwood, Christopher 137
Island of Terror 214
Islington studio 47, 49, 73, 97
It Started in Paradise 54, 209
ITC 87
Ivanhoe (TV series, 1958) 98
Ivanhoe (TV, 1981) 156, 220
Ivanhoe (TV series, 1996) 225

J Arthur Rank Productions Ltd 49, 58
Jack & Sarah 223
Jack and the Beanstalk: The Real Story (TV) 227
Jack the Ripper 162
Jackal, The 172-173, 225
Jackson, Glenda 130
Jackson, Gordon 45
Jackson, Pat 29, 31, 49, 54, 204
Jacob, Irene 173
Jacobs, Arthur P 132
Jacqueline 61, 210

Jacques, Hattie 98
Jagger, Mick 183-4
Jaggs, Steve 167-168, 169, 176, 177, 202
James Bond Fan Club 165-166
James, Sid 79, 92, 99, 103-104, 104-105, 177
James, Sue 177
Jane Eyre 216
Janni, Joe 84
Jasper Carrott Trial, The (TV series) 225
Javelin Films 49
Jaws 149
Jeeves and Wooster (TV series) 222
Jeffrey Archer – The Truth (TV) 228
Jeffries, Lionel 77, 94-95, 131, 136, 144
Jennings, Humphrey 29, 31, 204
Jericho 206
Jesus Christ Superstar (TV) 178, 226
Jewison, Norman 135, 139
John, Rosamund 35
Johnny Leyton Touch, The 213
Johns, Glynis 51, 57
Johnson, Richard 110, 165
Jolie, Angelina 170, 182, 191, 194-5
Jonathan Creek (TV series) 225, 226, 227, 229
Jones, Catherine Zeta 176
Jordan, Neil 168
Joseph and His Amazing Technicolor Dreamcoat (TV) 178, 226
Joseph, Teddy 62, 88, 92, 155
Jourdan, Louis 166
Journey Together 30, 31, 168, 207
Juggernaut 218
Jumping for Joy 142, 210
Jurgens, Curt 117
Just Cause 224
Just Like a Woman 166, 222
Just My Luck 67, 211
Justice, James Robertson 51, 59, 74, 77
Justin, John 31

K-19: The Widowmaker 187, 227
Kafka 223
Kaleidoscope 215
Kanin, Garson 30
Karaoke (TV series) 172, 224
Kaufman, Philip 178
Kazan, Elia 63
Keaton, Michael 162
Keep Smiling 207
Keith, Brian 137
Keller, Frank P 30
Kelly, Sam 165
Ken Russell's Treasure Island 224
Kendall, Kay 53, 74
Kenny, Chris 161
Kenwright, Bill 176
Kerr, Deborah 130
Kerrs, Curly 116-117
Keys, Anthony Nelson 27
Khartoum 128, 214
Kicking the Moon Around 206
Kidder, Margot 150
Kidman, Nicole 174, 186
Kidnapped (1959) 212
Kidnapped (1971) 217
Kidnappers, The 57, 209
Kids are Alright, The 220
Kiel, Richard 191
Kilmer, Val 158, 173
Kind Hearts and Coronets 208
King Arthur 199, 228
King David 221
King Ralph 222
King, W G 14-15
Kinky Boots 229
Kirwan, Dervla 177
Kline, Kevin 171-172
Klugman, Jack 150
Korda, Alexander 22, 23, 25, 35, 45, 60
Kortner, Fritz 23
Kostal, Irwin 131
Kristel, Sylvia 105
Kristofferson, Kris 149, 155
Kruger, Hardy 80-81
Krull 220
Kubrick, Stanley 127, 135, 157, 159, 174
Kwouk, Bert 158

La Bern, Arthur 135
La Frenais, Ian 176
Ladd, Alan 55-56
Ladd, Sue 56-57

Ladies in Lavender 228
Lady and the Highwayman, The (TV) 222
Lady Caroline Lamb 217
Lady Chatterley (TV) 223
Lady Vanishes, The 146, 220
Lambeth Walk, The 23, 207
Lamont, Peter 113, 117, 120, 122, 123, 193, 203
Lancaster, Dinsdale 145
Lancashire Luck 22, 206
Lancelot and Guinevere 94, 213
Landen, Dinsdale 145
Lansbury, Angela 146, 158
Lara Croft: Tomb Raider 182, 185, 227
Lara Croft: Tomb Raider – The Cradle of Life 191, 228
Lasky Studios, Islington 15
Last Curtain 206
Last Days of Pompeii, The 158, 221
Last of the Summer Wine (TV series) 98, 107, 172, 177, 200, 224, 226, 229, 230
Last Orders 184, 227
Last Yellow, The 226
Last Year in Marienbad 110
Launder, Frank 33, 35, 45
Laurentiis, Dino De 88
Laurie, John 45
Laverick, June 68
Lawrence of Arabia 85
Lawson, Wilfrid 10, 128
Laye, Dilys 69
Lazenby, George 115
Le Carré, John 163
League of Gentlemen, The 87, 212
Lean, David 28, 33, 35, 37-39, 45, 140, 163
Leavesden Studio 121
Lee, Auriol 97
Lee, Bernard 59, 79
Lee, Christopher 42, 59, 79, 116-117, 131, 133, 136
Lee, Jack 29, 59, 84
Lee, Laurie 31
Left Hand Drive (TV) 223
Left of the Line 29, 207
Legard, John 28
Legend 119, 159, 221
Legend of the Werewolf, The 138, 218
Legend of Young Dick Turpin, The 214
Leigh, Jennifer Jason 174
Leigh, Vivien 21
Lenny Henry in Pieces (TV series) 227
Lenya, Lotte 110
Lesley, Carole 92
Leslie, Eddie 69
Lester, Richard 94, 147, 151, 152, 153
Let Him Have It 222
Levin, Drury 11
Levin, Lloyd 182
Levy, Stuart 98, 102
Licence to Kill 121, 165
Life & Lyrics 230
Life for Ruth 93, 94, 213
Life on the Ocean Wave, A (song) 99
Lighthouse 226
Lightning Conductor 23, 207
Lights2 230
Limbo Line, The 215
Lime Grove Studios 32, 47
Line of Beauty, The (TV series) 229
Lipman, Maureen 105
Lipstick on Your Collar (TV series) 223
Listen to Britain 31, 207
Little Britain (TV series) 230
Little Shop of Horrors 159, 221
Little White Lies (TV) 225
Live and Let Die 115-116, 218
Live it Up 213
Living Daylights, The 120-121, 221
Llewelyn, Desmond 111, 123
Lloyd, Euan 25, 39, 42, 55-56, 147, 156-157
Lloyd's of London 27
Lloyd's Pinewood Fire Guard 27
Lloyd Webber, Andrew 196
Location Catering 165
Loch Ness 171, 224
Lodge, David 69
Lom, Herbert 79, 146, 158
London Film Critics' Circle Awards 106
London Belongs to Me 208
London Melody 19
London Symphony Orchestra 32
Long Duel, The 215

Long Memory, The 209
Long Shadow, The 212
Longitude (TV) 226
Look Back In Anger 109
Look of Love, The (song) 130
Lord Rank Research Centre 136
Loren, Sophia 129
Losey, Joseph 159
Lost 210
Lost World, The (TV) 227
Love Among the Ruins (TV) 219
Love Bites: Perfect Blue (TV) 225
Lowe, Arthur 146
Ludlum, Robert 173
Luenberger, John 140
Luke, Lord 32
Lumley, Joanna 143, 158
Luxford, Bert 103-104, 105, 111, 112-113, 115, 116-117
Lyons, Stuart 141

Ma Femme est une Actrice 227
MacDonald, David 29, 30
Macdonald, Richard 153
MacDougall, Roger 22, 23
Mackay, Fulton 71
Mackendrick, Alexander 22, 23
Mackintosh Man, The 218
MacLean, Alistair 133
Macnee, Patrick 142, 143, 175
Macrae, Duncan 57
Mad About Men 210
Madame Sin 217
Made in Heaven 209
Madeleine 45
Madonna 172
Magee, Patrick 130
Magnificent Seven Deadly Sins, The 217
Magnificent Showman, The 214
Magnificent Two, The 215
Major Barbara 25, 27
Make Mine Mink 212
Malkovich, John 169
Mallet, Tania 113
Malta GC 29, 31, 207
Malta Story 209
Mamoulian, Rouben 87-88
Man for All Seasons, A (TV) 222
Man in a Suitcase (TV series) 128, 178, 215
Man in the White Suit, The 23, 28
Man in the Moon 212
Man of the Moment 67, 210
Man Who Cried, The 226
Man With the Golden Gun, The 116, 139, 218
man with the gong 11, 176
Mankiewicz, Joseph 89, 136
Manley, Peter 80, 93, 141
Mann, Anthony 127
Mann, Christopher 33
Mansfield Park 226
Marat/Sade 130, 178, 215
March of Time, The (newsreel magazine) 41-42, 88
March, Elspeth 49
Marie Antoinette 229
Margaret, HRH Princess 141
Marina, HRH Princess (Duchess of Kent) 28
Marks, Leo 87
Maroc-7 215
Marriott, Moore 10
Marsh, Billy 65
Marshall, Alan 139, 140
Martial Kind of Men, A (TV) 223
Martin, Steve 159
Mary Queen of Scots 30
Mary Reilly 169, 223
Mason, James 147, 156
Masquerade 214
Master of the Game (TV) 158, 221
Masters of Venus (serial) 213
Mastership 10
Mathews, Denis 32
Mathieson, Muir 32, 41, 53
Matter of Life and Death, A 33
Matthews, A E 54, 57
Maugham, W Somerset 49
Mauretania, SS (ship) 16
Maus, Roger 156
Maxwell, John 32
Maxwell, Lois 191
Mayall, Rik 106

McCallum, Gordon 179
McClure, Doug 141
McCowen, Alec 135
McEnery, John 168
McEnery, Peter 125
McEveety, Vincent 147
McGoohan, Patrick 79, 110, 125
McGrath, Joe 130
McKenna, Virginia 81-82
McKern, Leo 60-61
McLaglen, Andrew V 147
McQueen, Steve 149
McQuitty, Bill 83
McShane, Ian 128
McVicar 220
Me and My Girl (musical) 23
Mean Green Mother From Outer Space
    (song) 159
Meddings, Derek 119, 146, 151, 153
Medina, Patricia 56
Medusa Touch, The 219
Medwin, Michael 77
Meet Me Tonight 209
Meetings with Remarkable Men 219
Memphis Belle 163, 222
Merchant-Ivory 172
Merchant of Venice, The (TV) 184, 227
Merlin (TV) 225
Merton Park Studios 10
Messenger, Dudley 94
Michaels, Lorne 183
Michell, Keith 62
Middleton, Guy 42
Middleton's Changeling 223
Midnight Menace 22-23, 206
Midsomer Murders (TV series) 226
Mikado, The 24, 207
Miles, Sarah 127, 159
Milland, Ray 137, 139
Miller, Arthur 62
Miller, Jonny Lee 170
Miller, Penelope Ann 166
Milligan, Spike 92
Million Pound Note, The 57, 209
Mills, Hayley 85, 91-92, 125, 128
Mills, Juliet 91, 99
Mills, Lady (Mary Hayley Bell) 91, 128
Mills, Sir John 85, 89-90, 91, 119, 128, 137,
    146, 176
Mind Benders, The 93, 213
Minder (TV series) 168, 223
miniature special effects 151
Minghella, Anthony 187
Mio in the Land of Faraway 221
Miracle in Soho 210
Mirad (TV) 225
Miranda 73, 227
Miss Julie 218
Missing, Believed Married 207
Mission: Impossible 172, 224
Mister Jericho 216
Mister Quilp 139, 218
Modine, Matthew 159
Monger, Christopher 166
Monroe, Marilyn 62-63
Moonraker 119, 146, 155, 220
Moonraker (novel) 109
Moon-Spinners, The 125, 214
Moore, Dudley 128
Moore, Roger 42, 94, 98, 110, 115-116,
    119, 120, 135, 138-139, 142, 147, 155, 158
Moore, Ted 113, 133
Moranis, Rick 159
Morden, Grant 11-12
More, Kenneth 53, 61, 74, 85, 119
Morecambe, Eric 29, 107, 127
Morley, Robert 21, 74, 127, 133
Morons From Outer Space 159, 221
Morris, Lana 66, 67
Morris, Oswald 135
Morse, Barry 137
Morton, Andrew 166
Most Dangerous Man in the World, The
    132-133, 216
Motion Picture Association of America
    44, 90
Mouse on the Moon, The 94, 213
Moving Story (TV series) 223
Mr Smith Carries On 207
Mrs Caldicot's Cabbage War 227
Mrs Merton & Malcolm (TV series) 226
Mummy Returns, The 183, 226

Munday, Arthur 85
Munro, Janet 94
Murder Elite 221
Murdoch, Rupert 165
Museum Mystery 206
My Dad's the Prime Minister (TV series)
    229
My Family (TV series) 188, 196, 227, 228,
    229, 230
My Friend Walter (TV) 223

Nail, Jimmy 176
Naismith, Laurence 136
Naked Truth, The 211
Nanny McPhee 198, 228
Nation, Terry 137
National Electricians' Union 51-52
National Film Finance Corporation 53
National Periodical Publications 149
National Provincial Bank 45, 49
National Velvet 144
Nature Boy (TV series) 178, 226
Neame, Ronald 33, 35, 45, 57, 65
Nearest and Dearest 136, 217
Net, The 54, 209
Nettles, John 143
Never Mind the Quality, Feel the Width
    136, 218
New Avengers, The (TV series) 142-143,
    144, 219
New Captain Scarlet (TV series) 196-7,
    228, 229
New Professionals, The (TV series) 177, 226
New York Critics Award 71
Newbrook, Peter 71
Newley, Anthony 55, 139
Newman, Nanette 128, 145, 170
Newman, Paul 23
Newton-John, Olivia 133
Nicholson, Jack 162
Nielson, James 125
Night of the Big Heat 215
Night of the Wenceslas, The (novel) 125
Night They Raided Minsky's, The 71
Night to Remember, A 82-83, 89, 211
Night Ride 206
Night Without Stars 208
Nightbreed 222
Nighy, Bill 176
Nijinsky 147
Nimmo, Derek 130
Niven, David 51, 110, 128, 130, 158
No Kidding 89, 212
No Love for Johnnie 89, 212
No, My Darling Daughter 91, 212
No Sex Please – We're British 218
Nobody Ordered Love 217
Nobody Runs Forever 216
Nolte, Nick 149
Nor the Moon By Night 211
Norris, Steve 185
North Sea Hijack 37, 147, 220
North West Frontier 211
Norton, Richard (Lord Grantley) 18-19,
    23, 24, 49, 158
Nothing But the Night 217
Noyce, Phillip 166, 173
Nurse on Wheels 213

O'Connor, Frank 31
O'Neal, Tatum 144-145
O'Neil, Paddie 69
O'Toole, Peter 130
Oakley Court 137
Obsession 208
Octopussy 119, 220
Odeon Cinemas 32, 44, 181
Odeon mnemonic 25
Odessa File, The 217
Old Curiosity Shop, The (novel) 139
Old New Borrowed Blue 176-177
Oliver Twist 33, 37-39, 139, 208
Olivier, Laurence 62-63, 127, 131, 136, 147
Omen, The 149
On Her Majesty's Secret Service 115, 216
On the Beat 69, 71, 213
Once a Jolly Swagman 208
Once Upon a Dream 208
One Day in London (TV) 126
One Foot in the Grave (TV series) 184, 227
One Good Turn 66-67, 210
One of Our Dinosaurs is Missing 218

One That Got Away, The 79-81, 89
Operation Amsterdam 211
Oram, John 145
Orient Express scene 111
Osborne, Jon 109
Osborne, William 194
Osmond, Donny 178
Ostrer brothers 22, 32
Our Fighting Navy 206
Outland 155, 220
Outpost (TV pilot) 222
Owen, Bill 98
Owen, Clive 201-2
Owen, Gareth 169-170
Oz, Frank 159

Pack of Lies 221
Page, Anthony 146
Pair of Briefs, A 213
Palache report 1944 32, 43
Palansky, Mark 202
Palin, Michael 171-172
Palmer, Lilli 28-29, 137
Paltrow, Gwyneth 167
Paluzzi, Luciana 114
Pandora's Box 23
Paper Tiger 37
Paperhouse 221
Parallel 9 (TV series) 166, 223
Parent Trap, The 91
Paris to Piccadilly (play) 65
Parker, Alan 139, 140, 156, 172
Parker, Cecil 62, 79
Parrish, Robert 130
Party's Over, The 94, 213
Pascal, Gabriel 24, 25, 27
Pasdar, Adrian 166
Passage Home 210
Passionate Friends, The 45, 208
Passionate Summer 211
Passport to Pimlico 52
Patric, Jason 173
Patriot Games 166, 222
Pavlow, Muriel 54, 61, 73, 77, 107
Payne, John 109
Pearson, Bill 155
Pearson, George 21
Peck, Gregory 57, 132
Peeping Tom 87, 212
Peers, Donald 93
Pelissier, Anthony 49
Penelope 202, 230
Penny Gold 218
Penny Princess 54, 209
Pentecost, Adelaide 28
People That Time Forgot, The 144, 219
Perfect Friday 216
Perfect Murder, A 225
Perier, Etienne 133, 135
Perkins, Anthony 147
*Persecution and Assassination of
    Jean-Paul Marat, The* 215
Personal Affair 209
personal appearances concept 42
Persuaders!, The (TV series) 135, 178-9,
    216
Pertwee, Jon 105
Pfeiffer, Michelle 163
Phantom of the Opera, The 196, 228
Phase IV 218
Phillips, Leslie 77, 105
Phipps, Nicholas 73-74, 76, 84
Phoenix and the Magic Carpet, The 168,
    223
Phoenix, Joaquin 178
Piccadilly Third Stop 212
Picton, Pierre 131
Pilkington, Andrew 165
Pinebrook Films 23-24, 158
Pinewood Films 49
Pinewood ghost 16
Pinewood Studios
    abortive sale as hotel 162-163
    accidents 52, 69, 113, 133, 140, 152,
        153, 167, 170
    bar area, importance of 84-85
    becomes studio facility 160
    Bond's natural home 123
    bought by Michael Grade consortium
        181
    British Comedy Society tributes 106, 107
    Carry On films exteriors 97
    Carry On films list 107

closure 1938 25
colour technology 24
commercials 161
Commissionaire Arthur Munday 85
construction 16-17
construction facts and figures 18
Deluxe Entertainment Services 176
Doctor films 72-77
007 stage 117-120, 172
end-of-picture parties 98
factory resemblance 60
female directors 60
female producers 73
50th anniversary 1986 51, 159-160
finance, initial 18
fire watching 29
fires 119-120, 136, 159, 175
first 'small' independent 97
first film 21
first live television 166
football club 139
'four-wall' 160
Hall of Fame corridor 106, 107
Heatherden Hall 11-15
Irish village 102
last fully serviced studio 158
name 16
opening ceremony 19
post-war re-opening 35
press boycott 81
rebuilding 1999-2001 177-178
renters 51, 95, 142
requisitioned by Army 27
restaurant 128, 139-140
robbery 58
Royal visits 28, 85, 87, 121, 141, 171
sound effects, wartime 30
stages 007 117-120
stages A-E 17
stage H 126
stages J and K 128
stages L and M 128
stages N and P 172
stages R and S 177-178
Stanley Kubrick Building 177-178
studio tours 144
10% pay cut 49
30th anniversary 1966 128
threat to close 1953 57-58
21st anniversary 1957 79, 82
wartime documentaries 29-30, 32, 204
wartime film shows 31
wartime film units 27
wartime musical recitals 32
wartime routines 27-28
water tanks 17, 83, 85, 117-119, 122
Wisdom, Norman, films made at
    Pinewood 71
Pink Floyd The Wall 156, 220
Pink Panther films 158, 166
Pinter, Harold 130
Pitt, Brad 168
Pitt, Ingrid 157
Planer, Franz 10
Planer, Nigel 105
Planet Cook (TV series) 229
Planet of the Apes 188, 227
Planter's Wife, The 54, 209
Play 227
Play It Cool 93-94, 213
Please Sir! 217
Please Turn Over 212
Pleasence, Donald 79, 158
Plummer, Christopher 131, 145
Plunkett & Macleane 225
Poet's Pub 208
Poirot (TV series) 224
Poitier, Sidney 173
Poldark (TV) 172, 224
Polish Air Force Film Unit 27
Pollack, Sydney 187
Pollyanna 91
Poole, Frank 139
Popeye films 41
Portal, Lord 32
Portal, William 11
Porter, Eric 146
posters 95, 101-102, 117
Potamus Park (TV series) 172, 224, 225
Potter, Dennis 172
Pottle, Harry 106
Powell, Michael 33, 35, 36-37, 45, 59, 87
Powell, Robert 146

pre-credit sequences 110
Prelude to Fame 208
Press for Time 71
Press Gang (TV series) 222
Pressburger, Emeric 33, 35, 36-37, 45, 59
Preston, Robert 156
Pretty Polly 215
Preventers, The (TV) 225
Prime of Miss Jean Brodie, The 216
Primitives, The 213
Prince and the Pauper, The 219
Prince and the Showgirl, The 62, 210
Pringle, Bryan 69
Prisoner, The 210
Prisoner of Honor (TV) 222
Private Life of Sherlock Holmes, The 133, 171, 216
Professionals, The 212
Professionals, The (TV series) 157-158, 177, 219
profit participation 23-24, 53
Project Shadowchaser 222
Proof of Life 182-3, 226
Prudence and the Pill 215
Prudential Building Society 25
Purple Plain, The 210
Puttnam, Lord [David] 139, 163, 168
Pygmalion 24-25, 207

QBVII (TV) 137, 218
Quaid, Randy 166
Quartet 49
Quayle, Anthony 59, 137
Queen of Swords (TV series) 227
Queen's Award to Industry 131
Queen's Nose, The (TV series) 227
Quest for Love 217
Quick, Diana 143
Quiller Memorandum, The 130, 215
Quills 178, 226
quota quickies 21-22, 43, 44

Raffi, Rudolph 142
Raft, George 130
Ragdoll 177
Raging Earth 223
Raising the Wind 212
Ranjitsinhji, K S 11
Rank Charm School 42-43, 47
Rank Film Distributors 139, 181
Rank Film Distributors of America Inc 84
Rank Film Laboratories 176
Rank Film Production Division 128
Rank Group 167, 181
Rank Hovis MacDougal Ltd 136
Rank, Joseph Arthur (Baron Rank of Sutton Scotney)
  unlikely film-maker 9-10
  religious films 9-11, 97
  annoyance at inefficiency 15-16
  Pinewood Studios Ltd 16
  buys out Lady Yule 22
  power as distributor 22
  Pygmalion decision 24
  Elstree studios purchase 32
  Gaumont-British purchase 32
  government concern at his power 32
  Rank Charm School 42-43
  children's films 43-44, 47
  financial press critics 44
  flour business 55
  Pinewood Studios 21st anniversary 82
  tribute to Charles Boot 82
  friendship with John Mills 128
  retirement as chairman 95
  Life President 95
  death 135
  memorial service 135-136
Rank Organisation
  bingo 95
  Bush Radio 51, 55
  cinema closures 95
  divisions sold in 1990s 181
  film financing abandoned 147
  finances 1948 44-45, 47
  holiday and leisure interests 95, 181
  ice cream sales 51
  last feature film 147
  move away from films 95
  Xerox 95, 181
Rank Precision Industries 55
Rank Rep Group 61
Rank Video Services 176

Rank, Jimmy 55
Rank, Lady 82
Rank-Xerox 95, 181
Rattigan, Terence 21, 49, 63, 85
Ratzenberger, John 155
Rawnsley, David 39, 41
Rawsthorne, Alan 31
Ray, Ted 41
Rea, Stephen 176
Reach for the Sky 61, 81, 168, 210
Really Useful Group, The 178
Red Beret, The 55, 110
Red Fox (TV) 222
Red Peppers, The 41
Red Shoes, The 36-37, 208
Redford, Robert 137, 139, 149
Redgrave, Michael 31
Redgrave, Vanessa 135, 159, 172
Reed, Carol 21, 30
Reed, Clive 52, 95, 130
Reed, Oliver 69, 94, 135
Reeve, Christopher 140, 149, 153
Reeves, George 149
Religious Film Society 10
Relph, Michael 87
Remick, Lee 137
Rentadick 217
renters 51, 95, 142
Rescue Robots (TV) 228
Restoration (TV series) 229
Return of the Frog, The 22
Return of the Musketeers, The 222
Return to the River Kwai 147
Return to the Secret Garden 178, 226
Revelation 227
Revenge 217
Revolver 229
Rhames, Ving 172
Rice, Anne 168
Rice, Lofty 179
Richardson, Ian 130
Richardson, Joely 171
Richardson, Ralph 127-128, 139
Riddle of the Sands 146
Riddle, Nelson 138
Rigby, Edward 21
Rigg, Diana 142
Riot at the Rite (TV) 230
Ripley Under Ground 228
Riverside Studios, Hammersmith 73
RKO 281 178, 226
Road to Damascus 229
Robbery Under Arms 211
Robards, Jason 71
Robe, The 58
Roberts, Julia 167, 169
Robin Hood 51
Robinson, Edward G 31, 204
Robson, Mark 55
Roc, Patricia 54
Rock Studios, Elstree 10
Rockets Galore! 84, 211
Rodgers, Richard 71
Roger Roger (TV series) 226
Rogers, Eric 99, 101
Rogers, Peter 49, 57, 73, 77, 89, 97, 98, 102, 105-106
Rogue Trader 225
Rollerball 139, 219
Romeo and Juliet 214
Rooney 211
Rose, Reginald 156
Rose, William 52, 53
Rosenfelt, Frank E 120
Rosenkavalier, Der 213
Ross (play) 85
Rossiter, Leonard 158
Rothschild, Evelyn de 139
Rothwell, Talbot 99, 104
Rough Cut 220
Royal Air Force Film Unit 27, 28, 29, 168, 204
Royal Film Performances 33, 141
Royal Mint 27
Rudin, Scott 187
Run a Crooked Mile 216
Runaway Railway 215
Rush, Geoffrey 178
Russell, Ken 135, 163
Russia House, The 163, 222
Rutherford, Margaret 21, 59, 66, 67, 94
Ryan, Meg 183

Sailing Along 206
Saint, The 173, 224
Saint, The (TV series) 115
Salkind, Alexander 149, 153
Salkind, Ilya 149
Saltzman, Harry 94, 101, 109, 114, 119, 125, 126, 131, 133, 142, 147
Sam's Game (TV series) 188, 227
Sanders, George 21
Sandwich Man, The 71
Santa Claus 159, 221
Sapphire 211
Savage Innocents, The 212
Sayle, Alexei 105
Scandal 163
Scarab Murder Case, The 206
Scarlett (TV) 223
Scavengers (TV) 224
Scheider, Roy 163
Schepisi, Fred 163, 171
Schnitzler, Arthur 174
Schumacher, Joel 196
Schünzel, Rheinhold 156
Scorsese, Martin 87
Scott, Ridley 119, 159, 178, 185
Scott, Terry 99
Scott, Tony 185
Screen Two: Mrs Hartley and the Growth Centre (TV) 224
Scroxton, H S 15
Sea Fury 211
Sea of Sand 211
Seagrove, Jenny 176
Séance on a Wet Afternoon 125, 213
Second Victory, The 221
Secret Garden, The 166, 168, 223
Secret Mission 33
Secret Place, The 210
Seekers, The 57, 209
Segal, George 130
Sellars, Elizabeth 45
Sellers, Peter 92, 94, 128, 130, 158
Seltzer, David 166
Selznick, David O 33
Semple, Mr 29
sequels filmed in advance 149-150
Serbedzija, Rade 173
Seven-Per-Cent Solution, The 219
Seven Thunders 211
Seventh Veil, The 73
Seventh Stream, The (TV) 227
Seymour, Jane 115-116, 162
Shackleford, Ted 170
Shaffer, Anthony 135, 136
Shafted (TV series) 227
Shakespeare in Love 167, 169
Sharif, Omar 158
Sharp, Ian 157
Shaw, George Bernard 24, 25
Shaw, Irwin 30
Shaw, Robert 110, 131
Shearer, Moira 36-37
Sheldon, Sidney 158
Shenson, Walter 94
Shepherd, Cyril 146
Shepherds Bush Studios 73
Shepperton Studios 45, 55, 141, 185
Sheridan, Dinah 48, 49, 53, 54, 95, 168
Sheriff of Fractured Jaw, The 211
Sherman Brothers 131
Shiner, Ronald 55
Shining Through 166, 222
Shipman, Dr 39
Shipman, Olivia 39
Shirley's World (TV series) 217
Shout, The 220
Shue, Elizabeth 173
Shuster, Joe 149
Siegel, Jerry 149
Silent Village, The 31, 207
Silver Dream Racer 147, 220
Silvers, Phil 102
Sim, Alastair 35
Simba 210
Simm, Ray 125, 141
Simmons, Bob 113, 115
Simmons, Jean 49, 73, 163
Simon and Laura 59, 210
Simply Red 172
Sims, Joan 84
Sinden, Sir Donald 49, 59, 61, 63, 74, 75, 77, 84-85, 107
Singer Not the Song, The 89-90, 212

Sink the Bismark! 85, 212
Sirens (TV) 227
Sister My Sister 223
Sixty Six 230
Skinner, Audrey 106
Skouras, Spyros 88
Sky Television 165, 178
Sky's the Limit, The 206
Sky West and Crooked 128, 214
Slater, Helen 153
Slayground 221
Sleeper, The (TV) 226
Sleeping Prince, The (play) 63
Sleuth 136, 217
Sliding Doors 225
Slipper and the Rose, The 139, 141, 219
Slipstream 221
Sloan, James B 15, 33
Smash and Grab 206
Smith, Maggie 147
Smith, Mel 175
Smith, Mike 181
Smith, Wilbur 138
Snatch 226
Snow White and the Seven Dwarfs 41
So Long at the Fair 73, 208
So This is London 207
Softley, Iain 170
Solomon 32
Some Girls Do 216
Some Like It Cool 93
Some Like It Hot 133
Something Money Can't Buy 54, 209
Sommer, Elke 135
Son of the Pink Panther 166, 223
Sons and Lovers 212
Sony Pictures 130
Soskin, Paul 61
SOS Pacific 212
Southern Television 51
Space: 1999 (TV series) 143, 170, 178, 218, 219
Space Precinct (TV series) 170-171, 223
Spaceman and King Arthur, The 220
Spall, Timothy 176
Spanish Gardener, The 210
Spartacus 127
Spencer, Norman 33, 35, 37-39, 41
Spender: The French Collection (TV) 223
Spengler, Pierre 149, 150
Spice Girls 125
Spider and the Fly, The 208
Spielberg, Steven 149
Spies Like Us 221
Splinters in the Air 206
Spooks (TV series) 196, 228, 229
Spooks of Bottle Bay, The (TV series) 224
Spot of Bother, A 23, 207
Spratt, Sir Lancelot (character) 74, 77
Springfield, Dusty 130
Spy Who Loved Me, The 117, 119, 142, 219
Square Peg, The 67-68, 211
Squaring the Circle (TV) 221
Squeeze, The 122
Squire, Ronald 57
St John, Earl 47, 52-53, 54, 65, 81, 89
St Paul: Faith Triumphant 207
St Paul: The Way of Salvation 207
St Swithin's 74, 77
Staffell, Charles 39, 41, 135, 163
Stanley Kubrick Building, The 177-178
Stanley, Kim 125
Star Wars: Episode 1 – The Phantom Menace 225
Star Wars films 93, 121
Stardust 202, 230
Steaming 159, 221
Stears, John 112-113, 115, 155
Steel, Anthony 42, 54, 61
Steiger, Rod 79
Steirs, David Ogden 158
Stephens, Robert 133
Steptoe and Son (TV series) 102
Sternhagen, Frances 155
Stewart, Hugh 29, 67, 68, 69, 107, 127
Still Crazy 176, 225
Still Crazy Like a Fox (TV) 221
Stitch in Time, A 69, 213
Stoke Poges Golf Club 113-114
Stolen Life 207
Stone, Oliver 194-5
Stone, Sharon 200
Stoned 229

Stop Press Girl 208
Stop the World – I Want to Get Off 214
Stoppard, Tom 163
Stormbreaker 229
Stranded (TV) 227
Strange Boarders 206
Strange Report (TV series) 216
Stranglehold 213
Strasberg, Paula 62
Street Singer, The 206
Strictly Ice Dancing (TV) 229
Strike It Lucky (TV series) 224
Strike It Rich 222
stunts 69, 115, 172
Subotsky, Milton 141
Sunset in Vienna 206
Supergirl 153, 221
Superman films 94, 144, 148-153, 159
  curse of Superman 150, 153
  flying sequences 150-152
  sets 151-152
Superman 149-150, 152, 219
Superman and the Mole Men 149
Superman II 146-147, 151, 152, 153, 220
Superman III 219
Superman IV – The Quest for Peace 153, 221
Surviving Picasso 172, 224
Survivor (TV series) 188, 227
Sweeney, Bill 28
Sweet Devil 206
Switch, The 213
Sword and the Rose, The 51, 209
Sykes, Eric 127
Syms, Sylvia 90
Szwarc, Jeannot 153

Take My Life 35, 45, 207
Tale of Two Cities, A 75, 79, 211
Tales from the Poop Deck (TV series) 223
Talk of the Devil 21, 25, 206
Tam Lin 216
Tamahori, Lee 189
Tani, Yoko 79
Tank Force 110
taxation, effects of 44, 119, 143, 146, 149, 155, 162
Taylor, Captain 177
Taylor, Elizabeth 87-89
Taylor, Gil 29
Teare, Andrew 181
teasers 110
Teddington Studios 199
Teletubbies (TV series) 177, 226
television growth 50-51, 58
10th Kingdom, The 178, 226
Terraine, Molly 42
Terry-Thomas 94, 127
That Lucky Touch 139, 219
That Riviera Touch 214
That's Carry On 105, 219
That's Entertainment 105
That's Your Funeral 217
There Goes the Bride 220
There was a Crooked Man 68, 212
Thewlis, David 168
They Knew Mr Knight 207
They Met in the Dark 33
Things To Come 23
39 Steps, The (1958) 146, 211
Thirty Nine Steps, The (1978) 219
This is My Street 214
This Man is News 23-24, 207
This Modern Age films 41-42
Thomas, Barbara 106
Thomas, Gerald 73, 77, 89, 97, 99, 103-104, 105, 106
Thomas, Jeremy 73
Thomas, Ralph 48-49, 51, 55, 61, 73, 74, 75, 77, 79, 85, 87, 89, 107, 125
Thomas, Serena Scott 166
Thompson, Caroline 168
Thompson, Emma 198-9
Thompson, J Lee 47, 58-59, 85, 132
Thomsen, Gordon 133
Thorburn, June 62
Thorson, Linda 142
Those Magnificent Men in Their Flying Machines 126-127, 214
3D (three dimensional) films 58
Three Days of the Condor 139
Three Fevers (novel) 10
Three Hats for Lisa 215

Three Lives of Thomasina, The 93, 213
Three Musketeers, The 149, 150, 151
3 Worlds of Gulliver, The 212
Thunderball 114, 117, 127-128, 214
Thunderbirds 193, 228
Thurman, Uma 175
Thursday the 12th (TV) 227
Tiara Tahiti 213
Tiger Bay 85
Tiger in the Smoke 61-62, 210
Time Lock 97
Titanic 82, 113, 122
To Paris, With Love 210
To Sir With Love 215
To the Ends of the Earth (TV series) 230
Todd, Richard 51
Tom & Jerry films 41
Tom's Midnight Garden 225
Tomlinson, David 31, 60-61, 73
Tomorrow Calling (TV) 223
Tomorrow Never Dies 114, 122, 225
Tomorrow's World: Live Lab (TV) 188, 227
Tony Draws a Horse 208
Tony nomination (Norman Wisdom) 71
Too Many Crooks 211
Toomorrow 133, 216
Tooth 228
Top of the Form 55, 209
Top Secret! 158, 221
Topo Gigio (TV pilot) 125, 214
Topol 135
Town Like Alice, A 59, 210
Toye, Wendy 60-61, 62
trailers 73
Trail of the Pink Panther 158, 220
Traitors, The 213
Trauner, Alex 133
Treasure Island (TV) 163, 222
Treasure of Monte Cristo, The 212
treble quota system 23
Trial and Retribution (TV series) 228
Trio 49, 208
Trouble In Store 55, 65-66, 209
True as a Turtle 62, 210
True Glory, The 30, 207
Trumper, John 29, 31
Tuchner, Michael 139, 156, 178
Tulip Fever 198
Tunes of Glory 91
Tunisian Victory 30
Turn of the Screw, The (TV) 224
Turn of the Tide 10
Turner, Fred 157-158
Turturro, John 168
Tutin, Dorothy 79
Twain, Mark 57
20th Century Fox 58, 87-89
20th Century Roadshow (TV series) 229
20,000 Leagues Under the Sea (TV) 173-174, 225
Twice Round the Daffodils 213
Twickenham Studios 22, 147, 160
Twins of Evil 217
twist, the 93-94
Two Cities Films 49
Two English Girls 217
200 Motels 217
Two Pints of Lager (TV series) 230

Udell, Ronnie 113, 114-115
UFO (TV series) 135, 170, 216
U.F.O. 223
Ultimate Avengers, The (book) 143
Uncle Tom Cobley pub chain 181
United Artists 19, 68, 71, 117, 131, 155
United 93 201, 229
Unsworth, Geoffrey 153
Untouchables, The 172
Up in the World 62-63, 67, 210
Up To His Neck 209
Upstairs and Downstairs 87, 211
Upturned Glass, The 73
Ustinov, Peter 30, 168

V for Vendetta 229
V1 and V2 missiles 28-29
Vacillations of Poppy Carew (TV) 224
Valley of Eagles 51, 209
Value For Money 59, 210
Vampire Circus 217
Vampire Chronicles, The (novel) 168
Van Dyke, Dick 131
Vanishing Man, The (TV series) 225

Variety Club of Great Britain 77
Vaughn, Matthew 202
Venetian Bird 209
Ventham, Wanda 135
Verne, Jules 173
Verrell, Bob 29, 42
Versois, Odile 61
Vertical Limit 184, 226
Vertue, Beryl 137
Vetchinsky, Alex 83
Vickers rostra 39, 41
Victim 90, 212
Victor/Victoria 156, 220
View to a Kill, A 119, 159, 221
Viktor und Viktoria 156
Villiers, James 136
Voight, Jon 172
Violent Playground 211
Vulture, The 215

Wagner, Robert 158
Walbrook, Anton 36-37
Walken, Christopher 155
Walker, Alexander 135
Walker, The 230
Walking Happy (musical) 71
Wallach, Eli 125
Wallis, Ken 115, 127
Walmsley, Leo 10
Walsh, Kay 39, 41
Walters, Julie 166
Waltz of the Toreadors 92, 212
Wanger, Walter 88
War and Remembrance (TV) 162, 222
War on Wednesday (script) 22
Ward, Simon 71
Wardour Street, relations with 42
Warlords of Atlantis 144, 219
Warm December, A 217
Warner Bros 168
Warner, David 146
Warning to Wantons 41, 45, 208
Wass, Ted 158
Watch Your Stern 89, 212
Watcher in the Woods, The 147, 220
Water Giant, The 227
Waterfront 208
Waterstone, Sam 155
Watkins, Alfred 33
Watling, Jack 31
Watson, Devina (Dizzie) 59-60
Wattis, Richard 84
Waxman, Harry 29
Weakest Link, The (TV series) 188, 196, 227, 228, 229, 230
Weaver, Sigourney 159
Weiss, Peter 130
Weller, Peter 173
Welles, Orson 130
Wells, Bombadier Billy 11
Wells, H G 45
Wessex Films 45
West, Simon 182
Western Approaches 31, 204, 207
Weston, Paul 152
What a Carry On 105
What a Girl Wants 227
What a Whopper 92, 212
What Changed Charley Farthing? 218
What's Good for the Goose 71
When Eight Bells Toll 133, 135, 216
Whirlpool 211
Whisperers, The 215
Whistle Down the Wind 90-92, 212
White Corridors 208
White Hunter, Black Heart 163, 222
White South, The (novel) 55
White Squall 224
White, Tom 33
White, Wilfrid Hyde 57
Whiteley, John 57
Whiting, John 84
Whitfield, June 97, 105
Whitman, Stuart 127
Who Dares Wins 156-157, 220
Why We Fight 28, 207
Wickes, David 147, 162, 166-167, 177
Widmark, Richard 157
Wilby Conspiracy, The 218
Wilcox, Herbert 18, 19, 22
Wilcox, John 133
Wild and the Willing, The 213
Wild Geese, The 147

Wild West (TV series) 228
Wilde, Cornel 94
Wilde, Oscar 51
Wilder, Billy 133
Wilding, Michael 54
Williams, Hugh 35, 42
Williams, John 135
Williams, Kenneth 57, 98, 101, 104-105
Williams, Robin 168
Willis, Bruce 172
Willis, John 119, 125, 127, 129-130, 131-132
Willis, Ted 65, 66
Willman, Noel 79
Wilson, Alf 50
Wilson, Frederick 45
Wilson, Harold 44, 119
Wilson, Joe 95
Wilson, Michael G 120, 122, 123, 189
Wind Cannot Read, The 75, 79, 211
Windkracht 10 – Koksijde Rescue 230
Windom's Way 158, 211
Windsor, Barbara 99, 101, 104-105
Winner, Michael 93-94, 179
Winslet, Kate 178, 183-4, 186
Winstone, Ray 196
Winter, Vincent 57
Winterbottom, Michael 176
Wintle, Julian 81
Wisdom, Freda 71
Wisdom, Norman Joseph 29, 55, 62-63, 64-71, 82
  British Comedy Society tribute 107
  films made at Pinewood 71
Wise, Ernie 29, 109, 127
Wiseman, Joseph 71
Wiseman, Tom 80-81
Wit (TV) 227
Without a Clue 163, 222
Witness for the Prosecution (TV) 220
Wodehouse, P G 69
Wolfit, Donald 158
Woman in a Dressing Gown 19
Woman in the Hall, The 208
Woman in Question, The 49, 208
Woman for Joe, The 210
Woman of Straw 126, 214
Wombling Free 144, 219
Wooden Horse, The 42
Woodward, Edward 157
Woodward, Shaun 203
Woolf, C M 10-11, 22, 24, 32
Woolley, Stephen 168
Work is a Four Letter Word 215
World is Full of Married Men, The 220
World is Not Enough, The 122-123, 178, 226
Wright, Basil 31
Wright, Tony 61-62
Wrong Box, The 128, 214
Wynn, Keenan 150
Wynter, Dana 85

X-Files, The 171
X-Men – The Last Stand 230
X-Perimental (TV series) 229
Xerox 95, 181

Yates, Peter 158
Year of the Comet 166, 222
Yentob, Alan 187
York, HRH Duchess of 171
York, Michael 135
York, Susannah 131, 138-139
You Bet! (TV series) 172, 224
You'd Better Go in Disguise 218
You Know What Sailors Are! 57, 209
You Only Live Twice 114-115, 117, 122, 127, 130, 190, 215
Young and Innocent 22, 135, 206
Young Person's Guide to the Orchestra, The 32
Young, Freddie 114
Young Lovers, The 209
Young, Robert 171
Young, Terence 51, 55, 94, 110, 111, 127
Yule, Lady 9, 10, 16, 22

Zeppelin 135, 217
Zinnemann, Fred 155, 173
Zoltan the Great 230
Zoo Gang, The (TV series) 137, 218
Zucker, David 158
Zucker, Jerry 158, 171

The cast of Carry On ... Up the Khyber *outside Pinewood's
Heatherden Hall — the building doubled in the film for the
British Governor's residence in Khalabar.*